D1348691

The Society of the Sacred Heart in Nineteenth-Century France, 1800–1865

The Society of the
Sacred Heart in
Nineteenth-Century France
1800–1865

by

PHIL KILROY

CORK UNIVERSITY PRESS

First published in 2012 by
Cork University Press
Youngline Industrial Estate
Pouladuff Road, Togher
Cork, Ireland

British Library Cataloguing in Publication Data
A CIP catalogue record for this book is available from the British Library.

ISBN-978-185918-499-8
Printed and bound by CPI Group (UK) Ltd., Croydon, CR0 4YY
Typeset by Tower Books, Ballincollig, Co. Cork
www.corkuniversitypress.com

Contents

Acknowledgements	vii
Abbreviations	ix
Preface	xi
Introduction	1
CHAPTER 1	
'One Musical Ensemble' The Society of the Sacred Heart, 1800–1865: The evolution of a community	9
CHAPTER 2	
The Society of the Sacred Heart: An educational model	85
CHAPTER 3	
The Society of the Sacred Heart and the Jesuits in the Lifetime of Madeleine Sophie Barat	133
CHAPTER 4	
Medical Biography in the Society of the Sacred Heart	167
CHAPTER 5	
The Spiritual Leadership of Madeleine Sophie Barat	201
Conclusion	235
Notes and References	239
Bibliography	297
Index	305

Acknowledgements

When writing these essays I drew on the expertise of librarians, archivists and historians in Paris and Rome. I would like to thank in particular the librarians and archivists of the Archives Nationales and Bibliothèque Nationale, Paris; the Archives de l'Archevêché de Besançon; Archives de la Compagnie de Jésus, Vanves. In Rome, the Vatican Archives and Archivium Historicum Societatis Iesu. I would like to thank the following in a particular way: Margaret MacCurtain who read the entire manuscript, in several versions, and who always gave me constructive, insightful criticism. I thank Sarah Curtis whose comments on Chapters 1 and 3 have been invaluable. Similarly, I thank Deirdre Raftery and Rosemary Raughter for their insights, especially with regard to Chapter 1. I have greatly benefited from Sara Wilbourne's enlightening comments on Chapter 1 and on the overall purpose of this book. In Paris I have appreciated exchanges on this project with Rebecca Rogers and Claude Langlois, and I thank Rebecca Rogers for her essay in Chapter 2. I thank Thomas Morrissey for his remarks on aspects of Jesuit history in Chapters 1 and 3, and Joe Ward for his comments on Chapter 3 regarding Jesuit life. In Trinity College Dublin I thank Jane Ohlmeyer and Dan Bradley for introducing me to the significance of DNA/forensic testing in medical/historical research. I am grateful to Mary d'Apice and Frederick Holmes for their essays in Chapter 4. I thank Maryann Valiulis and the students in the Centre for Gender and Women's Studies in Trinity College Dublin for the opportunity to present many of the ideas in this book at seminars.

Margaret Phelan, general archivist of the Society of the Sacred Heart, has helped me at every stage of the research and to her I am deeply grateful. I am also grateful to Maryvonne Duclaux, provincial archivist in Poitiers, France, as well as Chantal Kobel, provincial archivist of the Irish-Scottish province, and those archivists of the Society who have responded so readily by correspondence. Several members of the Society, Mary Loretto Busch, Sandra McSheaffrey, Mariajo Iribarren, Catherine Nowlan, Dairne McHenry and Maria Mullen, have read chapters of the book and made helpful comments which I have tried to integrate into the text. Nina Norell has followed the journey of this book over several years and I am deeply grateful for her insights. I thank Mary Maher for her translation of French texts, and Frances Deery for her translation of German texts. For many years now I owe François Vincent a real debt of gratitude for his professional assistance in French language and culture.

The communities of the Society of the Sacred Heart in the Villa Lante, Rome and in Avenue de Lowendal, Paris have given me gracious hospitality over many years. This has facilitated my research and writing, and to them I give my heartfelt thanks. I am grateful to successive General Councils of the Society of the Sacred Heart for their support, ongoing interest and encouragement. I thank Cork University Press for accepting to publish this book. Indeed, I appreciate all who have helped me, in the Society of the Sacred Heart as well as family, colleagues and friends. I hope this book will reply to the many questions and observations on the Society of the Sacred Heart which were expressed in conversations and written exchanges over several years.

Abbreviations

GA	Rome Society of the Sacred Heart, General Archives, Rome
AF	Poitiers Société du Sacré-Cœur, Archives Françaises, Poitiers
AN	Archives Nationales, Paris
AD Yonne	Archives Départementales de l'Yonne
ACM de Joigny	Archives Communales, Mairie de Joigny
ASV	Archivio Segreto Vaticano
AA Etr	Archives du Ministre des Affaires Etrangères.
AAFr.	Archives de l'Ambassade de France près le Saint-Siège, Rome
ARSI	Archivium Romanum Societatis Iesu
AHSI	Archivium Historicum Societatis Iesu
AFSJ	Vanves Archives Françaises de la Compagnie de Jésus
DS	Dictionnaire de Spiritualité
LA	Lettres Annuelles de la Société du Sacré-Cœur
SB	Sophie Barat

* The punctuation and spelling in the quotations from letters and manuscripts have been modernised.

Preface

Do you realise that you know more than you think you know? Do you realise that if you use all you know, and all the possibilities within you, that there is almost nothing you can't do? More serious than that is this fact: if you use more than you know that you know, the world will be a paradise.

When a nation or an individual creates things so sublime – in a sort of permanent genius of inventiveness and delight – when they create things so miraculous that they are not seen or noticed or remarked upon by even the best minds around, then that is because they create always from the vast unknown places within them. They create always from beyond. They make the undiscovered places and infinities in them their friend.

They live on the invisible fields of their hidden genius. And so their most ordinary achievements are always touched with genius. Their most ordinary achievements, however, are what the world sees, and acclaims.

But their most extraordinary achievements are unseen, invisible, and therefore cannot be destroyed.

This endures forever.

Ben Okri, *Astonishing the Gods*

Introduction

In the wake of the Counter Reformation and more intensely after the French Revolution, religious communities of women sprang up with astonishing rapidity in France. These communities shared a spiritual path, provided companionship and the opportunity to respond to the needs of society. This phenomenon invites analysis. It is intriguing to know how these women came together, agreed on their ideals and then set up structures and codes of behaviour which informed every aspect of their lives. On that basis they committed themselves to bringing their ideals to wider society, mostly by education and nursing. In that process, certain cultural transformations occurred, certain exchanges took place, between the social worlds these women had known and the one they created together in their community. One such community was the Society of the Sacred Heart, founded in 1800.

During the French Revolution, Madeleine Sophie Barat (1779–1865) and her companions created a way of life which attracted women from both the aristocracy and the poor class. Their calling was based on their spiritual equality, made all the more evident during the Revolution when uncertainty and violence had created social chaos and a certain, if temporary, blur between the classes. By the time the Bourbons had returned to the throne in 1815 and social order and class structures were restored, the Society of the Sacred Heart had already embarked on a genuine and brave attempt to seek resolution between the internal and external social worlds the members had inhabited in their childhoods. In working out their life together the members certainly experienced tensions and conflicts, within and without the Society. But over time they began to open new spaces for women's energies, new possibilities for independent

1

action, and they served the wider and indeed international community by the service of education.

These women merit research; the history of religious women has been well embedded in rigid stereotyping of nuns. The French historian Jeanne de Charry[1] considered Sophie Barat as 'the great unknown', and that, despite having a series of biographers in the late nineteenth and early twentieth centuries, she had remained a hidden and veiled figure. This was due in part to the canonisation process,[2] which began soon after Sophie Barat's death in 1865, and also to the genre and style of biography which obtained at that time. Two major biographies of Sophie Barat appeared between 1879 and 1884. One was written by her secretary, Adèle Cahier, and published in 1884. The other was published in 1876; this was written by Louis Baunard and commissioned by the Society of the Sacred Heart specifically in view of the canonisation process which began in 1872.[3] Contemporary witnesses appeared in church court hearings held in Paris and Rome, each testifying under oath. The regulations concerning canonisation required a biography of the candidate, providing evidence of the person's way of life and virtue, worthy of sainthood. The judicial body for the process then decided if Sophie Barat had exercised sufficient heroic virtue to merit the reward of canonisation. This investigation lasted from 1879 until 1925.[4] The outcome of the canonisation process was successful and Madeleine Sophie Barat was awarded first the title of Venerable in 1879, then Blessed in 1908 and finally Saint in 1925.

Thus, in a relatively short time after her death, the narrative and significance of Sophie Barat's life was locked into a framework which sought to meet and satisfy the requirements of the canonisation process. In many ways she was the ideal candidate for sanctity in the late nineteenth century, a time when the church sought to increase its hold and influence over education. Sophie Barat's contribution to the education of young women of the rich and poor classes in society was a useful example for the Catholic community. For its part, the Society of the Sacred Heart welcomed the possible canonisation of its founder. This would give it status within the church and wider society, particularly in the field of education. Such public, papal recognition would also facilitate the extension of the Society of the Sacred Heart internationally and provide a certain prestige when dealing with local bishops, clergy and secular authorities.

However, what the process of canonisation had to do with the actual life of Sophie Barat is another thing altogether. In the creation of the saintly figure of Sophie Barat, worthy of canonisation, hagiography inevitably took over and served to obscure her personality, especially her humanity. It also rendered invisible many of the deeper issues around the purpose of the community, the Society of the Sacred Heart, which she initiated in 1800 and governed as superior general for sixty-three years. The objections made by the devil's advocate, opposing her canonisation, signalled other, distinctive, highly individual aspects of Sophie Barat's life and the lives of her colleagues. But they were presented within the trapped confines of the process and its specific focus, and so their implications could not be grasped then. And so, by the time Madeleine Sophie Barat was canonised in May 1925, the content of her life story seemed well established. She became a distant, reserved figure; revered certainly, but for many quite inaccessible, as remote as her statue high up in the nave of St Peter's in Rome.

The style of biographical writing in the late nineteenth century also veiled Sophie Barat's personality. This tended to stress the public role of the subject, usually a political or military figure in society, and nearly always male. The inner life of the person, if considered at all, was considered in heroic, virtuous terms. The biography of Sophie Barat published in 1876 by Louis Baunard is a case in point. It was written specifically for the purpose of canonisation and presented her in heroic mode, without indicating either the depth of her inner journey or the extent of the personal challenges she faced in the course of her life. By contrast, Barat's former secretary, Adèle Cahier, was conscious that Baunard's biography did not reveal the true Sophie Barat. Soon after Barat's death Cahier had prepared a biography of her, initially to preserve the story of her life for future generations in the Society, and later on in view of her possible canonisation. However, it was considered inadvisable to present a biography written by a member of the Society for the canonisation process. For this reason, Louis Baunard, a young priest trained in theology and in literature, was asked to prepare the official biography. Adèle Cahier was required to hand over the vast material she had amassed on Sophie Barat to Louis Baunard and this cost her greatly. She doubted Baunard's competence for the task and she made her views known to the leadership of the Society.[5] When Baunard's work was published in 1876, Adèle Cahier was vindicated to the extent that she saw his errors in print. She was further justified when a historian in Germany refused to translate Baunard's life of Sophie Barat because of its inaccuracies. For her professional satisfaction and integrity, Adèle Cahier recorded Baunard's errors in detail and deposited them in the General Archives of the Society.[6]

Nevertheless, it was Baunard's work which became the standard life of Sophie Barat for many decades, and it was reprinted a number of times and translated into several languages. Adèle Cahier's life of Barat was published privately in 1884 and remained unknown to the general public and infrequently cited, even in the Society of the Sacred Heart. Fortunately Adèle Cahier was well aware that Barat's life could not be adequately presented within the limitations of a biography written specifically for her canonisation. Besides, there were too many of Barat's contemporaries still alive, preventing some issues and individuals coming into the public domain. In December 1871 Cahier wrote to a friend expressing reservations over how much to include in her biography. She had written two substantial chapters on the major crisis in the Society of the Sacred Heart from 1839–1851 and its impact on Sophie Barat. She decided finally that she could not publish them. These chapters remained in the Archives of the Society of the Sacred Heart, unexamined until 1993. Adèle Cahier also prepared a vast collection of manuscripts and correspondence concerning the life of Sophie Barat, especially during this critical period, 1839–1851. In fact, she left an archival map of this material, obviously prepared for future researchers. This material, now in the General Archives in Rome, has meticulous cross-referencing, indicating the range of sources available and how they were catalogued. Adèle Cahier had concluded that she must preserve all the material for a future moment when the full story of Sophie Barat could be told.[7]

This proved to be the case. Sophie Barat's process for canonisation in 1925 gave a certain definition to her biography and it appeared that there was no more to discover. In any event, religious archives at this time tended to be seen more as relics than as material for scientific research. Within that perspective, Barat's reputation as a saint was preserved, and new biographers tended to use Baunard as their source, as well as the conferences of Barat,[8] and ten volumes of her letters which were published between 1920 and 1965. Jeanne de Charry has pointed out how carefully these letters were edited, omitting three subject matters: Sophie Barat's dealing with her family; her (vast) concerns around finances for the schools and communities; her expression of personal feelings.[9] Apparently such concerns were not considered worthy of a saint. In fact, the only unedited, published letters of Sophie Barat in print in the early twentieth century were her official letters to the Society, her public voice as superior general.[10]

Possibilities for new research on Sophie Barat arose in the middle of the twentieth century when the Society of the Sacred Heart commissioned

Mary Cecilia Wheeler to catalogue its immense archives and open them to the public.[11] Jeanne de Charry published her definitive history on the 1815 Constitutions of the Society of the Sacred Heart, and critical editions of the correspondence of Sophie Barat and Philippine Duchesne, and of Sophie Barat and Joseph Varin.[12] The Society also appointed Claire Dykmans[13] to coordinate a team from the Society whose task was to transcribe the 14,000 original letters of Sophie Barat in their entirety. When these three tasks were completed, the Archives of the Society of the Sacred Heart revealed remarkable resources for the history of women in Europe and the Americas from the mid-eighteenth century until today.

In addition to these new resources, by the mid-twentieth century, the art and craft of biography had evolved and historians brought to it rigorous scientific training, enriched by the insights and approaches of several schools of historiography. These insist on the use of primary, unedited manuscripts in the construction of a biography, placed in historical context, and with a particular focus on the interface between personal and public life.[14] New approaches also came in the field of women's history which emerged from the late-nineteenth century and steadily established itself as an essential discipline in the world of academic research. For centuries women had been either ignored or rendered invisible in writing the narrative of history. If they were acknowledged at all in the records, it was weighted in favour of noble women, or exceptional individuals, or more often as part of the sub-narrative, the sub-text of history, almost always in the minor role.[15]

Historians of women have challenged this narrative, the patriarchal construct of history which for so long was considered the norm. Indeed Sophie Barat was presented for canonisation within that construction of history and within that perception of women. Now the biographer observes how a woman creates the narrative of her life, writes her text, and has her own sub-texts, her rules and criteria for judgement and choice. Once seen in this light, and not in deference and reference to the male model or archetype of history, then a woman's life can be liberated into its own truth. When a woman holds the major voice in the biographical narrative a radical shift in interpretation becomes possible. Then the biographer can track how women approach one another, how they work in the private sphere, and how they gain public voice; how they deal with their relationships, with both women and men; with their feelings and their power systems, and their power struggles; how they resolve issues, allow themselves to be changed, modified at times, or perhaps refuse to move to where they do not wish to go, where they know it is counter to their perception and values.

Most of these developments in the field of history have occurred since Sophie Barat's canonisation in 1925. In the light of that, the bicentenary of the Society of the Sacred Heart in 2000 seemed the right time for a new biography of its founder. The sheer volume of primary material on Sophie Barat made available for research in the archives of the Society of the Sacred Heart in Rome, Poitiers and St Louis was more than adequate for new research, but it was only the beginning. Using the Society's material, research led to further manuscript material on Barat held in the National Archives in Paris, in the Départments and Diocesan Archives in France, in the Vatican Archives, and in other libraries, archives and embassies in Paris and Rome. On the basis of this extensive material, a new biography was commissioned in 1993 and published in 2000.[16]

Following the publication of *Madeleine Sophie Barat. A Life* (Cork University Press, 2000) comments from reviewers, from the academy and members of the Society of the Sacred Heart showed that there were topics which caught the interest of readers. The biography generated further questions around stereotypes and myths in history.[17] Queries arose on how the form of community arose, how class issues were dealt with in the Society, and especially how (or indeed if) the members resolved the tensions inherent in a spiritual vocation which all held in common and equally but yet was lived out in two social ranks in community. Many were interested in the philosophy and activities around the education of young women in the nineteenth century; others asked about issues of power and authority within and between communities in the Society, and with members of the clergy, especially the Jesuits. Readers were curious too about Sophie Barat's health, how she managed to sustain her task in life into old age while battling with recurrent illnesses. Interest was also shown in her style of leadership, how this was exercised, what were her values, and how had these marked the history of the Society. Such topics were difficult to respond to adequately either in emails, letters or short conversations at conferences. They touched both individual and corporate biography and a new study was required, with a different focus.

This new book of five essays focuses on aspects of the Society of the Sacred Heart in nineteenth century France. It discusses the collective and individual biographies of the members, as well as the public and private life of the Society during this period. It is in that crossover place between the personal and the public that the lives of these women, their community and their educational work, their hopes and aspirations, their successes and failures, can be seen and assessed. The first essay shows how the community was created from 1800 by Sophie Barat and her companions. It explores their family origins and social backgrounds, how and why they gathered together and reached agreement on their goals and on how they would live them out. They gathered at a time when religious life was suppressed in France, and they created their model of community based on their experiences of family life, including its class structures, on their imagining of how a religious life could be lived in the future. They were also influenced by women who had experienced religious life prior to the French Revolution.[18] Certainly the 1789 Revolution itself was a common experience. It impacted on their families, on each of them personally, some by its idealism and many by its violence. They were marked, too, by the Enlightenment, and their consciousness was further awakened by the political and religious turmoil all around them. Their common wish to take part in restoring Christian life and values in France was articulated by their focus on the spirituality of the Heart of Christ, a statement of deep faith which had indications of political alignment with the Bourbons.

The social contribution of the Society of the Sacred Heart to the renewal of French society was the education of young women of the nobility and higher bourgeoisie, and the education of young women from the poor class. This combined focus opened new possibilities, new spaces for women, in the public and private spheres. The form of life in the Society of the Sacred Heart was attractive to many women, an alternative to marriage and the single life. In the context of the education of women in early nineteenth-century France, the second essay presents the educative vision of the Society of the Sacred Heart, articulated in three contemporary *Mémoires* (1823–4). One of the early educators in the Society, Marie d'Olivier, held radical views on education but little was known about her until her manuscripts were discovered in 1997 in the Jesuit Archives in Paris.[19]

The third essay is a study of the relationship between the Society of the Sacred Heart and the Jesuits in the lifetime of Sophie Barat. The Jesuit form of religious life, especially its structures of government, attracted Sophie Barat from the beginning. However, within the Society and among the Jesuits, the nature of the links between both congregations was often a source of debate and controversy. This essay shows the nature of these similarities and differences, especially those concerning the exercise of authority and power. While the early years of the Society of the Sacred Heart were marked by many friendships with the Jesuits, there was a change in attitude between the Society and the Jesuits, both in Paris and in Rome, after 1829. From this time the relationships became somewhat more formal and distant, although Jesuits continued to give the annual spiritual retreats in the communities and schools, as well as spiritual direction.

The fourth essay considers health care in the Society of the Sacred Heart. This was essential for the personal wellbeing of the members and for the tasks each one carried out. The most detailed health record is that of Sophie Barat, based on her 14,000 letters. In accordance with letter-writing conventions of her day, Barat spoke of her health and the health of members of the Society in most of her letters. These show in some detail how members of the Society cared for one another, and they also track how Barat coped with serious, chronic illness. The final essay discusses the spiritual leadership of Sophie Barat, its roots and origins, how it developed and motivated her in the course of her long life. It also discusses how she mediated her inner perceptions and reflections in practical leadership of the Society. The essay shows a leader at work, proposing definite stages in spiritual growth leading to enlightenment. Her teaching evokes the spiritual guidance present in the ancient mystery centres, found in all religious cultures and practised by the mystics. All propose a path of profound self-knowledge, leading to inner transformation. For Sophie Barat this path was the encounter with Christ and the gift of self for the transformation of the world. She walked this path herself and showed how powerful the witness of a human life can be when lived as honestly as possible. In the end, Sophie Barat embodied and mediated what she envisaged for the members of the Society of the Sacred Heart. Indeed, the individual and collective biography of the Society came together in the style and content of her leadership. At their best, these strove to find a balance between the inner call of the individual and the need to sustain the wider community of the Society of the Sacred Heart.

'One Musical Ensemble'
The Society of the Sacred Heart,
1800–1865
The evolution of a community

> The Society is like a well composed choir, with voices singing in different parts yet forming one musical ensemble. We all have the same rule. Those among us who know the Heart of Our Lord best, whoever lives in the most saintly way, she is the one who fulfils most effectively the purpose of her calling.[1]

When recalling the early days of the Society of the Sacred Heart Madeleine Sophie Barat described how it grew in a spontaneous, even haphazard, way. She told how she went to Paris in 1795, at the age of sixteen, and over time met small groups of men and women in the city, working in secret to restore stability and Christian values in France. They were not alone in this quest. The fall of Robespierre and the end of the Terror had led to public debates on how to regenerate French society, deeply traumatised by the violence unleashed from 1789. But there could be no simple going back, no return to the past. Far too much had happened since the outbreak of the French Revolution in 1789 which had led to profound changes in French society. Individuals, families and institutions were shifted out of their familiar spaces and drawn into events and experiences which displaced them, either for a time or effectively forever. Religion in general, especially the Catholic Church, was held in public contempt. Churches had either been closed or used for secular purposes. Sacred spaces and ritual vessels had been violated and ancient church bells silenced. Sophie Barat recalled this experience:

> At the end of the Terror and of the abominations of the Revolution against religion and the Blessed Sacrament, all hearts vibrated together in unison: Make reparation to Jesus Christ in the Blessed Sacrament was the rallying cry. No two pious people meeting

9

together would talk without trying to find some means of bringing
Jesus Christ back into family life.[2]

With this as goal and inspiration, individual women all over France
began to emerge out of the maelstrom created by the Revolution. They
gathered in small groups and found ways to look after the vast needs
around them, either by starting small projects to care for the poor and sick,
setting up small schools, or teaching the catechism to children on
Sundays.[3] In time their initiatives emerged into the public domain, and
gained recognition during the Empire of Napoleon. The suppression of
religious life in 1792 had both cleared a space for new forms of religious life
to take root and provided the possibility of moving beyond the strict rules
for religious women laid down at the Council of Trent in the late sixteenth
century. Thus, from the beginning Sophie Barat's desire for spiritual regen-
eration in France was linked with educational projects.[4] Initially small
boarding and poor schools were set up in Amiens, Grenoble and Poitiers.
Then greater freedom arose when Napoleon, conscious of the need to
educate young women, gave partial approval to religious communities on
the condition that they would not make perpetual vows.[5] The future
Society of the Sacred Heart received such approval on 10 March 1807.

Who then were these women who gathered round Sophie Barat?
What inspiration brought them together? How had they found each
other? What did they create? How did they devise, experiment and gradually articulate the purpose of their personal and community lives? What
did each bring to the process? All had been profoundly scarred by the
Revolution. They shared either partial or total disintegration of family
life, loss of home and property, war and violence, fathers, brothers, husbands called up to serve in the armies, the threat or reality of
imprisonment, the death of family members by war, by guillotine, or
years of illness, isolation and, for some, exile. The Society of the Sacred
Heart was born out of deep personal experiences of loss and death,
which drew a small band of women to help restore, renew and conserve
religious values lost during the Revolution. Moreover, they lived through
the first years of the Society, 1800–15, in politically charged circumstances which impacted on them both individually and as a group.[6]

Social composition of the Society of the Sacred Heart 1800–1815[7]

The women who joined the Society of the Sacred Heart came from all
classes of French society, from the nobility and upper bourgeoisie, from

the lower bourgeoisie, including the families of lawyers, merchants, government officials, and from the artisan and poor classes. All had experienced life in the ancien régime and most had firsthand experience of the Revolution and Empire. Some lived through the brutalities of the Terror and had seen their families cut down by the guillotine. Others were forced into exile or driven into further poverty and dispossession. Most were single women, though a few were widows. Others again had been in religious life until its suppression in 1792.[8] Each had to cope with the Revolution as it affected them and their families and friends; some lived in considerable danger and acted with real courage. Many had tried to set up small projects in their neighbourhood, offering some form of care and service, especially to poor children. Initially they gathered in four cities of France, in Paris in 1800, and then in Amiens (1801), Grenoble (1804) and Poitiers (1806).

They met each other almost by accident, beginning in the closing years of the eighteenth century when a small group of women gathered in Paris. One of them was Madeleine Sophie Barat, destined to be the founder of the Society of the Sacred Heart. She came from a lower bourgeoisie family in Joigny, in Burgundy. Her father, Jacques Barat, was a wine-maker (vigneron), a skilled wine-barrel maker (tonnelier), and marketed his wines in Picardy. Her mother, Madeleine Fouffé, more formally educated than her husband, took care of the family business and managed the household affairs. Sophie was educated by her elder brother, Louis, who taught his sister what he had learnt in school and the seminary. When he was ordained a priest secretly in Paris in 1795 he persuaded his parents to allow Sophie to join him there that year, to pursue her education.[9] In Paris Sophie and Louis Barat lived as paying guests in Madame Duval's house, in the rue de Touraine in the Marais (now rue Saintonge). Octavie Bailly, from Forge les Eaux, near Rouen, also lived there. She planned to join the Carmelite community in Paris.[10] Marguerite,[11] Madame Duval's maid, and Marie-Françoise Loquet were also members of the group. Loquet ran a small school for young workers in her house in Paris. She taught children the catechism and wrote several religious novels.[12]

In the autumn of 1800 a priest arrived in Paris, Joseph Varin,[13] and he visited the group in the rue de Touraine. He brought news of a new community founded in Rome, called the Dilette di Gesù, who asked him to explore possibilities of founding a community in France. The origins of this community were linked to Varin's friend, Léonor de Tournély (1767–97), who before his death had predicted that a community of women called Society of the Sacred Heart would someday exist.[14] Varin suggested that the group consider becoming affiliated to the Dilette, and in a ceremony on 21 November 1800 the group committed to at least test it out, although there was little clarity around the next step. They continued their daily studies with Louis Barat and worked with the poor, all the while searching for a project they could begin together.[15] Then in April 1801 news came of two women in Amiens, Henriette Grosier and her aunt, Hyacinthe Davaux, who had started a boarding school for girls in the town. They told Joseph Varin that they needed help urgently in their school. Both were from Beauvais, and Hyacinthe Davaux had been Benedictine of the Abbey of St Paul at Beauvais prior to the Revolution. Henriette Grosier (1774–1842)[16] planned to become a Carmelite and considered the school only as an interim project until religious life was restored in France.[17] Their boarding school was growing rapidly and a poor school was planned for the autumn of 1801, so help was urgently needed.

In September 1801 Francoise Loquet went to Amiens, followed a month later by Sophie Barat, Octavie Bailly and Marguerite (Madame Duval's maid). Other women quickly joined them. Geneviève-Françoise-Nicole Deshayes (1767–1849)[18] joined the group in 1802, despite the opposition of her brother and some clergy. She was a native of Amiens and a cultured woman of some wealth.[19] Her maid, Catherine Maillard, who was barely sixteen, joined at the same time.[20] In the same year Adèle Jugon came from Paris, where she taught catechism in the parish d'Etoilles. She learnt about the initiative in Amiens from friends and newspapers.[21] Though she stayed less than a year, in that short time she recognised the leadership qualities of Sophie Barat and pointed them out to Louise Naudet, a member of the Dilette in Rome, who came to visit the little community.[22] Then in 1803 Adele Bardot from Joigny joined,[23] as did Marguerite-Rosalie Debrosse.[24] In 1804 a woman from Lyon, Barthélémy Roux, arrived in Amiens. She came from a family of weavers in Lyon which had experienced all the rigours of the Revolution. Barthélémy Roux heard about the new community from Joseph Varin and she decided to travel to Amiens and ask to join:

> Later she recalled that she arrived in Amiens with just a little box under her arm. The sister at the door took her for a trader (petite marchande) and wanted to send her away: 'Thank you; we do not need any pins.' 'I am not a trader,' replied Barthélémy, 'I have been sent by Fr Varin and I wish to speak to Madame Barat.'[25]

That same year Félicité Desmarquest also joined the community. She belonged to a rural, lower bourgeoisie family in Guillaucourt in Picardy, the eleventh of sixteen children, and she had received a basic education at home.[26] In 1805 two sisters from Soissons, Thérèse[27] and Josephine Pelletier,[28] joined and were followed by Augustine Huchon in 1811,[29] Marie de la Croix from Metz in 1812,[30] and Suzanne Labart (1790–1848) in 1813.[31] Women who had been in religious life before the Revolution also became interested in the initiative in Amiens. Anne Baudemont, formerly a member of the monastery of Sainte-Claire de Rheims,[32] was invited by Joseph Varin to join in 1802, along with another former member of the monastery, Thérèse le Franc,[33] and their friend from Rheims, Mlle Capy.[34] The following year Teresa Copina, an Italian, arrived in Amiens. She had belonged to an Italian religious community, Vergine del Vanzo, and had joined the Dilette di Gesù in Rome in 1799/1800. In 1803 she was sent to Amiens and later (in 1810) became the Mistress of Novices.[35] Félicité de Sambucy de St Estève, a former Ursuline of Clermont-Ferrand, joined the community in Amiens in 1807,[36] followed by Anne-Marie de Coërville who had belonged to the congregation of Sainte Genevieve[37] and Madeleine Raison (1761–1837) who had been a Benedictine coadjutrix sister.[38] In 1813 Clarisse Langlet, a sister of Notre Dame, asked to transfer to the community in Amiens. She came from Picardy and her father served in the army.[39]

Women from upper bourgeois, scholarly and legal families were also attracted to the community in Amiens, and they came from all over France. Catherine-Emilie de Charbonnel de Jussac (1774–1857) arrived in Amiens in the autumn of 1803 riding a fine horse and dressed in striking attire.[40] She came from landed nobility (noblesse terrienne de province) in Monistrol (Haute-Loire) and was educated by the Ursulines there. During the Revolution she took immense risks to protect her family, especially when her father was exiled, her brother imprisoned and shot, and her mother too imprisoned for a time. Similarly, Marie d'Olivier, who joined the community in 1804, came from landed nobility in Nîmes in the Vaucluse. She was a highly educated woman and in time would write educational novels and significant essays on education.[41] Cécile de Cassini, who entered the community in 1803, was the daughter of Jean-Dominique Cassini, Comte of Thury (1748–1845), director of the Observatory in Paris from 1784 to 1793. He was imprisoned in 1793 for his opposition to the Revolution, and on his release the family moved to Thury, Clermont-en-Beauvaisis (Oise) for safety. There he finished his topographic and trigonometric survey of France.

Comte Cassini's house became a centre where friends and neighbours came and discussed ideas and shared their reading. The circle included the Abbé Lamarche,[42] Madame de Rumigny from Amiens,[43] and the Prevost family recently returned from colonial service in St Dominique. Madame de Rumigny prepared Marie-Elizabeth Prevost for her First Communion and in 1808 Marie-Elizabeth decided to join the community in Amiens.[44] Cécile de Cassini initially stayed a short time in Amiens (1803–4). The life of a teacher did not suit her, and this was made evident when a child fell out a window during class and she did not even notice it. She had been completely absorbed by the stars.[45]

Further aristocratic elements appeared in the community when three of the de Gramont d'Aster family asked to enter in Amiens. The family traced its origins to the early Middle Ages, in the south-west of France (now Pyrénées-Atlantiques) and was of the court nobility (nobles de cour), with a residence at Versailles.[46] Eugénie-Cornélie de Gramont (1788–1846) entered in 1806, followed by her sister, Antoinette de Gramont (1792–1844) in 1811.[47] Finally, in 1813, their mother, the Comtesse de Gramont d'Aster, Gabrielle-Charlotte-Eugénie de Boisgelin (1766–1836), joined the community.[48] The de Boisgelin de Pléhédel et de Sainte de Cucé family in Brittany traced its origins to the twelfth century,[49] and in 1781 she married Antoine-Adrien-Charles de Gramont, Comte de Gramont d'Aster (1758–1795). Several members of the Boisgelin and de Gramont d'Aster families suffered during the Revolution, either at the guillotine or by being forced into exile. The de Gramont d'Aster family spent some years as émigrés in London, before returning to Paris in 1796.[50] Another mark of the ancien régime impinged on the community in Amiens when Marie du Terrail entered in 1803.[51] She had been orphaned during the Revolution and educated at St Cyr,[52] a school founded in Versailles by Madame de Maintenon in the seventeenth century for daughters or orphans of poor nobility. She was followed by Henriette Ducis,[53] a native of Versailles, who joined the community in 1804, influenced by her former confessor, Louis de Sambucy de St. Estève (1771–1847).[54] Prior to his ordination he taught religion classes in Paris at St Sulpice, attended by Eugénie and Antoinette de Gramont, when they had returned from London and before they went to boarding school in Amiens. After his ordination St Estève became tutor in Versailles to the de Quelen family, among them Hyacinthe de Quelen, future archbishop of Paris.[55] He became confessor to the community at Amiens from 1803, and his sister, Félicité de Sambucy de St Estève, a former Ursuline, joined the community in 1807.[56]

Within a few short years a new community had slowly emerged. Those who joined it came from all strands of French society, and from the towns and rural parts of France. They came from the poor class, the lower bourgeoisie, the artisan class; from the landed nobility, the court nobility, from the upper middle class, as well as from scholarly and legal families. There was an inherent challenge and tension in the combined impact of the de Gramont d'Aster and de Sambucy de St Estève families. They readily sympathised with women like Anne Baudemont and Félicité de Sambucy de St Estève, whose monasteries had been suppressed in 1792 and who hoped to restore their former way of life. This was in marked contrast to those, like Sophie Barat and Marie-Elizabeth Prevost, who had come to Amiens without any experience of religious life and were following their own intuitions, responding to what was around them. During these early years the members of the community struggled to articulate what they had come for and what it was they wished to do in the future. They found they were not alone in this search, that others beyond Amiens wished to join them.

The world beyond Amiens: Grenoble

While the community in Amiens was coming into being, another initiative was taking place in Grenoble, in the former Visitation monastery of Ste Marie d'en Haut. In 1792 the monastery was suppressed and the community dispersed. One of its members, Philippine Duchesne,[57] continued living her religious life at home, as well as working with the poor and destitute of the town, often at great personal risk. In 1795, when the Terror had abated, Philippine tried to persuade the community to return to Ste Marie d'en Haut, but they were too old, too dispersed or too dispirited to resume their life. Nevertheless, Philippine went back to the monastery to try to retain the space and after a time four young women joined her. This development was viewed with consternation by the townspeople in Grenoble and, in an effort to circumvent criticism, Philippine asked one of the local clergy to devise a rule of life which she could ask the bishop of Grenoble to endorse. By March 1803 the little group was officially called the 'Daughters of the Propagation of the Faith'.[58]

By then Philippine had heard of the Dilette di Gesù recently founded in Rome and had considered joining them, going to Rome if necessary. But learning of the Dilette foundation in France, in Amiens, she wondered if she could link with that community. She discussed the possibility with Joseph Varin and a colleague, Pierre Roger,[59] who were in the area and visited Ste Marie d'en Haut in July 1804. Varin in turn spoke with Sophie Barat and some months later, on 13 December 1804, Sophie arrived in Ste Marie d'en Haut to explore the possibility of affiliation with the community at Amiens.[60] The women in Ste Marie d'en Haut came from diverse social backgrounds. Philippine Duchesne was of the upper bourgeoisie. Her father, Pierre François Duchesne (1743–1814), was a lawyer and politician. A formidable product of the Enlightenment, he was a radical thinker, anti-clerical and politically influential. Philippine's mother, Rose-Euphrosine Périer (1748–97), was a highly educated woman and from a wealthy merchant family. Philippine was taught reading, writing, arithmetic and household skills at home, and she joined her brothers for some of their classes, too. In 1781, to prepare for her First Communion, she went as a boarder to Ste Marie d'en Haut and decided to enter there. When she asked her parents in 1788 for permission to enter the community at Ste Marie d'en Haut they refused. However, Philippine simply left home, went to the monastery and refused to leave. In the end her parents relented, but on the condition that she would make her final solemn vows only when she was twenty-five.[61]

Marie Rivet joined Philippine in Ste Marie d'en Haut in October 1802. She was a native of Grenoble and had been a Carmelite novice prior to the Revolution.[62] She was followed in November that year by Marie Balastron.[63] In 1804 Emilie Giraud asked to enter the community. Her father, an architect, died when she was a child and, when her mother remarried in 1802, Emilie Giraud was placed as a boarder at Ste Marie d'en Haut. Rather than return home, she asked to join the community.[64] Adélaïde Second also asked to enter in 1804,[65] followed by Henriette Girard, a native of Lyon, in 1805. She became Sophie Barat's travelling companion for some months in 1805–6 and kept a journal of their travels.[66] Around this time a widow, Marie-Louise de Vaulserre des Adrets, asked to become a member of the community. As a young woman she had been forced into marriage with a much older man. After her husband's death she devoted her life during the Revolution to protecting priests, émigrés and prisoners.[67] Françoise Leridon[68] and Caroline Messoria[69] arrived at Ste Marie d'en Haut in 1805, and after a gap of four years Angelique Lavauden, a native of Dauphiné, entered in 1809.[70] Bertille Chauvin, from Sophie Barat's village, Joigny, entered in 1812 having spent some years trying in vain to establish a community there.[71] Philippine Duchesne's niece, Euphrosine Jouve, entered in November 1812.[72] Two years later, in 1814 Christine de Crouzas[73] and Hélène du Tour,[74] both from Savoy, joined the community. They were followed by Octavie Berthold in 1815. She was born into a Calvinist family in Geneva and became a Catholic in 1806.[75] Finally, in 1816 Hypolite Lavauden, sister of Angelique Lavauden,[76] joined the community, along with Eugénie Audé who came from Savoy.[77] While records are sparse for the social backgrounds of most of these women, contemporary accounts of the early days of the community in Grenoble reveal some reasons for their choice in life.[78]

When Sophie Barat arrived in Grenoble in mid-December 1804 there were just five members in the community. Sophie spent the days over Christmas to get acquainted with Philippine and her four companions. In early January 1805 Sophie began to speak about religious life to them, and it was as much a learning experience for her as it was for the expectant little group. In 1802 the Dilette di Gesù had appointed Sophie leader in Amiens, yet that same year the congregation was suppressed in Rome. The community in Amiens chose a new name, the Association of the Ladies of Christian Education, and Sophie Barat remained the leader.[79] Sophie could no longer lean on the Dilette di Gesù for guidance, she experienced resistance from some of her companions, as well as from Joseph Varin and the chaplain Louis de Sambucy de St Estève. Faced with such challenges, Sophie Barat began to find her voice and this was further strengthened in Ste Marie d'en Haut when she articulated her views on religious life.[80] Having had no experience of religious life prior to the Revolution had caused conflict for Sophie in Amiens, and this happened too in Grenoble with Philippine Duchesne. Their divergent views emerged in Ste Marie d'en Haut when Sophie proposed making some changes in the monastery. One change concerned her wish to abolish the monastic grills so characteristic of Visitation convents prior to the Revolution. Grills symbolised the separation of the religious from wider society, the cloister required by the church since the Council of Trent for all women who took solemn vows of religion. In this context, Sophie Barat's decision to abolish grills represented a significant break with the past.[81]

Philippine ceded to Sophie's views reluctantly and could not understand why monastic grills had to be abandoned.[82] Proceeding further, Sophie asked the little group to drop the recitation of office in choir in favour of personal, silent prayer.[83] Again Philippine Duchesne resisted this change but agreed to try an experiment for some days. Immediately the townspeople in Grenoble criticised the community for not praying in the customary way in Visitation monasteries, and they objected to the removal of the monastic grills. They also resented that Sophie insisted on fewer visitors to Ste Marie d'en Haut and that she accepted only young women into the community. Besides, they considered Sophie far too young to be in charge of a religious community. She was twenty-five. All these criticisms exposed the tensions between the old and new forms of religious life, within the community and in wider society.[84] The struggle in Grenoble around the retention of grills and the recitation of Office signalled a growing definition of the archetype of religious life which Sophie Barat had in mind and which the Society of the Sacred Heart would adopt over time, essentially a blend between the old and the new.

While the group in Ste Marie d'en Haut had experiences similar to that in Amiens, of the Revolution and of the desire to renew religion in France, it was different in several respects. Only two, Philippine Duchesne and Marie Rivet, had experience of religious life prior to the Revolution. The other women came directly from their families and within a wide radius of the south-east of France, as well as from Savoy and Switzerland. The aristocratic element, so prominent in Amiens, did not exist in Ste Marie d'en Haut, although Philippine Duchesne's family was certainly from the upper bourgeoisie. Most of all, this new community in the south of France broadened the initial foundation in Amiens, and gave Sophie Barat a wider base for her leaderships. It also led to a further expansion of the Association, to the west of France.

Poitiers and Bordeaux

Sophie Barat received an invitation in 1806 to visit two groups of women, one in Bordeaux and the other in Poitiers, and see if they could be incorporated with the Association.[85] The group in Poitiers was formed initially by three sisters, Lydie, (the middle sister's name is unknown) and Pulcherie Choblet. They had fled from Soullans in the Vendée and set up home in Poitiers in 1798. With their considerable wealth they acquired the former monastery of des Feuillants in 1802 and began a girl's boarding school with the help of some women from the town.[86] They also continued their opposition to the Revolution and were imprisoned in Poitiers for some months for housing a priest on the run. Once freed, the eldest, Lydie Choblet[87] (1765–1832), returned to the school in des Feuillants, but the second sister died shortly after her release from prison, and the youngest, Pulcherie Choblet, decided to found a school herself in Tours.[88] By 1806 only two women were left running the school in des Feuillants, Lydie Choblet and Josephine Bigeu, a native of Poitiers who had been in the school from the beginning.[89] However, by 1806 they both accepted they could not carry on alone and began to consider ceding the building to the diocese of Poitiers. As a last resort, a priest in Poitiers, Louis Lambert, suggested that they contact the community at Amiens and request a visit from Sophie Barat.[90]

In response to this invitation Sophie Barat travelled from Grenoble to Poitiers in July 1806,[91] accompanied by Henriette Girard. The journey took almost three weeks. On arrival in Poitiers Sophie met Lydie Choblet, Josephine Bigeu and some women from Poitiers who had expressed interest in joining the Association of the Ladies of Christian Education. However, before making a final decision, Sophie went to Bordeaux to meet the second group of women who also had expressed an interest in joining the Association. These six women, led by Thérèse Maillucheau, despairing of finding a religious community, decided to form one themselves. During the annual parish retreat they left home:

> Let us take advantage of the mission going on then [in the parish] and let us resolve generously to leave our families without a word of warning. Everyone agreed to this plan. One of the young women, called Angélique, whose parents were dead, owned a vineyard in the area where there was a type of small hut. There they chose their hide-away.[92]

Despite the pleas of their parents, the little group refused to return home. They stayed in the vineyard for three months, creating their own form of community life. They became a source of curiosity and of derisive comment as neighbours went by on the way to church. But it was not a passing phase. Only the assurance of Sophie Barat's imminent arrival persuaded them to move to a convent in Bordeaux and await her there.[93] When she arrived Sophie warned the group and their families that she did not have the resources to begin a community in Bordeaux. However, she proposed to interview them all and select those suitable for a possible foundation in Poitiers. News of this spread quickly and over a period of several days Sophie Barat examined not just the six women from the vineyard, but many others. After interviewing at least thirty women Sophie invited eight to accompany her back to Poitiers, on the condition that each had the permission of their families to leave Bordeaux.[94] Once families had given their consent Sophie organised the journey to Poitiers. She sent the women in twos and threes, to avoid drawing attention to such an exodus. Thérèse Maillucheau's family were opposed to her going to Poitiers, and their agreement was essential, not just for Thérèse, but also for the four other women from the same village who had asked to join. Sophie Barat visited the Maillucheau family herself at Saint-André de Cubzac, not far from Bordeaux. Though Thérèse's father was distraught at his daughter's decision, once the family had met Sophie Barat they agreed to let Thérèse travel to Poitiers, at least for a trial period.[95]

In September 1806 Sophie Barat began to organise the new community in Poitiers. News spread in the town and gradually more women asked
to become part of the new venture. One of them was Susanne Geoffroy
from Tellies, near Poitiers. Before the Revolution she wanted to enter the
Carmelites in Poitiers but the prioress thought their life was not for her.
Susanne waited for a time, and when religious life was suppressed in 1792
she decided to start a community herself in 1793/4.[96] She was joined by
three women and they taught catechism to children, helped destitute
former religious and gave safe haven to non-juring priests. The group
expanded quickly and soon became caught up in leadership problems;
with some relief Susanne withdrew in 1799 to nurse her dying father. The
following year she began another community in Poitiers, Les Sœurs de la
Providence, with two of her original companions. They lived in a house
formerly owned by the Jesuits. This was enough to create opposition from
some of the local clergy who refused Susanne the sacraments. In 1802 she
left Poitiers and joined the newly founded community at Chavagne in the
Vendée. Then in 1806, on hearing of the new community starting in des
Feuillants, Susanne asked Sophie Barat to be accepted into the Association.

Three women, connected with Susanne Geoffroy, also joined the new
community in Poitiers. Josephine Bonnet, a member of Les Sœurs de la
Providence in Poitiers (founded originally by Susanne Geoffroy) asked
to enter des Feuillants in 1806.[97] Madeleine du Chastaignier from
Poitiers, and a member of Les Sœurs de la Providence, also joined Les
Feuillants in 1806.[98] Then Marie-Madeleine de Chasseloup, a widow
from Bordeaux, had been in contact with Susanne Geoffroy for some
years, and in 1807 she asked to join des Feuillants.[99] In 1806 Henriette
Bernard, from Niort, asked to enter. She belonged to a family of twelve
children and she was fostered as a child. Acutely aware of the poverty
around her, she began a school for poor children which had sixty pupils
by 1806.[100] She asked Sophie if the Association could absorb her school
and Sophie agreed it was possible once Henriette had completed the
noviceship and had made her commitment to the community.[101]

Several other women entered at this time but records for them are
sparse. Jeanne Gertrude Lamolière, a native of Saint-André de Cubzac
near Bordeaux, came with Thérèse Maillucheau in 1806,[102] as did
Marinette Guiégnet (c.1783–1808).[103] Similarly Mélanie Demelin[104]
and Brigette Berniard[105] entered in 1806, with Louise Macqué Olivier
from Bordeaux[106] and Félicité Boulard.[107] Elizabeth Boué (1777–1861)
from Bordeaux joined the community in 1807.[108] Sister [nn] Frossard
entered in 1807/8, at the age of thirty-two.[109] Gabrielle Benoit from

Niort entered in 1808,[110] and Marthe Maugenet[111] also entered around this time. Amélie Colas entered in 1811,[112] as did Célestine Desnos,[113] while Julie Barré (1780–1859) from Niort joined the community in 1812.[114] No dates exist for Gabrielle Hinard, and only the Christian names of two other women survive: Marie, maid to Lydie Choblet for many years and who asked to stay with her mistress; and Madeleine, who took care of the sheep. Both lived with the community but did not follow the novices training programme.[115] No information exists on the social backgrounds of seventeen other women who entered the community in Poitiers between 1806 and 1815.[116]

Sophie Barat led the group in des Feuillants through a programme of religious training similar to the one she initiated in Grenoble. She recorded the training process she used in the journal she kept in Poitiers from 1806 to 1808.[117] She prepared some of the novices for teaching in the boarding school, in existence since 1802. In 1807 Sophie bought a property nearby for a poor school and trained some of the novices for this school as well. As in Amiens and in Grenoble, the social milieu of the women who joined the Association in Poitiers was mixed. But there was more similarity socially between the backgrounds of the communities in Poitiers and Grenoble. In contrast, the community in Amiens stood out as more distinctive socially, certainly more aristocratic. In Poitiers and Grenoble, few came from noble, upper bourgeois families, or from families with land and wealth. Most appear to have come from lower bourgeois and artisan families; some were orphans and many came from quite poor families. Perhaps fear of the dominant position of Amiens led Madeleine Chastaignier, a novice in Poitiers, to ask Sophie Barat if they would have a monastic structure, the model prior to the Revolution. Sophie replied:

> I can put your mind at rest with regard to your concern about becoming abbesses or canonesses. We will be neither one nor the other, I hope.[118]

Evolution towards the Society of the Sacred Heart 1800–1815[119]

The women who gathered in Paris, Amiens, Grenoble, Bordeaux and Poitiers between 1800 and 1815 formed the original profile, the original archetype, of the future Society of the Sacred Heart. They had come together either as individuals or in small groups and they began to find common purpose and companionship together. They came from all walks of life, from all sections of French society and from all over France; and a few came from beyond, from Savoy and Switzerland.[120] All had personal, often quite painful, experiences of the Revolution. Most came from Catholic families and most had experienced the ravages of war, the loss of parents, sisters, brothers, aunts, uncles and husbands, either by exile, prison, guillotine or war. Some had lost their homes and possessions. Many of their fathers, brothers and uncles served in the wars and not all their families had fought on the same side. They had so many stories and life experiences to share, which led them to seek out one another.[121]

They were all born into radical change, into war, turmoil and danger. Some of them viewed the Revolution as a tragedy, from the beginning. Others experienced disillusion over what had begun with such promise in 1789 and then tipped so quickly into unimaginable violence. Whichever way they thought, these upheavals impelled them to set out on new journeys, to begin new projects. Their spiritual convictions gave them the courage to take risks and find opportunities for action. They searched around and travelled far to seek the company of other women of like mind, often in the midst of risk and danger. Motivated by a blend of spiritual searching and commitment to social action, they shared their ideals and skills. In a relatively short time, fifteen years, they had created several communities which combined a spiritual purpose with offering education to rich and poor women. Many were highly educated. Some like Sophie Barat, Josephine Bigeu, Susanne Geoffroy and Thérèse Maillucheau, were educated at home. Others had a combination of home and school, like Philippine Duchesne in Ste Marie d'en Haut, Catherine de Charbonnel in Monistrol, and Eugénie and Antoinette de Gramont d'Aster in Paris and Amiens.[122] Madame de Gramont d'Aster, speaking before she entered, noted her satisfaction with the education her daughters received at Amiens:

> The ladies [choir sisters] here are highly educated, some are of out-
> standing character and their education is accomplished. This institute
> appears to be excellent, and the members are devoted completely to
> their work of education, giving themselves to it with an extraordinary
> degree of sacrifice.[123]

The women who entered from the aristocratic and upper bourgeois classes had learnt how to play music, dance, to embroider, write letters and engage in social conversation, either within their families or in public. Others from lower bourgeois backgrounds also were educated and possessed social, practical skills; women like Sophie Barat, Thérèse Maillucheau and Félicité Demarquest. Others from that same class may not have had those advantages but they certainly brought essential skills with them as cooks, dressmakers, farmers, gardeners, nurses and homemakers. Some had been maids to the nobility and the rising middle classes, or had been seeking such employment when they encountered the Association; a few had been maids to the aristocratic women who entered and were pleased to join them on the new venture. Others again were truly poor, with few resources, but ready to take part in a promising project. The chaos created by the Revolution allowed women from these strata of society to actually live together and, for the sake of a spiritual ideal, aspire to transcend their social differences.

All that said, in the end we will never know all the motivations of the women who formed the new communities in Paris, Amiens, Grenoble and Poitiers between 1800 and 1815. Some may have wished to gain freedom from marriage, or have personal independence, or avoid the loneliness of a single life. Even more basically during the Revolution, some perhaps sought places where they could live in safety; maybe they had lost their homes and families. Besides, the depth of fear and violence experienced during these years triggered a shift in consciousness and provided space for new initiatives, new choices, to emerge. Probably a combination of these factors influenced the women who formed and shaped the Society of the Sacred Heart in its early years. They first belonged to a group called the Dilette di Gèsu (until 1802), which then evolved into the Association of the Ladies of Christian Education (1802–14) and finally became known as the Society of the Sacred Heart in 1815. In this community each had found they could use their skills and fulfil a spiritual vocation.

They had shown enormous courage and independence, especially in a world where men, in the homes, in church and in political society, were considered the ultimate source and reference of authority. Indeed, during the first fifteen years of its existence, the future Society of the Sacred Heart had to deal with men, mostly clergy, who insisted on their right to control and oversee their lives. This was the assumption within families, and just as the male members of their families took for granted their rights over the women in the home, so the clergy claimed rights over religious women and over their communities. Struggles with clerics were particularly acute in Amiens, but also present to a degree in Grenoble and Poitiers. To balance that, however, there were many real and lasting friendships, and shared aspirations, with those priests who also had suffered during the Revolution and sought to restore the church in France. But in the inevitable struggles around leadership of the Society of the

Sacred Heart, most of the community in Amiens colluded with those clergy hostile to Sophie Barat and her leadership. After years of tension, these issues were resolved in 1815, and in the long term the conflicts strengthened the founding members and enabled them to articulate their goals and aspirations.[124]

Social distinctions in the Society of the Sacred Heart in 1815

During the first period of the Revolution distinctions between the aristocratic and poor classes were blurred by social chaos. But class differences had not disappeared, they were merely in abeyance until a certain order and stability was restored. When Napoleon created the Empire in 1804 he moved towards the restoration of the nobility by establishing a hierarchy of titles. These were a blend of members of the pre-1789 Bourbon court and the new court of the Emperor. As in the ancien régime, so under Napoleon social mobility existed, based on merit and reward, and this allowed for advancement within the hierarchical structures. The evolution of the Society of the Sacred Heart from 1800 to 1815 mirrored this general movement in French society. As the communities in Amiens, Grenoble and Poitiers became more rooted and new members joined, a more conscious awareness of social status grew and influenced the organisation of communities and tasks.

In the early years of the Society, until about 1807, status and tasks in the community were fluid and could change. For example, when Louise Duneufgerman and Henriette Moura entered in Amiens they were first listed as coadjutrix sisters and later classed as choir sisters. Status was an issue for Geneviève Deshayes. When she entered the community in Amiens one of the first tasks given her was to sweep the area around the front door. She admitted that she lived in dread of her family passing by the door and seeing her do this. Her maid Catherine Maillard, who entered with her, was designated first as choir sister and only later, in 1816, was placed as coadjutrix.[125] On the other hand, Marguerite (Madame Duval's maid in the rue de Turenne in Paris) was listed as a coadjutrix sister from the beginning. In Grenoble and Poitiers between 1804 and 1806, Sophie Barat allocated posts in the communities and matched the task with the capacity of the person and in her journal made no comment about social status.[126]

However, when the Amiens community sought legal recognition from Napoleon in 1807, their petition stated that the community had 'Coadjutrix Sisters (Sœurs converses) who do not take part in the administration of the house'.[127] The same year an inventory of the community at Poitiers, drawn up by the Départment de la Vienne, described the status of some members as 'Domestic Sisters'.[128] Differences also had emerged between those who recited or did not recite the church offices (in Latin), although it is not clear if this distinction was based on those who could or could not read, or between those who knew or did not know Latin.[129] Clearly by 1807, when the communities were coming into the public domain and finding their place in the wider society of France, two grades or ranks in community had developed. One rank held leadership, recited office in church and taught in the schools. Those who belonged to this rank were called choir sisters. The other rank attended to the domestic tasks in the community and schools, and those who belonged to this rank were called coadjutrix sisters.

The community in Amiens, in contrast to Grenoble and Poitiers, was markedly class conscious almost from the beginning, and especially when Anne Baudemont, Teresa Copina, Henriette Ducis, Marie de Terrail, Félicité de Sambucy de St Estève, Eugénie de Gramont, Antoinette de Gramont and Madame de Gramont d'Aster entered. With the exception of Madame de Gramont d'Aster, who always supported Sophie Barat, this group created a lobby in the community, and it constantly challenged Sophie's leadership from 1802 to 1815. The community chaplain, Louis de Sambucy de St Estève, joined them and sought to supplant Sophie Barat and to assume the role of founder himself. While tensions certainly existed concerning conflicting views of religious life and around spiritual goals and educational aims, undoubtedly Sophie Barat's own class background was also a key reason for their resistance to her appointment as superior general for life. It explains some of the difficulty which Joseph Varin himself had in accepting Sophie as leader, beginning in 1802. It was only when Sophie was confirmed as leader for life in 1815 that both Joseph Varin and Eugénie de Gramont publicly acknowledged her as superior general.

Sophie Barat held a complex position as founder and superior general of the Society of the Sacred Heart. Though born into the fixed class structures of the ancien régime (the nobility, clergy and the poor), Sophie's education and leadership capacities led to her appointment as local leader in Amiens from 1802, then to her election as superior general for life in 1806. She was part of the movement of social mobility which had grown steadily in France from the Enlightenment, to the Revolution and Empire. Indeed Sophie Barat's pivotal position in the Society went further and her role was an act of social reversal, and this was symbolised in the relationship between Sophie and Eugénie de Gramont. Down the years and despite their undoubted friendship, Sophie's role and position as superior general was challenged again and again by Eugénie de Gramont. The history of these two women reflects both the idealism and tensions around the new community's social composition. Both women shared a common vocation, which brought them together from very different backgrounds. However, as founder and superior general, Sophie had stepped out of her social class and held authority over both choir and coadjutrix sisters, over Eugénie de Gramont and the members of the aristocracy in the Society. At different times and for different reasons, Sophie Barat was both a point of unity within the Society and at the same time a sign of social contradiction.

As the political situation in France stabilised following the Restoration in 1815, so too the Society of the Sacred Heart moved to a new stage in its development. It was ready to take part in the reconstruction of France, in the task of renewal and reconciliation after the impact of the Revolution.[130]At the second General Council[131] in Paris in 1815 the name Society of the Sacred Heart was used publicly for the first time. During the Council Sophie Barat presented draft proposals for a rule of life, for Constitutions.[132] The proposals were discussed and endorsed and this process enabled the members to reach common agreement on the purpose of their lives, on what they shared in common, and how they wished to go forward in the future. They articulated their vision which was centred on the spirituality of the Heart of Christ, and they were convinced that the love of God revealed in the Christ of the gospels was a powerful force for transformation in society. They chose four tasks as the means by which the Society could express this spiritual vision: education of the rich; education of the poor; retreat work; any other means which would advance the aims of the Society.[133] These works would be carried out in houses of the Society, established with the approval of government authorities and of the local bishops.

Composition of the Society of the Sacred Heart in 1815

By 1815 there were sixty-two professed religious in the Society. Of the sixty-two, forty-four were designated choir sisters and eighteen coadjutrix sisters. In addition, there were seventy women at different stages of training for religious life: forty-six were approaching their final commitment, seventeen were novices and seven were postulants.

Each house showed a healthy profile of growth and stabilisation, especially between 1808 and 1815:[134]

AMIENS:

1808: 14 professed, 18 novices. No distinctions noted
1815: 25 professed. Noted as 15 choir sisters, 10 coadjutrix sisters

CUIGNIÈRES/LATER BEAUVAIS:

1808: 5 professed. No distinctions noted
1815: 6 professed. Noted as 5 choir sisters, 1 coadjutrix sister

GRENOBLE:

1808: 9 professed, 14 novices. No distinctions noted
1815: 13 professed. Noted as 9 choir sisters, 4 coadjutrix sisters

POITIERS:

1808: 9 professed, 9 novices. No distinctions noted
1815: 10 professed. Noted as 9 choir sisters, 1 coadjutrix sister

NIORT:

1815: 8 professed. Noted as 6 choir sisters, 2 coadjutrix sister

GAND:

Although this community separated from the Society in 1814, some rejoined the Society between 1822 and 1832. Of the 18 from Gand who rejoined the Society, 15 were noted as choir sisters and 3 as coadjutrix sisters.[135]

The Society of the Sacred Heart: Description of the members

The text of the 1815 Constitutions described the initial acceptance and the training of new members in the noviceship, followed by the process leading either to final commitment of members or to their dismissal. The spiritual motivation of the women who wished to be admitted to the Society was considered of primary importance, and to be assessed at every stage of their training. Once that was present, at least potentially, then the specific tasks which each could fulfil in the Society were studied. The Constitutions described the members of the Society in several ways. The woman who asked to be admitted was called the *candidate* (le sujet).[136] When speaking of the Society as a whole, it was termed the *body* of the Society (le corps) and all were *members* (membres).[137] All, irrespective of rank and position were to treat each other like *sisters* (sœurs).[138] The following of Christ was their primary aim, and at this level they were united, without distinction. However, they were not equal at the level of functions and tasks:

> The Society is composed of two classes of persons, those destined for teaching, and those who are to be employed in household duties.[139]

Distinctions between these two 'classes of persons' were described in several ways. The choir sisters were destined either for the work of education in the boarding and poor schools or for posts of responsibility in the Society.[140] They were called *Madame* until 1833 when this title was replaced by *Mother*.[141] The coadjutrix sisters (sœurs coadjutrices) were destined for household duties within the community and schools and were not eligible for leadership in the Society.[142] Their dress code was different, and although all lived under the same roof, the mothers and sisters lived in separate parts of the house and normally met as separate communities, except on Sundays and feast days when they met together. They had ranking order for entry to the chapel, for seating and for processing to Communion during Mass. They ate in the same dining room, but were seated at different tables.[143] This way of organising their community life reproduced socially what most would have experienced prior to their entry to the Society, either within their families or in their former religious lives. Inevitably they were separated from one another by family backgrounds and social standing, by culture and education. But what they shared in common, whether they came from the aristocratic/upper bourgeois classes of society or from the poor class, was a common vocation, a common spirituality as members of the Society of the Sacred Heart.

The Constitutions described what was expected of those who wished to join the Society:

> Since the aim of the Society is to glorify the Sacred Heart of Jesus by labouring with zeal for the perfection of its members and the sanctification of souls, those who present themselves for admission must have the qualities which are suited to attain this twofold end. Of these the chief are: respectable parentage; a good education; an unblemished reputation; a modest demeanour, good health, an upright mind, sound judgement, an adaptable and docile disposition, a certain degree of knowledge and a willingness to develop those talents and virtues which are suited to their vocation. But above all, they should have a relish for holy things, a sincere desire to give themselves unreservedly to God, and complete indifference to places and employments to which obedience may call them.
>
> All these dispositions are equally required of those who present themselves to be coadjutrix sisters, with the exception of such instruction and talents as relate to the education of youth, and these must be compensated in their case by experience in household work, or at all events by goodwill and aptitude for acquiring it.[144]

There were similarities and differences in the religious training of the choir and coadjutrix sisters, the 'two classes of persons' in the Society.

The first stage of membership in the Society lasted three months for choir sisters and six months for coadjutrix sisters.[145] However, both ranks had two years' training in the noviceship, and both were admitted to final profession after a further five years in the Society. In preparation for final vows, both had three months (at least) to prepare for this final stage of commitment.[146] Differences between the ranks arose over the time for prayer. While the choir sisters had one hour of morning meditation, the coadjutrix sisters had a half hour meditation in the morning. The rhythm of their daily life was considered contemplative throughout the day.[147] However, it was also true that many of the coadjutrix sisters could not read and in consequence an entire hour of meditation could be difficult to sustain without the aid of a book. In this context they were not required to recite the office of Our Lady in Latin in choir;[148] and a choir sister read aloud to them for half an hour when they met together for manual work in the afternoons.[149]

Certain assumptions appeared in the text of the Constitutions. It was clear that the life of the choir sister was the model and norm for community life in the Society. For example, in the rules for the novices in the Society, obedience to all in authority was recommended, even to 'the Coadjutrix Sisters when they [the choir novices] are sent to help them in their tasks'.[150] Again, while novices were urged to view the choir sister professed 'as their mother[s] in Jesus Christ, and on all occasions give them marks of respect, deference and tender affection' they were also asked to be:

> full of consideration and charity towards the Coadjutrix Sisters, looking upon their lowly and hidden life with a secret appreciation and certain envy, and be always disposed to render them every service in their power as far as obedience enjoins or permits.[151]

This 'envy' of the life of the coadjutrix sister highlighted the ideal of two vocations within the Society of the Sacred Heart. The vocation of the choir sister was fulfilled by study and teaching or by holding offices of responsibility, all of which involved contact with `the world'. On the other hand, the coadjutrix sister was called to the inner, contemplative life, to the rhythm of daily household tasks, to a life of hidden devotedness, with time and space and silence, in imitation of Christ in Nazareth:

> Their state of life is all the more to be prized as removing them more effectually from all the occasions and danger of self-love, vain self-esteem and dissipation of mind, to which those are exposed who are engaged in study; and it should be the more dear to them because, as

it is humble, laborious and hidden, it renders them more like Jesus Christ their Spouse, Who chose to pass the first thirty years of His earthly life in obscurity and labour. It is therefore by attaching themselves lovingly to the humble and laborious offices of their state of life, through love of Jesus Christ, that they will find themselves united in a most especial manner with the sentiments and affections of His Divine Heart.[152]

Yet 'envy' of the coadjutrix sisters' vocation, contrasted with that of the vocation to teach, could be interpreted as anti-intellectual, indeed highly ambiguous, from the point of view of the choir sisters. However, in the context of the period and in keeping with views of the place of women in society, of women in the public domain, this was an apologia, rhetoric, to justify the service of education offered by the Society of the Sacred Heart. Indeed the choir sisters were warned that the study they were required to do for teaching could be a danger, a trap, luring them into arrogance, and they were reminded that their studies were only undertaken in preparation for their task of teaching. Though obliged to prepare themselves for teaching, the choir sisters were also urged not to study beyond what was necessary, and to 'be on their guard against the foolish pretension of becoming or appearing learned'. And yet they were to take their task seriously and not try to escape the demands of teaching and caring for children, nor take false refuge in practices of devotion, a fatal form of escapism.[153] By the same token, the description of the work of the coadjutrix sisters in terms of the hidden life of Christ could be considered as spiritualising sheer hard work and drudgery. Yet in the context of the Constitutions and ideals of the Society, this was an attempt to value and respect what the coadjutrix sisters did in the communities and schools.

Nevertheless, there was an inbuilt imbalance and even contradiction around the vocation of the coadjutrix sisters as described in the 1815 Constitutions. While the Constitutions asserted that both ranks were full members and shared the same vocation and spiritual value, only the vocation of those destined for involvement in education and leadership in the Society was fully described. That was the norm but, from as early as 1820, fuller description of the vocation and way of life of the coadjutrix sisters was being sought, and the members of the General Councils of 1820, 1826 and 1833 undertook to develop it more fully. The two-rank system in the Society was not questioned. For the Society of the Sacred Heart in early nineteenth-century France, the challenge was to maintain spiritual equality of the membership while living community structures which reflected the class system and consciousness of the day.

The Coadjutrix Sisters after 1815

After the consensus created during the General Council of 1815 in Paris the Society needed to move forward and deepen its roots. It was one thing to have put ideals on paper; the challenge in the future was to see if they worked. The signs were positive and the Society developed rapidly after 1815, building on what had been established between 1800 and 1815. This is evident in the minutes of the community council meetings held in Amiens which show how much growth had already taken place prior to 1815, how a certain rhythm of life in the community and schools had been established. Soon issues around the need for coadjutrix sisters emerged. The community council in Amiens met on Thursday 10 October 1816, to organise classes and surveillances in the school as well as the domestic arrangements for the community and schools. The council decided to have the schools and community laundry done outside 'given the few number of coadjutrix sisters, and the individual and common occupations of everyone in the community'.[154] The need for coadjutrix sisters grew even more critical some weeks later, on Saturday 28 December 1816, when the council discussed a request from Sophie Barat. She asked the community to release a professed coadjutrix sister, and specifically for 'Thérèse [Pelletier], as the new foundation in Paris urgently needed an infirmarian'.[155] The council agreed reluctantly and set about finding another infirmarian.

In Amiens there was a waiting list of three women who had asked to join the community as coadjutrix sisters, and one of them, nineteen years of age, seemed suitable. The council asked Sophie to allow them accept this candidate as a coadjutrix sister postulant, once they had investigated her background. The council made a further request to Sophie Barat.[156] More domestic help was needed in the community and schools and a young woman, Marianne Place, had already asked to be admitted to the Society. She had completed a month's trial and the council knew her background well. Antoinette Place, her sister, was already a professed coadjutrix sister in the community. However, they were aware that the family could not afford a trousseau and proposed that the community provide six nightdresses (chemises) and that her other needs could be provided from supplies in the house. Sophie agreed and offered to help by suggesting that Thérèse Pelletier need not bring her sheets and bedding to Paris.[157]

While coadjutrix sisters were not expected to make a financial contribution to the Society when they entered, choir sisters were expected to do so, even if it was a small sum. In January 1817 the council in Amiens noted that several young women had asked to join the Society as choir sisters. The council made the same background enquiries concerning these women as they had for the coadjutrix sisters.[158] On the question of finance, the council accepted a candidate of seventeen years of age and suggested that she pay 300 francs for the first year. Further payments would be negotiated with her family at a later date. The council also decided that if a woman over twenty-five years of age wished to enter the Society as a choir sister, the initial contribution required would be discussed with the family.[159] It is not clear why over twenty-five years of age made a difference; at this stage dowries or annual pensions would have been settled on family members, whether married or single.

In early February 1817 Sophie Barat visited the community in Amiens and reviewed the arrangements made by the council for running the house. In the course of this review Sophie suggested some changes. She asked that all laundry and baking be done within house, rather than in the town, and she asked that a coadjutrix sister be trained as a baker.[160] Before leaving on 19 February 1817 Sophie assigned the duties of each coadjutrix sister in the community and school:[161]

HOUSEHOLD TASKS OF THE SISTERS

Sister Catherine [*Wartel*]
Doorkeeper, housework, knitting, washing dishes, ironing. She is responsible to Madame [Lucie] Piorette for these tasks. She lights the fires in the community room and the fires for the male teachers (des maîtres)

Sister Prudence [*Barbot*]
Helps in the Linen Room of the Choir Sisters and the boarders; dresses the boarders who get up late; supervises the male teachers ; housework

Sister Martha [*Vaillant*]
Combs the hair of the boarders; cleans the students' dining room; cleans St Désiré dormitory; sweeps St Grégoire and lights the heater; after dinner sweeps the classroom and lights the heater (poêle); cleans the lanterns and candlesticks (chandeliers); carries water to the kitchen. Watches her time so that she can do handwork in the community room in the evening.

Sister Antoinette [*Place*]
Cook; distributes the bread

Sister Francoise [*Feldtrappe*]
Combs the hair of the boarders; cleans Sts Agatha and Geneviève dormitories; polishes the following areas in the chapel: the shrine of the Sacred Heart, the choir stalls in the chapel, the tribune; polishes

the community room; carries water to the kitchen; works in silence in the evening in the community room.

Sister Rosalie [Cardon]
Infirmarian; prepares the oil lamps and candle lamps (les quinquets et lampes); clean Sts Innocents dormitory; cleans the room of Madame Leméré and of Madame Antonia; mends the infirmary linen; when there is no one ill, works in the evening in the community room.

Sister Marie [Polie]
Sweeps the classrooms in the morning and lights the heater; polishes in the small house, in the house of the professed, and in the rooms of Madame [de Gramont] d'Aster, Madame Le Franc and Madame Ducis; gathers wood; works in both gardens and in the flower garden; tidies the courtyard and the common areas; carries water to the kitchen; works in the evening in the community room.

Sister Marianne [Place]
Helps in the community storeroom; looks after the community dining room; works in the evening in the community room.

Sister Josephine [Leclère]
Helps in the kitchen; bakes the bread; carries water to the kitchen.

The duties assigned by Sophie Barat show how the coadjutrix sisters provided the essential infrastructure in the community and schools. Each coadjutrix sister had her individual tasks: cooking, nursing, gardening, looking after poultry, managing the dairy, dressmaking, baking and laundering. Coadjutrix sisters also shared work in the kitchen and laundry, and most did the dishwashing after every meal in the community and boarding school. Every day they cleaned and lit fires in the classrooms and community rooms and brought in wood for them; they also cleaned and lit fires in the rooms of the choir sisters; corridor lamps had to be cleaned daily and prepared for use in the evening time or earlier if in winter. The coadjutrix sisters cleaned the individual rooms of the choir sisters, brought water to their rooms and emptied the chamber pots and commodes, either in the rooms or closets. They swept and washed the floors in the dining rooms, kitchen, community rooms, music rooms, corridors, stairs and basements, courtyards and entrances, laundry rooms, bakery, outhouses and yards. They waxed the chapel floor, polished it regularly and dusted the chapel daily. Some of the coadjutrix sisters helped in the boarding school dormitories each morning and evening, cleaning the girls' shoes and combing their hair. Others taught dress-making, laundering and ironing to girls in the poor school, and some gave classes of instruction in the poor school. The more experienced coadjutrix sisters taught their skills to other coadjutrix sisters, especially to the new entrants. The assistant superior in the house held overall responsibility for the coadjutrix sisters, and in their specific tasks the coadjutrix sisters were accountable to a choir sister. For example, the cook was responsible to the storeroom keeper (dépensière)/ bursar; and those who worked in the school were responsible to the headmistress.

However, Sophie Barat asked that some tasks in the house be shared by the coadjutrix and choir sisters. She suggested that everyone in the house help with the laundry, from the assistant superior to the most recently admitted postulant, choir and coadjutrix. If necessary, the community and schools laundry could be done in stages. Sophie Barat specifically requested that outsiders should not be employed in the laundry, even if help in the house was short. Under exceptional circumstances, the coadjutrix sisters could continue working beyond midday, when they normally stopped for prayer. That time of prayer could be taken back later on by cutting short their recreation time by fifteen minutes. Her overriding concern was to avoid having strangers work in the house. This only led to gossip in the town, reaching those ever curious with regard to the happenings in the community and school. It could also have been an economy measure since income was always a problem.

Following Sophie Barat's visit to Amiens, the council made further arrangements for the community and school laundry which show how the two-rank system developed in these years.[162] For example, Sister Catherine (Lamarre or Wartel) was in charge of the washing and ironing. When doing a four-day washing Madame Véron helped her in the laundry, instead of teaching writing in the poor school.[163] Then when Sister Catherine was doing the ironing, Madame Le Franc replaced Madame Véron for the morning class in writing, again to allow Madame Véron help with the ironing. The council also organised other domestic tasks both for the choir and coadjutrix sisters. For example, although the coadjutrix sisters took care of the vegetable gardens, a choir sister, Madame Duneufgermain, was responsible for the superior's garden, the orange grove, as well as for the flower vases and the care of flowers in general.[164] The choir sisters funded day-to-day repairs and improvements in the house and school from their personal finances which they brought with them when they entered the Society. For example, renovations needed in the school dormitory in Amiens were financed by 4,000 francs from Madame Franciosi and by 1,000 francs from Madame Alteyrac. This practice was maintained in the Society during the lifetime of Sophie Barat.

The Choir Sisters after 1815

In April 1818 Sophie Barat visited the community at Beauvais. Founded originally in Cuignières in 1808, it transferred nearby to Beauvais in 1816 and became a thriving foundation with an aristocratic reputation. On the occasion of a religious vows ceremony held in Beauvais in 1816 town authorities noted that most of the members of the Society came from the higher echelons of French society.[165] The community at Beauvais ran a boarding school of over eighty boarders. The poor school numbered four hundred, and every Sunday between four and five hundred women attended classes given by the choir sisters.[166] The 1818 records of Beauvais describe in some detail how the lives and duties of the choir sisters had developed after the General Council of 1815.[167] Typically, choir sisters held all the key offices in the community, of superior, assistant superior, bursar, mistress of novices and mistress of postulants. Similarly they held the posts of headmistress of the boarding school and of the poor school. A choir sister was also in charge of the storerooms of the community and school infirmary, and of the community and school linen rooms. Choir sisters took charge of the music for liturgies on Sundays and feasts days, as well as for the ceremonies of reception into the noviceship, and the taking of first and final vows. They also played the organ, supervised the daily offices sung in choir, and the offices prescribed for funeral services.

Most choir sisters worked in the boarding school, according to their aptitudes. Some were involved in teaching and preparing their classes. This included copying material from books for use in their classes, correcting the work of the students and keeping charge of their copy books. They also prepared the students for First Communion and Confirmation, and taught church music (organ) and singing. For feast days of the church they prepared religious readings and made special decorations in the chapel and in the school, in the classrooms, dormitories and on the school corridors. In the course of the school year the choir sisters guided the retreat days of the students (usually in Advent and Lent), and chose the subject for reading during silent meals in the school dining room. Choir sisters taught the art of letter-writing and took charge of the library and supervised the use of books in the school. They taught the students deportment and prepared them for public speaking which helped them take their place in society with poise. They learnt in particular how to present compliments, bouquets and good wishes in public. Choir sisters trained the students to read poetry and to present extracts of plays. They made an annual inventory of the class texts used for teaching, checked they were returned by the students, and in this way they built up their teaching resources. Over the years they made collections of literature for teaching purposes and for use on prize days and other public events. They wrote out sets of fables, especially La Fontaine, for recitation in the classes and they also retained an inventory of these.

Choir sisters supervised the boarders at meals, at recreation, in church, in the study room and in the school dormitories. They slept in the dormitories and supervised the boarders when rising and retiring. Choir sisters also worked in the poor school, teaching basic reading, writing and arithmetic, as well as the church catechism. When coadjutrix sisters taught sewing, mending and laundry-making in the poor school, these classes were supervised by choir sisters. Choir sisters, experienced in teaching, acted as mentors of young choir sisters learning to teach either in the boarding or poor schools. A choir sister was in charge of reception and received those who called at the hall door either as visitors or on business. She designated where they could be received and if necessary remained present during the visit. Choir sisters were responsible in turn to check the buildings each evening, to ensure that all lights and fires had been extinguished and all doors locked. During the midday and evening meals choir sisters took it in turn to read religious texts to the community, usually a life of a saint or some aspect of Church history.[168] They also read to the Coadjutrix Sisters during their afternoon meetings.

Choir and coadjutrix sisters shared some tasks, though they relaxed in separate community rooms. For example, everyone knitted, embroidered, sewed, mended and did general handwork, and yet within these similar tasks there were some differences. The coadjutrix sisters mended cloths for use in the kitchen; they knitted stockings, made soles for shoes; they made new dresses (habits) for the community and new uniforms for the students; they also shared their skills and experience with one another. The choir sisters made petticoats and either knitted or crocheted the hems; they made bouquets of dry flowers for the chapel and house; some wove carpets and others embroidered cloths for use in the church; they taught each other embroidery; they learnt how to sew flowers and taught each other that skill; they sharpened the pens for the pupils. They also made shoes and mended clothes, including the linen of the chaplain and the sacristy.

The community records for Amiens and Beauvais in 1818 indicate how the two ranks were listed in community, according to rank and responsibilities. When tasks were assigned to individual coadjutrix sisters, their christian names were noted in the lists, and when choir sisters were assigned tasks, their family name was used. For example, in

Amiens Geneviève Deshayes was called Deshayes, and Marie de la Croix was known as de la Croix. However, Marianne Place was designated Marianne, and Barthèlemy Roux, Barthèlemy.[169] This practice mirrored society at the time generally in Europe, when cooks, maids, nannies and nurses were usually called and remembered by first names only, or occasionally by their function, and hardly ever by their family name. Madame Sister Duval's maid, Marguerite, who entered in Amiens along with Sophie Barat, was called Marguerite Boulangère (the baker).

Development of the way of life in the Society after 1815

In a relatively short period of time the Society of the Sacred Heart had reached a certain rhythm and symmetry in its way of life. This was facilitated by the decision of the General Council of 1815 to choose the apostolic model of religious life, created originally in the sixteenth century by the founder of the Jesuits, St Ignatius of Loyola. While the spiritual inspirations of the Society of the Sacred Heart were different from those of the Jesuits, the Jesuit model of religious life suited it well. The model was based on strong central government structures with a superior general appointed for life. This centralised authority structure fostered the union of all communities and it also facilitated exchange of personnel. In years prior to 1815 the monastic model of religious life had been preferred by some members of the future Society of the Sacred Heart, both in Amiens and Grenoble. This model retained independent foundations which were linked only by spiritual origin, history and a shared spirituality, such as the Cistercians or Carmelites. Sophie Barat considered that this model would be an obstacle to establishing the identity of the Society of the Sacred Heart. In December 1815 she commented on the actions of Louis de Sambucy de St Estève, the chaplain in Amiens, who for many years had opposed her leadership and made a bid to replace her as founder:

> All former members of religious congregations are accepted in his house. Yet he knows quite well that in the Society we believe that, while not excluding [such religious] we need to exercise great caution in admitting them. You will readily understand that a house open to receive religious from all the orders could not preserve its own spirit for long.[170]

And yet Sophie Barat recognised that the apostolic and monastic models were not mutually exclusive, and over time the Society established a way of life which had this blend. The fact that Sophie had no prior experience of religious life gave her a certain freedom to develop a way of life which suited the experiences and aspirations of the members. Coming from her experience in Joigny, it could be said that Sophie Barat created a type of village way of life, where each had her place and rank, and where the gifts of the members could be used for the sake of the community, the schools and the other works undertaken in the public domain.[171] Besides, the lives of most women during this period were quite monastic, whether they lived at home or within marriage or as single women. They too lived in ordered settings, with definite rules and regulations with regard to their personal lives, and all their choices were firmly controlled by male parental figures: father, brother, uncle or guardian.[172]

When the Society of the Sacred Heart chose aspects of the Jesuit form of religious life in 1815, it did so with several modifications. Clearly the Society was not a clerical order. Neither could it generate financial support and income from priestly ministries, or attract substantial donations or endowments like the Jesuits had enjoyed for centuries.[173] As far as possible the Society of the Sacred Heart, as a new community of women, had to be self-sufficient and self-reliant. This was essential for growth and economic independence, especially after the Napoleonic Code of 1804 when the economic rights of women were curtailed. In the early years Sophie Barat and her companions had few financial resources to hand and at times they needed to borrow heavily.[174] With few exceptions, the dowries and pensions brought in by the choir sisters were meagre; some families had lost a great deal of their wealth during the Revolution, and others never had it. Most often families agreed on an annual pension to be sent to the community where the family member resided. Sophie Barat's letters show how families often offered wine, fruits, nuts and grain either in lieu of money or to supplement a small donation. Certainly the families of Sophie Barat and Thérèse Mallucheau regularly offered wine after the autumn harvest.

With regard to the structure of community life, prior to 1815 the Society had gradually developed two ranks within the community, that of choir and coadjutrix sisters. Again, this could not have been modelled entirely on the Jesuits, who since the sixteenth century had established four grades of membership: some were professed as priests and they took four solemn vows; some were professed as priests and took three solemn vows, and were considered as coadjutors in either spiritual or temporal matters; others were received as scholastics and in time made profession as solemnly professed members who took either four vows of religion or three vows; finally, 'the fourth class consists of those who are received indeterminately for whichever grade they will in time be fit'.[175] This fourth grade was further described in the Jesuit Constitutions as temporal coadjutors.[176] However, the model of the coadjutrix sister in the Society of the Sacred Heart could only be based to a degree on that of the Jesuit coadjutrix brother. Rank in the Society was not based on clerical status, but determined by a combination of class, education, talent and capacity. The records in Amiens and Beauvais for 1816 and 1818 show the two-rank structure in place and gaining certain stability.[177] Experience would develop and modify this structure over time. Its first challenge came when Philippine Duchesne and her companions sailed to New Orleans in 1818 to found new communities of the Society in Louisiana.

1818: The Society in Louisiana – Transferring a model

From her childhood in Grenoble Philippine Duchesne had dreamed of going on the missions to the Indians, and finally in 1818 Sophie Barat agreed to let her go, accompanied by Octavie Berthold, Eugénie Audé, Catherine Lamarre and Marguerite Manteau. Sophie had asked for volunteers for this mission and chose these four women to accompany Philippine to Louisiana.[178] They set sail from Bordeaux on the *Rebecca* and crossed the Atlantic, confronted each day by new realities beyond anything they had experienced or imagined. On arrival in New Orleans in June 1818 Philippine was both enthralled and shocked, and she wrote a graphic account of her many first impressions to Sophie Barat. One of them was her reaction to slavery of the black people, held in contempt by the white population. This appalled her. She soon discovered that the white people refused to do menial work, saying 'We have the same colour of skin as you.' In her indignation, Philippine asked Sophie if the Society could admit students of colour to the boarding schools. She quickly noticed that white people refused to educate people of colour in their schools. Philippine argued that if the Society followed suit such an action could not be reconciled with the fourth vow, taken at final profession by choir sisters, committing them to the education of the young. She also asked if women of colour could be admitted to the Society.[179] Sophie Barat replied to this query with a brief, clear directive:

> Do not make the foolish mistake of mixing the white and people of colour (les blanches avec les noires). You would have no more pupils. The same applies to yourselves. No one will join the Society if you accept coloured novices. Later on we will see what we can do for the black women. The essential thing at the beginning is to win confidence and attract [white] novices and students.[180]

Philippine was not alone in experiencing the shock of change. Each one had been jolted out of their familiar worlds, first during the long sea voyage from Bordeaux and then on arrival in New Orleans. Perhaps Catherine Lamarre (1779–1845) was the most deeply affected. Catherine was a founder member of the community first set up in Cuignières in 1808, which transferred to Beauvais in 1816. During the preparations for the General Council in 1815, when the Society was beginning to establish its structures in a more formal way, Catherine Lamarre's rank was changed from choir to coadjutrix sister. She was attracted to the missions and when there was rumour of a possible foundation in the French colony of Martinique she asked Sophie Barat to go there. This plan came to nothing, but when Philippine was planning the mission to Louisiana, Sophie Barat asked Catherine Lamarre if she would consider going there. She agreed then but admitted later that the thought of going as far as Louisiana had frightened her.

On the voyage out from Bordeaux to New Orleans Catherine appeared to be disturbed and for some weeks Philippine feared for her sanity. She wrote to Sophie:

> She [Catherine Lamarre] often repeated that she had told Fr Sellier, Madame Prevost, and indeed you yourself, that she did not feel that she had the courage to go so far away. I responded by saying that I was sure that you would not have chosen her if she had not been willing to go and even asked to go. On this point she repeated that *she had indeed asked to go to Martinique because she thought it was near; but she had always felt repugnance for Louisiana.*[181]

As the *Rebecca* passed by Martinique and journeyed on to New Orleans, Catherine Lamarre must have felt that she had gone beyond the inner and outer boundaries of what she could safely imagine. Further shocks awaited her. The little group had to wait some time in New Orleans before proceeding up the Mississippi to St Louis. During this time they stayed with the Ursuline community, who offered to have their clothes washed by the black women they employed. Philippine Duchesne asked Catherine to wash some clothes alongside these women:

> After several difficulties she came to tell me that she did not like working alongside the black women, and that in this country the white people do not work with the blacks. I answered her by saying that these women have souls too, redeemed by the same Blood [of Christ] and received in the same Church. If she was not willing to work with them it would be better to return home on the next vessel leaving shortly,

since we came here for the black people. She only recovered her composure in the evening.[182]

When the little band reached St Louis they found that, as in New Orleans, domestic work was despised by the white people and done only by black people. Yet in the Society of the Sacred Heart, domestic work was done by the coadjutrix sisters. This situation only compounded the tension for Catherine Lamarre and indeed for Philippine Duchesne. She learnt that for some time Catherine had aspired to teaching, and being ranked as a coadjutrix sister in 1815 had frustrated that hope. Philippine asked Sophie Barat for advice:

> Think about sending us more Coadjutrix Sisters. The situation of black women here is the same as in New Orleans, and all white people are equal. Catherine Lamarre continues to dream of teaching and yet knows nothing about it.[183]

But Catherine persisted. She told Philippine that two priests in France had encouraged her to consider teaching; Sophie Barat herself had promised she would be involved in education in Louisiana. Catherine Lamarre had every reason to hope that this would happen since some coadjutrix sisters in the Society in France were involved in the poor schools, went to the villages and stayed for some weeks to instruct the children and prepare them for First Communion. This happened in Niort and in Catherine's former community in Cuignières.[184] In addition to her disappointment, Catherine Lamarre was fragile and she felt unable for the heavy work expected of a coadjutrix sister, especially in a new, frontier situation. She attempted some small educational projects of her own, teaching a mulatto slave girl, teaching singing to a woman and hearing the children's catechism. Philippine considered her unstable and wondered should she be asked to leave the Society or at least to live alone.[185]

Philippine had her own concerns and challenges to face. Immediately on arrival in New Orleans in June 1818 she realised that the community would need lighter clothing and, following the custom in France, she bought a different quality of dress for the choir sisters and for the coadjutrix sisters:

> We bought dresses in black cotton, light with a single white thread (the doctor and the community here insisted on this).[186] The Coadjutrix Sisters have violet colour cotton which is almost black.[187]

Clash of cultures, class and race

However, within a few months Philippine began to see the two ranks in the Society quite differently. In March 1819 she wrote to Louis Barat, Sophie's Jesuit brother, commenting on how few differences she noted between the two ranks in the Ursuline community in New Orleans. The only exterior difference she could see was that only one rank, the choir sisters, recited Office. She began to wonder if the rank of coadjutrix sister as described in the Constitutions of 1815 could ever work in Louisiana.[188] By July 1819 she had concluded that it could not, and she told Sophie:

> It will be impossible to have the two classes of religious here; all wish to be equal. There will be inevitable differences because of variety of talents, of education and tasks. But if you said to someone here that on entering the Society that they had come to serve, this would be unacceptable, even to a Native American. Several Americans have asked for information about the Society. They should enter as Coadjutrix Sisters, but they already enquire if the cooking is done by weekly rota, each one taking a turn.[189]

However, Philippine thought she had found a solution. Some women of colour, freed black women, expressed the wish to live in a religious community and Philippine proposed these become linked to the Society as commissioner sisters. The Society in France had begun to develop a group of women, called commissioner sisters, for those who wished to be affiliated to the Society but not required to live full religious life. They made a yearly commitment to the Society, and while they did not live in community, they had accommodation in the house. They had definite tasks allotted them, in particular shopping for the community and accompanying those who travelled.[190]

> Under this title [Commissioner Sisters] they could render services as important as those done by the Coadjutrix Sisters. It would be difficult for them to work alongside the Coadjutrix Sisters, as all whites are equal here.[191]

In November 1819 the bishop of Louisiana, William Dubourg,[192] wrote to Sophie Barat about the relevance of having coadjutrix sisters in Louisiana and indicated that there was no point in sending out more from France. While women could be found locally for the Society, social inequality in the community was unacceptable. The bishop suggested that physical health, instead of rank, should be the criteria for deciding who in the community should do heavy work, which in any event required intelligence:

> It is difficult here to retain the position of the Coadjutrix Sisters as
> given in your Constitutions, a position which would be contrived in
> a country where inequality of social background is not admitted,
> except that based on difference of colour.[193]

He suggested instead that Sophie Barat consider a proposal he had already
discussed with Philippine Duchesne. The bishop knew of many women
of mixed blood, of Indian or African origin, who were caught into prosti-
tution. Many of them wanted another life and some would be open to
religious life. The bishop wondered if the Society would accept these
women, not as members of the Society (at least initially). They could
dress differently from the coadjutrix sisters but do their work. He
assumed Sophie Barat would concur. The following month Philippine
wrote to Sophie Barat reiterating Bishop Dubourg's views on rank in the
Society. She asked Sophie to consider Dubourg's proposal and accept
women of colour, at least to work alongside the coadjutrix sisters.
However, she observed that their acceptance and formation even at this
level would be a long process, and that their form of dress should be different. Yet, even as she asked for this proposal to be discussed in Paris,
Philippine continued to press Sophie to consider admitting black women
fully into the Society, as either choir or coadjutrix sisters. She thought
they could start as coadjutrix sisters, and, if some proved to be gifted for
the work of education, they then could transfer to the rank of choir sister.

There were vast implications in both these questions posed to Sophie
Barat, and as Philippine reflected further she saw other difficulties. In
December 1819 she admitted to Sophie that the issue of vocations in
Louisiana was bigger than just the position of the coadjutrix sisters:

> Sadly I see that *equality* is the obstacle to many vocations, even if we
> had just one rank; ability etc will always make a difference and pride
> always finds something to complain about. Some would wish to
> teach who know nothing about it. And if the class teachers also do
> housework, where would they find time [for both]? And how [could
> they] manage their personal cleanliness? And if they did not do
> housework, then distinction already exists. All things considered, it is
> best to stay as we are and be open to having fewer voca-
> tions . . . When the *Superior* takes her turn in the kitchen, some will
> want to take their turn as *Superior*.[194]

Letters took time to cross the Atlantic. Four months later, in April 1820,
Sophie responded to Philippine and told her that she had decided not to
send any more coadjutrix sisters to Louisiana, since she seemed to prefer
receiving young women of colour as commissioner sisters. However,

Sophie only accepted Philippine's plan on condition that they were 'not known as members of the Society of the Sacred Heart'.[195] Furthermore, Sophie Barat made it clear that she did not agree either with the bishop or with Philippine on the question of the rank of the coadjutrix sisters.[196] Sophie Barat knew Bishop Dubourg had strong views on most things:

> I am afraid he will draw you away from our views and that, since he is used to creating rules as he goes along, he will want to create something new with you, too. I understand that you cannot follow all our customs to the letter and that we have to take into account place and circumstances. But at least we have to tend towards uniformity. To do the opposite would create a great difference between your foundation and ours. I sense your pain and how much you must be suffering now. If only we could actually meet, then we would be able to talk about your cherished plans with the love we all have for your community and especially for you.[197]

A month later Sophie Barat repeated her wishes, briefly and succinctly:

> Keep both ranks in your community and make them distinct. I will write at length about this before long.[198]

Sophie Barat's views prevailed and Bishop Dubourg accepted the Society's decision to retain the two classes of members in Louisiana.[199] However, the decision continued to be tested as in February 1821 when three young women asked to join the Society. Two were American and one French and their designation as choir or as coadjutrix sisters had be determined. In making such decisions Philippine knew that Sophie Barat would take account of the special circumstances in Louisiana and allow her to test a certain social mobility within the communities. One of the Americans, Eulalie Hamilton (1805–88), was an orphan and Philippine suggested the best way forward for her:

> She is 16 years old and looks after the kitchen with astonishing ease and gets on with everybody. While she would be very suited to studies, it is better for her spiritual growth to remain in the background for a little while. She has an excellent memory and will quickly learn all that is necessary for her to be a Choir Sister, if you allow this.[200]

Changes in rank went in both directions; some entered as choir sisters and later were changed to the rank of coadjutrix sister.[201] Social, national and racial backgrounds within the communities in Louisiana were also varied. In 1833 the community of four at St Charles, Missouri, consisted of a Creole from Lower Louisiana, an American from Philadelphia, a French woman and an Irish woman.[202] Thus, since the Society arrived in Louisiana the two-rank structure was critiqued, and while she was open to certain flexibility in a new situation Sophie Barat was not prepared to change the system. In any event, she had no authority to do so; only a General Council could make such a change in the Society.

Strengthening the model in France 1819–1833

Issues concerning the coadjutrix sisters had also arisen in France. In 1819 Louis Barat, then based in the Jesuit community in Bordeaux, preached the annual retreats to communities of the Society in the west of France. He also wrote a series of letters that year to the communities of Poitiers and Niort commenting on different aspects of life in the Society of the Sacred Heart. One of his letters dealt with the worth placed on the tasks assigned to the members, and Louis Barat asked why some in the Society appeared to value only those involved in teaching:

> Those for example who work in the kitchen, in the linen-room, at reception, have real difficulty in accepting that their work is just as valuable as those members of the same community who are charged with teaching the catechism to the students [in the boarding schools] and in the poor schools. St Teresa [d'Avila] was right to say that to be suited for religious life we need at least to have common sense. Indeed, it is difficult to carry out tasks we do not understand, and the subject in question here requires above all certain intelligence. It means that we need to be convinced that the cook can do as much for the salvation of souls as the superior of the house.
>
> The merit of each one is not in her rank. For example, say there is a conference arranged at five o'clock in the evening for the senior girls, to be given by a teacher in the poor school. Several Coadjutrix Sisters cooperate for this good work. The person in charge of reception takes the trouble to open the hall-door many times. The cook prepares supper for the Choir Sister responsible for the conference.
>
> Each of the three fulfilled her task well, at least exteriorly. The young girls from outside leave greatly edified and hold the teacher in the poor school in great esteem, and they praise her outside on every occasion. Echoes of such flattery are reported back and are heard by the doorkeeper and even by the cook. From this come jealousies, or at least the beginnings of regret that they are not involved in such a worthy task as Christian instruction. The poor souls! The quality and eminence of tasks count for nothing before God. It is the right intention from a humble heart which does all, whether one is opening a door, sweeping a dormitory or preaching.[203]

Louis Barat appealed to the ideal of the 1815 Constitutions, to the spiritual equality of the members whatever their tasks in the Society. However, in

1815 the life and vocation of the coadjutrix sisters was briefly described in
the Constitutions and it was clear that the life and vocation of the choir
sisters were both the norm and point of reference. Such social comment was
in keeping with the structure of French society as existed then in France.
However, the questioning of both Philippine Duchesne and Bishop
Dubourg on the place of the coadjutrix sisters in the Society led Sophie
Barat to reflect on the need to give the coadjutrix sisters both a deeper spiritual formation and affirmation of their way of life within the Society. This
was the point Louis Barat was making in his letters to the communities in
the west of France.

In 1820 the second General Council of the Society addressed both
the lifestyle and training of the coadjutrix sisters. In particular, this
Council drew up an order of day adapted to the daily tasks of the coadjutrix sisters and designed to support them spiritually. It took into
account that many of the coadjutrix sisters had come from varied backgrounds and in many cases lacked even a basic education.[204] Over the
years further recommendations concerning the coadjutrix sisters were
made by the General Councils. For example, normally coadjutrix sisters
worked in silence but if recreations had been cancelled too often, then
the coadjutrix sisters could talk during their work, as long as three were
present. On Sundays they should have more free time and their community recreation could be prolonged if a choir sister was present. While
the need to walk as a form of recreation was recommended for the choir
sisters, the coadjutrix sisters, who spent most of the day on their feet,
were advised to rest during recreation. Occasionally, on certain days in
the year, called community manual work days, the choir sisters joined
the coadjutrix sisters for Rosary and spiritual reading.

Common spirituality, separate tasks

As well as addressing specifically the spiritual formation of the coadjutrix
sisters, the early General Councils tracked the evolution of the community model in the Society. While continuing to examine what was
common to and what was different in each rank in the Society, the General
Councils underlined the spiritual equality of the members in terms of their
vocation and full incorporation into the Society. This was highlighted in
1826 when the fourth General Council decided to create a single noviceship for the Society in Paris.[205] The council also decided that choir and
coadjutrix sisters would prepare for final profession together, also in Paris.
Sophie Barat wanted to create a strong central base in the Society, and
before she accepted women into the Society she wished to meet them per-

sonally, especially those who asked to make final profession. This was an ideal which became impossible to realise since the Society expanded so rapidly. Over time Sophie had to admit that her dream of having both common noviceships and common stages for final profession in Paris was simply not viable.[206] However, until the mid-nineteenth century some choir and coadjutrix sisters spent short periods (perhaps only a few months) of their noviceship or of their stage prior to final profession (probation) in Paris, often at Sophie Barat's personal invitation.[207]

While the common spirituality and common call of the members was asserted by the General Councils, differences between the two ranks were apparent in several ways. The form of final commitment taken by the choir sisters differed from that of the coadjutrix sisters. Both ranks took the vows of poverty, chastity and obedience when they made their commitment (first vows) after the two-year noviceship. However, at final profession choir sisters, in addition to the vows of perpetual poverty, chastity and obedience, took a fourth vow devoting themselves to the education of youth.[208] This vow signalled the distinction of tasks between the choir and coadjutrix sisters. From this followed the further differences which impacted on all aspects of community life.[209]

On entering the Society each one dressed according to the rank they were assigned. Such distinctions mirrored French society in general in the early nineteenth century, and women entering the Society would have found them familiar. The General Council of 1815 described the dress (the habit) of the Society in some detail: all wore black wool dresses, with a pelerine (cape) for the choir sisters and a shawl for the coadjutrix sisters, with white coifs and black veils.[210] Subsequent councils made further changes in dress. In 1826/7 the council decided that the choir sisters (only) were to wear a black bandeau around the forehead, to cover their hair. The veil material of the choir sisters was to be of light quality, while that of the coadjutrix sisters was to be of thicker texture. The same applied to the white veils of the choir and coadjutrix novices.[211] The trousseau required for entry to the Society was itemised at the fourth General Council in 1833.[212] Those to be admitted as coadjutrix sisters were asked to bring a bed, a curtain, a mattress, a bolster, two eiderdowns and a bedcover (garde paille) with them. With regard to those entering as choir sisters, it was assumed that in general they would have greater financial resources than the coadjutrix sisters. In 1837 alone Sophie Barat noted that forty women who had entered the Society as coadjutrix sisters were unable to bring a trousseau.[213]

While future choir sisters bought the same items as the coadjutrix sisters, they were requested in addition to bring a pillow, two mattresses (one of which would not be for their use), a prie-dieu with a built-in cupboard, a table, two chairs and a silver goblet (which would not be for their use). Both coadjutrix and choir sisters were asked to bring sheets, towels, underwear, nightdresses and day dresses, including aprons and pockets. However, the choir sisters were asked to bring greater quantities of each of these items, often at least two-thirds more.[214] Each was asked to bring what they would require during the trial period of some months (the postulancy), after which they would wear the dress of the Society, with white veils. The coadjutrix sisters brought two black shawls; the choir sisters four black pelerines and two pairs of black gloves and two black underskirts. Choir sisters were recommended to buy their trousseau from the retailers used by the Society in Paris, another signal of difference.[215]

Material for the choir sisters' dress was to be wool, while that of the coadjutrix sisters was 'of black material, more ordinary than that of the choir sisters', and coadjutrix sisters should never wear the dress of the choir sisters.[216] The headdress of each rank was also distinct. The veiling of choir novices and professed (black after first vows) were of a lighter quality than that of the coadjutrix novices and professed. The shoes worn by the choir sisters were a type of black slipper which could be wrapped in strong material in winter. The shoes of the coadjutrix sisters were of leather, but those who found them too painful and rough to wear could get softer footwear.[217] At final profession, the choir and coadjutrix sisters were given different silver crosses, and choir sisters received a gold ring and the coadjutrix sisters a silver ring.

Order of rank was defined in detail for daily life in the community. This was apparent when entering and exiting the chapel, as well as for processing to communion during Mass. Professed choir sisters went first, followed by the choir sisters aspirants and novices. They were followed by the professed coadjutrix sisters, aspirants and novices.[218] Frequent communion was not customary in the nineteenth century and in the Society communion during Mass was permitted on Sundays, the first Friday of each month and the feasts of the Society. On their feast day (St Alphonsus Rodriguez, a Jesuit brother) the coadjutrix sisters were permitted to receive communion. However, for communion on other days, each one had to get permission from the superior. While choir sisters could be given a permanent permission by the superior, this did not apply to choir and coadjutrix novices and aspirants, nor to professed coadjutrix sisters, who were obliged to ask permission weekly.[219]

Such distinctions within the community were evident to visitors, families, pupils and parents. Yet for most, at least in France, they could not have been unusual or remarkable. What may have struck these observers was the combined activity of these women, choir and coadjutrix, committed to their spiritual ideal and devoted to the education of youth. They saw choir sisters, who taught either in the boarding or the poor schools and provided leadership, and coadjutrix sisters, who provided the infrastructure for both communities and schools, in the kitchens, laundries, gardens, farms, infirmaries, linen rooms and sculleries. Those who watched the Society at work could see that each one had her place in this village-type community they had created and where each made her contribution to the life of the community. However, in Louisiana the clash of culture and race continued to be a challenge for the Society of the Sacred Heart.

Further challenges in Louisiana

The Society expanded to Lower Louisiana in 1821 and founded a boarding school that year in Grand Coteau (Opelousas) and then a boarding school and orphanage at St Michael's in 1825. A new challenge arose in 1827 when a community, the Sisters of the Cross, in La Fourche, Lower Louisiana, asked to transfer to the Society of the Sacred Heart. When Sophie Barat learnt that most of the community did not know French nor could they teach in the schools, she only agreed to their incorporation into the Society on certain conditions. The Sisters of the Cross were to be received individually into the Society, not as a group. Each one would make a noviceship and if accepted would be admitted as a coadjutrix sister. The orphanage at St Michael's would transfer to La Fourche and while the community at La Fourche could accept boarding pupils from the lower middle class they were to be educated separately from the orphans. Sophie also asked that the level of studies in the boarding school at La Fourche remain lower than at the boarding schools at St Michael's and Grand Coteau. Finally, Eugénie Audé, the superior at St Michael's, was given overall responsibility for the new foundation, and Hélène Dutour was named the local superior of the new community at La Fourche, largely composed of coadjutrix sisters.[220]

Hélène Dutour faced immense challenges and had few supports. In her efforts to build up the new community, the new school and orphanage, she put aside the conditions laid down by Sophie Barat and changed the rank of the members from coadjutrix to choir sisters. Yet none were prepared for teaching. This inevitably led to tensions and rivalries between La Fourche and the two schools and communities in Lower Louisiana, something which Sophie Barat hoped to avoid. All lived in frontier conditions and had worked hard for the development of their school and community and they feared that Hélène Dutour's ambitions for her foundation would threaten the prosperity of St Michael's and Grand Coteau.[221] In 1829, at the request of Sophie Barat, Philippine Duchesne made a visit to the houses in Lower Louisiana and sent a report to Paris. She listed twenty-four proposals for change. Among them was a request that the coadjutrix sisters be permitted to learn to write and that they wear the same light clothing as the choir sisters, on account of the heat. Sophie Barat agreed to both requests.[222] But Philippine was well aware that these two requests could not resolve the tensions that existed in the region, not only between La Fourche and the other communities but generally between choir and coadjutrix sisters in the area. She noted in 1830 and again in 1831 that the coadjutrix sisters were being badly treated by some choir sisters:

> I could be wrong, but I find that in Grand Coteau they are too ready to discourage the Coadjutrix Sisters who have little experience of [social] *differences*. Four who have come [to the Society] have saddened me by the sight of their unhappiness, and the bad effects that followed. Since the end of May three have returned to their families. Much reflection is needed before sending others to Grand Coteau.[223]

Clearly the problems Philippine Duchesne encountered indicated how difficult it was to transplant a European model in the New World. This model could not mirror society in general in Louisiana nor be easily understood. Besides often those who lived it in community held to it so rigidly that they oppressed each other. Besides, the reality of what the communities were struggling with in this new culture was hardly understood in Europe, and the correspondence between Philippine Duchesne and Sophie Barat shows the two women grappling with their respective polarities.

Issues of class distinctions and social mobility in the Society

The issue of class distinctions in general in the Society arose during the 1833 General Council. From her experience of founding communities in Turin and Rome, Louise de Limminghe (a Belgian aristocrat) was particularly aware that the reputation of the Society was linked with the French nobility and upper classes, and she wished at least to modify that reputation which stemmed especially from Paris. In 1821 Marie de Flavigny (later le Comtesse d'Aghoult/Daniel Stern) was a pupil in the school at the rue de Varenne, where Eugénie de Gramont was head-mistress. Marie de Flavigny was impressed by the grandeur of the house (the former Hôtel Biron), and of the religious who:

> under their black veil, their cross of silver on their breast, and their long rosary at the side, took care not to forget their family back-ground. Most of them were from old families, and some of very noble blood. With rare exceptions, they only accepted pupils from the aristocracy, either from the court or province nobility.[224]

At the General Council of 1833 Louise de Limminghe proposed that in the Society the 'de' before family names be omitted, as a mark of sim-plicity. Members of the council discussed the proposal but rejected it. The majority considered that the change would create too many legal difficul-ties with their families, and could affect the dowries and legacies donated to the Society.[225] Besides, within the consciousness of the day, such a step was unthinkable. Class structures in France, after the 1789 Revolution, the Restoration of 1815 and the 1830 July Revolution, still remained the norm in the nineteenth century and persisted until the First World War. But the General Council of 1833 made a small, symbolic gesture of change by deciding that in future choir sisters would be called Mother (Mère), and not Madame.[226] Certainly Louise de Limminghe's proposal in 1833 which aimed at lessening the aristocratic reputation of the Society of the Sacred Heart, and especially that of the rue de Varenne, did not lead to a critique of the two-class system in the Society.

Yet while maintaining the two-rank structure in the Society, Sophie Barat always retained a certain flexibility regarding the allocation of rank, based on evident capacity.[227] Allocations to rank were the responsibility of those who first admitted women to the Society, usually the local supe-riors, and a great deal depended on their good judgement. Later on, if Sophie Barat perceived that a woman who was ranked as a coadjutrix sister had leadership or teaching capacities, she asked her to consider moving rank.[228] Early in 1830 Maria Cutts (1811–54), an English woman, a convert from Protestantism, arrived in Paris:

> Her desire to imitate Our Lord poor and humble led her to ask to be accepted in the capacity of Coadjutrix Sister. Every aspect of her life would have made her a Choir Sister, but her spiritual attraction was accepted by the Society. Since she was strong she worked from morning till night at the most difficult tasks.[229]

After some months in the Society her leadership gifts were evident and Sophie Barat asked her not only to consider changing to the rank of choir sister but also to joining the communities in Louisiana. It was her choice, and Maria Cutts was reluctant to change. Finally she decided to accept Sophie Barat's invitation, and after her final profession in 1836 she went to Louisiana. She proved to be a key leader there until her early death in 1854. But she never lost her attraction for the life of the coadjutrix sisters and whenever possible she took part in their tasks.[230]

Attraction of the vocation of the Coadjutrix Sister

The vocation of the coadjutrix sister was admired for its contemplative spirit, lived out in a hidden way within the houses of the Society. As a way of life it attracted some women of noble birth who asked to enter the Society specifically as coadjutrix sisters. Among them was Pauline de Saint André de la Laurencie de Villeneuve (1804–40). She was born in Saint-Jean d'Angély, in the département of Charente-Maritime (formerly Charente-Inférieure) into a noble family which originated in the sixteenth century. Pauline had two younger sisters, Adèle and Sophie, and when they were small her parents were involved in a scandal (unnamed) which effectively shattered the family home. The three children were sent first to a boarding school in Paris for some years, and then their grand-aunt brought them home, to the boarding school run by the Dames de Chavagnes in Saint-Jean d'Angély. While there Adèle became ill and died, and Pauline took on the mothering of her younger sister, Sophie.[231]

In 1834 Pauline decided to offer her life for 'the conversion of my father and mother', [232] and seek admittance as a coadjutrix sister in a religious community. She heard about the Society in Bordeaux and asked to enter there as a coadjutrix sister. The superior suggested that she should stay with them while they contacted Sophie Barat for advice.[233] Sophie invited Pauline de Saint André to come to Paris to discern her vocation but cautioned her to travel to Paris in normal dress.[234] Sophie Barat met Pauline de Saint André, who had no dowry or no member of her family present with her.[235] Sophie agreed to allow her enter the Society as a coadjutrix sister and decided that Pauline de Saint André would make her noviceship in Montet, Switzerland, and be known there as Sister Elizabeth. In 1836, as the time of noviceship drew to a close in Montet, Sophie Barat pointed out to Pauline de Saint André that she had the ability to teach and to take responsible offices in the Society; there was time to change her mind before taking her first vows. But Pauline de Saint André confirmed her wish and made her first vows as a coadjutrix sister.[236]

After her first vows Pauline de Saint André was sent to Italy, first to the community in Turin and then to Pignerol. A year later her health began to deteriorate rapidly and by the spring of 1840 she became terminally ill. She asked Sophie Barat if she could visit her family in France, and while agreeing to the journey Sophie suggested she wear the habit of a choir sister for the occasion. Otherwise, she would offend the family, who had never understood either her rank in the Society or her desire for a hidden, contemplative life.[237] However, the proposed visit proved beyond the energies of Pauline de Saint André and she died in Pignerol on 14 September 1840.[238] On her death, Sophie Barat asked the community to record their memories of Pauline de Saint André and conserve her writings and family papers, as well as testimonies from her spiritual director and friends, in the community archives.[239] Sophie Barat hoped that in time the life of Pauline de Saint André would confirm the contemplative spirit of the Society and affirm the vocation of the coadjutrix sisters.[240]

Good health was not always a deciding factor when discerning vocations to the Society, either of the choir or of coadjutrix sisters. Sophie Barat accepted some women as coadjutrix sisters whose health was not robust but who patently had a call to the contemplative life.[241] On the other hand, when some aristocratic women asked Sophie to allow them follow the path of Pauline de Saint André their requests were firmly refused.[242] For Sophie Barat the choice made by Pauline de Saint André was exceptional. A family name was important, signifying class and status, and this had to be honoured and esteemed. Pauline de Saint André felt her parents had so dishonoured the family that their salvation was in peril. Her vocation was to redeem them by a life of humility and prayer, and she found it possible to do that in the Society of the Sacred Heart as a coadjutrix sister.

However, Sophie Barat could not allow the social structure within the Society of the Sacred Heart be put off balance. To weaken that would draw the incomprehension of aristocratic families, who often sought excuses to block daughters who wished to enter, or so harassed and undermined them afterwards that they were forced to leave. It was not always a question of money, since some aristocratic families had merely their name to offer as a dowry, having lost lands and wealth during the Revolution. In 1855 the superior at Warendorf (Westphalia) asked Sophie Barat for a French teacher:

> I could offer you one of our orphans in Conflans from a noble family which has fallen completely on hard times. She is sixteen years of age and it appears she has a vocation. It is not really appropriate that she becomes a Coadjutrix Sister since she is gifted and would be of better service to the Society as a Choir Sister. But those in charge here,

unaware of her vocation, put her in the orphanage. In view of this, it is better that she leaves France and does her studies separately. She speaks French well and she could help in the care of the little ones. She could look after them; speak to them in French etc. However, it is not necessary for her to do housework, as she has to gain the respect of the children and she will have most contact with them. See if this young woman can be of service to you. They want her in Ireland, but she would be more appropriately occupied in Warendorf, as your parents want French to be taught.[243]

Ever vigilant with regard to admission of women to the Society, either as choir or coadjutrix sisters,[244] as the time drew near for final profession in the Society, Sophie Barat often intervened personally in their formation. If it was clear that a choir sister was not suited for leadership or for teaching, Sophie Barat would suggest that she move to the rank of coadjutrix sister or leave the Society. Even if a choir sister had brought a substantial dowry with her, Sophie Barat still would ask her to change rank or leave if she proved unable to fulfil the tasks of a choir sister. However, Sophie Barat also lamented constantly that it was often not possible to implement this option as the person had been too long in the Society without proper discernment, and to change her status then would discredit her in the eyes of her family. In this case, and if it was too difficult to return home, Sophie arranged that the choir sister could remain in the Society for life but not be admitted to final profession.[245] Similarly for the coadjutrix sisters. If there was a doubt concerning a vocation, Sophie Barat usually made several attempts to assess the vocation of the coadjutrix sister or asked the local superiors to treat the process with both care and realism.[246] If it became clear that there was not a call to full membership of the Society, Sophie offered either to allow them become a commissioner sister, if that position was open in a community,[247] or, if they did not wish to return home, she would try to find another religious community more suitable for them.[248]

Crisis and consolidation of the Society of the Sacred Heart, 1833–1851

The General Council of 1833 was an opportunity to look back over the course of thirty-three years. From 1800 Sophie Barat and her companions had gradually created a model of religious life, which had specific spiritual goals and coherent community structures. Their form of life was a blend of the active (apostolic) and monastic religious life which created a self-sufficient village type of life, where each had her place and task. Just as there was a two-rank system in the community, the Society had introduced a two-fold system of education which combined schools for the upper classes and schools for the poor. Finance in the form of legacies and pensions, mostly from the aristocratic and upper bourgeois families, sustained both choir and coadjutrix sisters financially, and normally fees for the boarding schools ensured the viability of the poor schools.[249] This combination of schools encouraged a certain economic stability. The Society was much in demand. Parents in particular were attracted to the Society's boarding and poor schools which by 1833 provided education for hundreds of young women.[250] Many young women were drawn to the Society, attracted by its spirituality and form of life. It offered them opportunities and choices other than marriage or the single life, and they could join either as choir or coadjutrix sisters. The model on paper was serene and classic, and was expanding beyond France and beyond Europe, and was becoming known internationally.

From her experience as superior general, by 1833 it was clear to Sophie Barat that the Society needed new structures of government to cope with such rapid expansion. The structures created in 1815 reflected the needs just then,[251] and even by 1820 Sophie was concerned about the rapid expansion of the Society which made increasing demands on her daily letter-writing (which she loved) and constant travel. Certainly by 1833 demands on her energy were beyond her strength and affected her health and she knew she could not carry on indefinitely without new governing structures. She also recognised with reluctance that she could not possibly retain direct contact with all the members of the Society. She sensed she was losing touch with the second and even third generations of women. Clearly good governance required new structures and these could only be introduced by a General Council of the Society, due in 1839.

Sophie Barat intended adopting the Jesuit structure of government for the Society, and divide the Society into geographical areas (provinces) with leaders (provincials) appointed by her. From 1833, with the help of a small group in the Society, Sophie planned to propose this change in 1839.[252] She asked Jean Rozaven, assistant general for the French province of the Jesuits and resident in Rome, to advise on how to proceed. In 1835 he invited her to Rome:

> You should bring with you two or three of the people you trust most and who are best placed to help you with their advice. Choose them in view of the common good, with no concession to human respect, whether or not they are assistant generals or councillors. With the advice you will get here you will draft the relevant changes to be

made [to the 1815 Constitutions] and have them approved by the pope.[253]

In addition to the need for new structures of government, Sophie Barat had other concerns which also needed to be addressed in 1839. These regarded the quality of the choir and coadjutrix sisters accepted into the Society. Sophie had met far too many young women who had been received into the Society without adequate assessment.[254] She complained that candidates, especially the coadjutrix sisters, were all too often accepted for the type of work they could do; or they were allowed to enter on account of their wealth and social position, especially the choir sisters. In many cases the evidence of a genuine religious vocation was not present.[255] The temptation to accept women as choir sisters was linked with the rapid expansion of the Society. The number of students in the schools was increasing, and the Society received constant invitations to make new foundations in Europe and further afield. These pressures led to overwork, and, in the urgent need for new members, conditions for admission were diluted and in some instances ignored. Sophie Barat feared that the Society was in danger of losing its path, its inner spiritual purpose.[256]

Another of Sophie's concerns was the actual numbers of coadjutrix sisters accepted into the Society. From at least 1815 she repeatedly asked local superiors to maintain a balance of two-thirds choir sisters and one-third coadjutrix sisters in their communities.[257] By 1833 Sophie was aware that if the admission practices in the Society were allowed to continue as they were, soon there could be almost as many coadjutrix sisters as choir sisters in the Society.[258] It would then only be a short step before the balance in the two ranks could actually reverse. This would dramatically impact not only on the inner structure of the Society but also on its work of education in the boarding and poor schools. Such a serious organisational dilemma needed to be discussed at the General Council in 1839 as a matter of urgency.

And Sophie Barat's concerns were well founded. By 1843, when statistics were first recorded, there were 413 coadjutrix sisters and 407 choir sisters in first vows (termed Aspirants). Furthermore, there were 175 coadjutrix novices and 156 choir novices.[259] By contrast, there were 148 professed coadjutrix sisters and 405 professed choir sisters in 1843, clearly showing that the crisis lay in the younger age group in the Society. Obviously the solution was to enforce strict screening of all candidates at the moment of entry, and in that discernment to take into account Sophie Barat's constant request to maintain the two-thirds/one-third balance. Again, as in the case of the choir sisters, this proved extremely difficult to implement. The Society was growing rapidly and its schools were much in demand, and the number of women asking to enter the Society as coadjutrix sisters was matched by the ever increasing need for domestic workers and skills.[260] Many communities would not have the financial resources to employ more outside help, and the temptation was to accept those who wished to enter but did not necessarily have a vocation.[261] The inbuilt tension between trying to provide adequate domestic help while at the same time maintaining the one-third/two-thirds balance in the community was difficult to resolve, especially when the contemplative ideal of the vocation of the coadjutrix sister was attractive to women.[262]

Another aspect linked to the same problem was the number of choir and coadjutrix sisters who asked to leave the Society after their final profession, which confirmed Sophie Barat's awareness that originally vocations had not been adequately discerned. Leaving the Society was stressful for each who left, for their families and for the Society. It was bad for the morale of the members and bad for the reputation of the Society of the Sacred Heart. Although the superior general had the authority to release members from simple vows (the first vows taken after the two-year noviceship) only the pope could release members from final vows. For Sophie Barat the most effective way to deal with this issue was to insist, yet again, on consistent observance of the Society's admissions/dismissals policies, as laid down in the Constitutions, and in this way put a halt to the steady stream of petitions going to Rome requesting release from final profession. This was a lengthy, expensive process which the Society was obliged to follow for each one.[263] These were the key issues around personnel which Sophie Barat wished to present at the next General Council, along with the need to change the government structures of the Society.

Reactions to the Sixth General Council of the Society, Rome 1839

The sixth General Council of the Society opened in Rome in June 1839 and met for three weeks. Proposals to create provinces and provincials in the Society as well as the possible residence of Sophie Barat in Rome were quickly passed.[264] However, the momentum for change had taken over and this led to further decisions taken to model the Society of the Sacred Heart more closely on the Jesuits. In less than three weeks forty-six decrees were passed modifying the 1815 Constitutions, and the decisions affected both choir and coadjutrix sisters. When the wider body of the Society learnt of the changes, reactions in the Society were diverse. Most welcomed the creation of provinces and provincials in the Society as necessary for good governance. But the forty-six modifications to the 1815 Constitutions were controversial. Many doubted that three weeks alone was sufficient time to effect such enormous changes to the 1815 Constitutions,[265] and they were astonished at such rapidity; some compared the Council to 1789:

> Your Council has imitated the Assembly of 1789: in a few days it has reduced the edifice to ruins. But when one destroys what was sacred in the eyes of all one exposes oneself to the destruction of one's own work in due time.[266]

One of the most severely criticised changes was the decree which proposed that solemn final vows, including the vow of stability, would be taken only by choir sisters, and after ten years of preparation. The coadjutrix sisters would not take final solemn vows, only the first vows at the end of the noviceship. This new decree was lifted directly from the Jesuit Constitutions, and reflected the Jesuit practice of retaining the right to dismiss their spiritual and temporal coadjutor members (that is, their coadjutrix brothers) if they proved to be unsuitable to the overall goals of the order. The coadjutrix brothers made three public, but not solemn, vows of obedience, poverty and chastity.[267] Clearly the General Council of 1839 adopted the rules for Jesuit coadjutrix brothers for the coadjutrix sisters in the Society of the Sacred Heart:

> It is very important for the Society that the Coadjutrix Sisters can be dismissed when they behave badly. And even though this extreme measure will only occur very rarely, it is good that they know this can happen. Those who cannot be held by the highest motivations will be controlled by fear. Since dispensation from final vows is reserved to the Pope, this process entails long negotiations and a lot of unpleasantness for the Society.
>
> It is necessary, therefore, to tell those who are admitted as Coadjutrix Sisters that they cannot hope to make vows other than those taken at the end of the Noviceship. They are vows of religion and are sufficient for their spiritual good. The Coadjutrix Sisters have the assurance that they will never be sent away if they behave properly, according to their holy calling. [268]

Both the tone and spirit of this decree was in marked contrast to the tone and spirit of the 1815 Constitutions, and was used as a mechanism to address the growing imbalance in numbers between choir and coadjutrix sisters, as well as deficient admission and dismissal practices in the Society.[269] As superior general of the Society, Sophie Barat was not at liberty to reveal in public the frequent difficulties she had experienced, petitioning the Pope to annul the final vows of members of the Society. Nor could she indicate publicly the numbers of choir and coadjutrix sisters who either asked, or were asked, to leave the Society. For these reasons, in her official letter in July 1839 to the Society Sophie Barat did not mention the disciplinary aspect of the decree on the coadjutrix sisters at all. She simply noted that in the future the coadjutrix sisters would take only simple vows at the end of their two year noviceship.[270]

Decree on the Coadjutrix Sisters

However, Sophie Barat could hardly hope for acceptance of such a sudden, radical change. The 1839 decree on the coadjutrix sisters opened a debate concerning simple and solemn vows which generated sharp criticism within and without the Society. While Jean Rozaven in Rome wished to incorporate the Society of the Sacred Heart as far as possible with the Jesuits, his Jesuit colleague in Paris, Joseph Varin, accused him, along with Sophie Barat and the members of the Council, of destroying the very foundations of the Society of the Sacred Heart. He accused them of treating the coadjutrix sisters shamefully:

> I know what has been said, I hear the complaints made against the Coadjutrix Sisters. Yet, if they have at times given cause for dissatisfaction, whose fault is that? Oh! If only they had been given proper noviceship training, if care had been taken to teach them religion correctly and to form them in the spirit of the Society, as the Constitutions required, we would have to praise them for their exemplary conduct.[271]

Sophie Barat asked Elizabeth Galitzine, secretary general of the Society, to reply to Joseph Varin. She did so with the help of Jean Rozaven:

> It is true that the Coadjutrix Sisters will no longer be admitted to final [solemn] profession, yet how necessary this step was . . . and why should we not be allowed to adopt what was so wisely decreed by you [the Jesuits] whereby the brothers are not admitted to final profession; nor are they less religious for that. But at least, when we are in the sad position of having to send them out of the Society, we do not have the distress of having to apply to the Pope as has already occurred, if they have taken the vow of stability.[272]

Other reactions emerged in the Society. A founding member, Genevieve Deshayes, asked in dismay if anyone:

> ever ordered a Dominican to become a Carmelite? Or a Jesuit to become a Capuchin? The pope would not force adherence or impose

his authority by coercion, without the possibility of objecting to the Decrees which a small group of councillors drew up, approved and declared to be obligatory on all. They wish us to be perfect and suggest, or rather direct, that we imitate the Jesuit Constitutions. We are not challenging those Constitutions, but everything has its own perfect form, each religious order its own spirit. Women are not men and France is not Italy.[273]

Such reactions showed that objections within the Society were not only to the decree on the coadjutrix sisters but also on the wider purposes of the 1839 General Council, to incorporate the Society of the Sacred Heart more closely with the Jesuits. For those weeks in Rome the General Council members felt all plans were possible, and Sophie Barat admitted her failure in leadership, that she and the Council had made serious errors of judgement:

> The Society is badly shaken. We have acted in every way with imprudence. We must proceed more slowly and hide our plans. This has happened, but what troubles I am going to reap! [274]

However, she could not renege on the urgent need for new forms of government for the Society, or on the need for rigorous entry and dismissal processes for entrants to the Society. These were urgent and necessary, and during these years Sophie Barat made her point again and again:

> I believe . . . that we must not accept women who really do not have what is needed to understand religious life and live it. Later on these would frustrate rather than help [the Society]. How much I prefer to have those who have difficult characters but who have soul and energy, to those wet hens that do us no good![275]

> Look at what our Society has become in twenty years. It has become unrecognisable! And what worries me most is that I cannot send away all who damage us . . . We have hardly any novices in rue Monsieur [Paris], very few postulants, and yet I prefer that to having numbers who are not truly religious. The source of vocations appears to be drying up. The best are in Heaven.[276]

Sophie certainly regretted the manner and the tone of the decree on the coadjutrix sisters, but she also complained that it had been seized upon and used as an emotive tool by her critics, especially Eugénie de Gramont and Joseph Varin. She insisted the decree was necessary:

> People were wrong to have informed the Coadjutrix Sisters so quickly about matters concerning them. It was aimed directly at new entrants. The older sisters and those who are giving satisfaction can

hope to make their final profession. But if they are accepted do not go back on what has been decided. At the end of the day all the vows are the same. Before God there is no difference. At least the situation regarding the Coadjutrix Sisters can be managed which will be a great help.[277]

Further reactions to the Decree on the Coadjutrix Sisters

As the outcome of the 1839 General Council reached France, an old friend of Sophie Barat, Césaire Mathieu, archbishop of Besançon, commented on the decree concerning the coadjutrix sisters:

> No more solemn vows for the Coadjutrix Sisters. What a retrograde step for these poor women, many of whom are saints and most of them so good! Why must there be such an enormous distinction between the choir and the lay religious in the humble Society of the Sacred Heart?
>
> I am afraid that [in Rome you] have been led in this matter by a badly thought out wish to resemble the Jesuits; [you did] not consider sufficiently the basic differences which have to exist between an order of men and a community of women . . . Was there no true friend there, able to give good advice and point out such simple observations and divert the members of the Council from collectively rushing into such a chasm? [278]

While Césaire Mathieu understood the need for new forms of government in the Society, the decree on the coadjutrix sisters was quite another issue. He noted how the tone and content of the 1839 decree on the coadjutrix sisters were radically different from the spirit of the 1815 Constitutions. The latter clearly stated that while there were 'two classes of persons' in the Society, those who taught and those looked after material needs, both shared the same vocation and were equal spiritually. In this context Césaire Mathieu found the terms of the 1839 decree 'very harsh'. He argued that:

> Since final vows are suppressed for the Coadjutrix Sisters, it can no longer be said that, according to Article 7 [1815], for the tasks of the Society there are two different classes of persons, but both are equal regarding the obligations of conscience. It is also very cruel to say that the Coadjutrix Sisters need to know that they can be sent away at any time. Do they not carry out the most laborious tasks in the house; wear themselves out taking care of the material needs of the schools? Should their position be considered the same as maids in service? Surely the seven years testing time, which can be extended, is sufficient [to test their vocation]?

I know that sometimes there are the Coadjutrix Sisters who go astray, who create problems and these have to be dealt with sharply in order to prevent trouble. But the majority of the Coadjutrix Sisters are so excellent, so humble, so perfect, and the only consolation they have for all their immense labours is the joy of being fully and definitively vowed to God. Should the entire majority of Coadjutrix Sisters be made to suffer for the faults of a few individuals?

For my own part, I have to say that in all my visits [to houses of the Society] I have been singularly impressed by the Coadjutrix Sisters. Tears have often come to my eyes when I have been interviewing these simple and noble souls, seeing with what generosity and what religious perfection they serve the Lord.[279]

Reactions within and without the Society to the decree showed how central the vocation of the coadjutrix sister was in the Society. It also revealed how much of the initiative Sophie Barat had lost during the 1839 General Council. She became the butt of criticism in the Society and beyond:

Undoubtedly my procedure was forced, for this is not my usual way of acting at all. Also, some call me a sleeping-watchdog, that's the word they use.[280]

In November 1839 Sophie Barat wrote another letter to the Society to explain the content of the decree on the coadjutrix sisters. It was modelled on the Jesuit coadjutrix brothers. Like them, the coadjutrix sisters of the Society of the Sacred Heart would automatically become fully professed members at the end of ten years in the Society (coadjutrices formées):

They will be as sure of remaining in the Society when they reach this status as they would be had they taken the vow of stability. Simple vows are perpetual in nature, following the Bulls of the Popes, as perfect in religion as the professed who take solemn vows. So our dear Sisters can be reassured that the Decree concerning them is not to their disadvantage. We know how much we appreciate their devotedness and attachment to the Society, and they can count fully on the affection of those in charge of the Society which has not changed in any way. [281]

Tensions between Paris and Rome intervene: suppression of 1839 Decrees

While Sophie Barat was composing this letter to the Society, controversy over the decree on the coadjutrix sisters was completely overtaken by a deeper crisis concerning Sophie Barat's possible change of residence, from Paris to Rome. Between the winter of 1839 and the spring of 1843 this question led to a protracted conflict between the Society of the Sacred Heart and two archbishops of Paris (de Quelen and Affre), as well as the French government which threatened to close all of the houses of the Society in France. Throughout the winter and spring of 1842–43 Sophie Barat worked with Césaire Mathieu, archbishop of Besancon, Antonio Garibaldi, inter-nuncio in Paris, and Luigi Lambruschini, papal secretary of state, trying to find a solution to the issue. In February 1843 Césaire Mathieu travelled to Rome and presented a possible resolution. This was considered in March 1843 by a group of cardinals appointed by Pope Gregory XVI, who advised the pope to suppress the 1839 Decrees until the next General Council of the Society, due in 1845. The pope took this advice and the decision automatically reinstated the 1815 Constitutions.[282]

Sophie had anticipated that this would happen and asked at least to retain the structure of provinces and provincials in the Society established at the 1839 General Council,[283] but this was refused on the grounds of being confusing and divisive. Returning to the 1815 Constitutions was a personal tragedy for Sophie Barat. For years she had planned to reform structures of the Society, as well as the admissions and dismissal policies for both ranks, and aspects of the life of the choir and coadjutrix sisters. Indeed the number of coadjutrix sisters in the Society was only one aspect of reform. Sophie Barat also considered permitting fewer choir sisters to take final solemn vows. Her goal was to maintain a strong inner core of spiritual energy in the Society, and find future leaders and spiritual guides within this group.[284] She had also intended to address issues around education, especially updating the Plan of Studies for the schools and the training of teachers.[285] But all had to be dropped and in the spring of 1843 Sophie Barat ended up with the same problems of government that she had begun to address in 1833.

Addressing reform in other ways: the Society after 1843

With characteristic realism Sophie Barat continued to govern the Society after 1843 and she attended to all aspects of its life, the communities and schools, care of properties and planning of new foundations. The Society expanded further internationally and the hegemony of France, especially of Paris, became even stronger in the Society.[286] Sophie persisted in demanding stringent admission and dismissal policies, convinced as ever that these were essential for the spiritual health and vitality of the Society. In the winter of 1843 she embarked on a thorough investigation of Louisiana, focussed especially on those recently admitted to the Society. She appointed Maria Cutts, a former coadjutrix sister, as her representative. She asked her to act decisively and without favour:

> You must reassess each of the novices, Choir and Coadjutrix, and each of the young professed, to be really sure about those who do not have a call to the Society, or who have truly serious deficiencies or characters which are too difficult for us to handle, etc. These are to be sent away from the Society.
>
> You can only proceed on this painful path of action after mature reflection, prayer and consultation. But having done all that, then you must act without pity, once you are truly convinced that were such persons be allowed to remain, they would be detrimental to the Society. There is nothing more to weigh up: Send them back to their families, or place them in other religious houses. If you discover that they cannot be sent away, either because of their health which has been damaged or seriously affected while in the Society, or on account of other equally serious reasons, then I wish to be told. In such cases, they must accept to remain in the Society without final profession, without the cross and ring.[287]

> The students could not value an order which admitted members who have neither a vocation nor religious virtue. I cannot tell you the damage and the serious consequences which have resulted from this.[288]

Sophie Barat's robust stance on the quality of vocations in Louisiana was applied to the Society in general, and her comments were frank:

> [Some enter the Society with] neither talent, nor refinement nor education and, worst of all, no religious vocation. If this goes on the Society will die out. We really need fewer foundations and more religious spirit and genuine integrity. Without these we will not achieve our goal and we will perish.[289]

> [Teresa of Avila] excluded them [unsuitable candidates] mercilessly from her order. It would be good if this examination and weeding out process was done during the time of noviceship, to avoid the serious problems which follow from release from vows . . . In some more religious countries release from vows leaves a taint which is like a lifelong dishonour for these women.[290]

> Yes, these women with little religious spirit, with only half-vocations do us harm! Please pay attention to this. Until my dying day this will be my: '*delenda Cartago!*' I will close all my letters with this.[291]

However, it was the quality of judgement displayed by local leaders which Sophie Barat criticised most of all. This included their criteria and motivation not only for admitting women to the Society but also for retaining those who were manifestly unsuited, and who often wanted to leave themselves.[292] She believed that it was far better, and indeed more just, to deal with weak vocations at the early stages of training, rather than wait some years. Often in the months before final profession it was left to Sophie Barat or her representatives to refuse admission to full membership of the Society. She knew that poor discernment of vocations damaged the individual, often wounded their families, and impacted on the communities and the schools. It also harmed the reputation of the Society, and most important of all, weakened spiritual energy.[293] It was that energy which Sophie Barat felt responsible to maintain by careful selection of members, certain that this safeguarded the Society and enabled it to fulfil its purpose. Then, once vocations had been discerned carefully and members had made their final commitment to the Society, Sophie Barat in return was attentive to their further formation, either through her letters, through visits, or by introducing measures at General Councils.

The life of Choir Sisters after 1843

By 1843 there were several generations of choir sisters in the Society. Their way of life had reached a degree of definition and young women encountered this lived experience even before they entered the Society. Their trousseau requirements had been laid down by the early General Councils of the Society and they could enter as choir sisters whether or not they had dowries, pensions or personal legacies.[294] The priority was whether they had the vocation, capacity and aptitude necessary for being a choir sister. In practice, however, women from the upper classes were endowed by their families, either outright with their inheritance or more usually by annual pension. When a woman decided to enter she brought this inheritance or pension with her, a welcome financial support and essential for the maintenance and development of the Society. However, the money was not actually accepted formally by the Society until the novice had taken her first vows. If in the meantime, or indeed later on, the family fell on hard times Sophie Barat mostly suggested that the monies received be returned, either in part or fully to the family. If the woman left the Society, even after final profession, the sum was returned in full, minus the interest accrued.[295]

From the earliest days of the Society each community was responsible to give a tenth of their income to the superior general, for the maintenance of central government and funding of new foundations. The dowries and pensions of each of the choir sisters, or at least portions of them, provided the finance for this tithe, and were also at the disposal of the communities where the individual lived, for both community and school-building projects.[296] Since each choir sister took her pension with her when she moved to another community (or left the Society) such practices often led to tensions between communities, or with the family of the choir sister concerned, or with central government in the person of the treasurer general and superior general. Such issues became even more complicated if the choir sister died; sometimes the family then made claims for money, some even claiming the ownership of school buildings. By 1851 it was clear that the Society needed to centralise all its finances for the purpose of better governance and to avoid conflicts such as these as far as possible.[297]

On the other hand, many families of the choir sisters had few resources to offer the Society and some paid the Society in kind, by sending wines and nuts, fruits and vegetables, according to season. Other cases arose, as when women were attracted to the Society but were prevented from entering on account of their responsibility to contribute financially to the education of their siblings. If Sophie Barat thought that a vocation in this instance was genuine, she offered a place in a school of the Society to one of the family. Over the years Sophie Barat asked the schools to reserve one place for her to fill and pay for at her discretion:

> At the moment I am paying five school fees (pensions) from my own funds. These are for the younger sisters of novices who could not enter until they had provided for their education. [Otherwise] they would have to become teachers (institutrices) in order to provide for their sisters.[298]

Class consciousness was an issue. Many choir sisters came from aristocratic, wealthy families and this led to family backgrounds becoming significant among the choir sisters. This element, present in the Society from the beginning, grew over time and in some communities a well-defined hierarchy of importance operated.[299] This development was inevitable since the education of the aristocracy was one of the works of the Society. Indeed the tasks of the choir sisters brought them into the public domain, either as holders of offices in the communities or as headmistresses and teachers in the schools. Parents and pupils drew attention to the family backgrounds of some of the choir sisters, and the Society became part of that world.[300] Of course, not all choir sisters were of aristocratic birth, but even one or two in a school or community was enough to create a reputation which sometimes did not match the actual composition of the community, with the exception of the rue de Varenne.[301] As a group, these aristocratic women were important in raising the public profile of the Society and in drawing attention to its work of education. All the more reason then for the Society to discern their motivation for admission carefully and for treating the issue of class at General Councils.

Choir Sisters and the General Councils of 1851 and 1864

In preparation for the General Council of 1851, Louise de Limminghe consulted the Jesuit superior general, Jan Roothaan, about the significance Jesuits put on the class of the person wishing to join them. In his experience noble birth and wealth were neither sufficient nor necessary for entry to religious life. Roothaan suggested that if any choir sister in the Society of the Sacred Heart took first vows and then proved incapable of responsibility and leadership, then she should not be allowed take the vow of stability (taken at final profession). This would automatically exclude her from being appointed to leadership positions and ensure that class did not dominate in the discernment of vocations.[302] This advice echoed Sophie Barat's own views which she had wished to introduce formally in the Society in 1839, by way of reform. Her project had failed then and by 1851 it was necessary that the General Council address the amount of attention some members of the Society paid to discussing the social status of some families. Comments made in community or in the schools, about families, their name, origin, status and wealth led inevitably to comparisons between the choir sisters.[303] The 1851 Council deplored such attitudes as contrary to 'religious spirit':

> It is noted with regret that some in the Society have a spirit contrary to that of the Lord. They have too great esteem for the family name, for noble birth (du sang), for connections with influential people, valuing their patronage and that of their own family. Honest people who like the Society have commented on this for our sake, aware that it could have consequences for us.[304]

From the beginning there were tensions sometimes between those choir sisters with either a pre-Revolution or a post-Revolution background, or between those who were court nobility and those originating in the provinces. Some noble families served under Napoleon and members of these families could be held in suspicion by families of the ancien régime. For example, the court aristocrat Armande de Causans clashed with the noble de province Aimée d'Avenas, both gifted women but from different grades of nobility.[305] Similarly, Madame de Gramont d'Aster, former lady-in-waiting to Marie Antoinette, was at odds with Marie d'Olivier when they lived in the community at Quimper.[306] These were the social realities of the day which each one brought with her when entering the Society, and they contributed to the diversity and richness of the communities, as well to the tensions. The General Council of 1851 asked that such social diversity within families should not dominate in the values and conversations of the choir sisters, nor should they allow wealth be used as a source of power and influence, either in the communities or schools.

Legacies, dowries and pensions

To try and lessen the matter of money within communities, the 1851 General Council addressed the matter of legacies, inheritances, dowries and pensions again. It proposed that all dowries, legacies and inheritances, and all pensions which exceeded 1,000 francs a year, be sent to the general treasury in Paris.[307] This was an ideal which was difficult to put into practice and the General Council of 1864 reintroduced the proposal, noting with some disapproval the Society's failure to implement it. Indeed members of the 1851 General Council learnt that in some instances women who wished to enter the Society as choir sisters were either accepted or refused on the basis of whether or not they had money to offer, quite contrary to the practice of the Society from the beginning. The General Council of 1864 asked that all monies be centralised in the central treasury of the Society (in Paris), rather than retained in the communities where the individual members lived. Once again, when put to the test it was deemed impossible to enforce legally. Instead, families tended to ask the Society to name the amount of dowry or annual pension required for entry to the Society and then sent it directly to the individual choir sister, who discussed its use either with Sophie Barat or the local superior.[308]

Sophie Barat always planned to centralise all finances in the Society, despite the opposition of families, of bishops and priests, the individual members and the legal advisers to the Society.[309] From her point of view, just as the government of the Society was central, symbolising the unity of all the members, so finance should be centralised and placed at the service of all. Such centralisation of finances would have given Sophie greater freedom to apply monies where needed. Instead, she had to respect the wishes of families who in donating money expected it to be used by the community where their relation lived.[310] While not achieving centralising of finance, Sophie Barat always insisted on her rights as superior general to move personnel from house to house, or from country to country. Just as Teresa of Avila was obliged in her day, so Sophie Barat had to remind families and clergy that financial gifts to the Society did not confer any family privileges and gave them no right to demand favours.[311]

But families did demand favours.[312] Even if a choir sister made her will in favour of the Society, it could be contested in law by the family. Occasionally when a choir sister died some families considered it their right in law to demand that her finances revert to them, including the finances offered originally as dowries. Some went to the extent of claiming that the fruits of the work done by their family member in the course of her life in the Society belonged to the family and were due after her death. By contrast, the Society held the view that all rights and fruits had been handed over voluntarily at final profession. Simple restitution was not possible or conceded. However, family interpretations led to court cases, often over buildings and properties. Some problems were compounded by the fact that not every choir sister made a will in favour of the Society, and even if she did it was not recognised by the state. Normally such cases were resolved amicably before they reached the courts and Sophie Barat sought to meet families half way.[313] But the cases which did go to court were usually won by Sophie, who had immense experience in dealing with the intricacies which surrounded such cases and she retained lawyers who were familiar with the legal material.[314]

Evolution of the roles of the Choir Sisters after 1843

The leadership roles of the choir sisters in the Society had developed over the decades, and through them they gained a certain assurance and confidence in their tasks. Their roles as teachers, headmistresses, charged with school studies or of school discipline, trained them for leadership. Equally, leading preparation for feast days in the community and schools, as well as teaching hymn singing and playing the organ, allowed them express their gifts.[315] Those choir sisters who were appointed to lead communities were given great scope for leadership. They were placed in situations where they dealt with government/local authorities, with bishops and priests, with parents and pupils. They were also responsible for the care of the choir and coadjutrix sisters particularly in the areas of spirituality. They had to provide proper nourishment for their community and school, a constant concern of Sophie Barat, since many young members of the Society, and some pupils in the schools, died from tuberculosis in the nineteenth century.[316] They were helped in their tasks by an assistant superior, who had particular responsibility for the coadjutrix sisters, and by three or four other choir sisters who were named as her councillors.

Choir sisters who were the bursars in communities and schools also exercised leadership. They maintained the buildings in good repair, supervised the adaptation or extension of buildings and sent the annual returns to the central administration in Paris.[317] Individual choir sisters were named to head all the work areas of the house, and linked closely with the coadjutrix sisters in the kitchen, dairy, linen room, sacristy, infirmary, reception, food storerooms, as well as the farm and gardens. Choir sisters also supervised the lay staff who worked in the house, in the gardens and on the farm,[318] and they accompanied the coadjutrix sisters if they worked alongside the lay staff in the community parts of the house. A choir sister was in charge of visitors and her task was ensuring that individual members of the community or school were accompanied during a visit. This took place in a parlour near the front door, and it was considered particularly important for the young religious to be accompanied if the visitor was a priest.

In the second year of their noviceship the leadership aptitude of each choir novice was assessed. Most were destined for teaching either in the boarding or the poor schools. In addition to learning how to teach basic subjects, the choir novices were taught music, drawing and the art of writing, of embroidery and flower-making. They were also taught correct deportment and encouraged to take adequate exercise to balance the time taken up by studies.[319] The Plan of Studies was their source of reference and it had been updated several times since 1804. Their training continued in the communities after their first vows, and mentors were appointed to help each one develop her teaching skills. Sophie Barat regularly addressed the importance of the education carried out in the Society, and reminded superiors that when choosing teachers in the schools that it was not a questions of rank or seniority but of knowledge.[320] She complained about the weak level of studies in the Society and was concerned about the quality of education in the schools. Aimée d'Avenas, in charge of studies in the rue de Varenne, was appointed to write textbooks for use in the Society. She also visited schools to examine the level of studies and to observe the standard of teaching. Sophie Barat was aware that parents were progressively demanding higher standards in studies, and that in time the state would demand the right to inspect the schools:

> This weakness is all the greater since we believe in conscience that we
> must refuse to be inspected by the University. If we weaken in the art

of teaching we provide ammunition to be used against us. That is what happened in one of the towns of France where the parents were the first to arouse the interest of the inspectors, telling them that we needed their inspections.[321]

The passing of the Loi Falloux in 1850 relieved the Society from the immediate pressure of having the choir sisters inspected by the state as the law permitted members of religious congregations to teach in their schools without a state certificate. However, Sophie Barat knew that the choir sisters needed proper teacher training and that they should be as well trained as their lay colleagues. In preparation for the General Council of 1851, she set up a commission of choir sisters to examine the content and quality of studies in the Society, especially in the boarding schools.[322] Sophie Barat also asked each school to put its documentation in order, verifying the agreements made with government authorities and with bishops since its foundation.[323] A revised Plan of Studies was published in 1852, in the wake of the 1851 General Council, with the understanding that setting up a teacher-training programme for the choir sisters would be treated as a matter of urgency.[324] Teacher training was taken up again during the General Council of 1864 and only realised after Sophie Barat's death in 1865.[325]

Sophie saw it as her responsibility to prepare choir sisters for leadership in the Society, and to follow them up once they were in office. She did this without the help of adequate governing structures to match the Society's rapid expansion, and mainly through her letter writing.[326] She knew that many of the challenges these women faced in different parts of the world were daunting; they could be liberating for some and overpowering for others.[327] But while she continued to help the local superiors in their leadership tasks, after 1851 Sophie Barat concentrated particularly on forming the geographical, area superiors, called Vicars, and she trained them in their respective offices.[328] She explained how they should visit communities and schools, how to lead spiritually and manage personnel, and always to pay particular attention to the health and wellbeing of the members.[329] During their visits they should look to practical matters concerning care of the properties, and in particular care of the animals, the cows and the sheep, as well as the orchards and gardens.[330] They were to examine the financial state of the community and school and Sophie Barat demanded high ethical standards regarding finance and fair treatment of employees; she especially abhorred debts and injustice.[331] In all, she asked the Vicars to use their judgement in situations, to take necessary decisions and learn to be accountable to her for them.

The life of the Coadjutrix Sisters after 1839

The coadjutrix sisters also received attention and training for their varied tasks and offices in the Society, especially after the failed attempts of the General Council of 1839. The question of numbers for admissions as well as formation needed to be addressed.[332] In anticipation of the General Council of 1851 Sophie Barat drew on two sources for discussion on the coadjutrix sisters: the draft rule for the coadjutrix sisters drawn up in 1839, and the comments sent by members of the Society to the proposed decrees of 1839, called *Observations and Responses*. Sophie Barat had prepared responses to these comments and retained them for use at another, more opportune, time. Observations had been sent in regarding the 1839 decree on the coadjutrix sisters:

> *Observation No 10:* [*1842*]
>
> [re Decree of 1839] The Coadjutrix Sisters will no longer take the Vow of Stability, and can be sent away at any time. To act this way is severe and harsh, having exploited the youth and health of the Coadjutrix Sisters in the service of the Society.

A response to this Observation had been prepared for presentation at the 1842 General Council:

> *Response to Observation No 10:* [*1842*]
>
> 1. Experience proves only too well the wisdom of this measure. The lack of education among most of these good women makes them difficult to train. A great number of them are controlled only by the fear of being sent away.
> 2. Dismissal is neither severe nor harsh; the measure is not taken except in serious cases, as a last resort and for grave reasons. Indeed, they are the same reasons as for the dismissal from vows of a finally professed [Choir Sister].
> 3. Moreover the Society gives financial compensation to those who leave as Young Professed (Aspirants), equivalent in value to the amount of money they would have received outside, for the time they have spent in the Society.
> 4. We have never sent away anyone who has spent her best years and health in the service of the Society.
> 5. The Coadjutrix Sisters are in no way to be considered like servants. They are our Sisters, and they are our privileged Sisters in the company of the Lord; and they share our spiritual and temporal goods as much as the Choir Sisters.[333]

This issue was sensitive, and shortly before the 1851 General Council Adèle Cahier, secretary general of the Society, commented on the reaction the 1839 decree on the coadjutrix sisters had created within and without the Society:

> The point [Decree] regarding our Coadjutrix Sisters was condemned, and most would condemn and reject it again. The secular clergy in particular find it unjust and they discourage all vocations [saying] the Society would end up having just servants in the communities instead of religious.
>
> But we think that we can replace [the Decree] by prolonging the preparation time of the Coadjutrix Sisters, who are naturally more difficult to get to know and train. Generally for final profession we accept only those who are considered suitable based on the information given us and if they have been in the Society for ten years.[334]

Diocesan clergy often opposed the Society of the Sacred Heart, for several reasons.[335] They resented the independence the Society enjoyed in the dioceses and parishes due to papal approbation. Tensions often existed between the Society and the chaplains appointed to the communities and schools by the local bishops. Sophie Barat often lamented the lack of good confessors among the local clergy, and commented on their interference in the life of the community and schools.[336] Diocesan clergy tended to resent the Society's practice of asking Jesuits to be the special confessors of the communities at certain times of the year,[337] and to give the annual community retreats, the school and the past pupils retreats. All this increased the Society's reputation among the clergy for aloofness. When Marie Lataste entered the Society in 1846 as a coadjutrix sister her parish priest asked why she had joined such a group of snobbish women, who would only treat her as a servant. She replied by describing her experience:

> Your letter shows me how little you know about the Society of the Sacred Heart. The Society is composed of choir, or dame, religious, and of coadjutrix sisters. The first named are involved in the education of the young, and the second look after the domestic needs of the house. The difference between us is entirely exterior. We are all sisters in the Sacred Heart of Jesus. We make just one heart and one mind in the adorable Heart of Jesus. The Society is a body whose members have special tasks but all seeking the same end. This is the glory of the Heart of Jesus, the spreading of this devotion and the salvation of souls.
>
> The Society is like a well composed choir, with voices singing in different parts yet forming one musical ensemble. We all have the same rule. Those among who know the Heart of Our Lord best, whoever lives in the most saintly way, she is the one who fulfils most effectively the purpose of her calling.[338]

At its best, this was the ideal the Society had tried to establish from the beginning, based on the spiritual equality between the choir and coadjutrix sisters. Undoubtedly, this ideal could not take root easily in daily community life, down the years, as the letters of Sophie Barat and the minutes of successive General Councils show. The way of life could be critiqued from within and without. Yet what the General Council of 1851 sought was a balance between the shared vocation of choir and coadjutrix sisters, and the need to have practical, down-to-earth norms for living, and these were different for each rank. Rules already existed specifically for the choir sisters in the 1815 Constitutions, and in 1851 rules were drawn up for the coadjutrix sisters, to develop what was lacking in the 1815 Constitutions.[339] While they drew on those Constitutions for inspiration, they dealt with issues of admission, dismissal and training which had arisen over many years and which had so exercised Sophie Barat in 1839. The rules contained nine articles, drawn from the proposed 1839 Decree which in turn was based on the rules concerning Jesuit coadjutrix brothers.[340]

The Council, by way of commentary on the rule of the coadjutrix sisters, made several practical recommendations which were intended for both choir and coadjutrix sisters:

> Our Coadjutrix Sisters are not to be considered as servants but as true sisters, and they will always be called this with affection when they are addressed by name.
>
> They will be directed always with great gentleness, and by this good example be led to Christian and religious graciousness. Their home background prepares them less for this than that of the Choir Sisters.
>
> Superiors will ensure that they are not overburdened, and that they have the necessary time to fulfil all their spiritual exercises.[341]

> If the Coadjutrix Sisters, on account of their infirmity or of their work in the garden, in the farmyard etc, need warm clothes in addition to their woollen garments, then superiors will ensure they get what is best for them.
>
> Superiors will be aware of the tasks which can lead to the Coadjutrix Sisters having wet feet; sabots, galoshes or strong shoes are needed for protection from damp.[342]

The 1851 General Council acknowledged that the formation and care of the coadjutrix sisters, especially in the noviceship, needed to be improved and that some women had left the Society because of this. The issue had been on the agenda for the General Council of 1839.[343] For example, requests for better formation of the coadjutrix sisters had been sent in by the Le Mans community but arrived too late in Rome for consideration.[344] The community raised basic issues around training in personal hygiene and table manners. But more specifically, they criticised how the recreation time of the coadjutrix sisters was often curtailed, that their evening prayer was too long and that they were often exhausted and ill from overwork. They also criticised that the coadjutrix sisters recited a litany in Latin for Morning Prayer and suggested that it would actually be understood if it was said in French.[345] In Amiens another case was drawn to Sophie's attention by an old Jesuit friend. In 1849, Louis Sellier told Sophie he was concerned about the community at Amiens which appeared to be in disarray.[346] He had encouraged a young woman to enter the Society there as a coadjutrix sister. She was assigned to work in Neuville, a community attached to Amiens, and she had far too much work to do there. However, that in itself was not the source of her complaints. She was disappointed at the lack of commitment in the community to prayer and genuine work. She wanted to stay in the Society but needed a dedicated community for support and inspiration.[347]

At the General Council of 1864, the last held in the lifetime of Sophie Barat, it was noted once more that the coadjutrix sisters were not receiving proper spiritual formation for their religious life. Some had arrived at the stage of final profession without having the text and commentaries on the Constitutions and Rules of the Society explained.[348] The Council received complaints that in some houses of the Society times of prayer appointed for the coadjutrix sisters were not respected. Rather they were given other tasks on the dubious pretext that they prayed better when active.[349] Again it was suggested that the coadjutrix sisters have a general noviceship, where their formation for religious life and training in skills could be attended to properly. The Council considered this unviable, given the Society's expansion, but the local superiors who accepted women as coadjutrix sisters were required to provide them with a solid spiritual and practical formation.[350] They were to ensure that the coadjutrix sisters had two sessions a week, either on the Constitutions or on the catechism. Superiors were recommended to have individual, personal meetings with each of the coadjutrix sisters regularly, even though the assistant superior did so as part of her duties. Both the superior and her assistant were to care for the coadjutrix sisters, be concerned about their personal lives and their work in the community and school,[351] and ensure they were not overworked.[352] In a case in point in 1855, Sophie Barat asked if a coadjutrix sister could be nursed in Lyon:

Here in the rue de Varenne we have a wonderful Coadjutrix Sister who has lost her health by far too much heavy work. Her devotedness and love of work and her fine character led her to undertake work which nobody else would do, and now she suffers from severe pain in her hip. We think that your physiotherapist (rhabilleur) could cure her and that even your doctors would look after her better than ours. We ought at the very least try everything since she has sacrificed herself for us.[353]

Sophie Barat knew that the work of the coadjutrix sisters was onerous and demanding. She admired the skills they needed to fulfil their tasks,[354]:

With regard to the woman who is 30 years of age and a dressmaker, I am not sure if it would be to our benefit to accept her. We really need women for the heavy work and for tasks which need strength and intelligence. We need dressmakers the least; the employments which are not working are the linen rooms (vestiaires), the kitchens, the infirmaries and the care of household goods and foods (dépensières). At present several houses in the Society are suffering from these employments being badly run. All the same, if your dressmaker of 28–30 years of age, has good health, is intelligent, skilled, then you may receive her on trial. She will then take her place [in the Society] and be able to help us.

Since we are discussing the Coadjutrix Sisters, keep your eyes open for a good cowherd (vachère/cowgirl), who is suitable, a good worker, who loves beasts and cares for them well. She will be destined for the Mother House (rue de Varenne).[355]

Sophie Barat also knew that the two rank structure was out of tune with many currents of the day:

Accept all the women who offer to enter the Society as Coadjutrix Sisters and who have the qualities we require. Most of the secondary orders (ordres secondaires), founded to respond to all needs in society, attract this class (the poor). All become Choir Sisters (Dames) since they have only one rank, and now we cannot recruit them.[356]

Sophie was aware that society in France was changing, but at no stage during her mandate as superior general did she consider changing the two-rank system in the Society. She held to the monastic village model created in the early years of the Society, held firm when it was challenged in Louisiana in the 1820s, and maintained this position until her death. For her the ideal begun in 1800 of a shared vocation, lived out in a two-fold form of community living, remained valid, and it enabled the

Society to fulfil its chosen specific tasks. The fruits of that form of life were all around her and confirmed her conviction. The Society of the Sacred Heart had developed and expanded beyond all her expectations.

Choir and Coadjutrix Sisters: 1800–1865

When Sophie Barat died in 1865 the Society numbered 3,539 members: 1,958 were choir sisters and 1,581 were coadjutrix sisters. In 1870 Sophie Barat's successor, Josephine Goetz, asked each member of the Society to write down or dictate their memories of Sophie Barat. This would provide material for a biography, and could be used if Sophie became a candidate for canonisation.[357] Bearing in mind the focus of this request to the Society was Sophie Barat, the testimonies are revealing of the writers themselves, of their values, their sense of self and the purpose of their lives, the response to their vocation.[358] They saw in Sophie someone who reflected back their own aspirations, someone whose life was a confirmation of what they had chosen themselves, and who had left them with an ongoing sense of purpose. Their reflections show the two spheres of the Society, the public and the private, the outer and the inner, the two countenances of the Society, the choir and the coadjutrix sisters.

The memories of the coadjutrix sisters are lively and candid. Each either wrote her own memories or she dictated and signed them. The coadjutrix sisters recounted a series of stories and anecdotes concerning Sophie Barat, recalling what they had noticed over the years, their conversations with her or what other people said about her, but most of all her effect on them personally. Some remembered how Sophie had helped them discern their vocation, often while visiting houses of the Society. One recalled in detail how she had been fostered in a family employed by the Society, and how Sophie Barat had given her the help she needed over several years to overcome personal problems.[359] Others recalled that on her visits to different communities Sophie Barat had remembered their personal journey and knew how to encourage them further and this over many years.[360] If they could not understand French she got lessons for them, as she had done for a German postulant in the rue de Varenne.[361] Some had met her only once and were affected by her insight into their lives, especially when Sophie was an older woman.[362] Others had known her for decades and wrote extensive memoirs of these years. Many commented of the number of coadjutrix sisters who had been companions of Sophie Barat over the many years of her mandate as superior general.[363]

Several coadjutrix sisters remembered how their families used to send small gifts to Sophie, and how quickly she responded with a little token of gratitude.[364] They appreciated her respect for them and the courteous manner in which she treated them in everyday life,[365] and that she was concerned for their health.[366] During the 1839 crisis the coadjutrix sisters, especially in Paris, noted the tensions between Sophie Barat and some of the choir sisters. They commented on Sophie's social origins with a certain pride.[367] Some remarked that she treated the coadjutrix sisters more justly than Eugénie de Gramont did in the rue de Varenne. One coadjutrix sister, Virginie Roux, lived in the community at the rue de Varenne in Paris for fifty-five years and her memories of both the choir and coadjutrix sisters over these generations are lively. They give both the light and the dark side of community living, a rare contemporary glimpse into life in the Society, especially in the period 1836–50.[368]

The coadjutrix sisters identified with Sophie Barat's concern for the poor. They liked how she shared goods in community,[369] and valued her personal gifts to them of medals and rosaries, books and holy pictures.[370] In 1864 Sophie Barat sent a holy picture to a coadjutrix sister, Françoise Bruchet in Orleans:

> Can I interrupt you a moment and ask you to give this little picture to Sister Bruchet, if she is still with you? I have lost sight of her, since I have not reread the catalogue for a long time. She belongs to those in the Society of whom neither good nor bad is said, and these members are rare enough in our time. If she is still alive, help me to make up to her for my forgetfulness by offering this memento from her mother general. She has always been truly included in the prayers I offer to the Heart of Our Lord for all the members of our little Society.[371]

The coadjutrix sisters knew that Sophie Barat admired their form of life; she sometimes took part in their work or recreations, especially when she was older.[372] They knew that at different times in her life Sophie had expressed a wish to share that life, mostly by way of release from her responsibilities.[373] Many recorded her interest in their work on the farms, in the gardens and kitchens.[374] She watched them as they planted and harvested vegetables, fruits and nuts, gathering herbs, and took care of the cows and poultry.[375] The coadjutrix sisters knew that the hired farm workers and gardeners respected Sophie Barat because of her knowledge of the land and her just treatment.[376] She constantly picked wood for the fires while walking in the gardens.[377] Many coadjutrix sisters recorded Sophie Barat's fear of fire; she would ask that candles and lamps be kept under surveillance at all times, especially in the evening time.[378] Although she was the founder and superior general, the coadjutrix sisters knew that socially Sophie Barat was one of them, and that at times she was more at ease with them than with some of the choir sisters.[379] But they also admitted that they could be truly daunted by her stern manner.[380] They were proud that while she belonged to them, she had also moved beyond them and could be on the path to sainthood.[381]

The testimonies of the Choir Sisters

Josephine Goetz had suggested some guidelines when asking for the testimonies, but these the coadjutrix sisters largely ignored. They set down or dictated their memories spontaneously, just as they came. Consequently their reflections are lively, free and vivid, and they show the intimacies of their own lives in the Society and give many glimpses into the home life of the Society of the Sacred Heart. By contrast, the choir sisters tended to follow the guidelines suggested, such as the theological virtues practised by Sophie Barat: faith, hope and charity; her moral, religious qualities; her spiritual gifts and graces; her impact on the Society, how people in general regarded her and spoke of her, especially bishops.[382] As a result the memories set down by the choir sisters tend to be rather formal, even cautious in style. The choir sisters worked in the public domain of education and they presented the public Sophie Barat, the founder of the Society of the Sacred Heart, influential in the field of Catholic education in France after the Revolution. The choice of memories sent in by the choir sisters reflects the significance of their lives and the reasons they joined the Society.

Central to their memories of Sophie Barat was their appreciation of how she had trained them for their responsibilities as leaders of the communities and the schools. They admired how she oversaw the administration of the properties of the Society, as well as her grasp of financial and legal affairs. In other words, they paid tribute to her good governance. Many noted how Sophie supported them spiritually in their early years in the Society, and some had experienced this consistently over many years. She had confirmed their vocation and encouraged their gifts, had pointed out their mistakes and given them suggestions on how to learn from them. Some admitted that the reputation of Sophie Barat had reached them long before they met her. They wondered if they would be disappointed when they entered and in fact they were pleasantly surprised to find her quite approachable.[383] They appreciated that she could listen to their point of view and change decisions in the light of what they said.[384] Her commitment to the work of education impressed them, to high standards and good teaching, as well as her care for individual children who found school life difficult for one reason or another.[385] They knew Sophie Barat valued both ranks in the Society and some deplored the snobbish efforts of some parents of the students to ennoble Sophie with de Barat as a title.[386]

Some choir sisters understandably felt constrained in their remarks by the fact that many of Sophie Barat's contemporaries were still alive in 1870 and were key figures in the Society. They had lived through the times of crises in the Society, especially the period 1839–51, and for their own reasons had opposed Sophie Barat. When commenting on these times, choir sisters tended to make general and guarded comments which could offend none. For example, Marie Prevost, one of the earliest companions of Sophie Barat, wrote a long, affectionate appreciation of Sophie Barat, but in such general terms that nothing emerged of the several crises they had both experienced over the years from their time together in Amiens in 1804.[387] Others, instead of writing their personal memories, cited the testimonies of people outside the Society: past pupils, parents (especially the nobility), families and the clergy.[388] In all, the choir sisters affirmed the way of life Sophie Barat and her companions founded and which they also had chosen. They felt proud of what they had undertaken and would continue to do so in the future. The prospect of Sophie Barat being canonised could only affirm them, and to have her declared saint would honour all.

The testimonies of both coadjutrix and choir sisters tell the story of many women who had found contentment in their vocation and were sure of their place in the Society of the Sacred Heart. Of course, there were many who did not write their memories, either from choice, forgetfulness or illness, or because they could only write negative memories about Sophie or the Society. Some may have been unhappy with the choice they had made in life; others may have felt trapped but could not imagine leaving the Society. However, those members of the Society who left their memories of Sophie Barat on record gave evidence of their engagement with life in the Society and of their personal contentment. The future of the Society seemed secure and they expected that it would continue to expand and prosper.

Friendship in the Society of the Sacred Heart

Over the years and generations friendships grew between choir sisters, stemming from their experiences of sharing work in the schools and in the communities, and many of these endured their lifetimes. Similarly, friendships grew between the coadjutrix sisters as they worked alongside one another over many years. Commenting on friendships in community, Sophie Barat remarked:

> I wish I could reply to the kind letters I received from the members of your Council. They gave me real pleasure. At least tell them how much the union that exists among them and with you touches and comforts me.
>
> However, since we are religious this mutual love, this divine love, has to be free of childishness and of the kind of pettiness we can leave to friendships in the world. In the Society we all need to be sincere with each other, yet noble and religious, not at all infantile or affected. All marks of affection have to be in keeping with and according to the Rules of Modesty which are wise. By holding to them the love that binds you all can only become more lasting and comforting, because the Lord is its binding force and purpose.[389]

Sophie welcomed these friendships as they could only further the happiness and effectiveness of the community, and she only intervened either if they impacted on leadership in a community or school or if they tended to exclude others or create dependencies and cliques. Sophie Barat confronted this particularly in the schools, and especially if pupils were being affected, by changing roles or by moving personnel elsewhere. Friendships also existed between the choir and the coadjutrix sisters. Some of these also grew out of shared work and community experiences, and some out of familiar class patterns of relating comfortably as maid and mistress. Though equal in terms of their vocation to the Society, their social realities did not disappear on entry. However, the nature of the tasks fulfilled by the coadjutrix sisters, providing the inner home life for everyone, meant that they knew the individual needs of each one. This often meant special care in illness and ongoing care afterwards, often for years.[390] In some instances it was a matter of course, that if a choir sister moved, sometimes the coadjutrix sister caring for her would move with her.[391] Of course, dependencies developed in some such instances and Sophie Barat confronted them, especially if she sensed a community or a school, or the wider Society, were being affected. Usually some form of separation had to be insisted on, unless those concerned accepted there was a problem and were ready to address it themselves.[392]

Sophie Barat herself relied on the skill of the coadjutrix sisters to enable her fulfil her task as superior general. She often needed prolonged physical care, especially after 1830 when her health began to deteriorate into a chronic condition. Prior to 1830 she tended to travel either alone (which was cause for comment in France) or with a member of the Society or with a friend. But in 1830, after the July Revolution in Paris, she moved to Montet in Switzerland, accompanied by a coadjutrix sister, Marie Patte.[393] From then on she and Marie Patte travelled together within France and beyond, and had several long trips to Rome, by land and by sea. Sophie called her 'my inseparable companion',[394] and she valued Marie's shrewd choice of inns and her quick assessment of carriages, routes and drivers. They shared a love of reading and knitting, and observers over many years noted the ease that existed between them, their mutual respect and companionship. For many years Marie Patte held a powerful position in the Society, which could be resented if access to Sophie Barat was denied, either on account of illness or as a mode of protection during periods of crisis or overwork.[395] When Marie Patte died in 1848 Sophie expressed her sorrow and deep sense of loss:

> I have just lost Sister Marie. She went to a better world on the 26 [July]. This is an immense loss for me. Certainly her love and care for me can never be replaced.[396]

And a few days later:

> I got back here [from Bourges] somewhat tired from my travels, to find myself without my Sister Marie's loving care and consideration.[397]

Inevitably personal relationships failed, either in the communities or in the schools. In these cases, Sophie Barat and the leaders in the Society had to try to prevent destructive situations taking root. A successful choir or coadjutrix sister could be resented in a community and prevented from exercising her gifts.[398] Sometimes a resolution was found by changing the tasks each of the parties had in the house, in the hope that this could modify the problem.[399] But if this did not work, then one or more had to move to other houses. Such actions had to be carefully thought out as changes could impact negatively either on the communities or schools, and indeed draw criticism from families, or from the parents of pupils if those who left had been teachers or heads of school. Sometimes the clergy also got involved and they worsened the situation even more by taking sides and lobbying Sophie Barat. Individual problems arose also within the communities between choir and coadjutrix sisters. These were often easily resolved by minor internal changes or a change of house in the course of the year. Sophie Barat noted that in general the relationships between choir sisters of noble birth and the coadjutrix sisters tended to be the most harmonious, as this reflected the class polarity in French society.

Conclusion

The Society of the Sacred Heart had its critics, not least the two-rank system in community. The artist and writer Pauline Perdrau took the image of the bee hive as a way to describe community life in the Society, the life of the choir and coadjutrix sisters. She suggested that the hidden work of queen bees in the hive mirrored the hidden work done by community leaders and by the coadjutrix sisters.[400] The worker bees, which left the hive each day in search of honey, mirrored the life of the teaching choir sisters. Just as the ongoing, interior work within the hive was essential for the making of honey, so life in the Society demanded mutual support, rhythm and substance, otherwise the entire project would fail. Perdrau argued that critics of the Society did not understand this and so judged the Society merely as:

> A group of ladies [Choir Sisters], reasonably cultured, aristocratic, whose servants were called Coadjutrix Sisters.
>
> No, no. We are not great ladies. We have our times for domestic work as well. Our superiors ensure that we are protected from the danger of exciting, ostentatious work [in the schools] by manual work, housework, sewing and sweeping. The religious, perhaps returning to community after spending time with visiting parents in the parlour, goes straight to wash dishes or peel vegetables afterwards.[401]

Pauline Perdrau took the image of bees as a way of describing life in the Society of the Sacred Heart. In 1846 Marie Lataste took the example of the orchestra:

> The Society is composed of choir, or dame, religious, and of coadjutrix sisters. The first named are involved in the education of the young, and the second look after the domestic needs of the house. The difference between us is entirely exterior. We are all sisters in the Sacred Heart of Jesus. We make just one heart and one mind in the adorable Heart of Jesus. The Society is a body whose members have special tasks but all seeking the same end. This is the glory of the Heart of Jesus, the spreading of this devotion and the salvation of souls. The Society is like a well composed choir, with voices singing in different parts yet forming one musical ensemble. We all have the same rule. Whoever among us knows the Heart of Our Lord best, whoever lives in the most saintly way, she is the one who fulfils most effectively the purpose of her calling.[402]

Yet, in the end only those who actually lived the life knew the full story, and their lives form the collective biography of the Society in the nineteenth century. Coming from all walks of life and backgrounds, they had found life together, centred on the spirituality of the Heart of Christ. This bond was strong and deep enough to inspire them personally and bond them together in Christ. They belonged to their time and were marked by the spirit of the Enlightenment and Revolution. By the quality of their lives and their choices they set in motion processes for change and transformation, and each one, choir and coadjutrix, probably never recognised the power they exercised and the influence they had in the communities and in the schools.[403] Certainly official power was exercised by those named to the various offices. But if heads of schools and superiors of communities, cooks and bursars, farmers and infirmarians, teachers and dressmakers were not in harmony and focused on the same ideals, then the entire household of community and school suffered and at times failed.

From the beginning each one's commitment in the Society was to Christ and to the ideals of the community, and this spiritual energy led them to work for the transformation of society through the education of young women. For their part the choir sisters opened up two avenues into the future, one which made space for the professional woman teacher of the future and another which prepared the path ultimately for the leadership of women in society. The lives of the coadjutrix sisters also served both these ideals. However, in addition by honouring the value of their vocation, the coadjutrix sisters ennobled domestic service which in the Society, at its best, was recognised as equal in value to that of teaching, and respected in the communities and schools. Sophie Barat's 14,000 letters bear witness to these shared ideals, to the relationships they created, as well as the vastness of the task they had undertaken, its difficulty and complexity and the inevitable failures. Her letters show individuals and communities in construction, always in movement, in tension and resolution, as relationships shifted and new challenges arose.[404] Nevertheless, from a modest project of a few women begun in 1800, a new community had evolved. It drew women from all levels of society, rich and poor, and together they educated young women in their boarding and poor schools, initially in France and then internationally. By any standards, then or now, this was a remarkable achievement.

CHAPTER 2

The Society of the Sacred Heart:
An educational model

People speak in several ways about them: some make fun of them especially on account of their description as *learned women* and because of the predictions they claim, as if they were announcing a new world and the good that they were called to do in the world. Others, though this was the smallest number, thanked God and praised his mercy when they saw a means which they considered adapted to the needs of the time, destined in the long term to prepare for the renewal of society, which they longed for with all their hearts. [1802][1]

Introduction

The first members of the Society of the Sacred Heart shared a desire to rebuild French society and especially the church after the impact of the Revolution. They gathered from 1800, initially in small groups, and set up small boarding schools and poor schools. In a relatively short time the Society developed its distinctive model of educating the nobility/upper bourgeoisie, and the poor class, and this expanded rapidly within France, Europe and the Americas. Normally the boarding schools and poor schools were located on the same property but housed in separate buildings. The model of combining the two schools in every foundation ensured a certain economic stability, since the boarding school pensions, along with the legacies of the choir sisters, sustained both the schools and the community. This model of education was adapted from the ancien régime.[2] Even after the upheavals of the Revolution, and the attempt to destroy the aristocracy, social class structures in France and indeed in Europe had hardly changed. Nevertheless, Sophie Barat and her companions knew that the world of education after

1800 could never be a simple re-invention of the past, a turning back to pre-1789. They were creating something new. From the early years in Amiens the founding members of the Society experienced a sense of excitement and adventure around the schools, 'which they considered adapted to the needs of the time, destined in the long term to prepare for the renewal of society which they longed for with all their hearts'.[3]

The Society presented its programme of education for the first time when it published the prize-giving booklet in Amiens in 1805.[4] It was based on the Plan of Studies for the boarding school drawn up by the community between 1803 and 1805, with the help of Jean Nicolas Loriquet, prefect of studies in the boys' school in Amiens run by the Fathers of the Faith. Loriquet also helped in the drawing up of class notes and of basic texts for use in the school.[5] The Plan of Studies described the timetable, the number and order of classes, as well as the content and the method of teaching. It covered a four-year course with the possibility of one or two more years of further studies for older pupils. The course of studies included religion, writing, reading, French grammar and spelling, arithmetic, history, geography and literature. A further Plan of Studies was drawn up in 1806 with similar content, but the curriculum was expanded to include Latin, foreign languages, arts d'agrément (music, dancing, drawing) mythology, domestic economy and handwork. Another Plan of Studies was drawn up in 1810 which contained some small modifications to the text of 1806. Similarly, a Plan of Studies was drawn up for the poor school. This was more basic in content and included teaching the catechism, basic reading, writing and arithmetic, and training in manual skills. The aim of the poor schools was to provide pupils with knowledge of religion and the means to earn their living.[6]

In her study of the education of women in nineteenth century France, Rebecca Rogers notes some of the difficulties teachers faced when trying to implement their educational goals. Among them she signals parental strategies and requests, institutional developments and the initiatives and limitations of the teachers themselves.[7] These three aspects of the Society's educational task were indeed daunting challenges for Sophie Barat and her companions. They grappled with them in various combinations and in differing cultural contexts either in France, Europe or the Americas.[8] From the beginning the major challenge was to have properly trained teachers, ready to lead and to teach in the schools.[9] The Society expanded rapidly, especially after 1815, and as the foundations increased in France and beyond Sophie Barat urgently needed capable women for the schools. While she certainly expected individuals to have a spiritual motivation for entering the Society as choir sisters, Sophie also expected that they would have basic education, or at least the capacity to learn and take part in the work of education in the Society. During the period of training (the novitiate) each choir sister was assessed and as many as possible were prepared for teaching. The older members of the Society acted as mentors and guides to the new teachers. They supervised the giving of classes, the preparation of texts and material for teaching, as well as the manner in which the pupils were to be treated.[10]

The Society's work of education attracted women in the nineteenth century. The Society provided them with new choices in life, and on entering they found communities of likeminded women who were motivated by spiritual values and ready to offer each other support and security. In the Society there were many fulfilling roles they could play in the schools, as headmistresses, or as teachers in boarding and poor schools, as carers of the children, in areas of discipline, health and general supervision, especially outside of class times. Others could be required to be administrators of school properties and buildings, of negotiating with parents, local government and church authorities, as well as managing the farms, providing food for the children, and keeping school accounts.[11] The schools of the Society had a more public profile than communities of religious women prior to the Revolution. Before 1789 convent education was carried out within the confines of a monastic community. All religious communities were suppressed in 1792. When religious communities of women were restored by Napoleon it was clear that convent education of girls would become a more public affair, although always within the strict limits placed on women generally in society by Napoleon and indeed on religious women by the church.[12] However, even within these limits, this more public presence of women religious in education from the early nineteenth century in France signalled the beginning of the professional religious teacher of the future. Many in the Society of the Sacred Heart were ready for this, were highly educated women in their own right and equipped to be part of this educational venture. One of them was Marie d'Olivier.

Marie d'Olivier, 1778–1868[13]

Marie d'Olivier was born in Nîmes in 1778 and entered the community at Amiens in 1804.[14] She made her first vows on 4 October 1806 at the age of twenty-eight. She had been ill during her time in Amiens and after her vows she was sent to Poitiers, in April 1807, where she recovered quickly. She began teaching there and organised a prize-giving ceremony in the boarding school, modelled on what she had seen in Amiens. Poitiers, founded in 1806, had developed rapidly, and by the autumn of 1807 a poor school was opened alongside the boarding school. The following year the Society made a foundation nearby in Niort and Marie d'Olivier helped there in the development of a boarding school and poor school. The beginnings were difficult and it was a struggle to maintain both schools, though Sophie Barat was particularly anxious to retain the poor school:

> The children in the other [boarding] schools are not without resources; their wealth will allow them to have a good education. But for the orphans, it is total loss. Truly, the poor do not touch our lives enough.[15]

During these years in Amiens, Poitiers and Niort, Marie d'Olivier gained valuable teaching experience, and she began to develop her gifts as a writer. She was articulate and there is evidence that Emilie Giraud, the superior of the community in Niort, found Marie d'Olivier a difficult colleague. There is no indication regarding the issue between them, except that the school in general was experiencing discipline problems at the time.[16] However, some years later, when a new foundation began in Quimper in 1817 and Marie d'Olivier moved there, the same pattern emerged. The superior of the community, Madame de Gramont d'Aster, complained to Sophie Barat about Marie d'Olivier, but again no details exist of the particular problem.[17] Then in 1822 Marie d'Olivier went to La Ferrandière in Lyon, to teach in the rapidly growing school and to prepare for her final commitment in the Society of the Sacred Heart.[18] Sophie Barat visited the community in August for Marie d'Olivier's final profession and found her transformed.[19] Certainly from the time she went to Lyon Marie d'Olivier's gifts were recognised and she was given leadership roles in the community and school. The 1824 house journal of La Ferrandière noted that Marie d'Olivier was assistant mistress of novices, in charge of half of the first class, taught religion to the second division and was a community councillor.[20] In the light of these developments, the tensions Marie d'Olivier experienced in Niort and Quimper could have come from how she articulated her ideas and perhaps threatened the community with more change than they could manage. At the same time, there were often tensions between the choir sisters based on class and family origins, and this may well have obtained in Quimper where Madame de Gramont d'Aster was superior.[21]

While she was in La Ferrandière Marie d'Olivier began to draft her ideas on the development of education in the Society of the Sacred Heart. Clearly these ideas had been germinating in her for some time, and between 1823 and 1824 Marie d'Olivier presented her views in the form of three *Mémoires* (position papers) addressed to Sophie Barat. She had also begun to write some moral tales, or educational stories, intended for young women, and she planned to publish these in journal form. While assuming the priority of educating young women in the Christian faith, Marie d'Olivier wanted students to learn how to think and reflect and be capable of holding their own in conversation, either at home or in public. She envisaged the Society educating in a much wider context than simply that of the rich and the poor classes. Her vision was to have three boarding schools. One for the nobility and upper bourgeoisie (premier pensionnat); another for the middle classes (deuxième pensionnat); a third one for the lower classes who would not be asked to pay fees but who would learn manual skills and use them to pay their fees. Furthermore, and if the Society had the resources, she wished to open day schools (non-fee paying), nursery schools, training schools for teachers, and Sunday schools. Later, she would add a library and an infirmary to this overall plan. Finally, to provide further assistance for young women when they left school, she proposed publishing a journal regularly. This would be called *Annals* and would contain material to help young women in the course of their lives; it would also contain a section for readers to ask for advice by correspondence. Marie d'Olivier intended this publication not only for past students of the Society but also for women in general.[22]

There is no evidence of Sophie Barat's response to the three *Mémoires* addressed to her, or indeed that she ever actually received them.[23] However, in 1826 Marie d'Olivier moved to the community in Paris, to the rue de Varenne (Hôtel Biron), the year the Society requested papal approval of its Constitutions and formal authorisation of the Society from the French government, both of which it received in 1827. A General Council of the Society was held that year in Paris to deal with both measures and with the ordinary business of the Society. Members were invited to table their queries for discussion during the Council, and Marie d'Olivier asked whether the Society would consider undertaking the education of the middle classes. Delegates at the council discussed this possibility:

> The Council does not reject this project, but decides that, for the time being, this undertaking is impossible.[24]

However, an exception was made for Marie d'Olivier and the Council discussed the possibility of her leading an educational pilot scheme in Beauvais. To this purpose Marie d'Olivier was appointed superior of Beauvais in 1828 and given the scope to test out her educational plans there. At the time of its foundation in Beauvais in 1816,[25] the Society made an agreement with the local authorities to provide free education for the poor, in return for its right to run a boarding school and to retain the property in perpetuity. In practice this agreement proved to be fraught with difficulties and these were particularly acute when Marie d'Olivier went to Beauvais in 1828. After two years of disputes, a form of mutual agreement between the Society and the town authorities was reached in 1830 which allowed Marie d'Olivier to proceed with her plans for the future. Aware of the difficult conditions in Beauvais, Sophie Barat continued to support Marie d'Olivier even though finance and personnel were limited in the Society.[26]

While developing her plans in Beauvais, Marie d'Olivier was convinced that the quality of education in the Society needed to be more rigorous. She saw her writing as a chance to discuss this within the Society and hopefully in the public domain.[27] She asked Sophie Barat to allow her to publish her work and in response Sophie asked her to send her work to Nicholas Loriquet for his comment and advice. She also explained that publishing her work just then would be imprudent. The Jesuit schools in France were on the point of being suppressed by the government, and since the Society of the Sacred Heart was associated with the Jesuits, any publication by the Society could draw unnecessary attention to it.[28] Besides, Sophie had questions concerning the quality of Marie d'Olivier's writings:

> We correct her work here, for her tales are rather like steel which has to be drawn from the earth and polished. She has no notion of the deep subtlety in the expression of thought today, as well as speech and the choice of epithets. She belongs to the age of Louis XIII which has to be modernised now. What a happy age that was; why has it gone from us?[29]

Nicolas Loriquet commented positively on the work of Marie d'Olivier and made detailed suggestions for making improvements in view of publication.[30] After several exchanges and revisions, Marie d'Olivier's first book, *Les Trois Paulines*, was published in 1834.[31]

As superior of the community and in overall charge of the schools at Beauvais, Marie d'Olivier presided over the rapid expansion of several educational activities on the property, all in separate buildings.[32] First there was a fee-paying boarding school for the aristocracy and upper bourgeoisie which initially was financially stable. A second boarding school existed for the middle class which required lower fees, but some students paid nothing at all. In addition, there were three other works, an orphanage, a nursery for children between two and four years old, and classes for 250 girls (held usually at weekends).[33] All three were free. However, over a period of several years adequate maintenance of the property was neglected. In time some of the school buildings began to fall into serious disrepair and the town authorities refused to pay their agreed contributions for maintenance. The situation came to a head when the roof of the second boarding school collapsed in 1839.[34]

This event exposed the serious financial situation existing in the two boarding schools. For a time before the collapse of the roof of the second boarding school, numbers in the boarding school for the aristocracy had begun to shrink, for two reasons. Some aristocratic families had decided to send their daughters to the second boarding school, attracted by the lower fees. But other aristocratic families took their daughters away completely, precisely because the class distinctions were not being strictly observed. With her educational project collapsing around her, Marie d'Olivier appealed first to Sophie Barat for money, then to the bishop of Beauvais, and finally to the pope. She argued that she had to retain both boarding schools, claiming that both were the source of income for the other works on the property.[35] Neither the Society nor the bishop of Beauvais, nor indeed the pope, were in a position to finance the repairs and Sophie Barat decided that the only solution was to revert to the original model in the Society of a single boarding school for the aristocracy.[36] In this way the orphanage, the nursery and the free classes could be retained.[37]

Bitterly disappointed, Marie d'Olivier found Sophie Barat's decision impossible to accept and she asked that it be rescinded. She compared her position and mission to that of Philippine Duchesne.[38] In 1841, to resolve the impasse, Sophie Barat asked Marie d'Olivier to leave Beauvais and move to Lyon, to the school she had taught in at La Ferrandière.[39] But by then Marie d'Olivier had other plans in train. Perhaps anticipating that she might have to leave Beauvais, she wrote to the bishop of Nîmes, Jean-Francois-Marie Cart, about a possible foundation in his diocese.[40] Two years later, in 1841, she contacted the bishop of St Flour in the Cantal, Frédéric de Marguerie, who showed interest in a possible foundation in his diocese at Lavorr where the project was supported by the Comtesse de Bassignac.[41] When this appeared to be viable, Sophie Barat made it clear to Marie d'Olivier that she could only be part of the

project for a time, in order to train others for it. It could not be designated a work of the Society of the Sacred Heart.[42] A prospectus for the
new school was drawn up, identical to the previous educational plans of
Marie d'Olivier. She also hoped to found a new religious congregation
devoted to her plans.[43] Some months later the Comtesse de Bassignac
withdrew her support for the project in Lavorr, and Marie d'Olivier
moved to Saignes in the same diocese, in the hope of establishing herself
there.[44] This project also failed. At that point Sophie Barat asked Marie
d'Olivier to make a decision, either to return to the Society or to leave.[45]
Clergy and friends warned Marie d'Olivier that leaving the Society could
compromise any future initiatives she might wish to undertake.
However, she had made up her mind and she severed her connections
with the Society of the Sacred Heart. A protracted, and at times acrimo-
nious, financial negotiation followed.[46]

Her loss to the Society of the Sacred Heart was immense. Marie
d'Olivier brought not just original educational ideas but also a lively
analysis of the content of the education offered in the schools of the
Society of the Sacred Heart. The Society was much the poorer without
that critique and insight, at a time when there was an opportunity to
make a radical contribution to education.[47] Marie d'Olivier lost a great
deal too. She cut ties with the many friends and companions she had
known since 1804. They had supported each other in the task of education, and she had carved out her place in the community. She had been
a central figure in the Society, a community leader, an innovator in the
field of education, and she was a delegate at the crucial General Council
of the Society held in Rome in 1839. But by 1842 her life had changed
profoundly and she left the Society to return to her family in Nîmes. All
her life Marie d'Olivier continued to consider herself a member of the
Society of the Sacred Heart, and from time to time wrote to Sophie
Barat asking for some financial support to publish her journals and
books.[48] She was also a regular contributor to the publication *Mémorial
Catholique*, and on her death in 1868 she was described in that journal as
a religious of the Sacred Heart.[49]

Manuscripts of Marie d'Olivier[50]

Mémoire on Education, presented to Mother Barat, January 1823[51]

I believe that I am bound in conscience to convey to my superior, my
mother and teacher, the views I hold for the glory of God and the good
of the Society of the Sacred Heart. For a long time now I have had the
desire and indeed the need to do this, but have held back. I ask myself,

what she would think of me, the lowliest in the Society, daring to give advice to her? Would she not think that I was a presumptuous person, with an over-active imagination? Would she not wonder how I could dare to meddle in things that are not my business, offering advice on issues that are so serious, so important and so delicate?

However, I recognise that fears of such censure are prompted by vanity, which is afraid of having its feelings hurt, and I have no grounds for letting such considerations stop me. In the final analysis, if it happened that I was curtly rebuffed would it be such a great disaster? That is all I have to fear, and even in this case I would have followed the promptings of my conscience, I would have acquitted myself before God, and therefore I should not have any regrets.

In one way, it is not beyond the bounds of reason to suppose that some of my views might be adopted. The people I address are totally dedicated to the glory of God and to perfecting their service to Him. If my ideas are just and true, they will welcome them. They are disposed to receive the truth wherever it may be presented to them, and to consider ideas in themselves, regardless of the little authority of the person who puts them forward. It is like a wise king who seeks the wellbeing of his subjects and will not disdain to listen to the observations of the lowliest of them, if such opinions contribute to his over-riding objective and desire: the good of his people.

From my own observations of the world and my reflections on the state of society, I am struck by one thing: the profound ignorance which exists with regards to matters of religion which, after all, is the most important knowledge for mankind. This ignorance is greater now than in any time in past centuries, and it is easy to see the reasons for it. I will attempt to discuss a few of these reasons in the following discourse. This increase in ignorance must necessarily result in a greater disintegration of moral standards. Who could fail to notice this fatal result, no matter how short a time they have lived in this world and considered the major events taking place there?

It is natural for a well-bred and upright person to deplore a fall-off in moral standards, but those who are inspired by their faith and their love of God feel particularly distressed by this. They feel an earnest and constant need to work to remedy these ills, [but say:] I can't do it; I have no ability to do this: such is the language of indifference or of ignorance. Every Christian has the means and must indeed work to repair the harm being done to our religion, since it is chiefly by prayer that one can remedy it. Every other means is powerless without that. Prayer is the most essential, the most necessary and the most infallible means. Happy are those to whom God has given the gift of prayer, and who use this gift faithfully. They alone with good reason can believe that they are serving God and religion. Nevertheless, it is part of God's will and the ways of Providence that we might also serve our religion by external acts and by worldly means. To view these acts in isolation from God, to see them as an end in themselves, is ignoble and lacking in enlightenment; but to dismiss them totally is dangerous recklessness, which is due to a lack also of enlightenment, except in very special cases.

We tend to put too high a value on external acts. The greatest and most admirable achievements, as judged by men, are but the natural and often necessary result of the unseen presence of God's love which has made man in his true perfection. But worldly man admires the results and gives no thought to the far more excellent cause which brought them about. Moreover, it happens only too often that certain acts, good in themselves, can be carried out for the wrong, or even for bad, reasons, or indeed for a combination of these reasons, and how can these be judged in the context of our faith? Such acts may be seen as brilliant by men who are unjust and who have a poor appreciation of real goodness. These acts may seduce both us and others. They shine, it is true, but with a fraudulent gleam, and to the eyes of absolute truth, they are worth nothing, or very little.

Happy are those who love God and who pray, because they alone are taking action, even if it appears to the world around that they are doing nothing. Nevertheless, as I have observed, neither is it not acceptable to simply turn away from doing those outward acts that Providence puts in our way; it is a weakness either to regret that one is not given a chance to carry out these acts, or to value them too highly when they have been executed. The perfect Christian should be ready to undertake these acts in a spirit of zeal, fidelity and perseverance, but without commotion and without undue haste, and to postpone or abandon them without vexation or regret. These acts may gain the admiration of the world, but this is a vain and contemptible reward, unworthy of real virtue; it makes them more to be feared than desired by the perfect Christian.

However, as a true Christian is not motivated by such superficial and base motives, he should not refrain from carrying out any external acts because he feels contempt for the vainglory which may be associated with them. The enlightened Christian knows that it is only when he is praying to God that he is serving Him. When he is performing external acts, he knows that they are of secondary importance, less perfect, incomparably less beautiful than prayer, but he tries to attach to them a feeling and a purity of motive which alone makes them good works. The unseen fire which is in his soul, and which was put there by God, should inspire all his actions, whether the results are visible to the eyes of others or not. I have felt the need to develop these preliminary reflections, because I am going to propose some things which in the public view could be considered very important, and which might stir up feelings of earthly glory. However, since the person to whom I address myself fears more than admires such glory, I felt it was not futile to put my views to her.

In human terms it is a great task to promote an informed understanding of religion in a far-reaching way, and in so doing contributing effectively to the improvement of moral standards, to the peace of families, and, following on from this, to the happiness of society. But what makes a Christian heart beat with joy is to serve God and to please Him. To please the Heart of Jesus, that loving and generous heart, that is what enflames and animates the soul of his faithful spouses; that is what makes them rise above themselves and enables them to deal with worldly esteem or contempt, with equal indifference.

> Oh adorable Heart of Jesus, fount of goodness and love, source of all generous and pure feelings, all-loving heart, to whom I have dedicated myself. It is to obey You and to please You that, in spite of my weakness and my lowliness, I am going to seek for the most natural ways to increase Your kingdom. With regard to the spiritual ways, that is to say, the truest ways, You yourself have inspired them in the heart of the privileged ones whom You alone know. May I, as a reward for my labours, hope that one day You might teach me the words of love which the human mind does not know how to teach, and which will put me in the ranks of those who truly serve You.

I have said that the century in which we live is more ignorant in matters of religion than the centuries which precede it. The principal causes of this unhappy occurrence are (1) the growth of intemperance and dissipation, which has taken up part of the time destined for education, (2) the great importance that is given in education to both the accomplishment arts (les arts d'agréments) and mathematics, (3) the shallowness of studies and (4) above all, the destruction of all religious institutions and the shortage of priests, the number of whom has decreased in a frightening manner in the space of thirty years. One must also add to this list the large number of frivolous or bad books which have replaced the good, or at least the better, ones; and especially the large number of elementary classes taught by people without learning or principles, pretending to teach what they themselves don't know – morality and religion.

Just to say in passing: education nowadays consists of the science of mathematics and of the accomplishment arts. This is the exquisite fare that we unwittingly lavish on young people, male and female respectively. This is what takes up those precious years that are assigned to education. Yet I ask every rational authority who has reflected on the needs and interests of human beings: what is a person, knowledgeable only in mathematics or in accomplishments, other than truly ignorant? This ignorance is all the more deplorable because unthinking people take it for real education, and we deceive ourselves and others by this false appearance. In education today, everything has to do with the things of this world, there is nothing about heaven. Must the immortal being accept that study which deals only with earthly matters is real education? We are fooling ourselves surely in limiting the education of males to the science of mathematics, and that of females to the accomplishments? The former is deprived of spiritual development, and the latter has a childlike mind which has never had the time to think or to educate itself.

We can see that all these causes are particular to our century. The evil is greater than it was in times past; therefore to counteract this we must employ more widespread and powerful means than used before. The principal means in our hands is the education of young people. Our aim must be first of all to multiply as much as possible the number of those we teach. Secondly, to perfect their education so as to make them more capable, not only of resisting the dangers of the world, but also of exerting a beneficial influence on society.

First of all, we must recognise that we live in circumstances that are very favourable to the growth of a religious order. All the old institutions have been destroyed in Europe. The needs of people demand that they be brought back; all governments feel the same need. Thus, in spite of the active opposition of the godless classes, these institutions will be rebuilt, and those which most correspond with the needs of the century and with the interests of people will have a more rapid and widespread growth than they could have had a century or two ago. The promotion of the glory of God and, of secondary importance, the glory of society demands that we must carefully research what are the most proper ways available to us to broaden and perfect the education of those entrusted to us.

Considering the actual state of society in Europe, one recognises that women exert a more active influence than ever before. Why? Because their relationships with men are more extensive and more frequent than ever before. Men of all classes, including those who rule the world, heads of state, writers of all sorts, military chiefs, all spend a part of their lives in the salons of women. It is at these meetings that the most serious subjects are discussed. Women are required to discuss them and often it is their point of view which prevails. It is not without apprehension that one sees such influence in the hands of a group of beings whose powers of reasoning are weaker, who are necessarily more ignorant but who are captivating because of their weakness. Enthusiastic by reason again of their weakness and endowed with the greatest willpower in the pursuit of trivial minutiae, their influence becomes dangerous. Let us not deceive ourselves: this willpower comes not from the strength but from the weakness of their intellect. They put a great value on things that do not matter, and that is why they pursue them with such ardour. We cannot destroy this influence but up to a certain point we can use it for the good by forming a very large number of rational, well taught, likeable and pious women. Indeed, there is no doubt that these women would have much greater influence since they would add to their natural qualities those of rationality and virtue, which have so much power over all hearts.

A question must be asked here: what is this perfect education which you propose for women? Is it not superfluous and dangerous to give them so much knowledge? Is it not sufficient that they know how to run their homes and practise their religion? What good would the rest do, but give them pride and ideas above their station, ideas which would make them incapable of carrying out their normal duties? Is this not the opinion of many wise people in the world, people who are accustomed to judging things according to the precepts of their religion?

I will begin by saying that my opinion is completely the opposite. I have adopted my views after much reflection, after having carefully studied both the world and my own heart, and the history of times past, insofar as I was capable of doing. And first of all, with regards to the authority on which such an opinion is based, let me say that I have noticed more than once that those who argue forcefully that a good education for women would be wasteful and dangerous tend to deviate from their supposed principles when it comes to the education of their own daughters. These are little more than idle arguments that are made to display their brilliance of mind and to have the pleasure of contradicting the opinion of others. Let us add to that several other equally specious motives. As regards persons of piety who share this opinion, perhaps they have never considered the drawbacks of ignorance when it comes to questions of morality. It appears to me that they have been influenced in their beliefs by a few unfortunate cases, and they have not taken on board that the lack of education for women in general causes great damage to their spiritual development. They leave it to others to deplore this evil. After all, to have too much education is the least dangerous of all the hazards that women will be exposed to, and it will always be the least common.

I am now going to present a few ideas for your consideration, mainly on the advantages of education for women, and secondly, on the particular need that they have of it in the times in which we are living.

Is not suitable education for women decreed as knowing religion more by practice than by an informed understanding, speaking little, talking about their households and their family, liking modesty and work? I agree that it is quite suitable, but should we imagine that it is so for many women, especially in the world in which we live? To think that it is suitable for them seems to me to be an illusion. Experience is the most persuasive of arguments. Let us consider what women were like thirty or forty years ago. Most of them were raised in convents and had pious habits instilled in them. They were brought up, no doubt, by respectable people, but by people who were in no position to give to others an education that they had not had themselves. Young women, therefore, left these sanctuaries extremely ignorant. They were quite defenceless going into a world which had been painted in dark colours for them. But this was totally false, because those who had told them about the world were like those who are colour blind. The first experiences of these poor creatures were no doubt disconcerting. They soon realised that their mode of expression, which was that of pious people, was out of place in the world, that their feelings and thoughts were not in harmony with those around them.

What should they do? One will say: let each live in the midst of the world as if one was not there, never allowing oneself to be seduced and carried along by the example and the opinions of another, constantly following the voice of one's conscience and reason. That is perfectly correct, but this is only possible for a person of very strong character. What happens, in reality, to almost all of them? Their feelings of piety soon weaken, and because their religion is not grounded in reason, they find themselves defenceless. They no longer have the appetite for religious practices, and the more empty their minds are, the more they give themselves up to the vain and dissipated life of the world in which they live. What do they talk about? What are the topics of conversation of women of the world who have been deprived of education? I would not dare discuss it. Conversations on changes in fashion and scandal mongering are the most innocent of what they go on with. We have heard these conversations and we have blushed. Yet, how many times have we heard resounding in our ears the following argument put forward by reputable men in the world: we would not ask for more than to talk to women in a rational and respectful way, but that is a language they do not understand. We speak to them in the language that they know and like. They force us to speak to them in this way.

Thus, by their vacuous conversations women damage themselves and those around them. Can we believe that women who place no value on, even disdain, education, will be seriously concerned with the cares and wellbeing of their household and their children? You certainly need not expect that from a woman who has given herself up to a life of dissipation. Such frivolous tastes distance them from the home; such frivolous tastes lead to ruinous expenses, such tastes cause them to devote all their time to the type of activity that is utterly trivial and vain. What I am saying is that they devote themselves to the minutiae of fashion which feeds and increases their flirtatiousness and dissipation. Having worked so hard to achieve little that lasts, they believe that they have achieved something remarkable, and they congratulate themselves as if they had actually done something praiseworthy. But I ask, in terms of their moral standards, is such activity not of less value than slumber?

I think I can sum up these reflections by saying that convent education was generally inadequate. Without a doubt it would be even worse today, because young women are entering a world where there is a lot less faith and a great deal more challenging of conventional wisdom than there was thirty years ago. However, I must admit that this education actually did produce some good mothers of families, but it would produce a lot less of them today, because of the times we live in. The extraordinary events of the Revolution, the various political movements, have excited the imagination and inflamed the spirits of the people. This is what we have noticed in the children born since then. Would it not be dangerous to leave such zeal unchannelled? Let me add that the spirit of this time is rational and daring. Faith is almost entirely banished from this world. How can young women entering this world preserve their virtue if they do not have values which are well thought out and solid; if they do not conduct themselves seriously and indeed if they don't have what is the absolute aim of a truly good education, if they do not have the ability to think? How are they going to acquit themselves, not only in the arguments which they hear in their social gatherings but also in their conversations with their brothers, their husbands, their cousins, and even their father? In other words, in the world in which they live and which they cannot and should not avoid?

It is therefore more necessary than ever that a woman, whether it be to defend herself against the dangers that society now presents or to do good to others, adds to her informed understanding of religion and her daily habits of piety, a solid education. This makes her conversation interesting and without danger for herself and others. She should have a cultivated mind. She must be able to talk on appropriate topics which are discussed in the world. She must not be a stranger to history and literature. Of all the modes of relaxation that women can pursue, reading good books is the one which is the least inconvenient and the most advantageous. The appetite for reading makes them happy to be at home; it enlightens their mind; it fortifies their soul; it makes them understand their duties; finally, it serves as nourishment for their imagination, keeping them from a thousand faults and often from a thousand vices.

Moreover, what we want for young people the majority of parents also want. They want it no doubt for reasons that are less pure than ours, but they want it a lot more intensely, they want it absolutely. They want their daughters to become pleasing people and they want them to learn how to converse in a pleasing way. This is the fashion and, so to speak, the need of the century. To speak and to write in an agreeable way, that is the ambition of both parents and young people themselves. But if we are influenced by a dangerous inflexibility in our attitudes and refuse to listen to their views, what will happen? Parents will not entrust their children to us, and the poor creatures will fall into the hands of other masters. They will teach human and worldly sciences without linking them to religion, which gives purity and a nobility to an otherwise empty study. It would be true to say that a dangerous but invisible instrument would be put into their hands, with which they could do nothing but injure themselves and others. Would it not be true to say that by our imprudent inflexibility, we would have become an accessory to such an unfortunate thing? I repeat, accomplishments and secular education are of prime importance to parents and there will be plenty of people who will give this to them, if we do not do it. And they will give them this education without any reference to the most essential study of religion. We cannot consider without alarm the evil that women thus educated can do. We cannot consider without fear the dangers they are exposed to by ignorance and idleness. Those who have seen it know it, but those who have not seen it can only guess at it.

We will regard the human sciences, therefore, as a means to acquire and conserve solid virtues. We will find in them nourishment for the imagination, which has become more necessary than ever. We will find a means to move them away from the futile arts which have become so common nowadays, from this passion for music which is not only a folly but a corrupting folly. Finally, the sciences will furnish us with the right which is so dear to us, the right to teach the only science essential to the soul. This science is being lost and those who truly love the heart of Jesus must seek to spread it with renewed effort, a science which they have the duty and the need to teach by every lawful means. So enlightened and thoughtful education is not only legitimate but very good in itself.

But it will be said: where will you get the resources you need for teaching? Do you not know that literature is corrupt, that almost all the sources of learning have been soiled? Do you not know that there is hardly any book that you can place without risk in the hands of young people? Do you not know that in the most admired works only too often one finds things which would damage morals and principles? You say that you want to give women some knowledge of history and of literature, but where will you find suitable history books? Do you find in the most recently written history books that necessary firmness of principle which will not lead young, inexperienced people astray? Where especially will you find suitable works of literature? Is there even one which you would dare put into the hands of a young person? Finally, is it not true that among all types of writers, you will notice that fatal weakening of principles which is afflicting our century and which produces a slackening of morals? Is it not true that the language of our literary people especially reveals a decrease in morals which is wrong for young people? Is it not true that those who announce that they are going to respect morality and modesty too often only prove one thing: that they themselves have no knowledge about morality and modesty?

We cannot deny these allegations. Unfortunately they are all too true. Nevertheless, we must not be discouraged. We must not hide the fact that there is a great amount of work to be done. The real needs of education and the state of our literature demand this. Inspired and helped by the Heart of Jesus we can achieve a great deal. This Statement on Education consists primarily in creating a certain number of texts which we lack now, texts which are not filled with false values. Secondly, we need to correct a great number of texts which have defective and false viewpoints, and replace them with useful and advantageous ones. But to whom would you confide such work? Alas, I do not know. Ministers and peers in these adverse times are almost all taken up with the necessary functions of government. We would have to undertake it ourselves, if Providence sent us a certain number of people who had not necessarily great talent but the ability to write, to judge – people of good taste, high moral principles and a knowledge of the world. However, all these qualities together are not easy to find in women, as we have often had occasion to remark. But let us repeat it: inspired and helped by the Heart of Jesus, we can achieve much.

With regard to the first of these texts, the most necessary and the most urgent would be a course of modern history for women, a course of literature also specifically for them, and finally, a course of natural history. It is not necessary to expand on the need for a course in modern history. A text is necessary to replace those written by authors whose intentions were not exactly genuine and who teach many erroneous facts. Nevertheless, these works which are widely read by women of the world, will also inevitably be read by our students once they are out of our hands. As part of this history course, one of the themes which we need to teach our students properly is a history of the popes. Not a cold, dry account, but written with feeling, written to inspire love and affection for the true leaders of the church. Women especially must be led by this feeling. Unfortunately, once out in the world they will hear unjust and imprudent attacks against the august pontiffs. It is therefore necessary that they should learn as early as possible to respect and to love the popes. There are many false allegations and treacherous fabrications, even in many highly praised books, and women must learn to recognise them for what they are. All they need is a short, abbreviated history, but, I repeat, one written to make them love the person who is a father for all Christians. The spouses of the Heart of Jesus have a concern to make him loved. They see in him a visible image of the One to whom they have devoted themselves. Finally, I believe that love and respect for the pope are a defence against all the errors in matters of faith that are so prevalent nowadays.

Let me confess I would have the greatest pleasure working on this task. I was born during the government of our benevolent King and from an early stage I learned to love him. This reverence would not only give me the courage but even the talent necessary to undertake such work. In second place, we have great need of a body of literature which contains pure norms and pure examples. No such work exists at the moment. It would be vain to tell young people to abstain from reading those kinds of novels which reflect the values of today's world; they would only obey us for as long as they were behind our walls. But beyond that, is it not the case that their parents, even the most Christian and enlightened, will put these works in their hands saying: these are the best, you cannot get any better. It is essential therefore that they be well taught and that they do not accept such works in an unquestioning way. Works of literature nourish and encourage the passions but what really incites them more is ignorance and empty-mindedness. This can be seen in the habits of the lower classes. However, the lower classes are safeguarded somewhat by the necessity to work which is a safeguard that others do not have.

It is necessary, therefore, to have a course of literature which would be suitable not only for young people, but would also meet the needs of women who live in the world, having regard to their needs and the position they hold in society. Is not such a course also necessary for our young teachers [in the Society]? Are they themselves going to choose those pieces of an author's work suitable for their charges? Are they capable of choosing them? Can they themselves recognise false values so as to be able to protect themselves and their pupils? Finally, will they not be affected also by reading material that contains examples that are injurious to their morals? We must be concerned about this, since they are our responsibility. We worry about everything which even in the smallest way could sully the hearts of those who are destined to be the brides of men, and yet we give no thought at all to those things which might affect the purity of the spouses of Jesus Christ. Ah! Without doubt, men owe us a debt of gratitude for the care we take to preserve the innocence of those whom they are going to marry.

But will not the Heart of Jesus bless us for the care that we take to remove from the gaze of the young virgins consecrated to Him anything that might in the smallest way hurt the purity of their hearts? At the same time, we must accept that they cannot live in happy ignorance of irreligious books, a luxury only given to those who do not look beyond their own selves. They will only be able to fulfil their vocation in a flawed way if they have not been educated themselves. It is vital that they receive instruction also as much and more than their pupils. At the present time, are we not putting several books in their hands which have many questionable morals? It is therefore urgent to work on suitable texts; the interests of the Heart of Jesus must urge us to undertake this most important work.

I have already mentioned that we need a course in Natural History. This book would not be difficult to write. It should have as its aim to lead the heart to God through contemplation of natural phenomena. At the same time it can provide an innocent pastime and stimulate a taste for simple habits and for country life. This book should be inspired by the work of Pluche,[52] with several differences however. It should not be as long, its information should be up to date since the natural sciences have made real progress since Pluche and it ought to be intended principally for women. Finally, it ought to include some excellent material found in several other works on the natural sciences to which women will not have access at all.

With regard to the second part of my plan, here are my thoughts. At one time there was a man whose conduct and principles were despicable, but who had wonderful literary talent and great genius. This man was called Photius.[53] He published a book called *The Library of Photius* where he analysed certain books and summarised others. He only retained the principal plot of these stories but he appraised them well. The abridged versions of the stories were so well done that the originals were overlooked. This is the model I would wish us to follow insofar as we can, but I would like to make a few modifications to this plan. This work would be titled 'Library of the Pupils of the Sacred Heart'. This would be really necessary because there are a certain number of books that we are unable to prevent women reading but nevertheless are dangerous in many respects, like the letters of Mme De Sévigné. In its present state, this book is a danger to moral standards. But some excisions and some commentaries would make this work useful in education. If we tell women not to read it, would they listen to us? We cannot think they would because it is too attractive to their longing, and that of their parents, of being able to read and write in an agreeable way. I will not list here the works which women should read, to replace those which are dangerous, popular and held in high regard. Have we not groaned when we have seen parents, even those who are enlightened and Christian, give certain popular books to their children, without even the slightest scruple? They are motivated by their tender love. They cannot resist the urge to give pleasure to their beloved children. It would be therefore desirable to have some interesting but light stories which would disguise their instruction and moral purpose in an amusing way and which would catch the imagination of young people.

This is the type of work which will be necessary to cleanse the sources of instruction. If it was carried out with flair, it would bring about a salutary reform in the morals of women. Without a doubt it would also increase considerably the respect and esteem which the Society enjoyed and which is necessary in order to achieve its aims. It is clear that it would contribute in no small way to the formation of good teachers for our schools, and since some of the teachers would come from the ranks of our pupils, it would ultimately contribute to the good of our Society. We need our teachers to learn History and Literature. We must not be afraid to recognise that they need to know how to converse in an agreeable way and have the gift of persuasion. In short, that their virtue must be clothed in agreeable forms and admired by important contemporaries. That is how the Society will expand. It will be invited to neighbouring countries where it is quite possible it will be successful. May it please God to give us the abundant fruits of salvation!

A thought stops me in my tracks: is there not a danger for those consecrated to God of being captivated by studying the human sciences? Will their souls not be imperilled? If we develop their talents, will it not develop their pride? Will their serious studies make them incapable of that union with God and with the inner life which should be the particular characteristic of the spouses of the Heart of Jesus? If such an effect should result from what I am proposing, I would have no difficulty in renouncing it. However lofty and however feasible might be the hopes which go with my proposals, I would believe that they would have been bought at too dear a price. However, I do not think that this would happen; indeed the opposite would be the case if we take a few precautions to preserve humility (which I am not going to develop here). For example, we must not allow just anyone to undertake these studies, because there is no doubt that, for some, studying would be damaging to their soul. I believe that studying will not damage our teachers, but rather they would find in it a means of advancing their inner life and their religious perfection. In effect, is religious life not a life of reflection? What hinders a life of spiritual perfection? Is it not our deplorable ability to greet those numerous vain thoughts which enter through the doors of our senses? A soul that is used to reflection, to comparing ideas, to exercising its judgment, even on things which are foreign to holiness, a soul animated by the views of its religion, has a different focus. Is it not obvious that it can rise above those who do not have the same discipline?

We worry that our teachers will be distracted by their studies, but I wonder if uneducated people, people who have an empty mind, are not distracted when they are praying? Without doubt, they are distracted all the time. The most trivial, the most miserable, the basest things are sufficient to distract them. It is conceit which is the source of distractions when praying. It does not matter how important or trivial *the task*. Indeed experience shows us that those who are busy with the most basic of tasks can find the means to take pleasure in doing it, to glory in doing it, and as a result, to be distracted by it. What distracts us is an excessive attachment to pleasure. It is certain that those who do not know how to taste the pleasures of the mind will draw more pleasure from their senses. I do not suggest that studying is a necessary requisite if one is to develop one's spiritual life. I am simply saying that it is a good, natural way, especially when it is not in any way damaging in itself. We also know that grace operates in hidden and mysterious ways and that often uneducated people are elevated to this spiritual life. How does this come about? By the power and mercy of God, which raises them up and teaches them without effort what the rest of us must learn by diligence, that is to say, by reflecting and meditating. I must repeat: there can be no inner life without meditation and reflection.

I must also add that the tendency to form judgements based on the opinion of others, the importance that is placed on trivia, the ability to get upset and be pulled down by the most insignificant details, all those things which are so hostile to the peace of the soul and to one's serenity, are they not particular features of a mind that is empty of ideas? To think of God is without doubt the most perfect of all human thoughts. But for those who cannot do this constantly or at least frequently, I would much prefer to see them occupied with study where reasoning is exercised and where the soul is fortified, rather than thinking about a thousand puerile, ridiculous and vain things. Now while these thoughts might be very harmless in themselves, I cannot hide the fact that they lead, by a fairly steep slope, to other thoughts which are not so innocent and which are injurious to the virtues of both charity and purity. This leads on to the question: if it is true that study enhances one's inner life, why deprive even one of the spouses of the Heart of Jesus of this means of spiritual perfection? In reply I would say that it is only a means for those to whom Providence gives it. Everyone cannot give themselves up to study in the Society. Indeed quite a number do not have the ability for that. For some of them, it would be injurious to the soul and Providence calls these people to holiness and spirituality by other means. Yet it is clear that in our Society there must be a certain number of truly educated and enlightened people who will be able to influence our decisions and important discussions. That is how we can say that the Society of the Sacred Heart is truly enlightened even though it cannot be so in every one of its members.

Moreover, it is certain that an enlightened Society [of the Sacred Heart], which values and encourages good study and the development of the mind, will find that this approach is a defence against that fateful laxity we see many religious societies falling into and against that dangerous apathy which attacks their heart and causes death. This truth becomes more obvious in the light of experience. Let us place side by side the Society of St Francis and that of St Ignatius. The founder of the former was more angel than man. His Society spread with extraordinary speed but its collapse came in an equally rapid way. St Bonaventure, its head, signalled that sadly after the short space of thirty years there was a marked falling off of zeal and standards. Let us look now at the Society of St Ignatius. Could its friends or even its enemies, and there were plenty of them, accuse the Society of a fall in moral standards? The Society was subject to two great trials, prosperity and adversity, and it emerged intact. Even after all these years, do we not find in that Society the same spirit of obedience and regularity, fervour and zeal, the same love of its task as at the time of its foundation? Certainly, it is most admirable. I believe that God wants us to understand by this example that study preserves moral standards and that the Jesuits were wise to use this human means with discernment.

In addition, I have had the ambition to model our Society on this generous and highly regarded Society (the Jesuits), in so far as the weakness of our sex allows us. It is not a question of creating a new model but rather imitating what has been practised with such brilliant success. If there are different and new circumstances today, as no doubt there are, they make our work all the more necessary. The Society of St Ignatius is being reborn today. After long and violent storms, it is still inspired by its wonderful models and by its moving and noble memories from the past. It will imbue the world again with the perfume of its talents and virtues. If we are worthy of it, if we are similar to it in our goals, it will recognise us as its sister and will aid us in our work. We will have the joy of helping them in our turn, and in this concerted way, we will win a great number of souls for our beloved Lord.

I still have a number of other views which I will develop in detail in a second *Mémoire*, if Mother [Barat] makes this request. All cannot be done at once but it is necessary to design in advance the edifice one proposes to build. We can then work slowly or quickly on it, depending on the means that Providence provides for us. But if we are working according to a preconceived plan we will make progress and not waste time. In thinking about this magnificent edifice, I have been filled with joy and hope. Happy the one who gets to construct this structure, but happier still is the one who puts her heart into it. But I ask what could prevent anyone putting their heart into it? Surely the heart of a Christian is sufficient? What then will be the heart of a member of the Society of the Sacred Heart?

Let me make one final observation. Experience proves that if the plan imperfectly sketched here was followed faithfully it would necessarily result in an increase of respect, esteem and even wealth for the Society. Without doubt these things are contemptible but they only serve as a means to our end. We will renounce approval when we will no longer have the duty and the need to influence people. We will disdain wealth when there are no more poor people to relieve, no more children to raise free of charge, no more churches to build to the Sacred Heart. In the meantime, since these advantages follow naturally from our efforts to carry out our duties as perfectly as possible and from actions inspired by the Heart of Jesus, we will receive them calmly and watch carefully to attribute them to Him alone. Moreover, this growth in revenue will allow us to lower the fees we receive from our students, and by virtue of this many more will be able to afford our education. These vile riches will therefore serve to acquire a far more precious wealth, souls which we will offer to God.

I must repeat how essential it is to have a certain number of teachers who are trained in the art of conversation and who have refined, cultured minds. This is very desirable when we are dealing with the children of the upper classes but with the poor as well. In this century which is in love with the mind, in this century when the freedom to judge is universal, in this century where no one is listened to if they do not possess the ability to please, now more than ever it is not permissible to neglect the means of reaching people.

I must now ask this question. If our Society carries out this plan, will it not be in demand in foreign countries where the governments as well as the upper classes feel the need to improve the education of women? We will go into the centre of France where there is need for serious, sound education to protect women from the natural negligence of morals there. We will go to the north where heresy dominates, where civilisation is backward and where so many strive with effort and commitment to advance it. With education as our passport we will have the right to teach there what they doubtlessly fear to learn. We will have the duty and the authority to teach even those who would like to reject education.

Let me sum up. Young people destined to take their place in the world need a carefully planned education and a cultivated, refined mind. In this way they are better able to defend themselves against the temptations, old and new, of this corrupting world. They will be better equipped to look after their families, their friends and all who surround them, and they will be motivated to use the influence they will have in the world in the service of God. The Society of the Sacred Heart of Jesus must ensure that its young teachers receive a very thorough education since they are destined to exercise a certain form of apostolate throughout the world. They must have cultivated and refined minds if they are to mould their students. They must be able to inspire confidence in families. During recreation, they must be able to direct and guide the conversations of children and young novices newly arrived from the outside world in a rational and beneficial way. In short, they must be in a position to advance the important work of the Society. The Society also needs well-trained teachers in order to expand and propagate, to maintain and increase the respect it enjoys and the esteem which I believe it will be given. This esteem is due not only to its educational work but to its aim of making known the One whose glorious name it carries and the heavenly society to which it seeks.

Finally, the last and most important consideration of all is this: the religion of Jesus Christ, unknown, unappreciated, forgotten, scorned, no longer can count very many disciples. This divine religion, brought from heaven by the son of God and established at the price of His blood, is going to be lost among men. It appears that our unfortunate countries, old Europe, now want to hand the celestial torch on to the New World. This is why the church cries out in sorrow. This holy bride of Christ, this tender and respectable mother, can no longer find any faithful children. In vain she calls them to her, but there is no answer. Some of them are ungrateful and unnatural, they fight against her; others are cold and indifferent, they do not care about the wrongs done to her, and don't even think about defending her. In her last extremity, the holy church needs the few children who still love her to rise up to show their love and defend her.

Praise be to God we are among those children. The misfortunes of our mother have inflamed our love for her. Her moving cries of pain have echoed in our heart. We have seen her almost abandoned by her children, and we have come to swear even greater loyalty and total devotion to her. We have seen her despised by all and we have felt the need to honour her in a more elevated and solemn way. We promise again, and we love to repeat this promise: we will serve her. Who can stop us? We will serve her in the lowliest or the loftiest of employments. What does it matter, as long as she is looked after? We will not feel ashamed by the former, nor filled with pride by the latter. No work is too big or too small to serve her. Everything we do is an honour for us; everything satisfies us, so long as it is in her service. Her interests are ours; her glory is ours; her suffering is ours. If our task appears too great, love will help us achieve it. If our task seems too small, love too will help us carry it out. We will never say: we are weak women, our talents are weak, our health is weak, and our virtue is weak. No, we will not say that at all. She is our mother, she needs to be looked after and we are her children. Our hearts will make up for whatever deficiencies we may have, for those who love can do everything. We will not be held back by the fear that people will mock or persecute us or kill us. No, we will not let fear stop us, because she is our mother and we love her with a child's love.

I have opened my heart completely to the respected mother [Barat] whom Providence has deigned to give me as guide and teacher. I do not fear to put these thoughts to her because she shares them. In her profound wisdom and in the light of her experience, she will judge to what degree my hopes can be realised. I still have several ideas to expand, but this is enough for today. I believe I have done the will of God in writing this document to my superior. If in the follow-up we find ourselves in agreement with what I have written, or if my superior asks me, I can further elaborate on the ideas developed here.

Hidden Objectives: September 1824
HIDDEN OBJECTIVES OF THE STATEMENT ON EDUCATION, AND A BRIEF SUMMARY OF THE PROPOSAL SUBMITTED TO MOTHER BARAT

Our true and chief motive is to find worshippers of our Lord, but it would be imprudent to state this openly in this century of indifference. To work to spread the flame of God's love is the real objective of the spouses of the Heart of Jesus, but we cannot say that [since] we would be considered fanatics and visionaries; we would not be read, our aim would fail. We must therefore employ more roundabout ways which I hope will lead all the more surely to the desired end. Therefore we will promise genuine though lesser advantages. This is what I have tried to do in the Prospectus. It has a tone of worldly piety which is popular in the present century, with fine words like honour and virtue. These will not frighten anyone away and can be interpreted by each person as they wish. The Prospectus is therefore only an inducement. All it contains is true but it falls far short of stating all our thoughts. First of all, let us inspire confidence, let people read about us, and then we will proceed little by little with our strategy which I am about to present now.

This world puts a great value on trivial concerns. If we dare state the true aim of our work, which is the reign of Jesus in our hearts, people will shun us disdainfully. But if we speak about study, education, good works, good manners and behaviour, nobility of heart and soul, they will listen. All these are really good in themselves, we can praise them freely; but in our eyes they are secondary and a mere preparation to lead us onwards. We will not state that we want to attack certain pernicious practices which contribute greatly to the corruption prevalent in this century: reading novels, immodest clothing, performances and balls. These three are the greatest destroyers of women's morals. We will not state that, but we will nevertheless attack them anytime circumstances allow us, making use of the weapons of religion, of reasoning and sentiment and even by making fun of them which so often wins the day. We will not state that we want to win the hearts of our readers so that we can guide their behaviour. This is true but it is solely for their good that we have this ambition. There are great spiritual aspirations in our overall plan which we are only giving a brief glimpse of here. We will not state them because we would frighten the people we want to reach. In the overall plan there are also great worldly aspirations. We will not mention those either because we would annoy those who are ambitious for the same rewards as ourselves, but for less pure reasons.

We will quietly instruct our young teachers but must take care not to say how much they need it. Nevertheless, we must not pretend either since it is true that they need to be instructed on the dangers contained in certain books. I know that some of them, whose intentions and virtues are no doubt very pure, have permitted reading material and speeches which contained real hidden venom. I would like to think that no one has been tainted by this material but do not dare so to believe. I think it is the result of their extreme naivety. In our century such an approach can have serious drawbacks for those responsible for the education of children. Most of our teachers, ignorant of what the outside world is like, cannot understand the type of dangers which their pupils will be exposed to every day. It is necessary to develop in life the ability to reflect and judge if one is to be on guard against such literature and be able to recognise the seeds of evil it may contain. If you cannot recognise this, how can you fight against it? And if you cannot do this, will evil not get stronger?

Therefore, we can conclude that our young teachers, who are too naive and ignorant of evil than is acceptable in their job, should themselves receive a formation that is normally beyond their range. Moreover, their own reading needs to be guided. Is it not the case that some of them have been badly influenced by poorly chosen reading? Since they are teaching others should they not be in a position themselves to be able to distinguish good from bad, truth from error? This is what I say, but their own self-respect should enlighten them a good deal more frequently. Teachers of twenty years experience, teachers of women, know what is necessary to produce a first-rate class, but do they know the world and literature? Do they know how to guard themselves from the dangers of both? Generally they do not and they should be educated in this knowledge up to a certain point, with prudence and caution.

For the record, I can see another positive outcome with regard to our young ladies. By suggesting subjects for conversation their leisure time could be an opportunity to make them more rational in their thinking. Let us not hide the fact that a gathering of women tends to disintegrate into idle gossip. How much more desirable it would be and beneficial to the perfection of the soul if leisure time could be used to speak about God. Or if one could not speak all the time about Him, to speak about their studies which for us are a means of attracting souls to God, the hopes and successes of the church, the works of zealous Christians and the sciences recommended and encouraged by the church which raise the spirit and perfect reason. Other topics might be about ways to combat vice, to encourage virtue, to perfect souls, to perfect oneself, to grow in the love of God – in a word, to speak about rational, serious and useful things.

Would not such conversation be advantageous to these young ladies? Apart from the good it would do to their soul, it would help form their judgement and their mind, would make them better able to pass on these qualities to children, would give or conserve in them a certain veneer of education which people seek, indeed demand of those to whom they confide their children. It should also be noted that even though discussions on science or studies might not be meritorious in themselves, they would have the advantage of keeping them away from personal discussions which might easily lead to sin. Some extracts of the letters received from America will be included. We will add certain reflections inspired by them but we will not say that we wish to attract certain generous souls who feel the need to make great sacrifices to God, people such as St Louis de Gonzaga, who had this attraction. We will not say that in the service of God we need people who are intelligent, who enthusiastically pursue excellence, even though not entirely for pure motives, whether they know it or not. They are like spirited horses. If they are left to roam free, they will go astray. If they are led by a firm, strong hand they will be more useful than any others in the service of the Master.

I have noticed that there is a movement among the Protestants which is favourable to their conversion [to Catholicism]. A man of my acquaintance, who knows Germany well and who travels frequently, told me lately that he had been struck by the general shift towards Catholicism by all those who read and think. Would we be flattering ourselves to think we could exert such an influence? Why not? It is not a question of reasoning with them theologically, for all the [Christian] virtues have been developed. Rather it is a question of touching their hearts, putting them in a frame of mind to make them open to an initial exploration of Catholicism. In this way, by preparing their feelings, they will be touched by the truths of Catholicism which they have rejected. That is what we can do. We will not state publicly, however, that we have this discreet, glorious ambition to bring back to our holy mother [church] some children who have strayed away. But this hope is in our heart.

We want to establish links between the members of the Society of the Sacred Heart by communicating with greater facility the events, the successes, and the tribulations of each house. Thus when this Society expands significantly, if it so pleases God, it can always say truthfully 'Cor unum et anima una in Corde Jesu (One heart and one mind in the Heart of Jesus)'. We want to indicate, advise on and recommend good works, a task which we would not know how to do all alone! Dedicated souls are sadly aware that there are a great number of tasks which they cannot accomplish. It will be necessary then to persuade others to undertake them. We want to make people wary of and avoid bad reading material. We must research good material. I do not hesitate in saying that on this point alone, our Journal is necessary. In our century women want to read everything, but they are less forewarned than men about the dangers of reading. In general, the paucity of their education has made them scarcely capable of reasoning by themselves, and the power of their emotions makes them more susceptible to being led astray by others.

Every day in this world dangerous ideas are being put forward and no one dares reply to them. We will reply in order to alert our children. People are doing things which are harmful morally speaking, without even thinking about it. We will demonstrate the weakness of such practices. Do not our children need this sort of instruction before they go out into the world? How will they get it if not through this Journal? Will it be from their teachers who for the most part are ignorant themselves, or from their parents who have already been seduced? We want to involve our students more actively in their education, instruct them and make them part of our great design. By presenting the Journal in a noble, gentle and attractive manner, we would like to enlist the aid of people from every class who could assist us in different ways. We want to combat the prejudice against religious life, which is so widespread today. We wish to strengthen those whom God entrusts to us with arguments contrary to worldly thinking, to human affection and the frailty of their own hearts. There are a certain number of people who seem suitable to serve the Society in an effective way. I know several but I do not know how to retain them. They would need explanations, enlightenment, and encouragement. That is what they would find indirectly in this Journal and much more easily than in any other way.

We want to make the Society of the Sacred Heart known for what it is and put an end to the false ideas that people have of it. In this century, where everyone is restless, where so many people are setting up establishments and enterprises of every kind, where people are bewildered by so much discussion and contradictory reasoning, it is books which will speak to the mind in moments of rest and relaxation. We are not well known in Lyon, as several clergy of this town have told me. If we are not known in Lyon, where we have been for the last five years, what is it going to be like in Marseilles, in Toulouse or elsewhere? We have to influence opinion in advance, if we wish to find pupils, friends and benefactors when we arrive. We see houses being dedicated to the Divine Heart being built everywhere. However, we have the ambition to take exclusive ownership of this admirable name through which wonders will be worked. Should we then have some distinguishing work that others will not be able to imitate, which will single us out and give us the distinction that we seek? We would like the Jesuits to consider us as belonging to them. We want to find in the Society of Jesus kindness, help, fatherly care and advice. Should we not endeavour to walk in their footsteps, as well as overcome the natural weakness of our sex and receive from the Heart of Jesus some lofty incentives for doing well?

We want to obtain protection and favour from ecclesiastical and civil authorities, necessary for the development and prosperity of our order. We must persuade the former that we serve the cause of religion. We must persuade the latter that we can be useful in promoting good education and good moral standards and consequently peace, happiness and the well-being of the state. But for these claims to be convincing what more suitable, legitimate and powerful course of action than to work with real commitment? Firstly, to serve our religion, in accordance with the spirit of our vocation and the desires of our heart, and secondly, which follows on from that, to provide a good education and high moral standards.

Perhaps you might say that our methods are extraordinary. But let us look at the state of religion in France and in Europe; it is almost lost. The ignorance of people in general and of those who would pretend to be knowledgeable in matters of religion is really frightening. Those fortunate people, whom the goodness of God has touched and who have been in the shadows of a cloister since their childhood, cannot understand it.

I received certain information on parishes where for some years now a frightening fall-off in the most basic religious practices has been observed. With this state of affairs must we not do something outstanding? Do we estimate objectively the dangers to our pride, inherent in such an undertaking? Moreover, our course of action may be astonishing to human eyes but considered in itself and in relation to God it is not. It is natural, legitimate and reasonable: that is enough. Caution is a good thing, but carried too far it becomes an obstacle to every great undertaking. St Ignatius says: 'when we want to do great things, we should not be too cautious.' This project is reasonable because it is in keeping with the spirit of the age. We must attract souls by offering them inducements which they value. In all his undertakings St Ignatius took the attitudes of his time always into account and then put his plans before God.

Let us consider the progress of the other religious orders. They have grown faster than ours, and yet circumstances today have never been so urgent. The conditions which favoured the growth of the other orders no longer hold weight in this century because today has no faith. A new approach is necessary as long as it is genuine. Our proposed course of action is exceptional and so much the better, for that is why it will succeed. If respectable, well educated men or saintly churchmen offer the public a work fundamentally the same as ours, will they succeed? Most probably not. Our century is particularly ignorant and arrogant. It does not think it needs being taught but it ardently desires to be entertained, intrigued, and moved to sympathy. We must reach them that way. People are conceited and begin by rebelling against those who appear to be superior to them. But women, nuns, whom they never see anywhere and who are not in competition with anyone, will not inspire distrust. Our century is also obsessed with novelty. Novelty pleases, what is extraordinary will carry people along with it. Those women to whom especially we offer our proposal are perhaps the least corrupted members of society. Nevertheless, they have a great need of renewal. We will try to direct their vanity towards honest and honourable things, and make them our defenders and our supporters in the world through the success of our work.

Perhaps all the good that we envisage may not come about. That is indeed possible but will no good at all come from it? Will there not be a single soul who hearing our voice returns to God, or though serving him already will not try to serve him better? Will there not be some sins shunned, even one? I would think so. God will give the success that he wishes to our good will, but first we must give evidence of our true and sincere good will ourselves. I know that undertaking a venture like this requires certain strength of mind, which is not common, especially amongst women. The Heart of Jesus can impart this strength to the weakest of people. There is a great fortitude that goes hand in hand with an intensity of faith and an intensity of love. It sees the dangers but neither weighs nor counts them. Without doubt, women are capable of this fortitude. Would the spouses of the Heart of Jesus not have it?

In this century courage is more necessary than ever to manage a great undertaking like this, and let us admit that this is generally lacking in people whom Providence has marked out to be influential. We are advised: be prudent, be cautious. Follow the methods of those who have attained authority. See their successes. And yet the enemies of goodness are not holding back cautiously and they are succeeding in their scheming. But the prudence that comes from God is different. It says: risk nothing which might displease God, risk everything to please him. If you work for him, will he not help you? And if he helps you, could you be afraid? That is obviously true prudence.

If this work is in keeping with the will of God, which I have every reason to believe it is, there is no doubt but that it will meet with keen opposition. The enemy of salvation will employ those who are similarly like-minded to challenge it. They will even succeed by cunning and subtle manipulation, by using those who are very different to them to challenge us, religious people who belong to Jesus. These people would be shattered if they realised how they were being used. Yes, the dangers which a book like this might pose will be highlighted, exaggerated and multiplied. But in the final analysis, what are these dangers reduced to? To a few words: what will people say? So long as it is not ridiculous, anything that is said cannot hurt very much. Truth has a certain strength which is natural to it and which penetrates hearts. Those who defend mistruths need very great talent to attain their ends. I am convinced that even with mediocre talents those who defend the truth with uprightness, with feeling, in a spirit of peace, with true detachment from all personal passions, will make an impression on a great number of minds.

However, it is indeed possible that there will be a certain commotion

– will the enemies of good ever stop rising up against those who do good? Should we give up because of that? Perhaps we will be libelled, persecuted even. Despite this, as long as the holy truths which God has come to teach reaches and penetrates a few hearts, our goal will have been achieved. It is also unheard of that a good book can be completely destroyed by hostility. I imagine that there will be an outcry. It will be nothing more than a hollow noise which alarms weak souls only. For those who act, not by their own strength but by the strength of God, all they need to do is continue on to their goals, calmly and with confidence, and the noise will quieten down and fade away. The worthwhile truths presented in the work will remain. The good that one cannot do in one place and at one time will be felt in another. There will be detractors, but will there not be a few upright and honest minds that will be able to judge which side is right? Will it not do some good? Will the Heart of Jesus not grant us some conquests, even from among those who declare themselves to be against us? These criticisms can even turn to our advantage, if God wishes it. Yes, and will the Heart of Jesus not take account both of the good that we do and the good that we would like to have done? Will He not reward us for both the success that we will have and for the success that we will not have? Will He not see with pleasure that the spouses, in their desire to make Him known and loved, are prepared to risk their reputation, just as they would risk their life for Him? They are prepared to be taken for mad women in the eyes of the world, if it draws some souls to Him.

And if the Heart of Jesus views our work and our motives with pleasure, is that not the truest, gentlest, most noble and greatest of success? I have exaggerated the dangers on purpose, so as to face up to them. However, in my opinion, such dangers do not seem very likely. It is not the opposition, libel and persecution that we may encounter that I really fear, but the esteem, the recognition, the praise, the wealth which could follow on the success of our undertaking – those are real dangers for a Christian soul. However, I think we will get through this danger, invoking the name of Jesus. I feel that this undertaking is so big that it is natural that it should worry the spouses of a crucified Lord. But to put off doing it on the sole basis that it is immense, would this not be a weakness that would show too little confidence in God again, too little zeal in working for His glory? In order to serve God in a great way, especially in these demanding times, will we not have to be able to face up to scorn, learn how to confront human respect, that dangerous malady which attaches itself to the most noble of actions?

I feel that holy and reputable people will ask if the natural reserve of women and Christian humility allow us to carry out our task. It is the first thought that comes to mind, but after some consideration and self questioning you realise that there is a natural female modesty which is purely external, which is associated with self-respect, with the desire to please and to be appreciated. This state of mind is not totally bad, but it should give way to a way of thinking of a higher order, which is to give the greatest glory to God. As for Christian humility, what does that mean? Pleasing or displeasing our fellow man counts for nothing; pleasing or displeasing God counts for everything. That is what humility is all about. We can undertake the greatest acts for the love of God. Humility will not be damaged by that, indeed it will be strengthened. If we undertake even the smallest acts for love of creatures then humility is at risk. Then humility gets lost and we do vile things.

But can we flatter ourselves that we are able to convince people, when we come up against the prejudices that are prevalent in society? One widely held prejudice is that women should not write. Men believe this and indeed most women also. Men do not like their spouses to spend their time writing. They want them to occupy themselves totally with the care of their home and their family, and to give their attention to pleasing their husbands. Moreover, men consider that thinking and using their minds is not flattering to a woman's femininity. They are conditioned to view women in this way. Perhaps they want to feel superior in every way to those they have power over. But I believe they will have a different attitude to women that they know they will never marry, women who are not destined to entertain or amuse them, and women whom they can only consider as teachers of their children. I think that they will find it not only a good thing that they write, but I am convinced that in this particular case, they will generally judge us more favourably than they judge other writers. This will be due to their natural feeling of protectiveness, indulgence and interest that they have towards us. We cannot doubt that the seriousness of our views on female morality will find support amongst men and that in the bottom of their hearts they will *feel gratitude* to those who undertake to spell out the rules of morality to their wives, rules which the world considers harsh.

Why should women feel alienated from those women who write? Here, I think, is the reason. They think these women have pretensions and a sense of superiority which they find annoying. Women writers also have a means of finding the kind of success which is denied to them, especially in the pursuit of their own interests. But when it comes to those women whose life in religion puts themselves beyond the range of ordinary interests, who are permanently separated by a barrier from a society ruled by self-importance and who neither could nor would steal those things which they hold dear, then I think that these women would think it appropriate that they write. I also believe that their self-esteem would be flattered that one of their own should have such gifts, and they would bask in her reflected glory. Make no mistake about it, women are more enamoured of the faculties of the mind than men; they are less industrious but more enthusiastic. Therefore, they would in some way make common cause with us, they would support us, they would love us, and they would trust us. I will not develop these thoughts in greater detail, other than to say that, since these women exert great influence in the world, what good could we do if we guided them to a certain degree? This seems very possible to me.

In addition, though we have consecrated our lives to Jesus Christ, do we still consider ourselves to be women? What I mean is, are we still weak, still taken up with minutiae, dependent on the opinion of others, concerned only about men and vanity? Please God no. Were we not reborn on the day of our profession? We must believe it. We must keep certain qualities of our own sex – gentleness, the gift of persuasion, compassion, an outward frailty, but we must take from the opposite sex, qualities such as spiritual courage, strong-mindedness, consistency in our reasoning and firmness of character. We must not therefore think of ourselves as women, but as the spouses of the Heart of Jesus. This title must raise us in our own eyes and in the eyes of others, and it is in the Divine Heart that we will in fact find everything necessary to serve Him greatly, provided that is what we want. Are we not, in a word, missionaries? Are we not charged by the mercy of God, to spread and make known the sacred truths that God came to teach to men? We cannot fulfil all the functions of the ministry, but should we not fulfil with fervour and devotion those functions that the church allows us to carry out? Men who are consecrated to God can no longer cope with the work in the vineyard of the Lord. This vineyard is decaying. Ah! Let us cultivate that part of it which belongs to us, with greater courage. Let not the fear of self-respect stop us. Let us not consider if a certain course of action is extraordinary, but rather if it is pure and legitimate, if it is appropriate to make God loved. Indeed this is not to be questioned.

Say to the little circle around us: love God, because it is the whole purpose of man. In order to prepare them for this sublime lesson, say: study your religion and your duties, be true, kind, good, diligent, full of uprightness and honesty, modesty and charity; Do whatever good that you can do – is this not obviously an appropriate way to make God beloved? The Journal will not have a different message, only the circle will be bigger and the message will not be delivered by human voice as this is not feasible for a wider circle. So it will be written and printed so that it can be read more easily and reproduced many times. I ask myself before God and examining things in the light of faith, if there is a difference between giving instruction to ten people or ten thousand? Is the latter less legitimate, less valid in making God loved? What makes the latter action preferable and in a certain respect necessary is that the number of people who are working in the service of God is unfortunately very small and absolutely insufficient. It is necessary therefore that they multiply and perfect their mode of action and their methods, that they redouble their efforts and transcend themselves.

At the present time, almost all have turned their minds away from the eternal, religious truths. If we love God we have to constantly put those truths before people whether the time is favourable or not. To do this we must use everything Providence has given to us by way of intellect, talent, imagination, perseverance and other qualities, gifts which were not given for any other purpose. We must use even those means which human wisdom rejects but which God permits. Moreover, though I have no doubt in this respect, I question if a work that is carried out from the purest of motives and feelings could be totally without success? No, without doubt and I have no fear in saying it, it is impossible that it could be a failure. I make this appeal to all informed by the true light of faith. Alas! Our houses in America are languishing. However, if there were more of them and if they were flourishing, what good could they not achieve in this new country where everything is growing so rapidly!

It is true that there are other books to write which seem more urgent in some respects, since they deal with basic religious instruction which is our particular task. But these books will take more time to write and will only do a limited amount of good. The Journal would give us time to prepare and promote the books. Perhaps they could be written by others more suited than ourselves but keeping to our plans and principles. I insist that in whatever town the Journal is printed, while it would be advantageous to have the support of those in authority, the Journal should not be subject to the censure of those of questionable principles but depend only on the bishop for approval. If we cannot get these conditions in Paris or in any other city in France where we have our convents, would we not find them in Turin, under a government which is much more open when it comes to religious matters? Someday, if we have a house in Rome, I think that is where the Journal should be printed. This will be in French, of course, because France is the country that we have primarily in mind. If the Journal is to have a wider distribution, as French is the most prevalent language it will always be preferable to others.

I admit that my hope of extending the circulation of the Journal beyond France seems a bit ambitious. I know it but I cannot help thinking about the following fact. In Nîmes, a man of my acquaintance brought out a mathematics Journal. It had subscribers from as far away as Finland and yet this man was unknown. He had neither supporters nor friends, and he was dealing with a clinical and cold science which does not speak to the heart and which does not meet any true human needs. If this was the case with him, what could stop the Journal reaching neighbouring countries, reaching as far as England? There the time seems favourable for a certain number of people to return to the true faith, and the English government exerts very wide influence. What if the Journal was to appear in the vast state of Russia, where they are always well-disposed towards works of a certain talent from other countries and its principal attractions being precisely that it is unusual and different? If the Journal were to get as far as Russia, would it not be a great mission, one which would bear fruit? St Magdeleine de Pazzi, burning with fervent love of God, used to ring the bell to summon everybody to come pay homage to Jesus. Motivated by the same zeal, if she were in our place would she not carry out or approve our plan?

So the arguments that could be made against the Journal, and which I have considered, are weak to the point of being unconvincing, compared to the beauty of our goal. There are the risks to be run, but I ask what great task can one undertake without running any risk, speaking even in human terms? What risks are run by those who want to be honoured or even those who want to get rich? The history of man has given us proof of this. As for us, to what risk are we exposing ourselves? In our judgement an illusory benefit, a little bit of worldly admiration. And what do we hope to achieve? Pleasing the Lord by attracting many to him, a genuinely admirable benefit, preferable to all the kingdoms of the earth. But what if the work does not succeed? All we need do is abandon it. Let us even suppose that it was absolutely dreadful, could it damage the Society [of the Sacred Heart]? I do not think so. In every group of people there are bad writers; that does not stop groups from growing. There are some poor writers even among the Jesuits. That has not stopped them carrying out so much good work.

I must add that if this work seems advantageous, we must make haste to start. We may not have a more favourable time again for the advancement of the Society. This is especially so because of the vital reason that in all that is for the good of souls we should always act today rather than tomorrow, unless there are very good reasons for putting it off. In addition, I know several people in the world who I think would support this work effectively. If we delay a few years, some of them will be dead, [or] their position changed, their influence lessened or their attitude less positive. I do not fear to say it: this work is in the spirit of the Society which is essentially a spirit of zeal for the conversion of souls, the fostering of love for our sovereign Lord, a commitment of total devotion to His interests and to His glory. This is the spirit of the Society of the Sacred Heart and this is the spirit which must inspire and guide the Journal. This thought always occurs to me when I hear the summary of our Constitution being read or when I think of the Heart of Jesus.

Ah! If only we could gather to Him, to whom we are consecrated, some true worshippers who would serve Him generously and make Him served. If only we could lead some weak and mediocre souls away from evil and towards good. They are under alien influences, many of which are fatal. In this unhappy century in which we live, if we could only receive from the Universal Father of the faithful that solemn approbation and blessing which would make our hopes, our strengths and our plans prosper! May the Society of Jesus [Jesuits], seeing us working successfully for the salvation of souls, recognise us as one of its own. May I express all my thought? May we be a new branch, growing from that admirable tree planted by St Ignatius, a distinctive branch, the Society of the Sacred Heart. This branch would carefully preserve the saintly, gracious, touching qualities of the original order. It would also add new means which the needs of this century seem to cry out for. Ah! If this blessed branch exists one day, it is there that we will find our fathers and our teachers, our guides and our models.

I need to ask pardon from the Heart of Jesus for my resistance to making these thoughts known, for it seems clear enough to me that they come from Him. I ask pardon from the Divine Heart for my cowardice and for a certain aversion which I think comes from a love of peace and a form of subtle self-esteem. How often have I not had to compel myself to write something to my mother [Barat] and when she told me to develop my plan, I felt discouraged, intimidated, I did not dare do it. I tried to persuade myself that I had not got the time, that I had too many pressing tasks. Then I felt a vague fear which I yielded to for quite a long time. I needed the presence of P(ère) R. to give me a bit of courage and to inspire me to hastily sketch these rushed thoughts. Yet, several times during my prayer the thoughts of the good that such a project would do struck me more forcibly than ever. Then blushing at my cowardice, I promised our Lord with all my heart to do as much as I was capable of to get the plan accepted. But would my earnestness of heart survive when the motives for action were subjected to the scrutiny of reason? Yes, it did, and it is at the feet of my mother [Barat] and after careful thought, that I now renew my promise to the Heart of Jesus to contribute as much as I can, according to obedience, to have this work carried out. Nevertheless, I do not ask to take responsibility for this myself. God forbid it. I would need more talent, learning, time and especially humility than I have for such a task. I acknowledge that the work can and must be shared, but it is essential that whoever is put in charge of it should be chosen with great care.

I have written these lines out of love for the Heart of Jesus. All that remains for me at the present time is to beg the Heart of Jesus to choose the person for this work and to make that name known to the heart of my mother [Barat]. In this way the one who is chosen by the Divine Heart can do good for others without harming herself. May she have a soul noble and great enough to treat praise and criticism with equal indifference; a soul sensitive enough to be able to communicate to others the feelings which inspire her, and be able to clothe the truths she is advancing in an attractive way. May she be wise enough to know what to say and what is better to withhold, and the extent and the limits she should put to her zeal to do good. Finally and above all, may she be animated by a fervent love for the Heart of Jesus, so that this love is the only motivation for her work. May this love inspire her, enlighten her and strengthen her. May she place this love above her own self-importance and in the end may this love be the only reward for her in time and eternity. I end by saying that I cannot state with certainly if it is the will of God that this work be done, but I know for certain that it is only His will which motivates all that I do. I ask only that this holy and adorable will is carried out. I ask the Heart of Jesus to break down the barriers, in my heart and in the hearts of those on whom this work depends, to the carrying out of His will. Yes, all I ask is that the holy, merciful, generous and loving will of my God is carried out, and that the headstrong, vain and cold will of man will not win out.

I add a new thought to this finished work: We [Society of the Sacred Heart] want to get [formal] approval from the civil authorities and from the Vicar of Jesus Christ which must bring so many blessings on our work. These two approbations which are so necessary to us, even though in unequal measure, will influence each other. Which religious societies will be more likely to get both approvals? Without doubt those more attuned to the needs of the century, and with the best means of inspiring virtue, will be shown to have most obvious success. Moreover, are the established religious societies at this present moment sure of their position? Certainly not! After a century of destruction, we see them being reborn everywhere. The moment will undoubtedly come and perhaps it is not too far off, when the ecclesiastic authorities working in concert with the civil authorities, will turn their attention to these societies. They will approve some and abolish others, and may amalgamate others with those they approve. So it is important that our Society, which we believe merits being in the first category, should be known for what it is by those who have the right to judge it.

I regard the Journal as a banner which will single us out, which may not have the right to carry the name of the Society of the Sacred Heart, but at least will be an already acquired and recognised possession of the Society. It will be a means to earn the respect and the favour of certain important people who are biased against us. Finally, it is a preparation for the official approval of our order. Is it outside the bounds of possibility to think that the court of Rome, this court which is so prudent, wise and measured in its approach, would approve an order without knowing its ethos, its views, and its ways of operating? A flattering statement, a particular favour, these will easily be given to us. But official approval [from Rome] is too important a thing to be given lightly, especially to people who belong to a nation about which they have legitimate fears. A development of the aims of our Constitutions and their justification will be needed when we ask formally for approbation. It is important that when we take this step that we are not refused or that it is not dragged on. We must therefore prepare our minds in advance. So I see the Journal as an indirect validation and in consequence we will not be held in doubt. The Journal will be a skilled validation, if I can use that term. That is all I can say today on this point. May the holy will of God be done!

Prospectus. For Mother Barat, September 1824

Annals of Christian Women, or Journal of Education

A religious society devoted to the education of the young cannot consider without apprehension the dangers their students risk when they enter our corrupt world. No doubt, a great number of them retain and follow the values they received from us in their family life, concerning the laws of honour and virtuous living. But some of them, whether it be that they were withdrawn from us at too young an age or have a weak character or an unfortunate disposition, soon go off the straight and honourable path of holy virtue. Providence has chosen us to be spiritual mothers with the noble and worthy task of caring for these souls, so how can we not watch this without great sorrow? The affection that we have for these dear children makes us believe that our guidance, our instruction and our motherly advice ought to accompany and follow them out into the world to which they now belong.

That consideration has given rise to the idea of a regular Journal which would treat of such subjects as the duties of women, their calling, their interests, the dangers to which they are exposed, the prejudices against which they will have to fight, the studies most suited to them, the good that they are called to do. In a word, everything that is of interest to them in every aspect of their lives. Even if the work would help only one of the children that Providence has put in our care, we should still undertake it. But we flatter ourselves to think that it would be useful anyway even for our best students, that it would strengthen them in goodness and perfect their virtue. In addition, we cannot consider without compassion the huge number of young people whose moral and religious education was incomplete or completely defective. We hope that we could bring a few back to virtue. At first, they will understand little of our language, they have experienced such a small amount of it. But with the help of God on whom alone we count, we dare to hope that little by little a certain number of them will come to understand the essential truth that happiness is found only in virtue and that virtue is found only in religion. Alas! Several of these poor children only need to be introduced to this beautiful and holy virtue to practise and love it. Maybe some of them will awake as if from a sleep and say from the bottom of their heart: Ah! If we had only been told that before!

However, so that our young readers will not be frightened away, we will not always speak the language of stern morality. We will try to present a few pieces of fiction where we will strive to make the moral position more striking, more tangible, more pleasant and more moving. Secondly, from time to time, we will recount some of those heroic tales about human nature which contain an instruction that is so easy to grasp and which inspire generous imitation. We will quote in preference those tales which deal with women. The upheavals of the Revolution have given us a number of heroic tales which are not yet well known. Finally, we will promise our young readers that we will publish some letters from those among us who have gone to bring Christian education to young people in America. We cannot imagine how much these distant, dangerous missions, full of amazing happenings, naturally appeal to the imagination of young people. In the letters which we put before their eyes, they will hear our sisters themselves describing their work, their successes, their hopes and their sufferings, in a moving and simple way. This reading material, so interesting in itself, will no doubt encourage them to faithfully fulfil in their turn the much easier duties that Providence lays upon them.

It is not only young people that we have in view. Our work will embrace women of all ages and all ranks, since our pupils who get older and take up a position in society do not cease to be our children and the objects of our most tender concern. We will therefore have in mind the needs of women of every class, even those who were raised in a religion that is different to ours. Our words will be heard by those whose education is the most advanced and it is on their support that we can count most. We will offer our work not only to the young but also to their mothers. We need to influence and win them over too, and we intend to give them a few details on the events taking place in our boarding schools. In this way, when they feel their children are far away from them, they can sometimes imagine themselves to be in their midst and can take an interest in what they are doing.

We also want to be helpful to all those, either lay or religious, who are concerned with the education of young people, and to those mothers who are educating their daughters themselves. We will present our observations and reflections with simplicity and will be delighted to receive whatever communication they wish to send us. Several Christian mothers want and ask for advice on reading material for young people, advice that is well researched and based on the principles of true morality. We will try to give them guidance and we will give a few simple comments on the usefulness or the danger of certain books, of certain practices and of certain opinions.

In conclusion, we know that there are often women in the world who find themselves in positions that are infinitely delicate and difficult. Their heart is true but they lack strength, even perception. They need advice, they need a virtuous, sincere and objective friend to show them the road they should follow so as not to get lost. But where will they find such a friend? None of the people who surround them can inspire real confidence in them. We will be this friend for them. They will not even have to let us know who they are since they can write to us anonymously; we will reply to them through means of the Journal.

These are the essential ideas concerning the Journal. This Journal is necessary. We dare to say that men, though learned and articulate, would do it less well than us. There are certain things about the needs and the feelings of women that only a woman can understand perfectly. We have the courage to believe that Providence has given us a kind of mission for women. In consequence, the goodness of God will inspire us with ideas of what we should say to them and enable women to have some confidence in our words. Because of our consecration to God, we will never be rivals with them on earth. However, we have lived with them and we feel, as they do, both their needs and their sufferings. God has put a deep desire in our hearts to work to fulfil the needs of the former and to moderate the latter.

Perhaps people will be astonished at this time to see women who are without learning or talent, humble religious, daring to publish their feeble writing, daring to expose themselves to the censure of a sensitive public, a public that is too often hostile to their values. No doubt, our self-respect has also led us to ask: how do you dare do this? Without doubt, we have experienced the reluctance natural in our position, and our enterprise astonishes even ourselves! But it is the good of our contemporaries that we have in mind. It is the considerations of virtue and morality that engage us and the desire to serve God which motivates us. So self-respect should be sacrificed or rather forgotten.

As for any financial profit from our work, it will be spent entirely on pious works, details of which we will give to our subscribers: founding houses of education in France and further afield; aiding the poorer houses who cannot support themselves by their own resources; raising young people whose families have suffered a reverse of fortune; raising churches to the true God in this unhappy country where so many of them have already been destroyed; funding also in other places where it would be advantageous and helping the poor. In brief, any financial gain from this work will be used for charitable works of every kind. This consideration, no doubt, will excuse any weakness in our style, and we believe that it may give us subscribers and readers whose religion may be different to ours, but who cannot be indifferent to the joy of doing good and donating to charity.

Further matters for discussion need to include the price and conditions of subscription, the date when the Journal would appear, the interval that there would be between each edition, which I think should be at least a month. We also need to discuss the town in which the Journal will be printed, the address that we would give but at the same time not naming any one individual. All these things can be discussed with mother [Barat].

Commentary on the texts of Marie d'Olivier, 1823–1824 (Rebecca Rogers)[54]

MARIE D'OLIVIER: VISIONARY PEDAGOGUE AND TEACHER TRAINER

Marie d'Olivier's manuscripts offer a rare opportunity to peek behind convent walls and discover how a particularly eloquent woman religious envisioned girls' education and the tasks of religious teachers in post-revolutionary France. Writing in the mid-1820s, the author of these texts speaks about the need to combat the 'disintegration of moral standards' through a reform of girls' education, involving more rigorous training for teachers and the production of pedagogical materials, such as textbooks and an internal bulletin. The various proposals outlined in these documents reveal facets of girls' education that historians have yet to explore for the early nineteenth century. In particular they shed light on the Society's educational goals after the initial rule-books and programmes had been promulgated, and highlight the specific concern to train teachers capable of transmitting the lessons necessary to reform society. In her writing Marie d'Olivier testifies to a certain pragmatic realism about what might and should be accomplished, given parental demands and the political and religious climate of the time. Although her proposals were not put into action, they nonetheless illustrate how within teaching congregations religious women educators participated in a more general discussion about the appropriate way to educate girls in the new century.

As Marie d'Olivier's first 'Statement on education' indicates, the 1820s offered an opportunity for enterprising women religious given the destruction of religious institutes during the Revolution. Sophie Barat's Society of the Sacred Heart was just one of many new congregations that emerged in these decades dedicated to girls' education.[55] While the Napoleonic State established a framework for boys' secondary education, through the creation in 1802 of the *lycées* and *collèges*, and then the University in 1808 to oversee the accreditation and training of the teachers of these schools, little was done for girls. As a result, religious and lay women set up their own institutions with relatively little official oversight.[56] Lay women teachers, but not teaching sisters, were theoretically expected to obtain a *brevet de capacité* as of 1819, but a majority did not in the years when Marie d'Olivier was writing. Girls' education remained the domain of private initiatives despite a general perception that women's influence in society was widespread and critical because of their role within the family.

Marie d'Olivier begins her plea for pedagogical reform with the sort of general statements about the decline in religious standards that were common in these years. The Bourbon Restoration encouraged the resurgence of religious associations, and notably female religious congregations whose charitable and educational works were seen as reinforcing the sort of values the Monarchy sought to defend. Like lay women of her time, Marie d'Olivier explicitly highlighted women's educational role in order not only to make girls capable 'of resisting the dangers of the world, but also of exerting a beneficial influence on society.' She accepted the idea that women's 'powers of reasoning are weaker' than those of men; all the more need then to train their minds 'forming a very large number of rational, well taught, likeable and pious women'.

Her project was directed towards women of the upper classes who ran salons where men of the world spent part of their lives. These women needed to learn the arts of conversation, not just because of their role as mothers and spouses, but also in order to 'talk on appropriate topics which are discussed in the world.' In this fashion Marie d'Olivier justified a pedagogical programme aimed at improving morality both within the private and the public sphere.

To train girls to become cultivated, reasoned and religious women, Marie d'Olivier drew on her experiences of teaching in Amiens, Poitiers, Niort, Quimper, and then Lyon. She argued specifically for a need to study such subjects as history, literature and natural history, and to acquire a taste for the reading of good books. Far from condemning reading, she stated that it 'enlightens their mind; it fortifies their soul; it makes them understand their duties.' Such proposals were similar to those made by other women pedagogues of the time, but they reveal a specific religious imprint, notably when she defended the importance of teaching students 'properly' a history of the popes. This account, 'written with feeling,' in order to 'inspire love and affection for the true leaders of the church', was to aid the overall pedagogic project in defence of the faith. Marie d'Olivier offered her own services to write this particular text, which needed to be short and abbreviated compared to existing tomes.

In general, her Statement reveals a concern to produce appropriate didactic material for the Society's schools and ex-students. Given the specific religious concerns of the Society, members should have specially conceived reading material at their disposal, and not rely on commercially produced texts that might contain examples 'that are injurious to morals'. The journal she envisioned, the *Annales des Dames Chrétiennes ou Journal d'Éducation*, was a response to this need, like the proposed history of the popes. In this journal she wanted teachers throughout the Society to contribute material, letters from the schools established in other lands, light reading, inspiring examples . . . But she also wanted students to get involved in the journal and remain involved in the Society's activities thanks to their participation in this collective endeavour.

With this proposal she anticipated the sort of initiatives that would flourish a decade later during the July Monarchy, with the success of the image of the mother-educator. The pedagogue and writer David Lévi-Alvarès (1794–1870) was among the most influential individuals promoting girls' education and innovative didactic material. Following the success of his day courses in maternal education that he founded in Paris in 1820, he published a journal, *La Mère Institutrice*, between 1834 and 1845 that strove to help mothers in their educational task.[57] His journal printed pedagogical stories, information about cultural activities, as well as providing a format for the women poets and writers of this period, such as Victorine Collin, Marceline Desbordes-Valmore, and Fanny Richomme. It is noteworthy that Marie d'Olivier's proposal antedates this journal as well as the Annals for the Propagation of the Faith (1830) whose format bears similarities to what she advocated.

While Marie d'Olivier's concern to reform girls' education was shared by many educators of the time, her suggestions are particularly fascinating in that they illuminate the mechanics of a religious teaching order in a particularly candid fashion.[58] Particularly, she highlighted the absence of adequately trained women within the Society to carry out reform. As a result, her most ambitious proposal concerned the necessity 'to ensure that its young teachers receive a very thorough training since they are destined to exercise a certain form of apostolate throughout the world.' Proper training was necessary to 'mould their students' but also to 'inspire confidence in families'. While she did not go so far as to establish a specific training programme, she spoke firmly about the importance of teacher training, saying the rigours of such studies would not imperil women's souls or make them less perfect religiously. On the contrary, she argued: 'It is clear that in our Society there must be a certain number of truly educated and enlightened people who will be able to influence our decisions and important discussions.'

This recognition of the need for enlightened teachers, as well as the call for the creation of a journal, was a product of the Society's growth and success in these early years. As the number of houses multiplied in France and across the seas in America, leaders like Marie d'Olivier recognised the need for a central direction and firm principles to guide the different houses in their task. But she also recognised that the Society had competition, both from other religious orders and lay institutions. To succeed, the Society needed rational, intelligent, and courageous women capable of transmitting these same qualities to the girls they educated and they needed the means to advertise their actions and attract attention.

The three documents presented all highlight, as well, a pragmatic approach to the Society's goals. In arguing for a more academic education, Marie d'Olivier noted families wanted daughters to 'become pleasing people' who could speak and write 'in an agreeable way'. Their motives were less pure than those of the Society's, but in the end the religious goal warranted respecting contemporary fashion. The skills transmitted in the study of history and literature were 'a means to acquire and conserve solid virtues'. Similarly, she urged the outward espousal of gendered characteristics in order to pursue 'missionary' activities. In her 'Confidential objectives' she argued: 'We must keep qualities of our own sex – gentleness, the gift of persuasion, compassion, an outward frailty – but we must take from the opposite sex qualities such as spiritual courage, strong-mindedness, consistency in our reasoning and firmness of character.' This could only be achieved through a rigorous intellectual training programme. Finally, she recognised the need to form strategic alliances in order to achieve a great good; this meant in particular allying themselves with the Jesuits and seeking the protection and favour of ecclesiastical and civil authorities.

The vision of girls' education promoted in these documents was unquestionably conservative and harked back to Old Regime society where elite women played an important role within salon society, even if she defended the idea of teaching pupils from all ranks of society. In some ways the Bourbon Restoration sought to re-establish such a society, but it could not efface the fact and the memory of the Revolution. Marie d'Olivier recognised this and her plea for girls' education positioned women as moral reformers working within the family, while outwardly pursuing a more worldly task – that of producing agreeable and pleasant women who could entertain with their conversation. Her project carried with it, however, more liberal undertones: the concern to train a cadre of women teachers, whose influence would spread around the globe, and the concern to produce an educational instrument to spread the Society's influence with the creation of the journal.

As Phil Kilroy notes in the introduction, the fact that her proposals were not put into action represented a loss to the Society and undoubtedly contributed to its increasingly conservative reputation. Her proposal to create a journal had an enormous didactic potential, as the success of the Annals for the Propagation of the Faith would prove in the following years. The Society had the opportunity here to create on a smaller scale a woman-oriented Annals and it didn't seize the chance. Similarly a chance was lost with respect to teacher training. In France the development of more serious training opportunities for women teachers began in the late 1830s, and teaching congregations were at the forefront of these early normal schools. However, the Society only developed its own programme, the *Juvénat*, in 1866, despite calls for such a programme once again in 1850.[59] By 1866, the concern to provide a two-year programme in academic and religious studies was no longer visionary, as Marie d'Olivier's proposal had been.

Rebecca Rogers, Université Paris-Descartes

CHAPTER 3

The Society of the Sacred Heart
and the Jesuits in the Lifetime of
Madeleine Sophie Barrat[1]

Introduction

In 1826 a critic of the Society of the Sacred Heart, blending fact with fiction, claimed that the:

> Society of the Sacred Heart is for young girls and women what the Jesuits are for young boys and men. They are called *Jesuitesses* . . . The same luxury, arrogance, deceitfulness, pride, strategy and even ambition is found in the Society of the Sacred Heart as in the Society of St Ignatius . . . It is remarkable that wherever the Jesuits have houses, the Jesuitesses have theirs too: Paris, Amiens and Bordeaux.[2]

There was a certain truth in the accusation. There were close links between the Society of the Sacred Heart and the Jesuits which evolved and changed in the course of the nineteenth century. Madeleine Sophie Barat was acquainted with several generations of Jesuit provincials and communities in Paris and Lyon, and in the countries where the Society of the Sacred Heart had established communities and schools. The Society of the Sacred Heart looked to the Jesuits to give spiritual assistance in the communities, particularly the giving of the annual eight-day retreats, the three-day retreats twice yearly and the confessions of the community at specific times of the year.[3] The Society also asked the Jesuits to give school retreats and sometimes classes in religion in the boarding schools.

In general the assistance of the Jesuits was either supplementary or alternative to the services of the parish clergy, who for the most part were not trained to give retreats and spiritual direction to religious communities. The personal formation and education of the Jesuits, as well as their understanding of religious life, were valued in the Society and were a source of inspiration and encouragement. The house journals of the Society and the volumes of retreat notes, letters, conferences and books deposited in provincial and general archives of the Society of the Sacred Heart bear testimony to the ministry of the Jesuits in the communities, the schools and in the associations of past pupils (Children of Mary) in the course of Sophie Barat's lifetime.

When founding new communities and schools of the Society Sophie Barat appreciated if Jesuits were present in the country and could give the benefit of their experience and their support when planning a new project. She did not always agree with their views, nor accept their advice; at times she wished they would interfere less.[4] In preparation for the holding of General Councils of the Society or for advice in dealing with difficult issues, Sophie Barat consulted the Jesuit superior general in Rome, and as needed the Jesuit provincials in France, in Europe and North and South America and Canada.[5] As an international congregation the Jesuits had an extraordinary network which Sophie Barat called on regularly, though she carefully reserved her freedom to act in the best interests of the Society of the Sacred Heart. While her appreciation of the Jesuits is evident in her correspondence, she did not hide her personal views nor, despite her rhetoric, would she cede her independence.[6]

These qualities marked Sophie Barat's dealings with the clergy generally. Her experience as superior general from 1806 to 1865 taught her how to protect what she and her companions had created, and she consistently opposed the efforts of clerics to either interfere or try to take control of the Society. During the process for her canonisation, the devil's advocate accused Sophie Barat of being anti-clerical, citing as evidence her resistance to clerical authority.[7] This criticism was true to the extent that throughout her life Sophie Barat had to defend and safeguard both the Society of the Sacred Heart and her own authority with regard to two archbishops of Paris (from 1830 to 1848) several diocesan bishops and many priests, including Jesuits, who wished to assert their authority over the Society.[8] The task of procuring chaplains for the communities and schools was particularly difficult. Sophie Barat also had to intervene when clergy interfered and tried to take control of local communities, or remove her from office, or again when clergy attempted either to reform or refound the Society, or persuade a community to separate from the Society.[9] Nevertheless, while Sophie Barat learnt to be cautious of clergy in general, she readily recognised and appreciated that ties with the Jesuits were particularly significant in the life of the Society of the Sacred Heart from its origins in 1800.

Jesuit influences on the origins of the Society of the Sacred Heart

When the Society of the Sacred Heart was founded in 1800 the Jesuits did not exist as the order was suppressed in 1773 by Pope Clement XIV. However, several Jesuit influences stemming from France, the Hapsburg Empire and the kingdom of Piedmont-Sardinia played a part in the formative years of the Society. A first influence came through a French priest, Léonor de Tournély (1767–97), who formed an association of priests in 1792–3 which he called the Society of the Sacred Heart until such time when the Jesuits were restored in the church. His friend Joseph Varin joined the association which settled in Hagenbrunn, near Vienna.[10] In January 1796 de Tournély began to plan an association of women, also to be called the Society of the Sacred Heart. Like the priests' association, their inspiration would be drawn from the Jesuit rule but adapted, particularly to their non-clerical status.[11] The women would be contemplatives, involved in education and in nursing, but firmly cloistered, in accordance with the decrees of the Council of Trent. Initially the princess Louise-Adélaïde de Bourbon-Condé, abbess of Remiront in France and an émigrée in Austria, supported this venture.[12] Even though she withdrew from the project, de Tournély remained convinced that one day a women's association called the Society of the Sacred Heart would exist. He died suddenly in July 1797 and Joseph Varin was elected his successor.

In 1787 a second Jesuit influence came from Poitiers, in the west of France. There Susanne Geoffroy (1761–1845)[13] spoke to a former Jesuit in the town, Fr Drouard, about her desire to enter religious life. He advised her to wait. When she pressed him to be more explicit, he told her that in time she would enter an order, devoted to the Heart of Christ. He indicated that while its inspiration would originate in Germany, the order would be established in France, by a Frenchwoman:

> She who is destined to be the founder of this congregation in France is still playing with her dolls.[14]

Drouard had received this prediction from another former Jesuit in Poitiers, Charles Nectoux. Nectoux had foretold the horrors of the French Revolution, the growth of the counter-revolutionary movement and the triumph of religion (by the return of the Bourbons), all in highly apocalyptic terms. He described a future community of women in some detail, saying it would be devoted to the Sacred Heart, modelled on the Jesuits, and characterised by gentleness and humility.

A third Jesuit element in the origins of the Society of the Sacred Heart appeared in late eighteenth century Turin, in the kingdom of Piedmont-Sardinia. There Nicholas Diessbach (1732–98), a former Jesuit, trained spiritual elite of clergy and of lay men and women to help the Catholic Church survive the violent events let loose by the Revolution. Though based in Turin, Diessbach had entry to most of the courts of Europe including that of the Emperor Francis II in Vienna. The archduchess, Marie-Anne of Austria (1770–1809), sister of the emperor, and her ladies in waiting Léopoldine Naudet (1773–1834) and Louise Naudet (1770–c.1845) were attracted to religious life and adopted the Jesuit rule for their way of life. In time they would be called the Dilette di Gèsu and would found a community in Amiens in 1801.[15] Significantly, Diessbach met the priests of the Society of the Sacred Heart in Hagenbrunn, and so the intuition of Léonor de Tournély to found a Society of the Sacred Heart for women was passed on to Marie-Anne of Austria and the Naudet sisters.[16]

A fourth Jesuit element in the origins of the Society of the Sacred Heart came from Trent in the north of Italy, in the person of Nicholas Paccanari (1771–1811), then a layman. He established an association called the Fathers of the Faith, largely composed of former Jesuits and of new members who worked for the restoration of the Jesuits. Paccanari had the ear of Pope Pius VI.[17] When the Fathers of the Sacred Heart asked the pope for approval of their association, Pius VI asked them to merge with the Fathers of the Faith. Learning of Marie-Anne of Austria and the Naudet sisters, who sought a form of life inspired by the Jesuit rule, Paccanari provided a rule of life for an association of women to be called the Dilette di Gésu, (the Beloved of Jesus). The merger of Léonor de Tournély's association with the Fathers of the Faith took place in April 1799, and the Dilette di Gesù began as a community in Rome in June 1799.[18] By the following year the Fathers of the Faith and the Dilette di Gesù were ready for expansion into France, and Joseph Varin was charged with the task of heading that movement.

The four Jesuit influences came together in Paris in 1800 and impacted on Sophie Barat when she met Joseph Varin for the first time. Prior to her encounter with him she had decided to become a Carmelite, but this meeting led her to take another path, to Amiens to join the Dilette di Gèsu.[19] Events moved quickly, and to her own surprise in 1802 Sophie Barat was appointed leader of the community by Louise Naudet, then a delegate on a visit from Rome. This appointment was made against the views of Joseph Varin, who wanted an older woman appointed, and it signalled the beginning of a difficult relationship between Joseph Varin and Sophie Barat which was partially resolved in 1815, when Sophie Barat was confirmed as leader for life. Both maintained respect and even affection for one another, but in the course of their lives they often differed in their views. Nevertheless, Joseph Varin's key significance in the life of the Society of the Sacred Heart lay in his meeting with Sophie Barat in 1800 in Paris when he recounted Léonor de Tournély's intuition of a future Society of the Sacred Heart and the events which led to the founding of the Dilette di Gèsu. The presence of Joseph Varin at this key moment in the history of the Society was always acknowledged in public and in private by Sophie Barat and her companions.

Influence of the Jesuit Constitutions on the Society of the Sacred Heart, 1800–1815

In 1802 the little community at Amiens faced its first major crisis when the Dilette di Gèsu was dissolved, due to scandals in Rome surrounding the founder, Nicholas Paccanari.[20] Sophie Barat and her companions were left to find their own way forward. They decided a new name was necessary and chose to call themselves the Association of Ladies of Christian Instruction. The Association began to expand and new communities were created in Grenoble, Poitiers, Niort, Cuignières and Gand. As the communities evolved a power struggle developed within the community at Amiens, led by the chaplain, Louis de Sambucy Saint-Estève,[21] clearly intent on taking over the leadership of the Association. His power was increased when Joseph Varin, without consulting Sophie Barat, encouraged Saint-Estève to seek provisional approval of the Association from Napoleon. This was achieved in 1807, the same year that Napoleon suppressed the Fathers of the Faith as they were considered to be undercover Jesuits. Forced to flee Amiens, Varin, again without consulting Sophie Barat, asked Saint-Estève to write a rule of life for the Association.

Saint-Estève produced a text which was an amalgam of religious rules, with structures based on a monastic form of religious life. The spirituality of the Sacred Heart was not to be the focus of the Association, nor was the inspiration of Léonor de Tournély acknowledged. This was signalled when Saint-Estève and the community in Amiens began to celebrate their major feast as that of St Ursula, rather than the feast of the Sacred Heart. Clearly the Jesuit model of apostolic religious life had no place in this rule of life. Neither had Sophie Barat a place in Saint-Estève's plans, although he expected her to implement his rule of life in the communities. Placed in this position, Sophie Barat declared her instinctive resistance but agreed to discover the views of the membership beyond Amiens. Her intuitions were confirmed when one of the communities, in Gand, rejected Saint-Estève's work and withdrew from the Association. In search of a resolution to the impositions of Saint-Estève, Sophie Barat travelled to Besançon in 1812, where Joseph Varin had taken refuge, and placed before him the polarisation which had arisen in the Association and particularly in Amiens. He agreed with Sophie Barat that an alternative rule of life was necessary. Sophie then travelled to Paris and consulted with Jean Montaigne, rector of St Sulpice, and with Pierre de Clorivière, a former Jesuit. In the course of 1812 Sophie Barat, Joseph Varin, Jean Montaigne and Pierre de Clorivière met with Saint-Estève several times in Paris, but they failed to reach any consensus. Saint-Estève persisted in holding to his rule of life for the Association and departed for Rome to seek papal approval for it.

Sophie Barat then informed the five communities of the Association of this situation and in 1814 she decided to confront Saint-Estève directly herself. She wrote a formal letter to him in Rome, asking him to cease all negotiations there on their behalf. The communities of the Association, which she called the Society (for the first time), had made it clear that they wished to draft their own Constitutions and to hold their own General Council to decide their affairs:

> Indeed, to respond to the general desire of all the houses, with the exception of Amiens, which is less demanding on this point, *all* would prefer to have the rule of the Jesuit Institute adapted as far as possible for women, particularly since France has regained its freedom.
>
> There is still another point with which you must comply, concerning the name which we will adopt for the Society. You are aware that the [name] *Sacred Heart* has been agreed on by all with, it could be said, a kind of enthusiasm. It would be quite difficult to gain acceptance of another. So you will readily understand that, just as it is for the Society to submit its Constitutions to the Pope, it is also its responsibility to choose its name.[22]

Saint-Estève reacted immediately and informed Sophie of a conversation he claimed to have had with Pius VII in August 1814, regarding the question of women adopting the Jesuit Constitutions. Just as Urban VIII in the seventeenth century had rejected the efforts of Mary Ward, neither would the present pope allow women adopt Jesuit Constitutions. Nor would he permit Jesuits to become involved with religious women:

> My predecessors destroyed the Jesuitesses. I do not want them either,
> even less so the Ladies of the Faith.[23] I will never permit Jesuits to
> become involved with women religious; it is contrary to the rules of
> their founder.[24]

Saint-Estève also hinted that Jesuits in Rome were critical of Pierre de
Clorivière's involvement with groups of religious women in Paris,
including the Association of the Ladies of Christian Instruction at
Amiens.[25] Such innuendo and veiled threats on the part of Saint-Estève
were intended to stifle the wishes of the Association as expressed by
Sophie Barat, but they only helped to further clarify her position. With
growing sureness she wrote to the Jesuit provincial of Italy, Louis
Panazzoni:

> Allow me, on my own behalf and on behalf of my companions in
> four of the houses of the Society, as well as a large number of those in
> our fifth house [Amiens] (which has been under the guidance of M.
> de Sambucy) to beg you to persuade M. de Sambucy to suspend his
> proceedings. Ask him to wait until all minds and hearts are united
> by the common rules which the Society itself will ratify. It seems to
> me that our Society, having been founded for France and composed
> of French women, requires this delay in order to test what appears to
> be most suitable for it, in accordance with its goal, for the glory of
> God and the desire to bear the name of the Society of the Sacred
> Heart and be entirely devoted to this Sacred Heart.[26]

Clearly Sophie Barat, with the consent of most in the Association, was in
the process of decisively reclaiming the original vision of Léonor de
Tournély. For his part Joseph Varin responded to Saint-Estève's accusation, that the members of the Association wanted to be 'Jesuitesses'. He
reminded Saint-Estève:

> Your former friend, Mr L'abbé de Tournély, could and should be
> regarded as the original founder of this Society, since he initiated the
> project and the plan in Germany. Its realisation in France is truly
> only the result of that [impulse]. Mr de Tournély . . . never planned
> to have Jesuitesses, but only an association of women consecrated to
> the Sacred Heart and entirely devoted to education. They were to
> take from the rule of St Ignatius what would help them fulfil their
> goal. Thus, they are Dames du Sacré-Cœur and not Jesuitesses.[27]

At this juncture Sophie Barat recognised that the fundamental weakness
in her position was the absence of alternative Constitutions, which would
reflect how she and her companions wished to live. Work on this project
should have started in the winter and spring of 1814/15, but this had to

be deferred since Sophie was too ill. However, in early March 1815 she was well enough to travel to Paris and begin work on new Constitutions with Joseph Varin, Pierre de Clorivière and Julien Druilhet.[28] Even then, their work was soon interrupted by the dramatic return of Napoleon from exile which forced Louis XVIII to flee Paris. Napoleon's return to power proved to be short-lived, however, and the coalition of European powers completed his downfall at Waterloo on 18 June 1815. A certain political stability returned to Paris in the late summer of 1815 and Sophie Barat wrote to Pierre de Clorivière, suggesting that they meet that autumn. Uncertainty was creating unrest, and divisions within the communities were growing. Even Sophie Barat began to wonder if the project was viable at all and what decisions she personally might have to make:

> The remedy for this germ of division, which extends to nearly all the houses, is the one that you have recognised yourself. That is: to be in a position to offer members what most want, Constitutions drawn up according to the spirit of St Ignatius. This work, which everyone continually urges me to do, is the only thing which will stabilise the members, win back hearts and reunite minds. I admit that if I cannot hold on to the hope of seeing an end soon to our troubles, I do not know if I can in conscience continue to govern this Association.[29]

Sophie received a prompt reply from de Clorivière informing her that he and his colleagues were ready to resume work on the Constitutions.[30] By mid-September she had recovered sufficiently to return to Paris and work again with Joseph Varin, Pierre de Clorivière and Julien Druilhet until they finished the text of the new Constitutions. Although they leaned greatly on the Jesuit rule, rules of other congregations were also consulted, notably that of St Thomas de Villeneuve, the Ursulines and the royal school of St Cyr. The name 'Society of the Sacred Heart' was adopted throughout the text.[31] The next step was to have the new Constitutions formally accepted by the communities and Sophie Barat convened a General Council to meet in Paris in November 1815. There the new Constitutions were presented and explained to the representatives of the communities and were officially accepted by the General Council and Sophie Barat was confirmed as superior general for life.[32]

So concluded a tense period in the early history of the Society of the Sacred Heart. Led by Sophie Barat, it had evolved slowly, first from the dissolved community of the Dilette di Gèsu into the Association of Christian Education, and finally by 1815, when it officially took the name Society of the Sacred Heart. Several strands of Jesuit influence were woven into that journey, from the groups around Léonor de Tournély, Fr

Drouard, Nicholas Diessbach and Nicholas Paccanari. By 1815 the communities of women, led by Sophie Barat, had worked through many tensions and difficulties and found it possible to define their spiritual goals and assume their name. They now shared common roots and experiences and many lasting friendships had been forged. Similarly with the Fathers of the Faith. Many of them, including Sophie Barat's brother, Louis, entered the restored Jesuits in Paris in 1814. In the future the paths of the Society of the Sacred Heart and the Jesuits would interweave again many times. The familiarity of their shared experiences would sustain some of their relationships, and in time their differences would also become more marked.[33] But there was always respect and appreciation and acknowledgement of the past. Indeed, as the events of 1812–15 unfolded, Joseph Varin admitted seeing Sophie Barat as it were for the first time, in charge and exercising leadership effectively.[34]

Jesuit influence on the Society of the Sacred Heart after 1815

To consolidate the work of the 1815 General Council Sophie Barat and her companions decided to obtain papal approval for the Constitutions. It took some years to prepare a final text, and in 1824 Sophie asked a Jesuit in Rome, Jean Rozaven (1772–1851),[35] for advice on how to proceed. Neither had met, even though Rozaven had been a Father of the Faith until 1804. That year he joined the Jesuits in Russia[36] and ministered in St Petersburg. He returned to France in 1815 when the Jesuits were expelled from Russia and went to Rome in 1820 as the Jesuit assistant general for France. He was also a member of the Roman Curia and worked in the section concerning religious life.

Rozaven agreed to advise Sophie but on the condition that his role remained private. He underlined that it was crucial that Jesuits were not seen to be involved in the process, and he warned Sophie that in the minds of some in Rome the Society of the Sacred Heart and the Jesuits had become over-identified:

> The Jesuits certainly ought to be willing to help you in every way, according to our Constitutions. But, as you well know, you are under particular scrutiny and we are as well. In certain quarters it was widely believed that your order had a special relationship with us. In Chambéry, for example, were you not called 'Jesuitesses'? It was difficult for us to quell these rumours and the fathers [Jesuits] had to withdraw completely [from the Society of the Sacred Heart]. The same thing could happen in other places, too. In Amiens[37] there were

far too many contacts between the Jesuits and the members of the Society of the Sacred Heart. [They had] visits, meals together. Did it not transpire that one of your religious took arithmetic or history lessons, I do not know which, from someone who neither should nor could take on that kind of task?[38]

However, in 1824 Jean Rozaven had his own reasons for helping Sophie Barat receive papal approval for the 1815 Constitutions. During his years in St Petersburg, Rozaven had received the Princess Galitzine into the Roman Catholic Church. This conversion to Roman Catholicism was momentous since generations of the Galitzine family had served the Tsars and the family belonged to the Russian Orthodox Church.[39] Rozaven's contacts with Elizabeth Galitzine continued when he left Russia in 1815 and in 1824 she asked him to recommend an order she could enter in Paris.[40] Rozaven suggested the Society of the Sacred Heart.[41]

Tensions ensued around Elizabeth Galitzine's entry which signalled a changing relationship between the Society of the Sacred Heart and Jesuits. Rozaven instructed Sophie Barat on how to deal with his pro-tégée, even prior to her entry. He decided how Elizabeth Galitzine would administer her substantial fortune, especially the dowry she would give the Society of the Sacred Heart, despite Sophie Barat's express wish that Elizabeth Galitzine act in her own right.[42] Again, when Sophie asked Elizabeth Galitzine to continue her studies in view of the educational work she would do in the Society, and in particular the study of history, geography, literature and grammar, Rozaven opposed it. And although Sophie protested that studies were important in the Society of the Sacred Heart, Rozaven had his way.[43] His opinion of the place of women in society, especially of religious women, was quite clear: it belonged to the private sphere. He was openly critical of education in the Society of the Sacred Heart:[44]

> My thoughts on Madame Barat and her Society are quite close to yours, as you can judge from what I said to your sister. I think there is a bit too much grandeur (éclat) about its work, and while humility is not lacking in those who are in charge, the Society does not seem to have a sufficiently solid base. What I particularly dislike are these public examinations, which take place in their boarding schools. I find these totally out of place and not without pitfalls for both pupils and teachers.
>
> I can see neither necessity, nor useful purpose in a young girl, whose shyness and reserve ought to be her attraction, appearing in public and speaking with ease in the presence of one hundred or more people, only one of whom is her mother. All that she can gain

from this are vain plaudits for which she will pay dearly, if as a result her modesty should suffer and vanity find a place in her heart. I do not like when a young woman draws attention to herself. I would rather that her merits were ignored or remained unknown, except by those on whom she relies for her own happiness.[45]

Sophie Barat kept her counsel until Elizabeth Galitzine entered the noviceship of the Society. Then a deep silence descended. Rozaven received no information regarding the progress of Elizabeth Galitzine and he complained bitterly about his loss of contact.[46] But Sophie Barat quietly made it clear that she would retain her independence and put limits on interference in the life of the Society. At the same time, however, it was a delicate moment in view of Rozaven's agreement to help in the negotiations for papal approval of the 1815 Constitutions. To his credit, Jean Rozaven continued to help that process and in 1827 the Society of the Sacred Heart received formal papal approval of its C onstitutions.

The Society of the Sacred Heart and the Jesuits in Rome

While the negotiations for approval were in progress Sophie Barat voiced the possibility of a foundation of the Society in Rome and this was enthusiastically taken up by Jean Rozaven.[47] He and a fellow-Jesuit, Georgio Massa, approached Leo XII to suggest that he invite Sophie Barat to found a school for young Italian noblewomen in Rome. The pope agreed and conveyed his wish to the papal nuncio in Paris, Luigi Lambruschini.[48] Accordingly, in 1828 Sophie Barat received an invitation to found a house in Rome at the Trinité des Monts, a property owned by the French government. While it agreed to permit the Society to found a school in Rome in the Trinité des Monts, the French government insisted on strict accountability to the French ambassador in Rome and that the superior of the community should always be a Frenchwoman.[49]

Sophie Barat appointed Armande de Causans, then superior at Turin, to begin the foundation in Rome. On her arrival there in 1828 de Causans discovered that the Society of the Sacred Heart was assumed to be associated in some way with the Jesuits. She welcomed this, convinced it would help the Society become accepted in Italy. Meeting Cardinal Ostini soon after her arrival, she noted his enthusiasm for the Institute of the Sacred Heart, 'entirely modelled . . . on the Jesuits'.[50] Sophie Barat commented in a letter to Philippine Duchesne:

> They want to put us on the same level as the Society of Jesus. Is this possible for women? Time will tell.[51]

Sophie Barat had never considered any incorporation of the Society of the Sacred Heart with the Jesuits. But after the Society received formal approbation of its Constitutions in 1827, she asked the general of the Jesuits, Aloysius Fortis, for a form of spiritual affiliation with the Jesuits. She hoped this would strengthen the spiritual life of the Society of the Sacred Heart.[52] The Jesuit general's response came in September 1828, which Rozaven gave to Armande de Causans. She commented:

> Father Rozaven undoubtedly drew up the document, or at least negotiated it for us. He told me that each house should have a copy of it and keep it carefully hidden away. Prudence is necessary in such matters and more than ever in the times we live in.[53]

But Sophie Barat was aware that too close an identification of the Society of the Sacred Heart with the Jesuits could create problems for her. She was disappointed that a possible foundation in Florence had been refused in 1833 by Louise de Limminghe (then superior at Turin) simply because there were no Jesuits there. Sophie chided her for such lack of judgement, and said it simply was not true that the Society of the Sacred Heart existed only in towns where there were Jesuit communities:

> It is not at all necessary that there be Jesuit houses where we are established. There are many towns in France where this is not so. We get on quite well [without them], and I would even say that in these cases the Jesuits are freer to help us.[54]

The Jesuits and the Trinité des Monts, Rome

Once the new community had assembled in the Trinité des Monts Jean Rozaven was continually present. He supervised the extensive renovations necessary in the monastery and made detailed arrangements for the community and school, even to setting the school fees (which was reduced by the pope who found them too high). He organised audiences with the pope, with cardinals and bishops, as well as visits to the Gesù, the Jesuit church in Rome. While Armande de Causans admitted that Rozaven was helpful in the early days in the Trinité, she found his manner austere and forbidding. He was clearly used to being obeyed without question:

> Fr Rozaven has many of the qualities of Fr Sellier [a Jesuit in Paris].[55] They both have hearts which no human affection, however little, can touch. Nevertheless, the latter still lets slip some lively and vivacious characteristics which allow you to see human goodness combined with and transformed into burning love. But in the case of Fr

Rozaven, human nature is only born to die, whether we do it willingly or by force.[56]

Jean Rozaven once acknowledged wryly to Joseph Varin that he knew his personal manner was 'dry and cold, more likely to cause fear than inspire some trust'.[57] Yet Armande de Causans noted a chink in this armour of austerity. She observed Rozaven's absorption with Elizabeth Galitzine and remarked dryly to Sophie:

> For his [spiritual] daughter Elizabeth . . . I suspect he has a little weakness, but it is the only one. Apparently she is worthy of it.[58]

Certainly Elizabeth Galitzine's letters to Jean Rozaven were his pride and joy, and he showed them to Armande de Causans, ostensibly to encourage her in the way of perfection. This only irritated her.[59] Nevertheless, Armande de Causans recognised from the beginning that she needed Rozaven's cooperation to succeed in Rome. It soon became clear that the Trinité des Monts, a French foundation in the city, would not be sufficient for the Society to root itself on Italian soil. Supported by Rozaven she asked Sophie Barat to allow her to found a poor school and a noviceship, independent of the Trinité:

> This noviceship house (between you and me) is of greater consequence to the Society than the foundation of the Trinité . . . In brief, it will complete the task of making us more like the Jesuits, in the eyes of the public as well as in fact.[60]

When Gregory XVI was concerned that a poor school and noviciate would lead to a confrontation with the French government, both Armande de Causans and Jean Rozaven wrote a justification of the Society's request to have a poor school. They explained that it was an integral part of the Society's practice to have schools for the aristocracy and for the poor, if possible on the same property, but certainly in the vicinity. They assured the pope that a poor school and noviciate would consolidate the work of the school at the Trinité and serve the poor in Rome.[61]

Influence of Jean Rozaven in the Society of the Sacred Heart

From the early years of the foundation of the Trinité there were warning signs that Jean Rozaven had assumed he had the right to interfere in the internal life of the Society, not just in Rome. This was indicated in 1832 when he and Elizabeth Galitzine urged Sophie Barat to reprove Natalie

Rostopchine, a member of the Society at the rue de Varenne in Paris. She was a Russian émigré whose reported criticisms of the Tsar had led to difficulties for recent converts to Catholicism in St Petersburg. Eugénie de Gramont, superior at the rue de Varenne, resented this intervention on their part and commented on the growing influence of Jean Rozaven in the Society of the Sacred Heart.[62]

In the circumstances this was inevitable. Just as Sophie Barat had sought Rozaven's help in 1824 when seeking papal approval of the 1815 Constitutions, so after the 1833 General Council of the Society, Sophie Barat consulted him again on how to modify the structures of government contained in the same Constitutions. Some changes were required in order to deal with the Society's rapid expansion and the steady increase in the membership. Sophie Barat considered adopting the Jesuit model of government and dividing the Society into geographical areas (provinces), with leaders (provincials) appointed by her. She had also begun to weigh up the advantage of residing in Rome rather than Paris, as a signal of international growth and to gain a certain independence from Paris. She had adequate time to reflect on these possibilities since any modifications to the 1815 Constitutions could only be passed at the next General Council, due in 1839. To this purpose Sophie Barat set up a small group to plan for this council, and as secretary general of the Society, elected to this office by the 1833 General Council, Elizabeth Galitzine became part of the group.[63]

Rozaven responded to Sophie Barat's request for advice by inviting her to Rome, suggesting she bring along some members of the Society for the discussions.[64] This process began in 1835 and gave Rozaven even more involvement in the life of the Society of the Sacred Heart. It happened just at the time when questions arose in Rome concerning how cloister was observed in the Trinité des Monts which led to serious tensions between the Society and the Jesuits.

Growing tensions between the Jesuits and the Society of the Sacred Heart 1833–1838

From its origin in 1534 Jesuits were advised in the course of their ministry to be cautious in their relationships with women, lay and religious. Yet, arising out of the shared history of the Fathers of the Faith and Dilette di Gesù in Amiens, during the dangerous days of the Revolution and Empire, a bond had been created between the first generation of Jesuits in Paris and the Society of the Sacred Heart. It was different in Italy and while the superior general of the Jesuits, Jan Roothaan,[65] recognised the historical background regarding the Society of the Sacred Heart and the Jesuits in France, in 1833 he explained to Louise de Limminghe why the Jesuit community in Turin could not respond to all her requests for spiritual help in the community and school:

> Because of the relationship between some Jesuits in France with the Society of the Sacred Heart, many other countries began to consider the Society of the Sacred Heart as a kind of branch of the Jesuits. I do not know if this view at all pleases the Society of the Sacred Heart, but it most certainly is not acceptable to the Jesuits.

Roothaan also underlined how strict St Ignatius was concerning contacts Jesuits had with cloistered women religious, and would have been no less severe with regard to:

> *houses that have no cloister.* I am certain that if St Ignatius had not established his rule for all religious women, one would have been created in the Society of Jesus for the Society of the Sacred Heart.[66]

The issue brought up by Roothaan regarding cloister for women was important in Italy where it was observed according to strict rules laid down at the Council of Trent in the sixteenth century.[67] In France, by contrast, religious life had been suppressed during the Revolution and Sophie Barat successfully negotiated papal approval of the 1815 Constitutions which included a mitigation of cloister. In the context of the time, and especially in Rome, this was considered quite a radical innovation.[68] A clash of interpretation around this form of cloister, which had been negotiated for a French congregation, became inevitable when the Society founded a house in Turin in 1823. There the archbishop, Mgr Chiavarotti, tried to impose full papal cloister on the Society. This led to endless disputes between him and the local superior, Armande de Causans, and he threatened to excommunicate her. Pope Gregory XVI held the same views and made no secret of his preference for strict papal cloister for women according to the decrees of the Council of Trent. Yet when he met Sophie Barat in Rome in 1832 he did not ask her to change the 1815 Constitutions, accepting that the Society was an apostolic, not a monastic, religious community.

When Armande de Causans left Turin in 1828 to lead the foundation at the Trinité des Monts in Rome, she did not expect that the Society's observance of cloister would be an issue there:

> What a fuss they created in Turin over the question of cloister! I was happy to see that my view on the issue is in accord with yours, and that your opinion is to accede only to the actual circumstances as

they exist. Otherwise, what repercussions! We would place ourselves in a situation which would incur or bring about excommunications. These dreadful laws only concern orders which observe full [papal] cloister.[69]

However, as the Society of the Sacred Heart became more established in Rome the difference between the French and the Italian interpretation of cloister for women religious became more apparent. Some disapproved of Sophie Barat's practice of walking unaccompanied between the three houses of the Society in Rome. Catherine de Charbonnel, an assistant general of the Society, noted during a visit to Rome in 1834 how the Society was criticised for not observing Tridentine cloister and for having young superiors. Members of the Society were:

> religious women who describe themselves as cloistered though they have no grills. They travel abroad without a chaplain, and become superiors of houses before they are at least forty years of age, etc, etc. All this seems abnormal and almost suspect to them. Even details of the way we live contrasts with some customs [here].[70]

Sophie Barat found the strict interpretation of cloister in Italy difficult to understand:

> Grills. Nothing will ever replace them in their eyes! This only happens in Italy. What would they do anywhere else with grills?[71]

But opinions in Rome could not be ignored. Although Armande de Causans had made useful contacts with the church authorities and the Roman nobility, she had also made some enemies. News of her previous conflict with the archbishop of Turin followed her to Rome.[72] By 1838 the issue had become acute and criticism of the Society in Rome was focussed on Armande de Causans and the community at the Trinité. That year Louise de Limminghe and Jean Rozaven, along with some Jesuits in Rome, urged Sophie Barat to remove Armande de Causans from her post in the Trinité des Monts. Sophie happened to be in Rome then and while she accepted the gravity of the situation she resisted their pressure to dismiss Armande de Causans. She preferred instead to speak with Armande de Causans and plan a decision with her. Unfortunately this time was not available as urgent affairs in Paris forced Sophie to leave Rome quickly in May 1838 and she left Louise de Limminghe in charge of the Roman houses.[73] She cautioned her to act prudently:

> What are you going to do, and what decision will you make to remove these two [Armande de Causans, and her assistant,

[Euphrosine Faux] from the Trinité? Confer with the Fathers [Jesuits] again. It is not possible to send them away until they are replaced.[74]

But events overtook any amicable resolution. In July 1838 the Jesuits in Rome announced that they would not minister to the community at the Trinité, assuming that this decision would force the issue. In an effort to find a solution before the problem became intractable, Sophie asked Louise de Limminghe to go to the Trinité and talk to Armande de Causans and Josephine de Coriolis, headmistress of the school, and try to reach some accommodation with the Jesuits.[75] This public breakdown of relations could damage the reputation of the Society of the Sacred Heart in Rome:

> How sad it is that these petty disagreements have broken out between the two houses (the Trinité and the Villa Lante), and even between the most intimate friends (the Jesuits)! We should bear many painful things in silence, for with patience and the help of God they will be resolved. On the other hand, when hearts are aggrieved nothing can heal the wounds, and if these miseries come to light you know the consequences! So do all you can to reconcile both sides.[76]

The pressure and criticism led Armande de Causans and Euphrosine Faux, and the headmistress of the school, Josephine de Coriolis, to consider separating the Trinité des Monts from the Society, thereby creating an independent foundation. They discussed this with Gregory XVI and Cardinal Luigi Lambruschini, the secretary of state.[77] This is what Sophie Barat had wished to avoid and she was astounded to learn that Louise de Limminghe had not gone to visit the community in the Trinité, a short walk from the Villa Lante in the Trastevere across the Tiber:

> What! Did you leave them in their pain and humiliation and not visit them, speak to them, encourage them to contact the Jesuits? Is that what charity is? Had they been even more at fault you would still have had to forget everything and take the first steps towards them.
>
> This is not the way that you should support my authority and make it loved. You are well aware of my style of government and you criticise any who follow it. No, I will never condemn anyone without hearing them out, and I will not permit the extreme measures suggested to me. You yourself should have inclined gradually towards indulgence, but instead you follow the severe measures which the Jesuits proposed. I am deeply distressed by all this.[78]

By August 1838 Sophie Barat had lost patience with the Jesuits in Rome.[79] They had taken a position with regard to the Trinité community which she could not approve of in any way. She warned Louise de Limminghe:

> Maintain your independence, and imagine what I would do or what
> I would say in such and such a circumstance. Always seek advice, but
> be sure that it is in tune with my way of thinking. I assure you that it
> is not because I think that my advice is the best. Far from it, but God
> has promised me the help my responsibility demands. Because of this
> I advise you to follow my ideas and my way of acting.[80]

In an effort to resolve the impasse, Louise de Limminghe suggested that the Society in Italy observe the rules of cloister according to the Council of Trent. This Sophie Barat resolutely refused to even consider.[81] As far as she was concerned, the real issue for the Society was union between the communities in Rome, and an end to gossip and rumour concerning the Society, stemming especially from the Jesuits. Then to her dismay, Sophie then learnt that Gregory XVI had authorised Jean Rozaven to appoint a priest to make an ecclesiastical visitation of the Trinité community. His brief was to examine the quality of religious life and observance there, with a particular focus on the question of observance of cloister. While Gregory XVI may have authorised the visitation of the Trinité, Sophie had no doubt that it was Rozaven who had drawn the attention of the pope to the controversy and suggested the punishment. Sophie's reaction was swift:

> This is a blow for us in Rome. God's will be done! What surprises me
> is Fr Rozaven's choice of inquisitor. Exactly who is this priest?[82]

But Armande de Causans was not without powerful friends in Rome, especially among the cardinals. Cardinal Lambruschini, secretary of state, was a frequent visitor at the Trinité and his presence there increased notably that autumn. Sophie knew this and she had to tread a diplomatic tightrope carefully.[83]

Rozaven then proposed his compromise to Sophie Barat, that Armande de Causans remain in the Trinité but no longer hold the office of superior.[84] Sophie replied that the last thing she would permit was a public humiliation of Armande de Causans, either by demoting her or by forcing her to leave the Trinité in disgrace. If she left Rome she would leave with dignity and good standing. Rozaven rejected Sophie Barat's views and openly criticised her leadership in Rome. But Sophie spoke her mind:

> If Fr Rozaven is not pleased with us, I have to say here and now that
> I am not very pleased with him in this affair. This good priest hardly

considers my position nor does he even understand the situation of the Trinité. Besides I am following my conscience and I am at peace in this. I am convinced that if we hold to our plan that Madame de Causans will leave the Trinité, this in time will happen.

I assure you that while our friends [Jesuits] render us services, which I certainly appreciate, they also cause us an amount of problems by their dictates. When there are only two or three months to wait, we need to be patient and so avoid endless difficulties and unpredictable consequences.[85]

Despairing of reconciliation, Sophie Barat asked the Jesuits to withdraw from their involvement in the three houses of the Society in Rome. In any event, she was convinced that the Society could not survive such sustained criticism much longer:

It is they [the Jesuits] who will destroy everything, and all through lacking a bit more patience and forbearance. I confess that I would not like to be responsible for this situation.[86]

The impasse ended dramatically. Finally weary of the endless controversy, Armande de Causans and Euphrosine Faux packed their bags and left the Trinité during the night of 7 December 1838. They had planned their exit carefully, had informed the pope, the secretary of state, Lambruschini, and the French ambassador to the Holy See beforehand, but not Sophie Barat. She learnt the news some days later in Paris and commented:

You realise that from the beginning I foresaw the imprudence of the Jesuits. It is done now. They wanted to help, that is true, but the damage is great. Consider very carefully how we may repair the damage. [Tell] the Jesuits that union exists among us etc, so that they see that the Trinité and the two other houses are as one. It is advisable to deny anything to the contrary on this important point, or all is lost! But it is clear that the Jesuits have done us harm.[87]

Jesuit influence on the General Council of the Society, Rome 1839

While the dispute concerning the Trinité des Monts deepened, it was only a prelude to a much deeper crisis between the Society and the Jesuits in 1839, but this time it had a wider context and impact. Partly because of the crisis of leadership at the Trinité, and partly due to the situation in Paris at this time, Sophie Barat decided to hold the General Council in Rome, and not as usual in Paris.[88] Between 1835 and 1839 proposed modifications to government structures in the Society had been drawn up by Jean Rozaven, Louise de Limminghe and Elizabeth Galitzine, based on the Jesuit model. When the General Council opened in July 1839 Sophie Barat asked Jean Rozaven to present the proposed changes to the delegates. Her expectations for change in the Society were quite specific, and she described them in the winter of 1838 as 'a few changes and structures which the growth of the Society requires'.[89] The essential changes Sophie Barat sought were the creation of provinces and provincials in the Society, and discussion of the possibility of her residence in Rome. However, her goals differed from the bigger designs of Elizabeth Galitzine, Louise de Limminghe and Jean Rozaven. They planned to bring the Society of the Sacred Heart into much closer incorporation with the Jesuits and they presented their fuller plans to the delegates with enthusiasm and conviction. After three weeks of discussion their proposed modifications to the 1815 Constitutions were accepted unreservedly by the delegates. How such changes would be received by the body of the Society was quickly revealed.[90]

News of the General Council's decisions travelled fast and was heard with dismay in France. A founding member of the Society, Genevieve Deshayes, asked Sophie had anyone:

> ever ordered a Dominican to become a Carmelite? Or a Jesuit to become a Capuchin? The pope would not force adherence or impose his authority by coercion, without the possibility of objecting to the Decrees which a small group of councillors drew up, approved and declared to be obligatory on all . . . They wish us to be perfect and suggest, or rather direct, that we imitate the Jesuit Constitutions. We are not challenging those Constitutions, but everything has its own perfect form, each religious order its own spirit. Women are not men and France is not Italy.[91]

Joseph Varin reacted strongly and stated that the 1839 General Council was a deviation from the original vision of Léonor de Tournély. In a letter to Sophie Barat in August 1839 he expressed his astonishment, and in Paris he spoke openly of his opposition to the decisions of the Council.[92] In October 1839 Clement Boulanger, a Jesuit in Paris, wrote to Jean Roothaan and criticised the involvement of Jean Rozaven in the affairs of the Society of the Sacred Heart.[93] He argued that such indiscretions compromised the Jesuits in the eyes of the French bishops, most of whom in any event were critical of Sophie Barat's proposed residence in Rome. He also asserted that neither the French bishops nor the French government would accept the plan to incorporate the Society of the Sacred Heart more fully with the Jesuits; nor would they accept that Sophie Barat, like the Jesuit superior general, should live in Rome.

Roothaan asked Rozaven to write to the Jesuit provincial in Paris, Achille Guidée, and answer the charges made by Boulanger. In his letter to Guidée, Rozaven presented his actions as both minimal and secondary and in his own defence he was economical with the truth. He admitted that he had been approached by the Society of the Sacred Heart during the 1839 General Council, yet made no mention of the years of discussion prior to that date, nor of his links with Elizabeth Galitzine and with Louise de Limminghe in Rome. He confirmed that the decrees of the General Council had been communicated to him, but omitted to say that he had been present during the sessions of the Council and that he had presented documentation on the proposed new structures of government:

> I have a clear conscience and I am not worried about what they say. What does it matter to me that someone exaggerates and says *that I have overpowered the mother general and some others, and that I have imposed what I wanted on them*? I would laugh at this nonsense . . . the enemy of all good is seeking to kindle the fire of discord in a congregation from which the church expects great results . . .[94]

Guidée accepted this explanation:

> So you have refuted the absurd fantasy of Mme XXX [Elizabeth Galitzine] who alleges that Fr Rozaven intends to appoint a Jesuit as superior and confessor of each house of the Society of the Sacred Heart. You know how fertile an imagination this good lady has in creating fanciful ideas, but this one is too much and exceeds the limits of ridicule and absurdity.[95]

But Roothaan was uneasy at how the Jesuits were being dragged into the affairs of the Society of the Sacred Heart, and he asked that Jesuits cease contacts with any community or member of the Society of the Sacred Heart:

> I have known for years that the seeds of division existed among these women, that with their present *form* of government this division seemed inevitably to perpetuate and bring about deplorable consequences. At least that is what is said, and for that reason the mother general, on the advice of several of her councillors, thought a congregation [General Council] should be held.[96]

But Elizabeth Galitzine persisted in seeking fuller incorporation of the Society of the Sacred Heart with the Jesuits. At the 1839 General Council

she was elected as an assistant general of the Society, provincial of
Louisiana, while continuing in office as secretary general of the Society,
an extraordinary combination of roles. In December 1841, while on a
visit to Grand Coteau, Louisiana, Elizabeth Galitzine made a retreat given
by a Jesuit, John de Theux.[97] She told Sophie that during it:

> It came to me in prayer that in order to save the Society and to con-
> solidate its form of government once and for all, the mother general,
> like St Ignatius, should make a special vow of allegiance to the Holy
> See. All the mothers general ought to make this vow personally into
> the hands of the pope, and offer the Society [of the Sacred Heart] to
> his Holiness so that he can deploy the professed members of the
> Society for whatever mission he designates. The professed members
> of the Society will also make a vow to be ready to go wherever the
> Holy Father sends them.[98]

She also proposed that the superior general of the Society of the Sacred
Heart submit all decisions to the superior general of the Jesuits, since the
pope could not personally direct the Society of the Sacred Heart in every
detail of its life. In this way the Society of the Sacred Heart would be
protected:

> by the court of Rome and by the Society of Jesus. The Society of the
> Sacred Heart in fact will be dependent upon the Society of Jesus but
> without the formal title as such. In this way, all can be settled
> amicably, the Company of Jesus cannot take any offence at all.[99]

What was proposed originally by Sophie Barat as necessary changes for
good governance in the Society of the Sacred Heart had developed
rapidly into clashes of unimagined proportions. While the plan to introduce provinces and provincials was accepted generally in the Society of
the Sacred Heart, the question of Sophie Barat's residence became controversial within and without the Society. Many in the Society were
prepared to support the possible change of residence of the superior
general, and could see the reasons for it. For one, Rome was the centre of
Catholicism and the Society was fast becoming an international congregation. In addition, Sophie Barat's residence in Rome could
counterbalance the influence of the French bishops, especially the archbishops of Paris, as well as the dominance of the community in the rue
de Varenne in Paris, especially Eugénie de Gramont. Yet this proposal
that Sophie Barat should live in Rome threatened to split the Society
apart and involve the Jesuits in the dispute, both in Rome and Paris, as
well as the might of the French government. The situation very quickly

became politicised.[100] Tensions between Gallicanism and Ultramontanism, between the papacy and the archbishops of Paris, were played through in this internal crisis in the Society of the Sacred Heart and threatened its legal existence in France.

Initially neither Sophie Barat, Louise de Limminghe, Elizabeth Galitzine nor indeed Jean Rozaven saw the implications of having the residence of the superior general outside France. But they were clear to the archbishop of Paris, Denys-Auguste Affre (1793–1848) who informed the French government of Sophie Barat's proposal to move her residence to Rome. In the eyes of the government, the Society of the Sacred Heart was a French foundation, authorised by the royal ordinance of April 1827. The statutes of that ordinance declared that the 'Superior General lives in the main house in Paris', meaning the rue de Varenne.[101] The French government, always sensitive to the encroachments of any foreign power, especially that of Rome, promptly notified Sophie Barat that if she moved her residence to Rome, it would instantly suppress the forty-three houses of the Society in France.

In contrast, Ultramontane thinking considered the possibility of Sophie Barat's residence in Rome as entirely positive. In addition to signalling the Society's international status, it would also mitigate Gallican influences in the Society, especially in the community at rue de Varenne in Paris which since 1830 had given hospitality to the archbishop of Paris. However, within this Ultramontane position more extreme views were held by a few in the Society, especially by Elizabeth Galitzine. Her Russian origins and the price she paid for her conversion to Roman Catholicism led her to take this position. She actually welcomed the threat of the French government to suppress the foundations in France as the price of establishing the Society of the Sacred Heart beyond the confines of Gallicanism. She admired the Jesuits, was devoted to Jean Rozaven, and they both wished to associate the Society of the Sacred Heart as closely as possible with the Jesuits.

Resolution of the impasse 1842–1843

It was left to Sophie Barat to find a middle path between such polarities. In September 1842 she contacted an old friend, Césaire Mathieu, archbishop of Besançon, to discuss how to deal with the impasse. With his help, and that of the papal nuncio in Paris, Antonio Garibaldi, and the secretary of state in Rome, Luigi Lambruschini, Sophie Barat negotiated a compromise. To avoid confrontation with the French government and to safeguard the houses in France, Sophie agreed to retain her residence in France. Mgr Garibaldi conveyed this decision to the Minister of Religion, Jean-Baptiste Teste who accepted the resolution on behalf of the government and passed on the information to the French ambassador in Rome. Teste, who had on occasion lodged with the Jesuits in Rome, was aware of the influence some Jesuits exercised in the Society of the Sacred Heart. He drafted a letter for the superior general, Jan Roothaan, ready to be sent if the Jesuits in Rome blocked the resolution reached by Sophie Barat:

> If the Society of the Sacred Heart falls, the whole wrath of the French bishops and others would fall on the Jesuits, and their houses too could be suppressed. The letter is quite lengthy and well composed and contains matters which are very true, capable of making an impression and striking fear.[102]

Clement Boulanger, now provincial of the Jesuits in Paris, wrote to Roothaan and warned him that the involvement of Rozaven in the affairs of the Society of the Sacred Heart had greatly compromised the Jesuits in France, especially in Paris. Boulanger also informed the general that Archbishop Affre was irked by the support that his Jesuit colleague in Paris, Nicholas Loriquet, gave the Society of the Sacred Heart, especially in the field of education. He suggested that the Jesuits both in Rome and Paris keep their distance from the Society of the Sacred Heart.[103] At the same time Paul Tharin, former archbishop of Strasbourg, wrote to Roothaan:

> Without meaning to do it, in actual fact several of your Jesuits have brought this valued and effective Society [of the Sacred Heart] to the brink of destruction.[104]

Tharin warned Roothaan that the French bishops held Jean Rozaven particularly responsible for pushing through far more sweeping changes during the 1839 General Council than Sophie Barat had ever envisaged.[105] The influence of the Jesuits in the Roman Curia was well known at this time, and especially Rozaven's power over Cardinal Pedicini, the cardinal protector of the Society of the Sacred Heart. Tharin warned that if the compromise resolution, already agreed on in France, was not accepted in Rome, then blame would fall on the Jesuits. Roothaan responded with his view on the situation, arguing that for some years he had been trying to lessen contacts between the Jesuits and the Society of the Sacred Heart. Then, surprisingly, he admitted that he himself had got involved with the preparations for the General Council of the Society of the Sacred Heart in 1839, but never imagined that some members of the

Society of the Sacred Heart would take matters to such extreme lengths. In addition, he admitted that neither he nor Rozaven understood the implications of the agreement with the French government, enshrined in the statutes signed by the Society of the Sacred Heart in 1827. This was strange, since Rozaven had been involved in the process for seeking papal approval of the 1815 Constitutions of the Society of the Sacred Heart in 1826–7. Furthermore, Roothaan insisted that Rozaven only gave advice to the Society of the Sacred Heart, that he did not compose or sign the 1839 decrees. In frustration Roothaan admitted:

> I want to have nothing more to write about the Society of the Sacred Heart. I have always thought that women religious are like the vine which needs complete support. Their role cannot be like that of men. There have never been women Jesuits.
>
> Yet how can an order of women religious, dispersed in dioceses, with a superior general, remain at the same time in customary dependence on local bishops? There I admit we have a problem which I do not know how to resolve.[106]

On the other hand, the French ambassador to the Holy See, the marquis de Latour-Maurbourg, and the archbishop of Besançon, Césaire Mathieu, were convinced that Roothaan never knew the full extent of Rozaven's involvement in the affairs of the Society of the Sacred Heart. Writing to the Minister of Religion in Paris in November 1842, the ambassador indicated that most in Rome considered that the Society of the Sacred Heart had been badly advised by the Jesuits, particularly Jean Rozaven.[107] For her part, Sophie Barat knew very well that both Louise de Limminghe and Elizabeth Galitzine were at the centre of a strong lobby within the Society in favour of the 1839 decrees. The papal nuncio in Paris, Antonio Garibaldi, commented to cardinal Lambruschini, secretary of state in Rome:

> Mother Barat said that the agitation of the religious in France stems in particular from the belief that they [the lobby] have support in Rome, that the superior general [Sophie Barat] is disapproved of there, and that the Holy Father and Your Eminence wish the enforcement of the [1839] decrees, especially . . . the residence of the superior general in Rome. Mother Barat believes that these ideas were formed by Mother de Limminghe, and by a religious from the illustrious society, Father Rozaven.[108]

Sophie Barat admitted that she had managed the General Council of 1839 badly and that this had weakened her authority in the Society and left her leadership open to criticism.[109] Jean Rozaven was openly dismissive of Sophie Barat's style of leadership and his comments damaged her reputation in Rome. He also harmed her reputation in France. In October 1842, writing to the archbishop of Bordeaux, Ferdinand Donnet (1837–82), he criticised Sophie for postponing a General Council due to be held in Lyon in August 1842. He saw no contradiction in admitting that in fact the Council could not be held, since Cardinal de Bonald (under pressure from Archbishop Affre) had suddenly withdrawn his permission to hold it in his diocese. Rozaven also condemned Sophie Barat for returning to Paris to negotiate with both Archbishop Affre and the French government, and deal with the community at the rue de Varenne:

> Here [in Rome] it is regretted that the superior general no longer has the strength and energy to maintain her authority. Indecision and weakness have placed her in a difficult position from which she will have difficulty in extricating herself. Fear and faint-heartedness are poor counsellors. [She] has allowed herself to be intimidated by the threatening and domineering tone which the archbishop [of Paris] uses towards her. She believed him to have more power than he actually had. But women are easily intimidated. They need support, encouragement, protection, and the bishops are those who can provide this for them.[110]

Sophie Barat was aware of this criticism in Rome. It was clear that the same lobby (Louise de Limminghe, Elizabeth Galitzine and Jean Rozaven) which urged her to remove Armande de Causans from the Trinité des Monts in Rome now focused on Eugénie de Gramont and the community in Paris at the rue de Varenne:

> It is true that in Rome there is a kind of conspiracy against me and my way of working, and since they are acting in the name of the Holy Father I find myself constricted and no longer able to move. So, they are insisting that I remove Madame de Gramont from Paris, that I relieve her of all responsibilities and consequently that I destroy her reputation.[111]

Rozaven dealt Sophie Barat's leadership a further blow when he persuaded Cardinal Pedicini (cardinal protector of the Society), to write a threatening letter to Sophie, reminding her of her duty of obedience to the pope and posing a series of questions. Rozaven told Elizabeth Galitzine of his strategy:

> I very much agree with you that we must do everything to save the Society despite the mother general. But I fear that all our efforts will

only be futile and founder, due to the insurmountable apathy or weakness of the one who governs you. She only knows how to use petty means and petty stratagems, which in ordinary circumstances allow her to deal temporarily with a situation. But such means are totally inadequate and useless in serious matters where the salvation of the Society is concerned.

I have asked the cardinal protector to write a letter and I enclose a copy or translation. The mother general herself will certainly not tell you about this letter, that is why I am passing it on to you.[112]

Rozaven had indeed drawn up the letter for Pedicini to sign. Its tone, style and content took Sophie Barat by surprise, but it did not take her long to recognise the source of the letter and the hostility behind it. When the papal nuncio in Paris, Antonio Garibaldi, saw the letter he remarked:

I am also of the opinion that the cardinal protector, Pedicini, could not bring himself to write in such a forthright manner. He is a quiet, easy-going person; indeed I would say he is almost indolent.[113]

Contrary to Rozaven's views, from September 1842 to March 1843 Sophie Barat vigorously exercised her leadership in a manner which could best avoid splitting the Society further. During these months she had lost nothing of her forthrightness and in the privacy of her correspondence with Césaire Mathieu she expressed her views openly and in character. Learning that her assistants general refused to join her in Paris, she asked Mathieu:

Can you understand such assistants general? And what am I to do with such mentalities? It is so true that it only takes one with the capacity and even the virtue to upset all. Before Madame Galitzine was on the council the greatest harmony existed. Under pretext of her attachment to Rome she has egged the others on, and Fr Rozaven, who has such influence over the cardinal protector and leads him like a puppet, is himself led by Madame Galitzine. Everyone knows that he has a weakness for her. This is the nub of my changed situation. So we do not know women. [Until now] I have always controlled them. What is the solution? Only one and it is urgent: the abolition of the [1839] decrees.[114]

The Society of the Sacred Heart and Jesuits after 1843

The decision to abolish the decisions of the 1839 General Council was confirmed by the pope in March 1843. Once this had been announced Jean Rozaven moved swiftly to protect himself. He told Adèle Lehon, superior at St Rufine, that direct communication with Elizabeth Galitzine would compromise him with his superior general, Roothaan, and with the Roman Curia. Rather than meet Elizabeth Galitzine, or even write to her, he asked Adèle Lehon to explain his position:

> He will not be writing to you because he always wants to be able to say truthfully that since the sad state of affairs [the decision in March 1843] he had had no contact [with you]. His own position is more delicate than ever. He has been asked to state frankly that he is opposed to the decision of the Congregation, [but] if reports criticising the decision were heard they would certainly be attributed to him. This would compromise him seriously with the cardinals and with his father general. He asks you therefore to be more circumspect than ever on his account.[115]

But while Jean Rozaven took distance from the Society, neither Elizabeth Galitzine nor Louise de Limminghe could accept the decision approved by the pope as final. They continued to plan for the next General Council of the Society, due in 1845. Before departing for Louisiana in the middle of 1843, Elizabeth Galitzine contacted Sophie Barat's brother, Louis Barat, a member of the Jesuit community in Paris. His position was fully Ultramontane and he agreed with Elizabeth Galitzine that there was hope that the changes proposed at the General Council in 1839 could be put forward again in 1845:

> The best thing about this matter is the postponement of the assembly [General Council] until 1845. By that stage there will be hardly anything to fear, either from the legal or from the Gallican authorities, and there will be an opportunity to reinstate the authentic Institute, which will then be definitive.[116]

Elizabeth Galitzine never got the opportunity to realise her dreams for the Society of the Sacred Heart. While in Louisiana she contracted yellow fever and had a sudden, painful death in December 1843, at the age of forty-three, a tragic, lonely end to her life.[117] But in Rome Louise de Limminghe believed that the decisions of the 1839 General Council had only been deferred (not abolished) until a more auspicious time. Her views were supported by the princess Borgèse in Rome who denounced the Society of the Sacred Heart for its Gallicanism.[118] A frequent visitor to Paris, she was associated with Henri Lacordaire and Madame Swetchine in France. The princess retained cordial relations with Sophie Barat and visited her in the rue de Varenne,[119] but in Rome openly criticised Sophie Barat's Gallicanism. Her views were reported in the press:

It was mostly about you [Sophie Barat]; you have been particularly blamed and it is claimed that you showed serious weakness of character in the whole affair [1839], etc, etc; that you have made the Society exclusively French. Then she inserted certain phrases in parenthesis, like these: I have complete confidence in Madame de Limminghe. She is my friend. The mother general is for France but Madame de Limminghe is the mother general for Italy. Etc, etc, etc. I am also aware that Fr Jean Rozaven may have said something to the princess about our affairs. I am afraid that the Italian houses (except the Trinité and Loreto) will sooner or later be lost to the Society.[120]

Despite this spate of publicity, the heat of debate between the Society and the Jesuits in Rome gradually lessened after 1843, especially after the withdrawal of Rozaven from the affairs of the Society of the Sacred Heart, followed by the sudden death of Elizabeth Galitzine in Louisiana. In Paris the Society and the Jesuits had to tread a careful path as Archbishop Affre forbade the Jesuits to act as chaplains or in any spiritual capacity in the schools and communities of the Society.[121] Sophie Barat complained to Affre that the secular clergy he appointed to the rue de Varenne and to Conflans were not suitable, that both a school like the rue de Varenne and a noviceship community had needs quite different from those of a parish. Although Affre admitted his appointments were not always satisfactory, he still refused to allow Jesuits to minister to the Society.[122] He was predictably furious when Sophie Barat asked him to remove a chaplain from the rue de Varenne and subjected her to a stormy interview.[123]

Eugénie de Gramont, headmistress of the school at the rue de Varenne, maintained an extensive, often combative, correspondence with the archbishop over the appointment of chaplains. Until the appointment of Archbishop Affre in 1840 Eugénie de Gramont usually presented the names of the priests she wanted as chaplains in the rue de Varenne and Archbishop de Quelen had appointed them. But when she requested Archbishop Affre to appoint Jesuits to the school, at least for retreats and special feast days in the year, he refused.[124] In 1846, in a ploy to have Eugénie de Gramont removed from the rue de Varenne, the archbishop offered to appoint Jesuits to the school and communities if Sophie Barat agreed to dismiss Eugénie de Gramont from office. This Sophie refused to do and she sought advice of the cardinal protector of the Society, Cardinal Lambruschini, and papal secretary of state in Rome.[125] This double impasse was resolved only when Eugénie de Gramont became ill in the summer of 1846 and died that December, followed two years later by Archbishop Affre during the Revolution of 1848. Under his successor

Dominique-Auguste Sibour (1792–1857) the ban on the Jesuits was removed and they were free to minister in the schools in Paris.

The Society and the Jesuits in the final years of Sophie Barat's leadership, 1850–1865

In November 1850 the Society of the Sacred Heart celebrated its golden jubilee of foundation and Sophie went to Rome for the occasion. Two visitors came to the Villa Lante to convey their good wishes, Jan Roothaan and Jean Rozaven. The visit was formal, short and polite, and much appreciated by Sophie Barat. Rozaven was seriously ill at this time and he had made a great effort to visit Sophie. He died the following year. By this time Sophie hoped the time was opportune to re-open the possibility of having provinces and provincials in the Society. Before meeting Pope Pius IX to present her request she discussed her plans with Jan Roothaan and Cardinal Lambruschini.[126] While Roothaan supported her request, both Lambruschini and Pius IX were more cautious. They considered that the effects of the 1839 crisis within the Society were still too recent and that a radical change in the structures of the Society could draw the antagonism of the French government.

They proposed a more modest adjustment to the structures of government in the Society which did not require a change to the 1815 Constitutions. In the future the Society would be governed in geographical areas by vicars. These would be appointed by the superior general and they would have limited scope for their exercise of authority and be dependent on the superior general for all major decisions. It was a poor response to Sophie's request, a compromise which she reluctantly had to accept. Deeply disappointed she told Lambruschini that they were 'half measures which could not give the Society the solid foundations it needed'.[127] But she had no choice but to present this decision to the General Council held in Lyon in 1851 and persuade the Society to accept structures she knew were inadequate.

In the course of her governance of the Society, Sophie Barat continued to encourage the local superiors and headmistresses to request Jesuits for the community and school retreats. In a personal initiative she asked the superior general, Jan Roothaan, to permit a French Jesuit, Joseph Barrelle,[128] to be available for retreats annually in France and this was arranged. In the area of vocations to the Society, Sophie Barat always hoped that the Jesuits would encourage women to enter the Society and in many instances her expectation was well founded.[129] She was characteristically frank if she felt either this support was lacking or that the Society was being criticised by the Jesuits.[130] In 1852 she complained to the Jesuit superior general, Jan Roothaan, that some Jesuits in the south of France were actually discouraging young women from joining the Society of the Sacred Heart, even directing them to other congregations:

> What can we do if we do not have enough new members? How can we fulfil the plan that God seems to have for the Society of the Sacred Heart, by inspiring so many requests for foundations all over the world? How are we to maintain our mission to educate young people who represent the only hope for religious belief to regenerate society?

She further complained that when some Jesuits were invited to houses of the Society to give retreats to young women, they did not encourage them to think of entering the Society:

> But how could Our Lord, after using Jesuits to establish an institution entirely dedicated to the glory of his Divine Heart, allow them to undermine its very foundations? And how can those Jesuits, whom we ask in good faith to come and minister to those entrusted to us by God, [and] who come to us for guidance, actually turn them away from entering the Society of the Sacred Heart?[131]

Jan Roothaan responded quickly and told Sophie that he had written to the provincials of both provinces in France, asking them to ensure that Jesuits would not discourage young women from entering the Society of the Sacred Heart in the future. Sophie's complaint had been strongly expressed and Roothaan could not leave it without comment and in defence of his colleagues:

> I cannot conclude this letter without mentioning to you how deeply saddened I have been to read in your letter that the very foundations of your Society have been undermined by the Jesuits. I owe it to the Company of Jesus to state categorically that, as far as I know, our Society does not deserve to be blamed in this way. I am sure that you will agree with me on this.[132]

True to his word, Roothaan wrote to the Jesuit provincials in France, and tactfully left it to his secretary general, Philippe de Villafort, to convey their response to Adèle Cahier, secretary general of the Society of the Sacred Heart.[133] He explained that the Jesuits in France had conveyed their point of view to Roothaan. Some were critical of the Society certainly, but these were few. Others found some superiors of the Society of the Sacred Heart quite wary of Jesuits. Others still were demanding and selective with regard to which Jesuit they wanted for their communities and schools.[134] Sophie Barat accepted these views and wrote to Roothaan in early June 1852, acknowledging that the tone of her previous letter may have been somewhat too strong. She explained that it was a measure of her anxiety for the well-being of the Society. She was pleased to note a change of attitude among the French Jesuits and expressed her appreciation of this.[135]

Conclusion

In many ways Philippe de Villafort's letter to Adèle Cahier describes the relationship between the Society of the Sacred Heart and the Jesuits in the lifetime of Sophie Barat. Its tone indicates an ease in communication and certain frankness in explaining their respective positions:

> I am responding as quickly as I can to your letter of 14 April last. I begin by thanking your for the candour of your letter, which allows me to reply to you in the same manner. First of all, I think you will agree with me that most Jesuits, each in his own sphere, are generally well disposed to helping the growth of the Society of the Sacred Heart. There are some exceptions, I am told. Given our great numbers, it is possible that there are some Jesuits who are not positive towards the Society. Yet, if it is so, these are very rare. This may be due to particular situations, to a Jesuit superior or to a superior of the Society.
>
> Indeed, you must be aware that some of your superiors have maintained aloofness with regard to Jesuits which could be interpreted as suspicious. Certain Jesuits have found some members of the Society of the Sacred Heart over-demanding in their choice of individual Jesuits, refusing to accept the ministry of those priests who are available in a given area, insisting instead that certain well-known Jesuits come from longer distances for them. I know this is exceptional, but it does explain how some Jesuits feel towards the Society. And you do realise that Jesuits have not always received the same cooperation or the same welcome in some of your houses, Paris in particular.[136]

These exchanges between Philippe de Villafort and Adèle Cahier threw long shadows, back down the years. Since 1800 long journeys had been made by the Society of the Sacred Heart and by the Jesuits and at each stage strong individualities interacted. While they were distinctive religious congregations, both shared many common elements. They had similar spiritual convictions around the core elements in Christianity, especially a common acceptance of Christ at the centre of their lives. The spirituality of the Heart of Christ was the focus and inspiration of the

Society of the Sacred Heart, and the Jesuits had a long history of honouring the Heart of Christ and of promoting this spirituality. Each in their own sphere had tried to confront Jansenism, and yet many were personally damaged in their soul life by the severity and harshness of its doctrine. Both groups lived in a Europe which had undergone profound changes in the course of the late eighteenth and early nineteenth centuries. They had been deeply marked by the Enlightenment and Revolution, and most had taken a counter-Enlightenment and counter-Revolutionary stance.

Nevertheless their differences were real. The Jesuits were an older community founded in the sixteenth century by Ignatius of Loyola, and became a powerful force in the universal church. Although suppressed in 1763 they were restored in 1815 and quickly increased again in numbers and influence. The Society of the Sacred Heart founded by Madeleine Sophie Barat was a much younger community which grew rapidly in the early nineteenth century. The contrast was not only between a younger and an older energy. Jesuits were essentially a clerical community. The Society of the Sacred Heart was a community of women finding its way within the church, constantly dealing with deeply entrenched attitudes and assumptions of clerical power and dominance.[137] In that context, in the course of her life as superior general of the Society of the Sacred Heart, Sophie Barat clashed with the Jesuits over her mode and style of government. This was evident in the crisis in the Trinité concerning cloister for women in Italy, and during the prolonged crisis of 1839–51, when Jean Rozaven criticised her leadership as weak, hesitant, confused and inactive. At the root of his criticism lay a difference in the exercise of authority and obedience, as well as a clash over models of discernment leading to obedience.

However, Sophie Barat's exercise of leadership of necessity was different from that of the Jesuits. Her task was new, she had few models to learn from, and circumstances often compelled her to work on her own. During the sixty-three years of her life as superior general, she exercised her authority pragmatically, often within the reality of fast-changing situations, and she rarely invoked the authority given her, or the Constitutions of the Society. By instinct she sought the middle ground. Such a position gave her flexibility, and allowed her avoid impossible polarities. It was an exercise of the art of the possible and it enabled her to deal with clerical power constructively. It could look weak and ineffective, but in fact it was another model, her model, more focused on the issues, the situations and the capacities and possibilities of individuals and communities. In this way and in a world and time when women's power and skills in the church were not readily recognised or respected, Sophie Barat moved as she needed to safeguard the spiritual vision of the community she had initiated in 1800.

CHAPTER 4

Medical Biography in the Society
of the Sacred Heart

Good health was essential in the Society of the Sacred Heart if the members were to fulfil their tasks in the schools, farms, kitchens, infirmaries and in the daily round of domestic and community services. The 1815 Constitutions discuss in some detail the ways to maintain the health of the members of the Society. Indications of how these ways were lived out are found in each of the annual community and financial accounts, in the records regarding the farm, the kitchen and the infirmary, the daily life of the community, and are especially evident in the obituaries which record the illnesses and deaths of the members. All show care and concern regarding health, an aspect of intimate life in the Society which was mostly hidden from the wider world. In her leadership role Sophie Barat regularly addressed health issues, sometimes in her general letters to all the communities of the Society, and more especially with individuals and leaders of the communities. She discussed various remedies, qualities of medical care, and often suggested seeking second opinions and travelling distances to find cures. She assisted at some of the operations which members of the community had, either at home or in hospital, and she tracked the aftercare of patients. She helped those who suffered from depression by suggesting rest, a change of house or activity; and if some had to be hospitalised for a time or permanently she searched far and wide to find an appropriate place for them.

In her care of the communities and schools of the Society Sophie constantly recommended good food and a balanced diet. Her letters and records of her visits to the houses of the Society show how she paid particular attention to the farms, orchards, vineyards and vegetable gardens, as well as to crops and animals. She urged harvesting of fruit, jam-making and fruit bottling, which provided variety in diet over the winter months. Indeed, to the dismay of the inhabitants of the Faubourg St Germain in Paris, she transformed the classic gardens of the Hôtel Biron into an orchard and vegetable garden, and she bought cows from Amiens to ensure fresh milk for the infirmary of the community and for the children in the school. Any failing in health care in the communities and schools drew sharp comment from Sophie Barat. She constantly asked for preventative measures to be taken, rather than merely wait and react to an epidemic, and she was particularly concerned about the health of younger women in the Society and the children in the schools.

In her collection of 14,000 letters it is possible to follow Sophie Barat's personal medical history which shows her coming to terms with health problems, aided by her companions in community and by several generations of doctors. Through the prism of these letters, taken in conjunction with the Society's records, it is clear that the doctors who treated Sophie Barat also treated all the members, with rare exception. While most personal letters of the members to Sophie Barat regarding health have not survived,[1] details of Sophie Barat's health are found in her letters and they shed light on attitudes to health in the communities of the Society. In keeping with her contemporaries and with the social conventions of the time, Sophie Barat comments on her own state of health in almost every letter, and on her various doctors, on their diagnoses and prescribed treatments. Her views are frankly expressed and her descriptions of illness leave little to the imagination, something which may surprise the modern reader but was typical of her time.[2] This essay narrates the health history of Sophie Barat, and concludes with two essays which offer considered diagnoses. These are by a medical doctor who is also a historian; the other by a medical doctor and psychotherapist.

Early health of Sophie Barat

Commenting on her childhood, Sophie Barat remembered that while her:

> parents were not rich, they enjoyed a certain comfort. Jacques Barat cultivated vines and practised the double trade of vine-grower and cooper. Thus he was able to bring the children up adequately.[3]

Sophie's early development was also helped by the climate in Joigny. The town was built along the river Yonne and surrounded by woods, the air was pure and bracing, the food wholesome; the water of the area was reputed to possess healing qualities and wine was central to diet in the region.[4] Sophie Barat had a dramatic entry into life, as she was born two months prematurely on the night of 12 December 1779, in the midst of a fire.[5] Nevertheless, she grew up a healthy child, preceded in the family by her brother Louis (1768–1845) and sister Marie-Louise (1770–1852). As the youngest born in such special circumstances Sophie was surrounded with special affection by her parents, Madeleine Fouffé (1740–1822) and Jacques Barat (1742–1809). She was a small, lively child, full of talk and charm, doted on by her parents and older sister, clearly very intelligent, and these years gave Sophie a strong foundation which stood her well.[6] Looking back, Sophie recognised that until the age of seven she was thoroughly spoilt at home. However, this radically changed when her older brother, Louis, returned home from his priestly studies at the seminary in Sens. He 'took immediate responsibility for my education and became not only my Master but took over the place of Papa and Mama'.[7] In other words, Louis usurped the parental roles and effectively ended Sophie's childhood. His parents did not question this. They were ambitious for their children, and being a cleric gave Louis great authority within the family.[8] While awaiting ordination he was appointed to teach in his old college in Joigny.[9] Thus at the age of seven Sophie:

> was confided to the care of her brother, who was more concerned about the spiritual development of his sister than experienced in the physical care such a fragile and delicate child needed. He made her work without the breaks necessary for her age and suited to her physical strength. She was truly imprisoned; her body suffered always from the effect of this handling in childhood.[10]

Sophie's classes were full. Louis taught her to read and write, and she studied the scriptures, Latin and mathematics. Indeed she followed the programme of studies Louis taught in the Collège St Jacques in Joigny, and she did the homework he set the boys. This was pressure enough, but in a display of extraordinary poor judgement, Louis brought Sophie to witness several sessions of the exorcism of a young girl in which he played a leading role. Sophie was eleven at the time and this bizarre experience haunted her for years.[11] Sophie made her First Communion at the age of eleven and from then on Louis expected her to attend the 7a.m. daily Mass in St Thibaut's along with the college boys:

> I had to be ready to go to the schoolboys' Mass which was at 7am. One morning, when I really wanted to sleep, my brother came and asked: 'where is Sophie?' I heard him and in fear I buried myself in my bed-clothes. 'Do you think that she is so lazy?' said my mother. Taking this as a reply my brother said nothing further. But I cried out: 'I'm here'.

> So Louis said: 'get up immediately and be at Mass at the same time as I am'. I was so afraid that I took just five minutes to dress.[12]

Mass was followed by breakfast, after which Sophie went upstairs to her attic room to do the work Louis had set her. Each day brought her little respite or time to play. In 1793 this routine was interrupted when Louis was imprisoned in Paris for refusing to accept the Civil Constitution of the Clergy. At this point Sophie's studies stopped abruptly and more balance came into her life. She spent her time at home dress-making and helping her father in the vineyards and by the age of twelve was recognised in Joigny as a dressmaker and a *vigneronne*.[13] Louis's absence from home also allowed Sophie greater intellectual freedom. She enjoyed reading *Don Quixote*, read *Virgil* in Latin with delight, and was absorbed by the huge tomes of Samuel Richardson's *Clarissa*, a popular novel in France.[14] Madame Barat invited neighbours to her kitchen in the evenings and listened with pride as Sophie read *Clarissa* aloud to her guests.[15] But Sophie's new-found freedom was not to last. In 1795, following the fall of Robespierre, Louis returned home, exhausted after the harrowing experiences of prison. He could not remain in Joigny indefinitely as his presence would threaten the safety of the family. He planned to return to Paris and take Sophie with him to complete her education there. At first Madame Barat would not hear of it, but Louis gradually persuaded his parents and got his way.[16] Louis was ordained a priest secretly in Paris in September 1795 and returned home to fetch Sophie after the grape harvest.

Sophie Barat in Paris 1795–1801

Sophie Barat was sixteen when she left home in 1795. If her mother had last-minute hesitations about Sophie's departure these were swept away by her son's ordination that year. He had secured accommodation in Paris, in No. 4 rue de Touraine, in the heart of the Marais district, not far from the Bastille. This was a 'safe house' where Louis Barat's identity as priest was kept secret and from which he exercised a clandestine ministry in the city. With three other women in the house, Sophie Barat followed an order of day laid down by Louis. They led a life of silence, prayer, meagre food, fasting, study and little sleep. The day began with prayer, Mass and then breakfast on dry, rough bread. In the mornings they had no hot drink for breakfast and if they had not finished a piece of study from the previous day, then that had to be completed before they broke their fast. Classes consisted of study of the fathers of the church, mathematics, Latin and the scriptures. All works of literature, which had nurtured Sophie's imagination and affectivity, were completely forbidden. This transition marked the beginning of Sophie Barat's rapid deterioration in health. While at home in Joigny her parents were able to protect her from Louis' excesses, but in Paris she was quite alone.

Sophie was quick at her work, and to hold her back and allow the others to catch up, Louis gave her other tasks, such as learning long psalms in Latin by heart, especially Ps. 50, and then translating them into French. Nothing escaped his eye and if he saw that she was enjoying a particular piece of work, he would immediately change to something different. All spontaneity was curtailed. If he noticed that she was making something with evident pleasure and joy, he made sure she could not finish it. Once when she managed to finish something for herself he threw it in the fire. The same happened to a gift she made for his birthday. Her companions found Louis' treatment of Sophie bizarre and difficult to watch. Sophie herself felt singled out from the others and treated much more severely. He regulated her life in every detail, monitored her relationships, especially with men, heard her confession daily and denied her the gifts of special food sent to them by her mother from Joigny.[17] He struck her across the face when she greeted a (male) cousin in the street with a warm hug. It was a life of tyranny, at the level of body, soul and spirit.

In later years members of the Society of the Sacred Heart confirmed just how much Sophie's health suffered at the severe treatment of her brother. This had begun in Joigny but was accelerated in Paris and led to the effective ruin of her digestive system.[18] While living a life of rigid austerity himself and brutalised by his time in prison, Louis Barat demanded too much of his younger sister, without the consideration due her age, gender and health. At the physical, emotional and spiritual level Sophie paid a heavy price for this, all her life. When the results of his actions were pointed out to him later, it was clear that Louis never grasped the extent of the damage Sophie had suffered from his actions. Yet, by the age of eighteen Sophie had learning and skills to match the best of her generation, which prepared her for her task in life as founder of the Society of the Sacred Heart. Until the end of her life, however, she would have to face successive illnesses which tested her endurance to the limit.

From Paris to Amiens, 1800–1806

This unhealthy situation began to shift in the autumn of 1800 when Sophie, who had thought of becoming a Carmelite, met Joseph Varin, a priest recently returned from Rome. He told her about a new order of women in Rome called the Dilette di Gesù which wanted to make a foundation in France, possibly in Amiens. He urged her to consider joining this project and after some hesitation Sophie went to Amiens in 1801, to discover if this was to be her path.[19] In a short time and although she was the youngest, Sophie's leadership capacity was recognised and in 1802 she became leader of the new community. Almost immediately her health began to give concern. She lost her sleep and appetite, and a gynaecologic illness emerged which her contemporaries called a 'cancer'. This was extremely embarrassing for her and her reticence to talk about it made it difficult for the community to help.[20] In September 1803 even Louis Barat was dismayed at Sophie's physical state and told his sister, Marie-Louise, that Sophie needed a long rest at home in Joigny.[21] But Sophie could not leave Amiens then as one of the most gifted in the community, Mlle Capy, suffered a serious mental breakdown in October 1803. Despite their best efforts, the community were unable to cope and she had to be taken to the Salpêtrière in Paris. This breakdown weighed heavily on them and they also had to endure the criticisms of the local people in Amiens and those of the Capy family and local priests at Rheims.[22]

Sophie's health continued to deteriorate, and by the spring of 1804 she had become very ill indeed and was in danger of death. Joseph Varin urged her to go to Paris and consult the Sisters of Charity there,[23] a suggestion which Sophie resisted. She found it intrusive and she decided instead to will her body to get better. Varin noted this:

> I hope you will be more reasonable and that you will consent without resistance all that religion and common sense asks of you for the care of your health. You are aware of the reputation of Fr Lambert as a wise and enlightened man. When I placed your inconsistencies before him, he exclaimed: 'Is this then the virtue of the Dames de la Foi? Is this their spirit? 'Oh!' he added, 'this gives me a bad impression of their life! Fr Thomas, also enlightened and devout, thinks the same. I do not mention Fr Gloriot, who could not get over his astonishment. Certainly theology and reason condemn you; it is also certain that your obstinacy has especially troubled me. But let us forget all that. I forgive you willingly, on condition that you do absolutely all that Madame Deshayes prescribes for you, following the advice of Fr Bruson,[24] with regard to the treatment. So let us forget your faults and my little displeasure.[25]

Sophie's malady was now the subject of detailed discussion by at least five priests. This further invasion of her privacy, as well as the voyeuristic comments on her condition, were intolerable for her. But willing her way back to health would not work and her health continued to worsen. By March 1804 her last resort was divine intervention:

> We have to conclude that the pressure to obey [Joseph Varin] forced
> Madame Sophie to the only remaining protection of her vulnera-
> bility; she asked God to heal her illness, so that she would be spared
> having to expose her malady.[26]

No miracle came and in the end Sophie accepted she needed help and
went to Paris for a treatment which lasted several weeks. She stayed with
Madame Bergeron who ran a thriving hardware shop in Paris and from
there attended the Sisters of Charity by day. Her condition was alleviated
though not fully cured, and at least the treatment prevented further
deterioration of her illness. After six weeks in Paris Sophie returned to
Amiens, still needing care. It took another two years until she felt really
well again. That turning point came in August 1806 during a trip in the
south of France when Sophie was twenty-seven years of age and away
from the tensions in Amiens. By then she had been elected superior
general for life, she was beginning to find her feet and to assert her leadership, and she was travelling and making new foundations, in Grenoble
and Poitiers. Her growing friendship with Philippine Duchesne made her
visits to Grenoble enjoyable and she attributed her final cure to
Philippine's good care:

> You know the state I was in when I left you [Grenoble]. When I
> arrived in Lyon the heat of the journey had aggravated my illness and
> I became worse than last year. I was still in Lyon when all symptoms
> had disappeared, and yet I had done nothing to heal the illness. On
> the contrary, on the journey it had been extremely hot; I had had
> very little sleep, as well as bad food and dirty lodgings. At this time
> everything only added to my ailment, and yet all disappeared in a
> night. I am completely healed.[27]

While she felt healed in the summer of 1806 Sophie Barat did not emerge
from these years unscathed. Aspects of her health, especially her digestive
system, had been damaged for life in Paris and these she would have to
take account of again and again in the course of her life. For example, from
these years she had to accept her inability to fast, and this was a key com-
ponent in religious life at certain times in the liturgical year. In her capacity
as leader of the Society Sophie Barat felt duty bound to model religious
life for the members. As an inexperienced superior general she encouraged
monastic practices of public penance, long periods of prayer in the chapel
and a certain cult around fasting and eating less food. This was the model
she had learnt in Paris from Louis Barat and it reached an unhealthy level
in Poitiers in 1806. During a retreat there most of the food prepared for
the community was returned to the kitchen, uneaten. Many years later

Thérèse Maillucheau remembered that Sophie's example of fasting actually took away their appetites.[28] This was far too austere, and only when some members of the community collapsed did Sophie recognise that health had to be safeguarded if prayer and work were to be sustained. Clearly she herself had not found that balance herself, and only later admitted that she had devised a programme more suitable for enclosed Carmelites than women involved in schools and domestic tasks.[29]

In any event, she had placed an impossible model before herself. She was unable to fast, to spend long hours especially at night in the chapel, or work without respite. But she tried to do so, and regularly her health just simply collapsed and she was forced to take rest. It was Joseph Varin who managed to confront her in public over her unwillingness to accept her limitations around fasting. She was visiting a community during Lent and she asked to eat alone to avoid the community seeing that she was not fasting. Joseph Varin turned up unexpectedly in the house and was shown into her room. She hid her meal under the bed, but Joseph Varin saw the food:

> 'What do I see there?' 'But, Father (I was very embarrassed, and I admitted as much to him), Father, I am not fasting.' He said: 'How can you have such small ideas about your companions that you are afraid that they will think less of you. Come on now, call the community here.' Everyone was brought to my room, even those who were with the children. I certainly was very embarrassed.[30]

However mortifying the incident, it challenged Sophie to accept her frailty, a reality beyond the issue of fasting. Fundamental to her frailty was the long-term effect of the regime imposed on her by Louis Barat and her inability to become free of it and become more independent of her brother. In 1807, when considering whether or not she had sufficient health to spend nights in prayer, Sophie wondered if she should ask her brother's opinion about this.[31] But two years later, when Emilie Giraud in Niort told Sophie that Louis disapproved of her doing embroidery, Sophie took the opposite view:

> I am not in the least surprised that my brother prefers prolonged periods of prayer to your embroidery, and that he laments the time you give to it. Long ago he tore up all that I made, saying that it was time lost. You know how useful embroidery is to us and I want you to learn how to *nuance* this. It is not the quantity of work that I ask, neither do I insist on the time you give to it. Take the time you can for embroidery but make sure always that your spiritual exercises, grammar and the other subjects come first.[32]

Sophie was beginning to nuance situations, to find inner balance, learning by hard experience that her body crumbled under stress, either from work or from her own unreal expectations. A threefold rhythm began to emerge: intense work, followed by a collapse and gradual recovery. Over time her own intelligence and common sense came to her rescue. She became quite matter of fact about her ailments, and warned her friends that she would outlive them all, a prophecy she fulfilled.[33] However, as well as learning to accept her propensity for becoming ill, Sophie also recognised her capacity to recover; that given time and rest, her energy and health would return, at least for a time. By nature she was usually optimistic and kept hoping she would recover full health:

> It is almost pointless for you to worry about my health. You know that I am not ill for long. These are the attacks which you know about and which endure either for a long or short time. Our doctor considers that the nerves of my stomach are deteriorating and that over time they will wear out. It seems after this judgment that there is no cure and that I will have to put up with this illness which is often acute for as long as Our Lord so wishes. Since it is not terminal you are wrong to get so upset about it.[34]

The years 1806–16, when the Society of the Sacred Heart was coming into existence, were particularly stressful for Sophie Barat, and they were punctuated by exhaustion.[35] Sophie noted her symptoms regularly in her letters. Between 1807 and 1811 she suffered continually from fevers which affected her eyes badly and prevented her from writing letters, an essential tool in her leadership of the communities.[36] While she struggled to continue working relentlessly, in the end she had to take rest. In the summer of 1810 she took the waters at Vichy, and also spent some weeks resting in the countryside around Lyon;[37] in 1811 she rested in Poitiers and was urged to take goats' milk as a restorative.[38] Her eyes did not improve,[39] though she lived in constant optimism about their cure, and noted that in general her health was good. But in March 1813 she was ill again for a month in Grenoble and was nursed by Philippine Duchesne.[40] From January to September 1815 Sophie had a prolonged illness, during a crucial and particularly stressful period in the life of the Society, but by the early autumn of 1815 she had recovered. In December that year she was confirmed as superior general for life at the General Council of the Society of the Sacred Heart held in Paris.

New responsibilities, new demands

This endorsement of her leadership led to new responsibilities and more travel:

> Everywhere there is work to do and my little ailments drain my energies. In Poitiers, Niort and Bordeaux I was sick most of the time. On my return to Paris, after a night of travel in the carriage made difficult by shivering and thirst with fever, I had to go to bed for a week and could do no work. This is the pattern of my life.[41]

Her eyes continued to bother her:

> I am tired. I am losing sleep and I can hardly see. The fire I have in my blood affects my eyes. You can see this in my handwriting.[42]

She admitted to her nephew, Stanislas Dusaussoy, that she had done herself no good at all rushing around the country and then falling ill.[43] She linked this 'fire', this fever in her blood, with her digestive difficulties and felt doomed to have these ailments for life. She complained of stomach pains and had constant diarrhoea which weakened her and often prevented her travelling.[44] Rheumatism also dogged her, but she tended to complain only when it was worse than usual.[45] Expansion of the Society affected Sophie emotionally. When Philippine Duchesne left France for Louisiana in the spring of 1818 she became ill for some weeks.[46] In July 1819 Sophie wrote to her sister, Marie-Louise:

> I have been miserable. I have not been able to write for a long time without becoming overtired. Ask mother to forgive me if I do not manage to write to her for her feast. I have such severe stomach pains that I vomit everything I eat. Just now I cannot write without a great deal of difficulty. I will have to take care of this for a few weeks. So greet mother for me.[47]

These abdominal pains did not abate.[48] Her eyes continued to trouble her throughout 1819: 'my good eye continually weeps' and 'rheumatism in the eyes' often prevented her writing necessary letters of government.[49] While these illnesses exposed the weaknesses in her digestive system, undoubtedly the outcome of her brother's influence, they were also due in part to the responsibility Sophie Barat carried. She was the founder and leader of an exciting new enterprise in France which was rapidly expanding. She was learning her role and task, and much of what was being asked of her was new and unknown territory. It was a long journey from the simplicity of the life in Joigny to the leadership of communities of the Society, comprised of aristocratic women and of women from simple backgrounds. In addition to her leadership of communities and schools, Sophie Barat also took decisions to buy properties on behalf of the Society, and some of the transactions involved large sums of money. One such decision was the purchase of a large property in Paris. In 1820, with the support of her council, Sophie Barat took an immense risk and purchased the Hôtel Biron in Paris (now the Rodin Museum), on the rue de Varenne in the fashionable Faubourg St Germain. This would be the centre of government for the Society, as well as the noviceship and boarding school for young aristocratic women.[50] Finally, members of the Society looked to Sophie Barat for spiritual guidance, something she was eager to give. But this demanded time, and when one complained about a delay Sophie replied:

> I did not say I would not direct you anymore. I said that my head and eyes have been very sore for several months, and that I have had to confine myself to business letters only, and put aside those of spiritual direction.[51]

Catalyst for change, 1823–1824

In these years Sophie's health problems did not improve. She continued to suffer from chronic fatigue, fevers, colds, pains in the stomach, diarrhoea, sore eyes and headaches. All are listed with regularity in her letters.[52] By April 1822 she admitted that her entire body was wrecked:

> I wrote to you with difficulty as I was suffering greatly from rheumatism in the gut, and indeed my entire system is badly shaken. I'm afoot fortunately, but I suffer a lot when I try to work. My eyes simply refuse to function.[53]

Another blow came that year when her mother died.[54] Sophie had spent little time at home since 1795 and knew how lonely her mother had been when she and Louis had left Joigny and especially when her father died in 1809. Already weary from overwork and filled with grief, events in Grenoble in the winter of 1822/3 triggered Sophie's collapse. Despite Sophie's warnings, bad management there had allowed debts to accumulate over seven years and in the winter of 1822 the house crashed into bankruptcy. Sophie spent some weeks in Grenoble, reorganising the house and settling the most outstanding debts. Her health broke, and she became seriously ill, to the extent that some feared she would die.[55]

For forty-five days Sophie struggled with a tenacious fever. Her doctor in Grenoble, Dr Bilon, wrote to Dr Terral in Amiens:

> After forty-five days of illness and several crises which did not peak, Madame Barat is now convalescing. I have already allowed her some light food and she has remained up for about two hours. Unless there is a setback, and I have no reason to think there will be, Madame Barat will soon recover health, as her companions and all who know her so desire. The illness was a sinus infection (une fièvre muqueuse), complicated by gastritis and a rheumatoid infection. This could be called, if you prefer, gastro-enteritis, with irritation of the liver and of the muscular system of the body, to a degree severe enough to produce and sustain prolonged fever.[56]

At this juncture, when Sophie was convalescing and gradually resuming some of her work, Sophie met Joseph-Marie Favre, a priest from Chambéry in Savoy. This meeting flowered into friendship and Favre began to challenge Sophie Barat's lifestyle, urging her to find inner balance and moderation, in order to sustain her task in life.[57] He pointed out the signs of stress, poor energy, and the recurrence of her old aliments, rheumatism, sore eyes, headaches, nerves, fevers, insomnia, stomach pains, and a new symptom, gout, which she found painful.[58] Yet she listened to Favre's advice and in August 1826 she noted that her health had vastly improved.[59] She still complained of constant fevers, and noted in April 1828 that she had a fever lasting seventy-two days.[60] The fever may have been connected with her earlier illness in Amiens in 1802, with her menstrual cycle and the onset of menopause. On 12 July 1828 Sophie was prevented from travelling:

> I was ready to set out when the community protested and opposed my travelling. They said it was unwise, on account of the heavy rains and the bad chest I have just now. Besides, when I am a bit tired and there is dampness, then you can imagine how my body bleeds.[61]

Again in 1832, when she was fifty-three, Sophie Barat assured her friend, Eugénie de Gramont:

> Yes, you will see that I am following your advice. I will set out while expecting my period (la mauvaise femme). If it comes when I am travelling I am ready to go back. I must admit that I am afraid of getting it anywhere but doubly so in the Midi.[62]

A series of falls

Sophie's search for balance in her life continued to be tested. In April 1829 she complained of pains in her right arm which prevented her writing letters.[63] Then the following month, just as she was beginning to improve, she had a serious fall:

> I had to break off this letter on account of an accident which could
> have killed me. Fortunately my good angel saved me. I fell with all
> my force from the height of a table right on to the ground. My
> whole [left][64] side was bruised and I sprained my foot. I cannot walk
> nor move around. Being bled twenty times and confined to bed etc,
> all this has lessened the danger, but I am still very tired. You are the
> first I have written to since the accident, six days ago. Yesterday I
> went to Mass in a chair, to thank God for preserving me from a
> worse accident.[65]

Sophie's fall forced her to rest. Since she could neither write nor walk, and
because her entire body was too exhausted to make an effort, she decided
to 'rest my body and my soul; I will pray for you and all you are involved
in.'[66] She was beginning to learn how to use times of illness, to pray and to
consider future plans and decisions. The illnesses, which were real and at
first an apparent block to her government of the Society of the Sacred
Heart, actually began to give her space to reflect and consider how to go
forward when she was ready. She learnt to withdraw into her own world,
though she may not have consciously recognised what she was doing at the
time. She also admitted gratefully that being ill sometimes spared her
being caught into situations which could force her to act or compromise
her position.[67]

Healing was slow. During these months Sophie complained about her
difficulty in getting back to walking, and her weakness after so many
bleedings.[68] In August 1829 she had another fall, setting back her
recovery though apparently not compounding her previous injuries.[69]
This second fall heralded a further series of falls and by December 1829
Sophie noted: 'For several weeks now a seventh fall on the injured foot
has forced me to stay in bed or in my basket-chair.[70]

Certainly by the winter of 1829 Sophie Barat was in constant pain
and immobilised, and no doctor in Paris seemed able to treat her foot
properly. Bleedings and leeches were applied regularly, to no lasting
improvement, and Sophie feared she would be invalided for life.[71] She
tried to use crutches but only for a short time and spent most of the day
in a type of basket chair. This could be pulled around the house and
garden, but it was heavy and uncomfortable both for her and for those
pulling it. She could not write as much as she liked and indeed enjoyed,
and she was learning to rely on the services of others as secretary, usually
different members of the community according as they were free. There
was no relief from pain, no true repose and no prospect of recovery.

Forced to travel, 1830–1839

The July 1830 Revolution in Paris forced Charles X into exile and the Society of the Sacred Heart, closely linked with the Bourbons, was under threat from the revolutionaries. Sophie Barat and the community in Paris made plans for a swift exit from the capital and accepted the offer of the Marquis de Nicolay to join him in a chateau in Givisiers, Switzerland. On 10 August 1830 Sophie set out for Lyon with the help of Marie Patte, Eugénie de Gramont and Anna de Constantin.[72] When they arrived in Lyon they found the house at La Ferrandière under threat from the revolutionaries. By this time Sophie's foot was in such poor condition after the prolonged travel that she could not continue on to Switzerland. Instead she, Marie Patte and Eugénie de Gramont went to the hot sulphur springs at Aix-les-Bains from 13–24 September hoping the waters would cure her foot.[73] On 8 October 1830 they set out for Switzerland and stayed for a time with the de Nicolay family at Givisiers, a centre visited by many who had left Paris in July 1830.[74] By the end of October 1830 two properties suitable to the Society's needs, the Château de Montet and the Château de Middes, had been found. The latter was rented for a year until Montet had been renovated, and Sophie spent November and most of December there.

Two doctors in Givisiers advised Sophie to return to Aix-les-Bains for further treatments on her foot.[75] One of them, Joseph Claude Anthelme Récamier (1774–1852),[76] had been her doctor in Paris for several years. He was also the community and school doctor in the Hôtel Biron from its foundation in 1820, although Sophie was not always satisfied with Récamier's care of the community and seriously ill students, a view echoed by a student at the time, Marie de Flavigny, later the Comtesse d'Aghoult and novelist Daniel Stern.[77] Despite these reservations, Sophie Barat consulted Récamier frequently about her own health and the health of others, and a relationship of trust and mutual respect developed between them.[78] Even while travelling Sophie Barat consulted Récamier by letter with regard to her own health or the health of members of the Society or indeed of her own family. These consultations ranged widely, from minor illnesses to serious operations; his views on the health of some young women wishing to join the Society were also at times requested.[79] When he died in 1852 Sophie Barat told her nephew, Stanislas, that Récamier 'looked after me as he would his own mother'.[80]

Taking Dr Récamier's advice, Sophie set out for Chambéry in late December 1830. She had a disappointing setback on the journey when she fell again, for the eighth time, when she and her companions had stopped to rest at St Genin.

> As I was getting up from the sofa where I had been sitting, I reached
> out for a chair to steady myself and pick up my crutches. [But]
> someone pulled the chair so quickly that I lost my balance because I
> was already leaning forward. I fell once again on my injured heel
> which took the weight of my body, which as you know is not as light
> as air, [and] my heel snapped. I am in great pain.[81]

A week later Sophie gave Eugénie de Gramont further details:

> As I was leaning on the chair in front of me, with my knee already
> bent, the chair was suddenly whipped away from me seconds before
> I could see what was happening. So I fell again on this bent foot with
> the full weight of my body on it. I heard the ligaments in my heel
> snap and the pain I felt was terrible. I had to get back on the carriage
> and at Geneva I consulted a good surgeon who discovered that
> nothing was broken. He wanted to place leeches immediately on my
> foot and [suggested] that I remain in Geneva. This I did not dare do
> and I continued on my journey with my foot very inflamed. [In
> Chambéry] Dr Rey declined to use leeches and instead put a type of
> ointment on my foot. This provoked a small inflammation with lots
> of small spots which felt like needle points. It was a relief to have the
> swelling brought out on my skin.[82]

Sophie spent three months in Chambéry resting her foot, waiting for the
season to open at Aix-les-Bains, as the waters were only beneficial when
they were sufficiently warm, generally from April to September. Dr Rey
warned that the treatment could be long and painful.[83] Indeed in the
course of that year Sophie went to Aix-les-Bains three times: 5–22 April;
22 May–1 June; 22 July–13 August. She tried to remain optimistic,
promising herself dates when she would be ready to travel again; or
making the best of her situation, by remarking that her restrictions safeguarded her from many demands from communities.[84] But she was
frustrated:

> I tried to go to the right, then to the left, tra, tra, tra . . . and then I
> fell and I had to stay in bed for three months. This is how my life has
> been for two years, and if our Lord does not want this to change I
> must resign myself to it all over again.[85]

In Aix-les-Bains she stayed in the house of Dr Vidal who was in charge of
her treatments. Her surroundings were pleasant and beautiful. She had a
room on the ground floor of the house with a door out to the garden, to
a stream whose music soothed her and gave her peace. On Sundays she
returned to the community at Chambéry and caught up with her post
and business. The treatments she received were a combination of

immersing her foot in the waters and of having full baths. She had fifteen days of this regime, then a rest period of fifteen days in Chambéry, followed by a further fifteen days of treatments.

Her doctors in Chambéry, Dr Rey and Dr Despines, visited her at Aix and worked closely with Dr Vidal. Sophie found the hot waters, sometimes reaching 33–34 degrees, most beneficial; she did not take the salt waters which were cooler, reaching only 28 degrees at most.[86] By the last week of April, Sophie's foot was still rigid and her Achilles heel had not healed. Her ankle remained swollen and her left heel was shorter than her right by a good finger's width. Dr Rey advised a further round of treatments in Aix-les-Bains and Sophie returned there in early May. Despite these treatments her Achilles heel did not improve and she was unable to place her left foot on the ground at all.[87] The doctors continued to encourage her and to assure her that she would eventually walk again. But Sophie was disappointed and becoming weary having to explain in letters why she could not walk. After another three-week break in Chambéry, she returned to Aix once again in July and stayed until mid-August 1831. But there was no improvement at all. She walked a little with crutches, or with sticks, but never for long.[88]

Weight problems also impeded her recovery. From 1817 Sophie worried about her weight, and was surprised that she actually put on weight when she was ill, despite the fact that she was neither sleeping nor eating well. When advised to take goats' milk for her health, she refused on the grounds that it made her fat.[89] Sophie tended to share her concern about weight only with Eugénie de Gramont, but since they lived together in Paris between 1818 and 1830 comments on her weight only recur when she was travelling.[90] In 1831 she noted with dismay that at Aix-les-Bains that she actually put on weight since all exercise was denied her, but noted the following year with satisfaction that she had begun to lose a little weight.[91] In addition to this worry, Sophie grappled with her customary ailments, the fevers, rheumatism and persistent coughing. In early September 1831 she caught influenza. She perspired and coughed a great deal at night, complained that her back was sore and that her voice was faint and very strained. She began to spit blood, not for the first time:

> The second day I began to spit blood, though not as much as last year. Though I still have night sweats and I have to change my sheets in the middle of every night, at least the inflammation has decreased. My chest has become very weak. Dr Rey is going to give me a purgative tomorrow.[92]

The doctor also prescribed an expectorant with an opium base (sirop de diacode), which gave Sophie some relief from coughing and allowed her sleep better at night, though her fever continued.[93] But by mid-September Sophie accepted she would not be cured at Aix-les-Bains and she decided to return to Paris, via Montet in Switzerland.

On 15 September 1831 she left Chambéry on crutches, accompanied by two students from Grenoble. She was joined at Payerne by Dr Récamier who was also travelling to Switzerland to visit his wife in Fribourg.[94] Sophie arrived in Montet on 27 September and spent some weeks there. Always hopeful of a cure, she accepted to have her foot examined by a reputed local bone setter, but to no avail. Before leaving the area Sophie completed business in Fribourg and stayed with Madame Récamier for a time.[95] Although always on crutches, she felt able in early October to travel on to Paris. She planned to go via Joigny but warned her nephew Stanislas that she would not be able to visit her sister Marie-Louise:

> If you were not perched on the mountain I would be delighted to go to your house and stay there. But how could I climb up? I cannot do that with my crutches. Besides, how could I go to Mass on Sunday?[96]

Sophie arrived in Paris on 17 October 1831 and the condition of her foot had deteriorated so badly that she feared it would have to be amputated. Nevertheless, learning that she was expected in Rome in the course of 1832, for a visit planned since the foundation of the Trinité des Monts in 1828, she decided to travel to the south of France for the winter and proceed to Rome from there.[97] This plan seemed to suit her well and she noted that the further south she went the better her general health improved.[98]

In May 1832 Sophie visited the community in Turin and had a consultation with Chevalier Rossi, physician to the royal family of Piedmont, regarding her foot.[99] By this time her ankle bone was severely disjointed but Rossi managed to set the bone and he insisted on dressing her foot bandage daily to ensure the bone remained in place. After a short time and to her enormous relief, Sophie Barat began to walk again, at first slowly and with difficulty. To aid full recovery and strengthen the foot muscles Rossi prescribed and supervised her daily foot baths.[100] It took time for the foot to heal and to strengthen fully but Sophie Barat's years of immobility were over. Sophie shared this good news with her friends.[101] Rossi wrote two reports on the treatment he used to save Sophie Barat's left foot, one on 31 July 1832 and the other on 15 August 1832. He was confident that she would retain full mobility as long as she continued to wear a bandage to support her ankle.

Demands of administration and poor health

Despite her illnesses and physical disabilities Sophie Barat continued to lead the Society of the Sacred Heart during these years. Between 1828 and 1832 alone seven new foundations were made, one in Rome, two in Louisiana, three in France and one in Switzerland. In addition, several others were at the preparatory stages, involving constant letter writing and consultation. Sophie Barat's letters at this time, both of government and of a personal nature, reveal notes of strain and frustration, indicating how she struggled to keep up with the Society's rapid growth.[102] Family responsibilities increased at this time too in the measure that the health of her sister, Marie-Louise, deteriorated. Sophie continued to watch over her nieces and nephews and to ensure that Marie Louise had the care she needed.

While she no longer battled with immobility, Sophie's general health pattern had not changed. She continued to have serious digestive problems and complained constantly of being unable to retain food. She succumbed to chest infections regularly, had ongoing fevers, especially at night, and she was spitting blood. She had a poor appetite, suffered from headaches and what she called nerve pains, and was unable to sleep, all symptoms of stress and overwork. In the summer of 1832 Sophie's friend and guide, Joseph-Marie Favre, warned her not to overstretch her energies. He urged her yet again to find balance in her life between prayer, work and rest, as necessary for her emotional and spiritual health as it was for her physical wellbeing:

> Trust and the love of God gladden the heart, uplift the soul and make it capable of the greatest undertakings, whereas fear and mistrust depress and sadden the soul, shrink the heart, dull the spirit, ruin the health of the body and disturb rhythm of the spiritual life. God did not come down upon the earth to be feared but to be loved. Never push yourself to work to the point of crushing your body and soul, and rendering you incapable of all spiritual pursuit. Be joyful. Take a break each time you feel yourself becoming heavy, weary or tired; or, vary your occupations. Whoever does too much does nothing.[103]

However, Favre knew that Sophie had reached such a point of exhaustion that she needed a provisional structure to carry her until energy returned. He and Louise de Limminghe[104] drew up an order of day for Sophie, indicating when she was to rise and when to retire, when she was to work and when she was to relax. She was to accept the food set before her, and only reject it if it made her ill. She was not to fast, unless the doctor prescribed it for losing weight. In general she was to accept all the help offered her, even if she considered it as poor modelling of a superior general. They urged her to follow this plan until she was really restored to good health. With such advice Sophie set out from Turin for Rome in the autumn of 1832, accompanied by Louise de Limminghe and Marie Patte. On the way she stayed with the Countess Cherubini, whose daughter was at the school at Turin. While there Sophie burnt her foot badly on a warming pan and this healed slowly. She was bitterly disappointed to be yet again on crutches, remarking wryly that a superior general arriving in Rome on crutches would 'cut a poor figure in every sense of the word'.[105] When Sophie finally arrived in October at the Trinité des Monts in Rome she had to retire immediately. A few days later Pope Gregory XVI called to see her at the Trinité and to her embarrassment she could not greet him at the main door. Instead he visited her in her rooms and arranged for another meeting in the papal apartments when she was better.

But a burn was not a fall and by the spring of 1833 Sophie was fully mobile again and her health was improving. This was possibly linked with a comment she made at this time, noting that she felt better when she did not fast. She was finally learning to accept that she could not practise full observance, nor could she model it as superior general of the Society.[106] Yet in the winter months in Rome Sophie had constant colds. In 1835 she was ill from January to June,[107] and in 1837 a cold lasted seventeen days and developed into a sinus infection, though Sophie made little of it, remarking that everyone in Rome had it.[108] She began to comment on ageing at this period, that her energy was drained by constant fever and heavy colds, coupled with chronic digestion problems.[109] Favre warned her that she was damaging herself in a reckless way:

> I have learnt with great sorrow that you are in very poor health. Take some rest and relaxation as well as the remedies prescribed. Allow them [the doctors] to treat you as they think best and not according to your own wishes. Do you not need robust and vigorous health to fulfil the greatly increased and varied obligations, so complicated and *exhausting*, as those which you are responsible for? Heavens above, Mother, in running down your health by overwork, sleepless nights and mortification, are you not also weakening the whole Society? The devil only mocks your acts of penance which are becoming an obstacle to the exercise of your important responsibility.[110]

The pattern of colds continued in the winter of 1837/8,[111] and in February 1838 Sophie caught a really bad chill. She knew she needed more air and exercise but the weather in Rome was wet and cold. She felt caged and continued to overwork.[112] She admitted that she was not helping herself, but that she found Italian food difficult to digest. In April 1838 the doctor attending her in Rome told her that the problem was indeed diet. He gave her a three-week regime of sweet drinks, frog bouillon and wine, to build her up for the return journey to Paris due after Easter of 1838.[113] Sophie set out in the middle of May and assured Louise de Limminghe that she was well and was taking exercise.[114] But this positive report did not last long; the following week Sophie admitted she was ill again, and depressed, as she missed her friends. Just then Sophie learnt that Joseph-Marie Favre had become gravely ill and was dying.[115] By the time she arrived in Turin in early June 1838 Sophie was ill:

> My news is not great. Inflammation in my throat and chest has put an end to my regime, for a long time. How can I continue to take strong remedies when I caught a cold on the way and cannot shift it? I have a cough and too much work in hand. Also, the diet heats my system to the extent that I cannot speak any more. I have lost all appetite and nothing is able to calm the fire in my throat. All that, with so much work to do in this house, within and without. How I miss you for everything! I see my work increasing and my energies diminishing. No one to help me! The doctor here is helping me. Good Mr Favre is still alive, they say, but has hardly a breath of life left. He wrote too much during his life and now it is as if his brain has shrunk. He suffers a great deal.[116]

The next day Sophie had become more hopeful. The doctor, presumably Chevalier Rossi, in consultation with his colleagues, put an end to the diet prescribed in Rome. Instead, Sophie was instructed to sip 'eau de gomme' to sooth her throat. She continued to find it difficult to speak nor could she sleep, but the doctor assured her that in time she would fully recover. He found her blood count good, and in view of that applied leeches to her throat and chest. Within a week Sophie had begun to feel a lot better, her cough had improved and her sleep pattern was better. She was prescribed tepid baths which she found very helpful, and the doctors confirmed that the rash on her body, which had begun in Rome, was not scurvy.[117] While in Turin Sophie learnt of Joseph-Marie Favre's death. Her sense of loss was profound.[118]

Growing crisis in the Society

In early July 1838 Sophie travelled on to Paris and so escaped from the summer heat in Turin. Her throat had not fully healed and the doctor prescribed watercress juice which he assured her would heal her deeply rooted skin irritation.[119] When she reached Lyon she found her throat was much better, the skin had erupted and the inflammation had decreased.[120] However, the doctor in Lyon, Mr Laboré, advised her not to use her voice and allow the healing process to continue, an odd position for a leader. Sophie remarked wryly to Henriette Grosier that she moved through Turin and Lyon rather like a silhouette or a shadow.[121] She listened and wrote letters and continued to feel better. The constant fever, however, was tenacious and she could not seem to shift it. She vomited bile which the doctors treated with purges followed by quinine.[122] The quinine worked well in her system, though she found it exhausting.[123]

In August Sophie continued on her journey to Paris, staying in Autun en route. There she had two purges to release a large amount of bile, and this time she did not take quinine. She noted that her recovery was becoming quicker and she began talking about rebuilding her strength, that fever had left her body and she was sleeping better.[124] She arrived in Paris on 30 August 1838 and felt quite well after the journey.[125] Intractable administrative problems awaited Sophie in Paris, and she was due to convene a General Council of the Society that year, all of which did not make her return easy.[126] As she resumed her work the old illnesses returned – headaches, poor appetite and digestion and an erratic sleep pattern.[127] Dr Cayolle studied her health history and concluded that she had a stomach ulcer which could be treated with leeches. He gave Sophie a simple diet of vegetables and a little red wine mixed with water and he suggested she walk as much as possible. At the beginning the leeches did not help her digestion, and even taking a little of her diet was difficult and affected her sleep.[128] To reduce her workload Sophie agreed to postpone the General Council of the Society for some months, until the spring of 1839. She tried to take exercise and rest, but remarked that she carried her concerns with her, 'they journey with me'.[129]

Sophie persevered with the diet and her digestion began to function better and her general health improved, although her throat continued to be inflamed and it was a strain to talk.[130] While Sophie was preparing to call a General Council and she confided to her old friend, Henriette Grosier, that it would be her last: 'I feel spent.'[131] It was in this condition, and at sixty years of age, that Sophie Barat faced into twelve years of institutional crisis within the Society of the Sacred Heart. The Society was expanding rapidly and needed new structures of government to sustain its growth internationally. A signal of this internationality was a proposal that the administrative centre of the Society of the Sacred Heart move from Paris to Rome. The proposal alone led to tensions between the Society and the archbishops of Paris, and between the French government and the papacy issues around Gallicanism and Ultramontanism quickly surfaced. Moreover, there were internal problems in the rue de Varenne community in Paris, as well as in the Trinité des Monts community in Rome.[132]

1839–1845, Paris and Rome: The critical years

Sophie Barat's health in the spring of 1839 was generally good and she made plans to travel. She had decided to convene the General Council in Rome in July 1839 and set out for Rome in February 1839, visiting some of the houses of the Society en route. She travelled first to Switzerland and, even though the journey through the Jura Mountains in the snow was bracing, this did her good.[133] By the time she finally arrived in Rome in May 1839 she was sleeping and eating quite well.[134] But life in Rome was busy and stressful. The General Council of the Society, held in the Trinité des Monts, was a catalyst for unleashing a series of crises in the Society and by the autumn Sophie Barat struggled to maintain union in the Society. By October 1839 she was ill again:

> My health is far from good. I have lost the capacity to sleep and eat since the Council, and have recovered neither one nor the other since then. I cannot retain the little food I take, and I have to rest after every meal, except lunch. The day before yesterday the doctor was shocked at my weakness. The life I lead just now could not produce any other effect. It is useless to speak of this in public. Happily my condition does not prevent me getting about and working as usual. When I am burnt out, then it will be the end.[135]

Nevertheless, over the winter and spring of 1839–40 Sophie Barat continued to work with the unfolding complexities within the Society, and despite a fever in the early summer of 1840 she sustained her workload.[136] That autumn Sophie was back in Paris to face the full force of opposition to the decisions of the General Council of 1839, both from the rue de Varenne community and the archbishop of Paris.[137] In Paris she was amazed at her own resilience: 'I am well. By a kind of miracle the good God gives me strength in proportion to the tasks I have here.'[138] As ever, her digestion was problematic.[139] In December 1840 she caught a heavy cold which developed into a deep sinus infection. Sophie was confined to bed for several weeks and only returned to her desk in March 1841:

> My convalescence has begun but it is slow. Neither my sleep nor my appetite have returned and I am still very weak. How could I recover with so many worries and so much distress?[140]

But she did recover and this seemed like a miracle to Sophie, even though her sleep and appetite had not returned.[141] Her convalescence was filled with problems urgently needing resolution. By May 1841 she still could neither sleep nor digest food properly, she had a sore mouth and her nerves were on edge. Dr Récamier suggested that a change of air, outside Paris, could help her recovery. She decided to visit the communities at Amiens, Lille and Jette (Belgium).[142] But the weather in northern France and Belgium that summer was particularly wet and cold and this made travelling stressful and tiring.[143] Besides, her troubles went with her. Life had become bleak and lonely and the members of the Society seemed unaware (or she felt they were unaware) of the chronic state of her health and the weight of her burden:

> I am overwhelmed with work. I am still unwell and I feel that I will
> not recover. I have no secretarial help at all. On this latter point no
> one shows me any sympathy, and, rather than put themselves out, I
> am left to carry on as best I can. All this does not matter to me. I will
> do as much as I can. I am looking forward to the General Council
> [1842] and once matters are settled I will have nothing else to do but
> to prepare for my imminent death I believe. Our Lord will allow me
> the time to complete my task.[144]

The wet and cold weather continued and Sophie caught a heavy chest cold in Jette. She developed a bad rash and her digestive system collapsed.[145] After a week the cold had improved but the rash on her body was so noticeable that she felt obliged to keep to her room. She was assured by the doctor that the inflammation would decrease with diet and care. Sophie remarked wryly that she would return to Paris exactly as she left and with no improvement to her health.[146] Affairs in the Society just then were critical and Sophie Barat's critics judged her indecisive and weak.[147] To her relief, Sophie's fever began to abate in early August[148] and she felt well enough to return to Paris and deal with the tensions within and without the Society. She decided to go to Rome and set out from Paris on 16 September 1841, going to Joigny on the way, to visit her sister Marie Louise. While at home Sophie suffered another bout of digestive upsets:

> No doubt you will have heard about me from Joigny, which perhaps
> caused you worry? Indeed I arrived there very ill. Some hours of rest
> relieved me and since then I feel better. I found the family well. As I
> have no time to write to Joigny it would give me pleasure if you
> would do this for me; give them my news and tell them how
> delighted I was to be with them.[149]

Sophie travelled on south to Lyon[150] and then through Chambéry and Turin, Parma and Loretto and arrived in Rome in mid-October 1841. The same pattern emerged. She struggled to cope with work and was continually exhausted. She caught colds and fevers; she could not get rid of a throat infection, even when leeches were applied.[151] She sent to Paris for marshmallow root, which she took in the form of syrup; she found this helped her throat as long as the 'fire in my mouth' remained undisturbed.[152] She slept poorly and had little time for exercise or fresh air. Many in the communities in Rome were seriously ill, and Sophie remarked that the Trinité was like a small hospital.[153] While Marie Patte cared for Sophie's personal needs, her secretary, Elizabeth Galitzine, was in Louisiana. No one in Rome was either free or capable of helping Sophie with her work, not even 'a cat to write a letter for me'. She asked Eugénie de Gramont to try and find someone to help with her vast correspondence,[154] but no one came, leaving Sophie over-burdened and depressed by the weight of her task.[155]

In addition to dealing with the critical situation which had arisen in the Society since the General Council of 1839, normal administration continued. The Society continued to expand and between 1839 and 1842 Sophie planned or gave approval for others to plan new houses in Kientzheim (Alsace), in Nancy, Laval and Montpellier (France); in new territories in America, in Sugar Creek, New York and McSherrystown (Pennsylvania); and in Canada, to Saint-Jacques de l'Achigan, near Montreal; in Ireland, at Roscrea, and in England at Berrymead, as well as in Italy, in Loretto, Saluces, St Elpidio and Padua; and in Lemberg in Galicia (Poland) and in Mustapha (Algeria). Sophie also received many requests for foundations from all over the world: from Latin America (Peru), India (Calcutta), Australia (Sydney), Burma, north Africa (Tunis), as well as from countries in Europe. The Society had never been so sought after since its foundation.

In the midst of all these demands on her leadership, Sophie Barat continued to suffer from colds, fevers, sore throats, coughs and poor sleep. The doctors in Rome applied leeches to her throat with some success but they advised her to speak as little as possible and not move about Rome.[156] Sophie developed toothache in December 1841; her mouth was continually sore and she could only eat soft bread which she found indigestible. She found coffee too bitter and she asked for chocolate to be sent her from Paris.[157] Her goal was to manage her health as best she could, to continue in office until the next General Council, due in the summer of 1842, and resign her post then. Assessing her situation in July 1841,

Sophie remarked: 'It seems that from now on my life will be a continual convalescence.'[158] Sensing certain finality, Sophie wrote to Stanislas that month asking him to be the executor of her will, in case of sudden death.[159] During the winter and spring of 1841/2 Sophie fulfilled her tasks as she could and returned to France for the General Council. When Elizabeth Galitzine saw her for the first time in some months, she thought Sophie could be dead by Christmas.[160]

Resolution and respite

The winter months of 1842 into the spring of 1843 proved to be the most arduous for Sophie Barat. In the course of these weeks she found a resolution of the crisis which deeply divided the Society of the Sacred Heart from 1839. From her base in Paris, with the help of Césaire Mathieu, archbishop of Besançon and the papal inter-nuncio in Paris, Mgr Garibaldi, and Sophie found a formula to resolve the conflicts with the archbishop of Paris, Mgr Denys Affre and with the French government.[161] This was presented to Pope Gregory XVI and his secretary of state, Cardinal Lambruschini, by Césaire Mathieu during his *ad limina* visit to the pope in March 1843. Compromise had been reached and the Society of the Sacred Heart reverted to the Constitutions of 1815.[162] While this was a certain resolution to the immediate problems of the Society, it would take a long time for it to recover from the years of polarisation and division. At that juncture Sophie considered that she could not resign then, that the polarisation within the Society, especially among the first and second generation of members, was too strong for her to leave her post. She decided to remain as leader and try to restore unity in the Society. In that spirit she set about her task, wondering if she had the strength for it.[163]

Certainly the burden of leadership had lessened and Sophie's health stabilised. In June 1844 she spent a month in England, despite warnings of a hazardous sea journey. In fact Sophie travelled well and she noted with some satisfaction that most travellers on board were seasick and she on the contrary had a very good crossing.[164] In fact she felt so well after this trip that she began to plan a visit to Louisiana, considering that that could be an easier journey than travelling from Paris to Rome.[165] A minor mishap in mid-August 1844, when she fell and hurt her arm, prevented work and travel for some weeks.[166] By late October she was ready to set off for Rome, accompanied by Marie Patte and her recently appointed secretary, Adèle Cahier. They visited communities in stages on the way. Sophie caught a heavy cold in Lyon and spent the month of November recuperating before moving on in early December to Annonay and Avignon.

On her birthday, 12 December, the weather deteriorated while they were travelling between Avignon and Aix-en-Provence. Heavy snow fell and the Mistral made the journey even more uncomfortable. When they arrived in Aix the driver of the coach did not know where the community lived and he set the travellers down at some distance from the house. They walked in the snow and Sophie caught yet another heavy cold. The familiar pattern emerged again: nights of perspiration and consequently of insomnia; administration of purges followed by quinine; inhalation to ease the sinuses. She remarked to Eugénie de Gramont: 'We are back at the beginning.'[167] And to Césaire Mathieu: 'I am getting old. The slightest fatigue brings me endless maladies.'[168]

Nevertheless, a month later, on 13 January 1845, Sophie was better and able to continue on her travels, first to Marseilles and then to Genoa from where she embarked for Rome on 17 January 1845, arriving at Civita-Vecchia on the morning of 23 January. Winter that year in Rome was severe. Sophie fell ill again and was confined to bed for two months. She told Eugénie de Gramont that her cough and fever left her no rest day or night.[169] Leeches had been tried and a vesicatory was placed on her chest to alleviate the cough. While they gave her some relief, her coughing, fevers and constant night perspirations continued.[170] The same symptoms, the same ailments, the same treatments, all over again.

Sophie Barat's final years in Paris, 1846–1865

By 1846 Sophie Barat's health patterns were well established, and indeed chronic. But she continued to govern the Society of the Sacred Heart until her death in 1865. During these years, with rare exceptions, Sophie was ill from November to February /March each year, or at least confined to her room. She became accustomed to this and accepted it had become a way of life for her. The beginning of Sophie's winter retreat period was signalled when she succumbed first to a cold, which then developed into a fever and triggered her throat condition. Insomnia, coughing, persistent perspiration and chronic stomach upsets became a regular feature of her nights. Remedies were applied which upset her digestion and these were so interrelated by now that any doctor would have been hard pressed to know which symptom to treat. Commenting on her health, Sophie said while she could overcome colds and sinus attacks, she usually had fever at night with consequent insomnia and weakness during the day. She complained continually of having a dry mouth and sore throat, especially if she had to talk for any length of time.[171] Yet she was realistic and remarked to Eugénie de Gramont in 1846, 'basically my constitution is sound.'[172] Indeed she had recognised this as early as 1818: 'My constitution is basically sound and nothing but the years can destroy it, and I greatly fear I will survive you.'[173]

To help Sophie manage what had become a chronic state, Dr Récamier insisted she take prolonged rest during the day. He sometimes visited her unexpectedly in the rue de Varenne to ensure this was happening. If she was up and about he firmly ordered her back to her room, even if she was in the chapel. This was not always accepted with good grace.[174] From 1846 Sophie Barat travelled much less and except for one more journey to Rome in 1850 and a trip to Germany in 1856, her travel was confined to France. Even then the journeys were of short duration, and after 1857 she ceased to travel altogether. She lived in Paris and governed the Society from her rooms. She had secretarial help and the constant presence of four assistants general. This was the period of consolidation and institutionalisation of the Society. While her personal correspondence was predictably less in winter, Sophie resumed this each spring and peppered her letters with the conventional bulletin of health. No new symptoms appeared, but the familiar ones were as regular as ever.[175] In January 1858 Sophie told her nephew, Stanislas Dusaussoy, with some satisfaction that she had attended midnight Mass at Christmas for the first time in seven years.[176] Members of the Society and her friends sent her gifts of special foods to tempt her appetite, but most of these she refused graciously and passed them to the community.[177] But when she received a gift of pomegranates from Algeria, she accepted them gratefully; they soothed her throat which 'was always inflamed'.[178]

In February 1863 Sophie wrote to her niece, Sophie Dusaussoy (a member of the Society in Niort), thanking her for the gift of special cheeses sent to her and the community in Paris. She knew the community enjoyed them, but admitted:

> I cannot manage to take cheese now from any part of France. They are all too salty and often sharp in taste. My throat too is sensitive, all acidic foods or salted food aggravate my cough and this prevents me from talking. This is always painful for me. Indeed, I am reduced to having only dull, bland food. Yet many send me gifts to stimulate my appetite! Happily for the good of my soul none of them succeeds! Besides I need to make amends for the little extravagances in food of my youth.[179] Neither have I the possibility of having the opposite since I cannot tolerate sweet things. So I take this opportunity to send you some sweets and they will do your digestion good.[180]

However, there was one type of cheese Sophie could still enjoy, a special gougère made according to a recipe from Joigny. Agnes Verney, who cared for Sophie after Marie Patte's death, knew how to make it well and Sophie always enjoyed eating this.[181]

Final months of Sophie Barat

Sophie Barat noted that the winter of 1862/3 was exceptional for her, simply because she had no major illnesses. Even more remarkable, for the first time in years she had no sore throat. From the spring of 1863 she was afoot and able to deal with her post, sign letters, and delegate business to her assistants general.[182] That year too, in April 1863, she redrafted her will and her testament to the Society. The following winter Sophie reverted to pattern and she was ill during the last two winters of her life. By the spring of 1865 she had been confined to her room for four months.[183] Over that winter she wrote very few letters, but by February 1865 she took up her pen again, and wrote six letters that month, six in March, seventeen in April, and twenty in May. Early in May 1865, taking advantage of the warm spring weather, Sophie spent time in the garden of the rue de Varenne (the Hôtel Biron).[184] She maintained interest in the community and the school and was alert in her perceptions.

On the morning of Monday 22 May 1865 all appeared normal until breakfast time. Sophie had hardly started to eat when she began to feel quite unwell. Putting her hands to her head she moaned: 'My head! My head!' Her speech became difficult and she closed her eyes. When asked if a mustard poultice would help, she could barely signal her acceptance. She was brought to a comfortable chair first. She opened her eyes briefly and tried to speak, but her tongue had become paralysed. Sophie had had a brain haemorrhage (une congestion apoplectiforme) and she slipped slowly into unconsciousness and never spoke again. Doctors were sent for and three came in haste. They treated her with 'all the resources they had at their disposal'. By Tuesday morning the effect of her stroke had deepened. Sophie's eyes remained closed, and yet while she could not speak it seemed that she was conscious and understood what was spoken. To test this Dr Gouraud asked if she would bless the members of the Society and Sophie raised her hand. Yet when Dr Bauchet, another physician, asked her twice to bless the doctors treating her, Sophie's hand remained quite still. On Wednesday 24 May one of the doctors lifted her eyelid and met her candid, direct look. Sophie turned to Joséphine Goetz, her successor, looked intently at her and pressed her hand twice. Over the next hours her life ebbed gently away. At 11 p.m. on the evening of Ascension

Thursday, 25 May 1865, Sophie Barat died peacefully.[185]

Observations on the Medical History of Madeleine Sophie Barat.
(Frederick Holmes).[186]

Born prematurely in 1779 Madeleine Sophie Barat enjoyed a healthy childhood and developed into an intelligent young woman who was of short stature (150 cm height) but physically normal and sound. Her brother Louis, elder by eleven years, was an overbearing and stultifying influence in her young adult years and was never far from her thoughts until his death when she was sixty-five. Once grown and away from home, she developed a life-long pattern of intense mental and physical activity culminating in exhaustion of her physical faculties, requiring periods of convalescence before she was again intensely active. Even during these periods of convalescence she never ceased writing letters, which activity was the venue for her life and work of developing and extending the world-wide identity of the Society of the Sacred Heart of Jesus. It is possible that her brother Louis was at once her goad and her hairshirt.

In her twenties she developed a mysterious illness of a gynaecologic nature. We can infer that this was extremely uncomfortable and was something she perceived as a swelling, that she feared was a cancer. Within the limits of her modesty – perhaps considerable even for her time and station in life – she had desultory treatment with little good or lasting effect. In 1806, after a hard, hot, uncomfortable coach ride from Grenoble to Lyon she had sudden relief of her symptoms and they never returned. It is certain that she had a Bartholin's cyst or abscess at the entrance to her vagina and that it drained suddenly after the trauma of the coach ride, never to recur.

In the remaining nearly sixty years of her productive life, defined by the cycles of intense activity and then convalescence, she had a number of real physical problems that are documented in her letters. By her thirties she had developed soreness in her eyes, rheumatism, and prolonged bouts of fever for which there was no obvious cause. By age forty she complained of 'rheumatism of her eyes' and her episodes of fever continued. At age forty-five her eye soreness was occasionally sufficient to limit her reading and writing of letters. Before her fiftieth birthday she was having severe enough rheumatism – clearly arthritis – to prompt a diagnosis of gout. (As she was still having regular menstrual periods she did not have gout; Hippocrates, about 2,500 years ago, was the first to note that pre-menopausal women never develop gout.)

During her fifties she had night sweats with her fevers and also coughed up blood on more than one occasion (haemoptysis). On several occasions she was thought to have sinus infections and mouth soreness was mentioned as well. With these upper respiratory symptoms she often had 'severe colds' and usually had fever with these episodes. In her early sixties she had a rash over her whole body and sore throats were often noted.

The continual problem with eyes, often sore throat and mouth, periodic unexplained fevers, and at least one episode of acute arthritis lead one to a diagnosis of Sjögren's Syndrome, a relatively common autoimmune problem of middle-aged women. In Sjögren's there is slowly progressive damage of all of the salivary and lachrymal glands leading to the sicca syndrome, dry eyes and a dry mouth. It is not possible to overestimate the misery of chronically dry eyes for the sufferer. As the disease progresses, damage to fluid-producing glands lower in the respiratory tract may lead to acute and chronic bronchitis, surely part of Sophie Barat's problems in her later years. Sjögren's may be a disease entity unto itself or a syndrome accompanying rheumatoid arthritis, scleroderma, sarcoidosis, lupus, or other so-called autoimmune diseases. In Sophie Barat's case there is no reason to think she had anything beyond the Sjögren's itself.

In modern times the definitive diagnosis of Sjögren's is easily made by biopsy of the labial mucosa (inner aspect of the lower lip) and finding microscopic evidence of inflammatory cells in the minor salivary glands. I am sufficiently certain of the diagnosis of Sjögren's in Sophie Barat that if a labial biopsy were negative I would ask that a second biopsy be done. Without a positive biopsy we can't be absolutely certain of the diagnosis of Sjögren's; however, the clinical picture is so compelling that the diagnosis seems certain. I am disturbed by her several episodes of haemoptysis. The possibility of coexisting chronic pulmonary tuberculosis must be considered, particularly in light of her night sweats. However, it is unlikely that she could have had this for decades without becoming a pulmonary cripple or having a diagnosis of pulmonary tuberculosis made by one of the many competent physicians who saw her, particularly Dr Joseph Récamier, who knew her well. It is likely that the haemoptysis was a consequence of chronic bronchitis, itself the consequence of a dry bronchial mucosa from her Sjögren's.

An unrelated medical problem was the injury to her ankle suffered in 1829, which caused her instability of gait and a further series of falls, worsening that injury. No treatment was successful until 1832 when a surgeon, Chevalier Rossi, in Turin, got the fracture properly diagnosed and, with a regimen of daily dressings and immobilisation, got that fracture to heal and thereby restored his patient to normal activity and a normal gait.

The spells of abdominal pain and alternating diarrhoea and constipation that she suffered through much of her adult life were probably what is presently called functional bowel disease. It is quite likely that French physicians of the nineteenth century had a good feeling for managing this benign problem as do physicians of our own time. Her death in 1865, at age eighty-five, unheralded in any way, was from an acute intra-cranial haemorrhage (frappée d'une apoplectiforme), unrelated to her Sjögren's. Considering the scope and size of the mission Ste Sophie Barat's life represents, it is not amiss to compare her to St Paul and her physical affliction to his 'thorn in the flesh'.

Observations on the Medical History of Madeleine Sophie Barat. (Mary d'Apice).[187]

It was with much interest that I read Professor Holmes' diagnosis of Sophie's many and varied physical ailments. I should like, in my turn, to examine a little of the impact of her early and adolescent life experiences on her personality and emotional development. The roots of much that we recognise in her later life can be found in these formative years.

In doing this, it is not possible to ignore a number of factors in her life in Joigny. Those which appear to have had the greatest impact on her personality were the relationships with her parents and her brother Louis.

In the case of the former, the love and affirmation with which Sophie was surrounded from her earliest years would have developed in her the self-assurance and security needed to face the challenges met in her later life. While the acceptance she experienced as a child from both family and friends was a source of her ability to relate confidently to people in all stations of life from the aristocracy to the tradespeople.

A lively sense of independence transmitted to her so strongly by her Burgundian mother was to stand her in good stead in the years ahead when she struggled to unite a fractured and divided Society, first in Amiens and again in 1839. It was also what enabled her to cope, often unsupported, with the demands of a rapidly growing organisation.

Although, in her own words, 'thoroughly spoilt' by her parents and older sister, who treasured this youngest member of the family, this did not seem to affect her adversely. Any ill effects were, perhaps, negated by the subsequent treatment by her brother.

However, the intensity of the fear which surely would have been communicated to her from her mother in the face of the fire in Joigny that caused her premature birth could not have been without its impact on Sophie. Nor could the struggle for life by the fragile two-months-old premature baby who would not have had the support systems available today, or the care of her very ill mother. This, though no longer recalled, would remain an influential factor in her unconscious mind. It could well have had its repercussions in the severity of the struggles and fears experienced later in life. Again, the fear experienced by the whole family as they hid Louis from the authorities in post-revolutionary France and as they suffered through the years of his imprisonment must have deepened the levels of anxiety in Sophie, then in her early teens.

Madame Barat's exaggerated anxiety and scrupulosity (obsessive compulsive neurosis) would also have been communicated to her little daughter in a way that would influence her own reactions through much of her life. This predisposition to scrupulosity, increased by the Jansenist teachings rife at the time, caused Sophie much anxiety and pain when she found herself unable to meet the demands for sanctity imposed on her by Louis. It is also evident in the struggle she had later to accept her inability to live the life of mortification and prolonged prayer she deemed appropriate for her as superior general.

But it would seem that it was Louis' control over his sister, conceded to by her parents at the early age of seven, that had the most damaging effect on her emotional development. Madame Barat's obvious respect for her son's scholastic status and her awe of his power and position led her to give in to a regime for her daughter which would probably not have been tolerated by someone less fearful.

The sudden transition from the happy, carefree life Sophie had enjoyed to a harshly disciplined control quite unsuitable for her age and sex had lasting consequences. Although inspired by ambitions for the very best for his god-child, Louis' handling of Sophie damaged both her physical and psychological development. The abrupt change of lifestyle crushed her spirit, resulting in a deep insecurity and loss of balance in her judgement. This was to remain with her, adding to her tendency to scrupulosity until she finally began freeing herself of her brother's influence in her thirties. The demands she placed on herself and on others with regards to fasting, to prayer and to the workload expected in the early days of her leadership showed clearly a lack of judgement. It was difficult for her to accept her limited strength and to adjust her living accordingly, with the result that she was constantly on the verge of burnout. Only gradually was she able, with the help of others, to regain her balance and accept and adjust to her physical frailties.

Louis' domineering and uncompromising behaviour towards his sister, especially during the time she spent with him in Paris, constituted real abuse for this particularly sensitive and affectionate young person. Like any abusive behaviour it can, if maintained, give rise to a condition sometimes referred to as Prolonged Duress Stress Disorder (PDSD).

Apart from its physical symptoms of headaches, migraine, stomach and bowel problems, raised blood pressure, sleep disorders and loss of energy, all of which we find in Sophie, the psychological effects are also marked. Foremost among these are an increase in anxiety and fear, a sense of guilt, reactive depression and a loss of confidence and self-esteem. We so often see evidence of this in Sophie's later life, even though Louis' direct control had lessened.

Her self-doubt when named leader of the newly formed group which was to become the Society of the Sacred Heart was paralysing for her. The degree of stress this caused her at a time when the very existence of the group was threatened by the Paccanari trial led to a serious physical collapse. This was not helped by the embarrassment and obvious humiliation caused by Joseph Varin's invasion of her privacy by discussing her gynaecological problems with a number of priests. Sophie's extreme sensitivity in such matters would have added to the impact of this.

Perhaps the severest damage done to her sensitive nature was caused by the sessions of exorcism Louis forced his eleven-year-old sister to witness. The severity of the fears noted later by Joseph Varin could well have been caused by the post-traumatic stress resulting from this ordeal which was far beyond her emotional strength to endure. 'I do not know what your dear brother and mine could possibly have ordered you to do which was capable of bringing such trouble and anxiety to your soul,' [188] he wrote in 1801.

No one can suffer this type of abuse without it resulting in a marked degree of anger. For Sophie, there was no opportunity to give expression to this in any way. As a consequence, the anger would have been repressed by the fear-filled young girl, giving rise later to bouts of depression. There is evidence of these throughout Sophie's life.

In spite of the obvious negative effects of the draconian regime experienced from Louis' years of control, Sophie gained a level of education from him rare in women of her day. This enabled her finally to guide a developing educational establishment with sureness and a genuine confidence in her own ability to do so. One wonders, too, if the strength of character and the self-discipline Sophie acquired in these years was what helped her later to withstand the extraordinary demands made on her during her years of guiding the Society of the Sacred Heart. These pressures were particularly evident during the crisis in the Society in 1839.

With the progress of time and support of close relationships, especially that with Joseph-Marie Favre, Sophie gradually surmounted many of the repercussions of Louis' treatment of her. She regained the strengths so evident in her childhood, showing a remarkable independence and wisdom in her handling of the many complex situations of a rapidly growing religious congregation. She related freely and confidently to every class of society, to the hierarchy of the church, to the aristocracy, the needy and above all to the children, who loved her dearly. Sophie's friendships in later life were both deep and lasting, notably that with Philippine Duchesne on whom she relied so heavily. We find evidence of this in the countless letters she wrote over the years. Even the emotional imbalance of her relationship with Eugénie de Gramont was not unusual as such infatuation is, at times, experienced by women in the early years of midlife.

With Favre's guidance, Sophie's scrupulosity lessened as she learnt to overcome the Jansenist influences of her early life and to discover a loving and non-judgemental God. 'How can you mistrust a God who infinitely loves you, who wishes only for your health and happiness,'[189] he wrote to her in 1832. The struggle to embrace this Ultramontane spirituality was a slow process but it brought with it a freedom from the many doubts and fears that had governed her previous life.

CHAPTER 5

The Spiritual Leadership of
Madeleine Sophie Barat[1]

Introduction

In 1853 Madeleine Sophie Barat read a new biography of Joseph Varin:

> I was deeply moved by the many memories awoken in me, and also
> by my regrets! We cannot say everything. I have reproached myself
> sometimes for not recording so many significant things about us [the
> Society of the Sacred Heart] and which can only be known by us and
> can come from the original members. I am too old to do it now and
> besides, where could I find the time to do it [?] At least we are fortu-
> nate to have the essential information.[2]

But in fact Sophie Barat left 'essential information' in the form of a vast
archive of 14,000 letters, two journals and a testament. Since Sophie
Barat's process for canonisation began soon after her death all who possessed letters from her, within and without the Society of the Sacred
Heart, were requested to release them, thereby creating an instant archive
of primary documents. Adèle Cahier, Sophie Barat's secretary for many
years, carefully listed and catalogued this vast body of material which
shows Sophie Barat at her desk day by day from 1800 to 1865. The letters
follow the slow construction of the Society of the Sacred Heart and reveal
the spirit in which Sophie Barat governed the communities. Her public,
formal voice is heard in her letters to popes, bishops and priests, to the
families of the members of the Society or to parents of the pupils, or to
secular authorities. These letters have a format and rhetoric which allow
her to deal deftly with situations and realise her own goals for the Society.
Similarly, her general letters to the Society, usually to mark the preparation for and outcome of General Councils, also tend to be formal, quite
distant in tone. They are letters of government and administration.

By contrast, Sophie Barat's letters to the members of the Society and to her own family show her as spontaneous and, for the most part, unguarded. These letters are first drafts, sent uncorrected. Sophie Barat writes quite unconsciously and she never imagined so many of her letters would be preserved. She certainly never suspected that her letters would be examined minutely for the process of her own canonisation. It is in these personal letters that Sophie Barat's spirituality emerges as, day by day and year by year, she deals with people and issues in the Society. The comments she makes, the advice she gives, the decisions she takes, endless suggestions and proposals for discussion and exchange, all reveal her spirituality at work. Each letter contains a number of elements. It opens with a greeting and giving of news of the Society (including her health), followed by business/personnel matters, and usually ends with some spiritual reflection and advice. The letters read like written conversations, and some are very long.

Depending on the context, Sophie Barat's letters concern good governance of the Society, especially the vitality of the communities and schools. They deal with issues regarding the members of the Society, their personal needs and work issues. Some treat of acceptance or dismissal of members; others discuss legal cases arising from the dowries or pensions given by families to the Society. In her letters to community leaders and to headmistresses Sophie Barat shows keen interest in the level of education given in the boarding and the poor schools. She also deals with issues of health in the schools and in the communities, and is particularly attentive to the quality of food in both. When making appointments to leadership, either in the communities or schools, she discusses how these could impact the members of the community and on the students in the schools. She guides the community leaders personally and urges them in turn to care for the spiritual needs of the community. She constantly addresses the ongoing spiritual formation and practical training of the members as either choir or coadjutrix sisters. She deals with financial questions endlessly: the buying and selling of properties, negotiating with civil and ecclesiastical authorities, insisting on financial viability and avoidance of debt.

Letter writing was Sophie Barat's essential mode of communication with the members, along with visits to communities, which became rarer after 1850. As the Society expanded, Sophie's letters became more prolific. Despite being under pressure for time, her letters tend to be long and she admitted that she found it easier to write a long rather than a short letter. Her tone is direct and realistic, pragmatic and engaged, sometimes brusque and laconic, often full of wry humour. She can be abrasive and infuriated, especially if she sensed the recipient was not engaged fully on her task or again had not grasped the implications of either action or inaction in critical situations. And yet there can be a rush of tenderness and understanding in these same letters, a wry, self-deprecatory remark, in an effort to soften the bluntness of her observations. As she writes Sophie Barat quite naturally weaves in quotations from the Gospels and the Letters of St Paul. She cites especially from the Gospels, especially that of St John, and from most of the letters of Paul, particularly to the Romans, Colossians and Corinthians. She quotes Horace, Virgil and Ovid. She enjoys comparing situations she is dealing with to the fables of La Fontaine. She cites Teresa of Avila, Montaigne, Malebranche and Voltaire, even Napoleon, and she refers to the newspapers of the day, *La Quotidienne*, *Ami de la Religion*, and *Gazette de France*. Most of all, she has an endless source of French proverbs which allow her to make her points with freshness and realism.[3]

Sophie Barat's guidance of members in the Society of the Sacred Heart

From its foundation in 1800, the impulse of the Society of the Sacred Heart was to bring the message of Christ to a country torn apart by the Revolution. This aspiration was symbolised and expressed in the spirituality of the Heart of Christ pierced on Calvary. In the course of her life and leadership Sophie Barat returns to this as to the point on a compass and it is the basis of her spiritual teaching. She assumed that when women asked to enter the Society they were committed to grow spiritually and were ready to take the steps necessary to reach that goal. Her guidance at all stages of their journey is direct and clear, and she calls each from where they were to where they could be. Once this basic orientation has been established Sophie then invites the person to choose consciously to go onward and deeper on the spiritual path. By way of encouragement she often indicates the joy and fulfilment of those who respond to Christ in freedom and generosity.

But she continually warns that the price is costly, there are no short-cuts; only by following Christ all the way to Golgotha can each reach the joy of Easter. She develops this in various ways: she speaks of the polarity between the creature and God; she writes of how human nature is transformed by the Spirit of God; she notes the power of the Resurrection in our lives; she speaks of the action of Christ in our inner world and the impact of that on our inner being; she focuses on the Passion of Christ as

the source of growth; she urges individuals to move into that consciousness and live in that depth; she understands that human nature is not
destroyed in the process of spiritual growth, but rather transformed. In
the course of her guidance of the members of the Society, Sophie Barat
devises a path of self-knowledge and of generosity which leads to transformation in Christ. This path is present from the beginning but becomes
more assured and refined as she gains experience.[4] When read in the
context of her own biography, it is clear that what Sophie Barat asks of
the members of the Society she asks of herself. Her advice is practical and
basic, especially in the initial stages of spiritual development.

Path of self-knowledge

At every stage in life Sophie Barat insists on self-knowledge and on developing the capacity to reflect. She constantly points out the danger of
living a double life in the Society if members do not know themselves in
their light and in shadow. Without such awareness members of communities cannot understand the impact they have for good or ill on each
other. Sophie Barat asks that members accept personal responsibility for
their lives and their actions, in the communities where they lived and in
the tasks they undertook there and in the schools. Such frank advice was
essential for dealing with difficulties in relationships, differences of
approach and opinions, as well as differences of social backgrounds.
Otherwise intractable problems set in, either in a community or school,
and led to impossible polarities.[5] Sophie Barat could not reach each
member but she could train leaders, trusting that if each one was seriously
engaged on a spiritual life, insight would be given her, as in the case of
Marie de la Croix in 1828:

> I pray that the Lord may enlighten you, for it has to be said that you
> only know the good side of yourself while you do not know your
> faults well enough. The dark spirit is deceiving you and you do not
> realise it. True, your motives are genuine, but you are far from acting
> with caution and judgement. If you pray, the Holy Spirit will
> confirm what I am trying to convey to you. Though I do not believe
> myself to be divinely inspired, nevertheless I think I am right.[6]

Seventeen years later, she reminded Marie de la Croix:

> You must not plan on too grandiose a scale. Do not forget your past
> activities, so badly calculated at Lille, and then the renovations at
> Conflans, which were quite useless, and are still not fully paid for.
> This is how we ruin the Society, with so many false estimates. I am

reminding you of these facts, not out of bad temper. I have let that go as I placed all in the hands of the Lord. But I am reminding you of the past because we need to truly learn from our mistakes in order to avoid making new ones. Without that, what is the point of our experience? I hope that you will benefit from this.[7]

Some in the Society offered or expected to be leaders but did not have the capacity for this task. These had to be told this truthfully:

> Though you are unaware of this yourself, you are not free enough with regard to the office of superior. You know you have gifts and that you wish to do good. But although you have some essential qualities, you lack others that are necessary. You are not at all calm enough; you exaggerate both good and bad qualities; you are not interior enough, at all. You count too much on yourself and not enough on God; you want to do too much. In a word, your activity is too frenetic. Fulfil your present duties and you will render the Society a great service.[8]

To another, having a difficult time with someone in her community, Sophie Barat told her that the impasse would soon be resolved as changes were already in train. But in the meantime, her own task was to grow in self-knowledge:

> You need to know your deepest self, plumb the depths of your inner life, and be convinced above all of your own nothingness, and that you can only rely on God alone and his grace. This time of trial will pass. Only be faithful to humble yourself and overcome your temptations with regard to the person who torments you. When you get the opportune moment warn your superiors of the abuses you see.[9]

When Sophie Barat sensed that the person was committed to journeying spiritually, she offered endless encouragement, often for years:

> Your will is set on corresponding to Christ's love and not refusing anything. That is all the divine Heart asks of us. He does not ask that we become perfect all at once, but that we work towards this each day, in the measure that grace operates in us and the radiance of the Holy Spirit enlightens us. But alas, often we do not listen with the ears of our soul to this divine Word. Self-indulgence, over-activity and our other little passions place obstacles in our way. These obstruct the pathways of the Spirit's inspirations and lights which we would receive in torrents if we were committed.[10]

As part of their growth in self-knowledge, Sophie Barat asked leaders to reflect on how they used their power for the good of others. She told Irène de Ferry in 1862 that she was too uptight and somewhat rigid and cold in manner. Sophie asked her to bring this into her prayer and see what light she could gain, especially on how her leadership impacted on the community and school.[11] She linked her observations with complaints in the school about poor food, knowing by her own experience that issues around food and rigidity were often linked and indeed found in the same person:

> I hope the Lord in his goodness will come to help you in a role for which you would need to be a saint to fulfil honourably and perfectly. It is true that the way to become so is to seek only the glory of the Heart of Jesus and the good of those confided to us, by forgetting our own self and our personal concerns, Then aware of our powerlessness and our neediness, and how our faults can block the fruits of our mission, we bring ourselves to another level in order to cast ourselves into the arms of Jesus Christ in absolute surrender. Otherwise, if we rely on ourselves and our devices, we fall into a labyrinth from which we can never escape. So be full of trust in the One who has given you this charge. You will have His support and help from the moment you have recourse to His Heart with trust and love. Be more humble than ever. May this virtue exude from the very pores of your body, so to speak, and be in your words and in your contacts with all.[12]

Eliane Cuënot was treasurer of the local community in the rue de Varenne, Paris and had difficulty dealing with some of Sophie Barat's colleagues, especially the treasurer general of the Society, Henriette Coppens, and the secretary general, Adèle Cahier. Sophie accepted that the task was complex and offered her a possible way to resolve, or at least alleviate, tensions:

> I cannot recommend enough that you use all your religious spirit and tact when dealing with them, especially Mère Henriette [Coppens, treasurer general]. When she finds that she needs help, then offer your services and say Amen to everything graciously. Keep all your difficulties for me. Our good Master will help us when we only seek His glory and the fulfilment of His good wishes. Be the same with Mère Cahier. She really is working on her character. For your part, do the same. Normally we do not become perfect in a day. Imitate the silence of Jesus, the eternal Word. It is so true that silence is indeed more excellent than anything we could say, when we are not obliged to speak out.[13]

Sophie Barat continued to encourage Eliane Cuënot who felt that her work was unseen and unappreciated. In 1862 Sophie suggested she face this issue in herself rather than bury it in resentment. She could learn so much from this experience:

> I have been expecting news from you for some weeks and found the waiting long. I feared you were ill and sensed what was wrong. You are better now, so try then to be calmer. Your impressions are so intense and profound that they affect you physically. I ask the Heart of Jesus to give you an understanding and a love for the hidden life. If only you knew this gift of God! Then you would be happy to have some part of it. I have not much time and so I cannot develop this theme which is so attractive to an interior person who contemplates the Heart of Jesus.[14]

Sophie Barat knew how roles take centre stage and create power cliques within a community or school, and how this applied not just to leaders but also to all office holders such as the headmistresses, cooks, infirmarians, farmers, treasurers. By pointing this out to them all Sophie Barat fought to maintain consciousness of the fundamental purpose of their life, asking that they be honest with themselves and with her. When Marie de Tinseau wrote frankly about her struggles, Sophie responded warmly:

> You genuinely recognise your ignorance and even your mistakes, and with uprightness and resolute will you want to make up for them, avoid them by the greatest commitment in the future. You have grasped all this, you have accepted the humiliation of the past, and the self-sacrifice this asks of you in the future. I repeat, this is the real action of the Spirit of Jesus. Learn to appreciate this divine Light and walk only in its radiance. It will cost you, without any doubt, to watch over your natural impulses and not allow them to dominate or take action. But the practice of watching how you act, which you must consent to without limit and in complete inner freedom, will make this habit easy and reassuring. It is so sweet to obey the inspirations of grace which let the peace of Jesus permeate the soul. Is this not the most delightful of gifts which the divine Heart bestows on those He loves and who respond to the depth of His Love?[15]

Call to the contemplative life

As the Society grew in numbers and expanded rapidly, Sophie Barat feared that this could lead to it becoming a counter-image of the original vision she and her companions had in 1800. She feared a loss of soul energy, drained out by success, overwork and a mediocre inner life of prayer. She was truly distressed when Elizabeth Galitzine's niece was told by the Jesuits in Paris that she would find it impossible to live a contemplative life in the Society of the Sacred Heart:

> It is a mistake to think that only those called to an active life join the Society. If we lacked the contemplative life the active life would soon

become a lifeless spectre, and deprived of that vitality what good could we possibly do then? I am convinced that we lose our best candidates through the false notion that those who wish to enter our Society must be solely attracted to external work, yet almost all those attracted to the deal of the contemplative life have been successful with us. An order composed of these two attractions is spiritually strong and this strength becomes a great support for the active of the Society. This is what I feel compelled to establish in our Society before I die. By this means all will be renewed, we will maintain a strong contemplative life and this will not damage the works which the Society undertakes since unfortunately those entering with contemplative attractions are few. Moreover, the contemplative side of the Society will be a nursery for [future] superiors, mistresses of novices, etc.[16]

It was this inner life that Sophie Barat nurtured and encouraged in the Society, inviting the members to journey to the thresholds of their inner being, where shadows, doubles and counter-images are revealed and confronted. She encouraged any signs of growth in this direction:

It seems to me that you are more at ease within yourself. I ask this of Our Lord for you, I ask Him to allow this work to your benefit. If we so will, such a surrender to the good wishes of Jesus is the alchemy (talisman) which transforms everything into gold. This is a wonderful secret which we do not deepen sufficiently.[17]

If she saw someone hesitating to go forward, she would urge them to reach into their inner depths:

When will you be firmly rooted in Jesus, seeing only Him, *seeking only* Him, to such an extent that people and the self disappear, as if they were in the antipodes. It is in this way that our soul and its ways of operating become simple and we will have peace. But these backtrackings, these anxieties, these analyses, these attitudes, the judgements you make, all this army comes together (criss-crosses) in our inner world, and sometimes unhinges us. Yet when we can liberate ourselves from these foxes (deceivers) by keeping Our Lord constantly in mind, and surrendering to His good will, we create peace and harmony in the depth of our soul. And this happens, even after committing faults, when we accept them and make up for them by a life of tolerance and humility. So open wide your heart. You hold your inner self too rigidly. Generosity will develop this outlook. Do not refuse the Good Master anything deliberately and consciously.[18]

Sophie's friend, Louise de Limminghe, was often disheartened and trapped in a dark view of herself and of God. Sophie invited her to reach to another level within:

Please, and I cannot repeat this too often, open out your soul, you hold yourself in a double stranglehold. Your faults, which are only sheer fragility, upset you too much and constrain your heart! You must draw much more closely to the Heart of Jesus and not think about yourself. His glory, his work in people ought to be your dominant thought. A single disavowal of your failings is enough. Conserve all your powers of your soul for securing yourself in union and in love with Jesus! Believe that everything is useful for nurturing these virtues. It is like the way we throw dry wood, green wood, brambles and brushwood on the fire, these materials feed the fire, and their nature is changed on account of the action of the fiery furnace! Jesus acts like that in our souls, if we surrender our being entirely to Him.[19]

As members of the Society journeyed inwardly in prayer and sought to integrate this into their everyday life, Sophie warned them not to get caught in self-absorption or pride. She insisted on the need for a humble attitude in prayer, as the truest expression of integrity:

Once known and practised, this virtue draws the gifts of the Holy Spirit to a soul rapt in the beauty of God. The Spirit rests in a heart that is emptied of the self and of all the self-absorption which pride engenders. Then when our heart is free of all self-interest, the Spirit of Jesus acts in peace, and this good Master remains with delight within us, where He becomes our centre and principal guide. Such are the fruits of humility. But to conserve them, help them grow and consolidate, we need constant prayer and recourse to Jesus. So then, the habit of recollection needs to be acquired through the energy of our soul forces focussed on the things of God. Thus, once again we need to keep our contacts with people to what is strictly necessary and not to let ourselves be dispersed by worldly affairs.[20]

Similarly to Adèle Lehon, living through political upheavals in the Papal States in 1860:

More than ever let us draw close to the open Heart of Jesus. Let us meditate on His love, His charity towards all, and in our turn may we try to bring this wherever we have any influence. How many acts of sacrifice and patience are needed in the exercise of loving, and yet leaders must be the model! Ask this grace for me, as I do for you. Otherwise we will reap little fruit from our constant labours.[21]

Adèle Lehon was overwhelmed by personal struggles at this time and asked Sophie for advice:

Well, of course, we would be able to act more perfectly if we did not have strong feelings and if we were continually under the influence and guidance of the Holy Spirit. But this is not our privilege in this life. All the Saints have tried and only a few, very few, were exempt from the effects of the sin of Adam. So I am not at all surprised that you have regrets like so many others. Indeed, if the great St Paul said: 'I do the evil which I hate, and I do not do the good I love', then without doubt, while he did not do evil acts, he was inclined that way like all human beings tainted by original sin! So you should not be surprised by your weaknesses, by your failings. Who does not experience them? Nevertheless, like the saints we should fight them, lessen them, take the means to overcome them, and you know the means.[22]

Transformation in Christ

Instead of being disheartened by failure, Sophie urged the members of the Society to press on to the source of Christian joy and hope, the death and resurrection of Christ. This is the core of her spirituality; all her teaching and guidance leads to Golgotha, to Calvary where transformation takes place, a resurrection into new life. Her rhetoric and language insist on 'the Cross' in this context. Sophie Barat spoke constantly of the power of Christ's death and resurrection as the source of inner peace and transformation, if we have the courage to go into the depths. Writing to Adrienne Michel in 1816, Sophie called these depths a foretaste of heaven:

> We are alive, but our life is more divine than human. It is the tomb which the great Apostle [St Paul] talks of when speaking to the Christians of his time: *When you were baptised you were buried with Jesus Christ; you have died with Him and your life is hidden with Christ in God.* When we consent to be so purified, we may then hope before long to enjoy a glorious resurrection.[23]

Her letters speak of 'the Cross 'not as a place of arrival but of passage, of transition. In Holy Week 1831 Sophie Barat commented:

> The last few days have been so sad, mirroring so accurately our situation! Still, we shall be no less joyful for all that when we sing Alleluia, Jesus, Spes Mea, is reborn. He is the reason why we feel joyful. Let us be reborn with Him and we will partake in His glory, but how much more will we have to suffer before we can reach this ultimate outcome![24]

Again:

> Trust that your inner world will gradually be transformed, even the inner world of each of your community. For whoever is a channel [of God] has an effect on others in the measure that she is more in

harmony with the One empowering her to act. If she is at one with the Master acting in her, not placing obstacles in the way, then she bears astonishing fruit. This happens in the course of ordinary human life. [But] what could this mean when the source is Jesus Christ himself and His divine Spirit, when He finds a heart that is docile, empty of self-love, happy to suffer and not to have a life of her own anymore! Then she becomes the person described by the great Apostle [Paul]: she is hidden with Jesus Christ in God. She is buried in the tomb with Him in His death and she rises with Him, leaving her human nature in the tomb, like the silk-worm that Teresa [of Avila] talks about.[25]

To those struggling day by day to manage the challenges of life in school and community, Sophie Barat offered them a wider view and deeper purpose. 'The Cross' was the road to hope:

We will never enter into the Heart of Jesus if we want to do so by any other way than that of the Cross, because he opened His Heart only when he had died on the bed of shame and now the place of glory! So we must not get discouraged. What we have to do is work harder than ever to perfect the work we do with our students and primarily on ourselves. Let us courageously remove our faults, our obsessions, indeed all that can damage the work of the Society. Nurture in every way those in your care.[26]

During Holy Week 1853 Sophie wrote to Marie de Tinseau, telling her how she kept her and indeed the whole Society in her prayer during 'these days fully given over to the mysteries taking place between the arms of Christ'.[27] The mystery of Calvary remained Sophie Barat's continual source of meditation and contemplation. She commented how Mary Magdalene, who remained at the foot of the Cross, was:

the first person, with St John, to see, to experience the wound revealing this Divine Heart to humanity. We cannot doubt that Jesus disclosed to her the mystery of Love.[28]

On Good Friday 1865, a few weeks before her death, Sophie was still attentive to the spiritual journey of the members of the Society. The previous day (Holy Thursday), one of the community in the rue de Varenne, Blanche Ghirelli, had a heated exchange with Adèle Cahier, Sophie Barat's secretary. Sophie had witnessed the event and that night received an apology from the young religious. Sophie wrote her a note the following morning, Good Friday:

Thank you for your holy picture, which I received last evening, and for what you wrote to me. Your words are somewhat more humble than usual and this softened the pain I felt yesterday, witnessing your appalling behaviour towards Mother Cahier, who did not deserve your grumpiness. Your apologies should be addressed to her and not to me. I only received the side effects of your bad humour. So, if you have made no effort to apologise, hurry up and do so. Above all, do not delay. Yes indeed, dear Blanche, you are far from understanding the holy virtue of humility. Yet if we reflect on it seriously, we are poor specimens of religious, not to say bad, if we do not do battle to root out our dreadful arrogance. Now take this motherly correction well. I hope it will help you to work on yourself. If so, then let us say: Happy Fault.[29]

From her election as superior general in 1806 Sophie Barat's spiritual guidance was challenging. The consistency of her teaching and the frankness with which she expressed her views were hugely demanding. Sophie remarked that often the leaders of the Society were most offended by her continual demands for reflection and honesty, and they took this as her lack of confidence in them. But Sophie pressed on. Her letters to key leaders of the Society, Philippine Duchesne, Aloysia Hardey and Ana du Rousier, as well as Eugénie de Gramont, Louise de Limminghe and Elizabeth Galitzine, leave no doubt of the qualities Sophie Barat demanded of her colleagues. She called them continually to go beyond and even transcend their perceived capacities. She spoke bluntly if she felt they had been out of line, and tested them if she felt they had acted wrongly. When they made mistakes she called them to order, suggested remedies and pressed on. Only if they continued to repeat errors would she remind them of past failures. Otherwise it was over and forgotten; a fresh start had begun. These leaders were either representatives of areas (called vicars in the nineteenth century) or local superiors, directors of novices, school heads, bursars, and holders of offices generally. Many others in the Society also benefited from Sophie Barat's guidance in the course of their lives.[30]

Admission and dismissal of members

Sophie Barat's spirituality was evident when dealing with the admission and dismissal of the women who entered the Society. She insisted on the need to exercise a high quality of discernment when accepting entrants to the Society, ensuring in particular that they had the capacity and motivation necessary. This was essential for the good health of the Society.

Sophie knew that religious life was not for everyone, even if they wanted to live it. She was equally convinced of the need to send away those who had no vocation. Her letters show her acutely critical of the quality of discernment exercised by local leaders who were responsible for accepting candidates in the first place. Sophie constantly complained that first they accepted unsuitable candidates and then they were unwilling to face the difficult task of sending them away. When these women arrived some years later at the moment of final profession it was left to Sophie Barat to ask them to leave the Society. This was unjust to them and to the Society and often created problems impossible to resolve.

In the early nineteenth century the Society of the Sacred Heart was a popular life choice for many young women and opposed by their families. All the more reason for vocations to be properly assessed as in the case of Marie Tallandier (1833–63). She wished to enter the Society of the Sacred Heart, but her mother was opposed and asked Sophie Barat to refuse her daughter. Sophie explained that she could not act so arbitrarily, that both mother and daughter would reproach her at a later stage in their lives if she interfered with a life decision in this way.[31] When Marie Tallandier told Sophie that she was being forced into a marriage Sophie asked her why she was so opposed to this:

> I want to tell you my complete thought on your revulsion for the step you have been asked to take. I am afraid that you have heard imprudent descriptions of marriage and these have given you false or exaggerated ideas. You can save your soul, and even become holy in marriage. The Church offers us many Saints from this state of life for our veneration! You should not refuse just because you are afraid of risking your salvation! You would have to have other reasons [for refusing marriage] which belong deeply to your conscience. So, to enlighten you and help you choose finally what your vocation is, you need to make the retreat I have recommended. I have written to your mother so that she will send you here immediately. It is much better for you and your family to resolve your doubts and calm your anxieties, and help you discover the way of life through which the good God wishes to save you. For your part, search your own heart so that you will not have regrets later on in life.[32]

In other cases, some families were happy to deposit their daughters in the Society and often these were accepted by local leaders who exercised poor judgement at that critical moment. Later, if the Society asked such women to leave, a great deal of pressure was exercised by the family, sometimes through the clergy, to force the Society to keep them for life.[33] By contrast, other women entered the Society against the wishes of their family and were pressurised relentlessly to return home.[34] Matilde de Kersabie entered the Society in 1834 and after some years Sophie Barat sent her to live in Rome for a time. The family accused Sophie of sending her out of the country as a way of imprisoning her. Even when Matilde de Kersabie returned to France, family pressure on her remained so relentless that in the end, against her own wishes, she decided to leave the Society.[35] Sophie Barat knew this decision gave her little joy and for many years she continued to offer her encouragement and support:

> You hold first place in my affection, and you know why! These bonds of religion do not disappear. Even though your outer life has changed, I hope that the inner reality remains. You will always belong to the God who called you and who rescued you from many dangers. Hold on to the essentials of your vocation, by prayer and by avoiding a certain milieu of society, and by having worthwhile occupations.[36]

Sophie Barat usually discerned vocations shrewdly. She could perceive potential for growth, a capacity to learn and live the life of the Society. Equally she could sense if the person was not at all suited to the Society and in these instances was firm, sometimes to a point of brusqueness. She was wary of being pressurised to accept candidates on recommendations from within and without the Society. Even the proposals of Eugénie de Gramont, supported by the archbishop of Paris and a lawyer, would not sway her. Without notifying Sophie Barat, they sent a young woman from Paris to Rome suggesting she be accepted as a candidate for the Society. Sophie was not impressed:

> As for Mlle Celina, I cannot tell you the bother she has caused me since she arrived in Rome. This person has not the shadow of a vocation to religious life and I perceived this immediately. Now we are landed with this burden here and I will probably have to bring her back with me to France. I will advise her with all my might to return home to her mother, where indeed she will be best placed, rather than leading a nomadic life. So, if Mgr [de Quelen] thinks it appropriate to reply to the lawyer, Monsieur Semarquiers, his Grace can say that this woman left Paris of her own free will, that we, the Society of the Sacred Heart, have no plans ourselves for this young lady or for per- mitting her to lodge with us. We will enter very willingly into the wishes of her mother by urging her to return home. Indeed, this is what I will do myself when I see her.[37]

Such frankness left no one in doubt with regard to Sophie Barat's expectations of those who wished to enter the Society. These were intoned regularly:

I believe that we must not accept women who really do not have what is needed to understand religious life and live it. I would much prefer to have women with difficult characters but who have soul forces and energy, to those wet hens that do us no good![38]

[Some enter the Society with] neither talent, refinement nor education and, worst of all, no religious vocation. If this goes on the Society will die out. We really need to have fewer foundations and more religious spirit and genuine integrity. Without these we will not achieve our purpose and we will perish.[39]

[Teresa of Avila] excluded them [unsuitable candidates] mercilessly from her order. It would be good if this examination and weeding out process was done during the time of noviceship, to avoid the serious problems which follow from release from vows. In some more religious countries release from vows leaves a taint which is like a life-long disgrace for these women.[40]

Yes, these women with little religious spirit, with only half-vocations do us harm! Please pay attention to this. Until my dying day this will be my *delenda Cartago*! I will end all my letters with this.[41]

Everywhere the same mistake is being made and if it continues it will be irreparable: the admission of women who have no vocation. And there are plenty whose call is uncertain, many who are extremely mediocre and unable to grasp our commitments since they lack judgement. At present this weakness is being revealed all over the Society, it is being exposed everywhere. Because of it we are losing really fine women who go elsewhere to follow their call. I cannot tell you the numbers in the Society who should be sent away; some leave of their own accord. All such processes undermine the very foundations of the Society and damage its reputation.[42]

If we continue to accept such mediocre, unintelligent women the Society will be lost. Soon there will not be enough houses where they can be parcelled out. This is my daily Cross; how many complaints reach me from every quarter.[43]

Vigilance and discernment regarding entrants to the Society weighed heavily on Sophie Barat all her life, a concern typical of leaders of religious groups in every age and in every religious tradition. Sophie Barat knew that the true vitality of the Society depended on the quality of its members, not in the success of its works. The point of entry to the Society was key. All else followed, for once Sophie was convinced of genuine vocations, she took all steps possible to aid and ensure that these had the conditions necessary to live a spiritual life and contribute to the tasks of the Society. Her process was always the same. She guided them along a path of continual self-knowledge and self-giving, leading them gradually to a transformation in Christ which in turn impacted on their tasks in life. Sophie Barat offered them a spirituality which was pragmatic, consistent and insightful; it was healthy and challenging, and became more confident as she became wiser and more experienced. Her guidance of the Society arose out of her experience of the following of Christ, as it evolved over the years and shaped her spirituality, beginning with her birth in Joigny in 1779.

The origin of Sophie Barat's spiritual leadership, 1779–1865

That birth was dramatic. She was born at 11pm on the night of 12 December 1779, while a fire raged through the village of Joigny. As it drew near her home, Sophie's mother became so alarmed that, in Sophie's own words, she was 'thrust prematurely into the world by fire'.[44] For her parents, Jacques Barat (1742–1809) and Madeleine Fouffé (1740–1822), Sophie was a miracle child, and she grew up surrounded by their love.[45] Sophie had one elder brother, Louis Barat (1768–1845), and one elder sister, Marie-Louise (1770–1852). By all accounts Sophie Barat was a lively child, full of curiosity and endless questions. Later in life she recalled: 'I was only seventeen months old when I became conscious that I existed.'[46]

Sophie's spiritual development was shaped at home and in the parish. She attended Mass and devotions in the church of St Thibault each Sunday and on special feast days. These included the feast and procession of St Vincent in January, marking the planting of the vines, and the feast of St Martin in November, marking the wine harvest. Such festivals gave warmth and colour to life in the parish and maintained a sense of community. At her First Communion Sophie's mother gave her a present of her own prayer book which she had bought at the age of fourteen. It was called *The Manual of the Christian*, and contained the New Testament, the Psalms and the Imitation of Christ, in French, without commentary.[47] The work emanated from one of the scholars at Port Royal, Louis-Isaac Le Maître de Saci (1613–84), who had translated the texts. His aunt was Mère Angelique Arnauld de Port Royal, and for a time Le Maître de Saci was confessor to the community. The prayer book is an attractive work of devotion and piety and Sophie kept it by her until she died. At this time Port Royal published Biblical and devotional texts in French, representative of this phase of Jansenism (1640–1711) which sought a middle path between the severity of Calvinistic predestination and the perceived casuistry of the Jesuits. This new prayer book introduced Sophie to the Scriptures in French. Later as an adult the texts she cites most frequently in her letters come largely from the New Testament and Psalms.

Jansenism in Joigny

The region of the Yonne was considered the most deeply affected by Jansenism in France. Certainly its influence in Joigny was problematic and puzzling for Sophie growing up.[48] When Sophie's mother, Madeleine Fouffé, was a child there were two opposing camps in Joigny, those who followed the teaching of Jansenism and those who adhered to papal teaching, condemning Jansenism. Matters in Joigny came to a head in 1730 when the bishop of Soissons, Jean-Joseph Languet de Gergy, became archbishop of Sens (1730–53). He openly opposed the acknowledged leader of Jansenism, Charles de Thubières de Caylus, (1704–54), archbishop of Auxerre.[49] To lessen the strength of Jansenism in Joigny, Languet de Gergy filled the three parishes in Joigny, St André, St Jean and St Thibault with his nominees. Matters came to a head in 1732 when the parish priest of St Thibault formally denounced Jansenism in Joigny. This was repeated in 1736 by his successor. In practical terms this meant that members of the parish had to accept papal teaching or be refused the sacraments. This divided the parish. Those who adhered to Jansenism travelled to Auxerre to fulfil their Easter duty of confession and communion; and there were cases in Joigny of men and women refused the last sacraments unless they conformed. Both Jacques Barat and Madeleine Fouffé experienced this atmosphere of controversy in their parish of St Thibault as children and young adults. Sophie Barat recalled growing up within this atmosphere of tension and conflict, and how she had been affected by it.[50]

Much later, in 1856 when speaking to some young women preparing for their final commitment in the Society, Sophie Barat spoke of her childhood. She explained the double, even contradictory, message she had received as a child concerning the spirituality of the Heart of Christ:

> It is true to say that in life there are certain circumstances, certain events, apparently of little significance and with little effect on what Providence has planned as our destiny. It is good that you know I was born into a Jansenist family, very attached to this sect which has always been the declared enemy of the devotion to the Sacred Heart.
>
> [Louis Barat] found two very fine engravings in a print shop [in Paris] one representing the Sacred Heart of Jesus and the other the holy Heart of Mary. He bought them and sent them to Madame Barat, and forgetting her former prejudices [Jansenism] she welcomed

her beloved son's gift with joy. And despite the remarks of her family, for one of her sisters was particularly trapped in the error [of Jansenism] she had the two images framed and they remained there [in the kitchen] throughout the Terror, without ever being insulted, or even remarked upon in the frequent visits made to the house during these times.[51]

During the Revolution Louis Barat had been arrested and jailed in Paris and by some miracle had been saved from the guillotine. For Madame Fouffé the pictures were a token of God's love and protection of him and her family. Although it was dangerous to display publicly the symbol of the Heart of Christ during the Revolution – the symbol was linked with counter-revolutionary movements[52] – Madame Fouffé displayed both pictures in her kitchen for all to see.

Sophie Barat's spiritual development in Joigny and Paris

Ironically, it was Louis Barat, Sophie's brother, who imposed an austere, rigorist version of Jansenism on his sister which cast shadows on her childhood and seriously warped her image of God and of herself. He 'dreamed of making her a saint and for this reason did not neglect her education'.[53] Sophie later commented that Louis 'took immediate responsibility for my education and became not only my Master but also that of Papa and Mama'.[54] Louis Barat became Sophie's stern teacher in 1786 and she admitted she was afraid of him. This fear was compounded when he brought her to witness his role in sessions of exorcism in Joigny; she admitted that the experience had scarred her soul and haunted her for years.[55] Louis' position in the family was raised to heroic status when he was imprisoned for a time in Paris, and then ordained a priest secretly in 1795. But his absences from home were a source of relief for Sophie, when she could live a more normal life. She was free to work with her father in the vineyards, help at home and learn dressmaking, be with her friends as well as read the classics and the novels of the day.[56]

After his ordination Louis Barat decided to return to Paris permanently. He had found safe accommodation in Paris and he determined to take Sophie with him to complete her education along with three other women who were ready to form a study group. Under Louis Barat's direction Sophie and her companions lived a monastic life of silence, prayer, meagre food, study and inadequate sleep. The day began with prayer, Mass and then breakfast. They had cold water and dry bread for breakfast; if they had not finished work from the previous day, that had to be completed before they broke their fast. Classes consisted of study of the

Scriptures, the fathers of the church, mathematics, French and Latin. Nothing escaped Louis Barat's eye, all spontaneity was curtailed, and he was particularly hard on his sister. All works of literature, which had fired Sophie's imaginative and feeling world, were completely forbidden. Instead she learnt the Psalms in Latin by heart, especially the long, penitential Ps. 50, and then she translated them into French. If he saw that she was enjoying a particular piece of work, he would immediately change to something different. He regulated her life in every detail, even refusing to allow Sophie enjoy the gifts of food sent to them by their mother.[57]

In addition to controlling Sophie's physical and intellectual life, Louis then moved to imprison her spirit when he became her spiritual director. Using St Jerome as his model, Louis corrected every failing in Sophie; he exaggerated her faults and painted them in the most lurid colours. He required her to go to confession to him every day and insisted she confess the least fault in detail. His inexperience and rigidity led to torture for Sophie in the area of confessing faults, which falsified her judgement and filled her with a sense of guilt. He imposed penances and trials on a daily basis. Once in anger Louis struck her across the face, because she had hugged a cousin she had met in the street. His method was to humiliate her to the depths, often in public, and to require absolute obedience to him. In the process Sophie lost her self-esteem, her sense of worthiness and she often refused to go to communion. This experience of having her soul seared daily by examination of conscience remained with her for life and burdened her with scruples for many years. She remarked to her companions, who were dismayed at Louis Barat's treatment: 'I understand nothing; I no longer think for myself; if I'm told to do something, I obey.'[58] Some years later Sophie admitted: 'I cried a great deal.'[59]

Sophie Barat endured this austere life in Paris from 1795 until 1800, and it was only interrupted when she went home each autumn to help with the wine harvest. These years damaged her physical health and impeded her emotional development. Most of all, Sophie's spiritual growth was skewed by her brother's disastrous theology. From this period she became scrupulous, became unsure of herself and found decisions difficult. This was the price she paid for her education which indeed was unusual in women of her class then. Learning had been encouraged by her mother and by Louis Barat, but each in their different ways. Devotional Jansenism, mediated to Sophie in the prayer book her mother gave her, had nourished Sophie's spiritual life in Joigny. But Louis Barat's version of rigorist Jansenism had a destructive influence on her spiritual life which caused her immense personal suffering for many years.

1800–1815: Paris to Amiens

Sophie Barat's austere life in Paris finally came to an end in the autumn of 1800 when she met a priest, Joseph Varin. By this time she was twenty-one years of age and thought of becoming a Carmelite. But Joseph Varin invited her to join a new order of women recently founded in Rome, the Dilette di Gesù, and which wanted to start a community in Amiens. This was a crossroads for Sophie and she took some months to consider her choices. She could return home to Joigny, to the delight of her parents who wanted her to marry. Or she could take up this invitation to go to Amiens, albeit with some pressure from her brother and Joseph Varin to go there.[60] She decided finally to try the new community in Amiens and arrived there in November 1801. It proved to be a challenging experience for the community and Sophie's potential for leadership was quickly recognised. In 1802 the Dilette di Gesù named her leader of the community in Amiens, and no one was more surprised than Sophie at this appointment. Yet through working with others and fulfilling demanding tasks she regained some of the confidence and independence she had lost through Louis Barat's actions.

When community of the Dilette di Gesù disintegrated in Rome in 1802, Sophie had to take sole responsibility in Amiens and she discovered her capacities for leadership in crisis. She led new foundations in France, first in Grenoble and then Poitiers, and in 1806 was elected superior general for life of this new community. From 1802 to 1815 she survived continuous opposition to her leadership, mostly from the community in Amiens. And while this caused her real suffering, at the same time the challenges helped Sophie find her voice and inner courage. She gradually found clarity and she articulated the purpose of the community, placing at its centre the spirituality of the Heart of Christ. Finally in 1815, after intense debates within the communities and with some clergy, Sophie Barat was confirmed as superior general for life of the community now called the Society of the Sacred Heart.[61] She had found her place and her voice.

During these years when her leadership had been tested, friends were immensely important for Sophie in terms of human comfort and for her spiritual growth. Her correspondence shows how she was affirmed by many women in the communities, especially by Philippine Duchesne in Grenoble and Thérèse Maillucheau in Poitiers. In Paris she was helped by several priests, including Pierre de Clorivière, Philippe de Brouillard, Jean Montaigne and the Abbé Lamarche. The Abbé Lamarche affirmed the spiritual vision she held for the Society of the Sacred Heart:

I am your Society's oldest friend. Before its birth I gave all the encouragement possible to such a Society. I have followed all its developments. I have wept for all the tribulations it has endured. [I have been] deeply convinced for the past thirty years that religion in France would owe its renewal to the Sacred Heart (as I have publicly preached). I have always believed in the need for a Society to be *clearly called* the Society of the Sacred Heart, in order that the Lord operates his greatest miracle ever in France.[62]

During her years in Paris, Sophie Barat may not have imagined she was capable of articulating the spiritual purpose of the Society so clearly, when she wrote to all the members immediately after the 1815 General Council:

The Society at its origin was essentially founded on devotion to the Heart of Jesus and must be so dedicated and consecrated to the glory of this Divine Heart that all the works and functions it undertakes are related to that chief purpose. Such is the glorious and attractive aim of our little Society: we become holy ourselves by taking the divine Heart of Jesus as our model, trying as far as we are able to unite ourselves to His feelings and innermost dispositions; and at the same time we dedicate ourselves to extending and promoting the knowledge and love of this divine Heart by working for the sanctification of souls. I repeat, this is the destiny of the Society of the Sacred Heart which God graciously revealed at our origins.[63]

The Society of the Sacred Heart after 1815

The Society expanded rapidly after 1815, to Paris, to other cities in France, and in 1818 Philippine Duchesne set out for Louisiana. Further foundations followed in Savoy and Piedmont. Sophie Barat's life became intensely busy and she was regularly weighed down by illness and exhaustion. In 1823 her health collapsed under the strain of overwork and for a time she was in danger of death. When she had recovered sufficiently Sophie went to the south of France to convalesce and there, through her friend Louise de Limminghe, she met a priest, Joseph-Marie Favre (1791–1838).[64] Like Sophie Barat, Joseph-Marie Favre had suffered from Jansenist influences, and like her he had struggled with scruples since adolescence, around a sense of sin and worthiness for receiving communion. His scruples were compounded when he went to the seminary to prepare for the priesthood. Fortunately he encountered the theology of Alphonsus de Liguori which transformed his image of God from one of fear and remoteness to one of trust and intimacy. This led to comforting confessions and regular reception of communion. Graced with this inner liberation and peace, Favre took it as his life's mission to pass his personal experience on to others. Constantly challenged by his own colleagues in Chambéry and accused of heresy, he defended his position vigorously, in word and in writing.[65]

Sophie Barat met Joseph-Marie Favre at a critical point in her life. Her serious illness in 1823 indicated she was working beyond her strengths. But Favre was convinced that overwork alone could not have undermined her health so drastically. Her inner, soul life was in deep crisis and this had also drained her strength. He suggested that she had a double illness, of body and soul; these were closely linked.[66] In his letters to Sophie Barat, Favre drew attention to her endless battles with scruples which were a major block to inner peace and were a burden she had carried from her years with Louis Barat in Paris. But furthermore, Favre queried her lifestyle. Her responsibilities were complex. She was overworking, either attending endless meetings, letter writing and travel, all concerning the communities, schools and new foundations. He understood that Sophie was driven by the need to maintain personal contact with the members but wondered if the rapid success of the Society of the Sacred Heart left her at once flattered and uneasy. She was living in a milieu way beyond her social status and family background; she was constantly dealing with members of the nobility, church and state, including the royal family. To deal with all these elements, she had to find a certain moderation, a middle ground, a balance in her life. She could not sustain her current pattern, her inner world was in turmoil and her task as superior general was too chaotic. She would have to find a resolution to this dilemma.

Favre reminded her of the first retreat she made with him in Chambéry:

> Let go of everything which does not absolutely require your involve-ment in the exercise of your responsibility. By being united to God you will do more in a quarter of an hour than in a whole day's *pouring out* of frenzied activity. Neither is ENTHUSIASM the least of obstacles: restrain yourself and moderate your actions in such a way that you are more attentive to God than to the chaotic nature of your occupations, which, however necessary, are less important than your great spiritual ideal. Furthermore, your duty to God and to yourself comes before your duty to your neighbour. And you can only give out of what you have. Go to communion as often as you can; your poor soul needs it so much; every day would be best. Why do you find it so hard to be led?[67]

Such advice was a huge challenge for Sophie and she struggled to accept it. Her scruples seemed impossible to overcome; they haunted her continually. Louise de Limminghe asked Favre why Sophie had such battles with scruples:

> The pains, scruples and worries of your dear mother are partly due to her temperament and partly due to the false guidance she has been following for a long time. But they are due most of all to the dark spirit which aims solely to make her waste precious time by useless self-occupation and by making her examine her conscience endlessly, like a squirrel going round in circles.[68]

Favre assured Sophie that the only way forward was to believe in the power of Love to heal her and give her strength:

> Trust and the love of God gladden the heart, uplift the soul and make it capable of the greatest undertakings, whereas fear and mistrust depress and sadden the soul, shrink the heart, dull the spirit, ruin the health of the body and disturb rhythm of the spiritual life. God did not come down upon the earth to be feared but to be loved. How can you mistrust a God who infinitely loves you, who wishes only for your health and happiness? How can you mistrust your dear, kind brother Jesus, who has suffered so much to save you, who has made so many sacrifices, so that you could share in his glory and his treasures? How can you mistrust this loving and gentle heart that only wishes to be loved and to give love? Such mistrust can only come from the devil. Let it never be intentional.[69]

While Sophie Barat struggled with these inner demons her workload continued to increase. Aware that she could collapse under the pressure of such inner and outer tensions, Favre and Louise de Limminghe proposed an order of day to Sophie which would provide her with a rhythm of rest, prayer and work.[70] But by 1834 Sophie felt she was beyond her leadership task and should not continue as superior general. She asked Favre how she could possibly be in the right place. On the contrary, he suggested she was in exactly the right place, and that to fulfil her task she had to know and accept herself, and find balance and rhythm to her life:

> Who could doubt this, since you are called to it by God and the Society? It is for you to stay where you are and discharge your role to the best of your ability. Cast aside as genuine illusion all thoughts of abandoning this responsibility which God has entrusted to you, for this would be to follow a path of selfishness. Look back no longer lest you risk, like Lot's wife, being turned into a pillar of salt.[71]

This went to the heart of Sophie's life and commitment. Favre asked her if she actually believed in the Love of God, in the Love revealed in the

Heart of Christ, of which she spoke so eloquently to the Society and which was enshrined in the 1815 Constitutions. Where did she stand on this as founder and leader?

> I invite you, I beg you to set out on the path of love, obedience, trust and holy liberty. No more worries, no more deliberate turning back. Only joy, trust, love and courage in our good and loving Jesus who for so long has been asking for your heart. He only awaits the moment when you will quite gently, simply and lovingly, like a little child, abandon yourself to his sacred and loving care, with total, childlike trust, so that He can unlock and bestow upon you the inde-scribable treasures of His Heart which burns with love for you.[72]

The struggle for Sophie Barat was immense. Favre knew this and asked Louise de Limminghe to give Sophie every support to enable her carry on:

> You will expand the shrivelled heart of your beloved superior; you will advance the glory of the Sacred Heart and the prosperity of your new-born Society. I wish, I desire with all my heart to see this soul act in complete trust and simplicity and in particular, with complete freedom in the way of obedience, despite her futile fears, her endless doubts and her confused views. Such an open, courageous and obedient way of being would rid her of this shroud of scruples which almost completely overcomes her, diverts her from her most impor-tant tasks and distances her from the love of the Sacred Heart and from religious perfection.[73]

This inner battle was a crossroads for Sophie Barat. She was undoing an inner pattern of oppression which had begun at the age of seven in Joigny when Louis Barat took control of her life, and was further deepened in Paris when she no longer had the protection of her parents. Now it seemed an impossible task to truly let go of her self-doubt, the burden of guilt and anxiety, self-blame and self-punishment. Favre pointed out that in her own personal, spiritual life Sophie Barat was contradicting the purpose of the Society of the Sacred Heart. It was one thing to write and speak about a spirituality and quite another to incarnate it personally, day by day. That was her task, and Sophie must have wondered if she could ever resolve her inner conflicts. In what proved to be his last letter to her, Joseph-Marie Favre had only words of encouragement, though it appeared Sophie had not budged from her inner prison:

> I have learnt with great sorrow that you are in very poor health. Take some rest and relaxation as well as the remedies prescribed. Allow them [doctors] to treat you as they think best and not according to your own wishes. Do you not need robust and vigorous health to

fulfil the greatly increased and varied obligations, so complicated and *exhausting*, as those which you are responsible for? Heavens above, Mother, in running down your health by overwork, sleepless nights and mortification are you not also weakening the whole Society? The devil only mocks your acts of penance which are becoming an obstacle to the exercise of your important responsibility.[74]

Favre remained hopeful:

You must realise that only by a miracle of grace can your worthy Mother give up her long-standing tendency to guilt and penance which she has grown used to. It is a habit which must be treated like a chronic illness, with gentleness, care and patience. Sooner or later grace triumphs over all obstacles, no matter how great they seem.[75]

Inner resolution through outer events, 1839–1843

Favre thought that over time 'sooner or later grace triumphs over all obstacles, no matter how great they seem'. He died in 1838 and the following year, with no sign of inner resolution to her struggles, Sophie Barat faced the most critical period of her leadership. The Society needed radical reform of structures suitable to a growing international community. She had begun to plan for these after the 1833 General Council and proposed adopting the Jesuit structure of provinces and provincials. There were ominous signs that some of the houses in Louisiana and in Rome could separate from the Society. In Paris there were serious problems in the rue de Varenne, where the archbishop of Paris, Mgr de Quelen, had taken up residence. He had been invited there by Eugénie de Gramont in the wake of the July Revolution of 1830 and Sophie Barat was only informed afterwards. Sophie Barat considered the decision unsuitable and increasingly scandalous. Time proved her to be right. As she reached the summer of 1839, a few months before her sixtieth birthday, Sophie Barat's letters betray a tone of weariness and exhaustion.

Yet Joseph-Marie Favre's assurance that Sophie would finally overcome her inner doubts, scruples and anxieties came true in circumstances that appeared to be truly destructive for her and the Society of the Sacred Heart. These circumstances were around exterior events and issues of governance, not directly of spirituality. The fifth General Council of the Society opened in Rome in the summer of 1839 and the proposal to adopt the Jesuit structure of provinces and provincials in the Society was accepted without difficulty by the members of the Council. However, two proposals became immediately and unexpectedly divisive. One was that the superior general of the Society should reside in Rome, not Paris. The other, led by a small, effective group, proposed that the Society of the Sacred Heart be incorporated into the Jesuits. Within a few months the Society became polarised, mostly around the question of Sophie Barat's proposed residence in Rome. The Gallican lobby was led in Paris by Eugénie de Gramont, and supported by two archbishops of Paris, Mgr de Quelen (1778–1839) and Mgr Denys Affre (1793–1848), the French episcopacy and the French government. All firmly opposed Sophie Barat's residence in Rome. The Ultramontane lobby was led by Sophie's four council members (assistants general), and supported by the Jesuit assistant general for France, Jean Rozaven. This supported Sophie Barat's residence in Rome, the centre of Christendom, which would render the Society more international, less dominated by the influence of France, especially Paris.[76]

Sophie Barat was caught between these opposing views, and both criticised her for being weak and indecisive. She remarked wryly that in Rome she was considered Gallican, and in Paris Ultramontane. The Jesuits in Paris were divided. Joseph Varin at first criticised the move to Rome and later supported it. Sophie's brother, Louis Barat, also a Jesuit, held the Ultramontane view. Pope Gregory XVI did not take a position on Sophie Barat's residence in Rome, but he firmly defended her rights against the claims of the archbishop of Paris, Denys Affre.[77] The crisis point came when the French government threatened to close all forty-three houses of the Society in France if Sophie Barat moved to Rome. From its point of view such a move infringed the statutes granted the Society of the Sacred Heart in 1827 by Charles X, which declared that the superior general resided in Paris. Archbishop Affre and Jean-Baptiste Teste (1780–1852), Minister of Religion and Culture, joined forces and pressurised Sophie to accede to their demands. As the crisis grew Sophie's good name and integrity were publicly questioned in the Society, in the church and in wider society. She endured slow, public humiliation and loss of reputation, as well as doubts being openly expressed regarding her judgement and leadership. Some began to plan for her successor.

During her retreat in Rome in the winter of 1839 Sophie reflected on her life and recorded her thoughts in a little journal. They were written before the storms broke over her and she was thinking of retirement and death:

> NOTES FOLLOWING MY RESOLUTIONS:
> 1. I ask insistently of the Sacred Heart of Jesus, through the intercession of Our Lady of the Seven Sorrows, for the grace to make a final confession before I die.

2. To spend the last years of my life, if God gives me them, under obedience and hidden.
3. To receive as a gift from the mercy of Jesus for that the way of prayer which I had before and which I have lost because of my long infidelities.
4. To obtain also through the intercession of our sorrowful mother the grace and the facility to keep before me the sufferings and death of Jesus Christ by a sense of sorrow and of love for my sins and for those of the members of the Society.
   This petition includes all the sinners in the world. 1839.

PRAYER:

Jesus, my true, dearest life, listen to the heartfelt prayer of my soul: Give me the grace to die perfectly to my own self, so that you alone may live in my depths. May I keep an inner silence as deep as the dead, so that there you may speak to my heart. May I live in restfulness, so that you can do in me all that you will. Amen.[78]

Over the next few years these resolutions, made in the private domain, would be taken out and tested in public. Painfully slowly, from the winter of 1839 and over many months until the spring of 1843, Sophie Barat negotiated her way through a morass of problems. While trying to maintain a modicum of continuity and stability in the Society she trod a careful path to avoid further polarisation. Discussion with members of the Society was not an option as she was unable to convoke another General Council of the Society, either in France or in Rome. She had to find other routes to resolution. In August 1842 Sophie wrote to an old friend, Césaire Mathieu (1796–1875), the archbishop of Besançon. She outlined the problems and the urgent need to find a strategy to resolve the deadlock and reach a compromise solution. Césaire Mathieu was well acquainted with the current crisis and agreed to help. A small working party emerged – Sophie Barat, Césaire Mathieu and Antonio Garibaldi, the papal nuncio in Paris (already embroiled in controversy with Mgr Affre[79]). They established a link with the papal secretary of state, Luigi Lambruschini (1776–1854), a former papal nuncio in Paris.

In the winter of 1842 Sophie Barat and Césaire Mathieu devised a compromise solution with the diplomatic aide of the nuncio, Antonio Garibaldi, and this was circulated to the French episcopacy. Then Mathieu went to Rome in February 1843, officially on an *ad limina* visit, but in fact to present this compromise to the pope. In March 1843 a commission of cardinals was appointed by Gregory XVI and they accepted the proposal to abolish the decisions taken in the Society of the Sacred Heart in 1839 until the next General Council could be held. Césaire Mathieu, at Sophie Barat's specific request, asked that exception be made for the creation of provinces and provincials in the Society. To her great disappointment that request was refused. Nevertheless, a certain measure of stability was restored in the Society in the spring of 1843. Only then could Sophie Barat take the measure of what had happened to her since 1839.

Radical following of Christ

Sophie already knew the effects of Jansenism in her personal life but the events of 1839–43 led her to another level of self-knowledge. She knew her reputation and good name were damaged and she accepted that she had brought some of this upon herself. She had shown lack of judgement in not fully communicating her plans to the Society from 1833, and because of this her leadership was weakened. She also acknowledged that her freedom to act as leader had been curtailed for some time by the situation in Paris in the rue de Varenne, not just by the presence of the archbishop of Paris but also by her friendship with Eugénie de Gramont. Nevertheless, some situations and issues in the Society were not of her making and Sophie recognised that in some cases she was powerless to deal with them. She knew as well that issues of class were influential, not just in the Society but also in church and social circles in Paris and Rome. Some addressed her as Madame de Barat at this time, either in an effort to promote her socially or as a term of contempt. Such experiences of deep humiliation coupled with personal self-doubt flooded Sophie Barat's consciousness as she journeyed along this path. The experience was devastating and it radically shifted the ground of her being. It threw her into a new and different space interiorly.

Her correspondence with Césaire Mathieu on almost a daily basis, especially between November 1842 and August 1843, reveals Sophie Barat struggling to come to terms with what was happening within her:

> Allow me in sharing your cross to experience also something of its weight. Simon of Cyrene was glad to have something himself to suffer when he helped our divine Master on the way to Calvary. I can only be hopeful for your congregation. The present storm shows you what success means, and that of the Society is compromising its very existence. But in my opinion Providence is teaching you a lesson in humility. For that reason you must accept and carry this cross with great calm, great gentleness, in reverent silence and perfect trust.[80]

Every aspect of Sophie's life lay open to scrutiny. She asked herself again and again how and where she had gone wrong; what she had done to bring such calamities down upon herself and the Society:

> I have hardly any time for prayer during the day. I have to do it at
> night and I am worn out with fatigue and sleepiness. I believe the
> good God is punishing me for having abandoned my first call which
> was to Carmel. Can the cross of Jesus, the sufferings and humilia-
> tions I endure make amends for this? I have a lot of worries about so
> many of my failings and my natural reactions mixed up at this time
> of trial. Pray then that I obtain from the Sacred Heart of Jesus a
> merciful pardon of which I have so great a need![81]

Césaire Mathieu replied by return of post, urging Sophie to trust that, no
matter all the appearances to the contrary, God was at work in the actual
events unfolding. Her task was to take care of herself:

> There is a very appropriate word in Scripture which will comfort you:
> It says that giving alms is prayer. And how could the cross you bear
> not be a source of prayer, since Our Lord prayed on the cross for us!
> So then it is not necessary that you pray during the day, for you have
> not got the time; nor is it necessary that you, worn out with fatigue,
> prolong your vigils into the night. That would put you in danger of
> not having the strength necessary during the day. But hold fast to the
> cross in surrender and love, let it pray for you. This thought, which is
> very gentle and very true, will set your heart at ease.[82]

Yet each day brought new problems. Again, Césaire Mathieu advised her
to try and keep balance and perspective:

> The more complicated the situation becomes from outside, the more
> you need to proceed with simplicity. Accept the information which is
> given you, but do not let it reach the depths of your heart.[83]

Sophie Barat's greatest challenge came in March 1843 when Sophie faced
the task of initiating a process of reconciliation within the Society of the
Sacred Heart, especially with those who had opposed her from 1839.
Césaire Mathieu had hinted several times that she would have to take that
initiative herself.[84] However, when the moment came to act she baulked:

> If I could give you the details of their procedures I think you would
> advise me to maintain a bit of dignity still. They doubted my faith,
> my allegiance to the Holy See and insinuated this to others, without
> asking me for a word of explanation. It seems to me that it would be
> somewhat difficult for me to write to them now, apologise and show
> them trust. I will certainly take advantage of all the overtures they
> make to me, to show them good will, understanding and even that
> the past is forgotten. But to write to them first, I do not think so![85]

Sophie's feelings were raw. Since 1839 she had felt at best misunderstood and at worse judged and rejected by many of her companions. She had paid a high price as superior general, and for Césaire Mathieu to suggest she humiliate herself even further was intolerable:

But Césaire Mathieu responded quickly, to explain:

> In a serious case such as yours, when human prudence is stretched to the limits, it is clear that you must act in the noblest manner possible and that what looks like folly in human eyes is wisdom in the sight of God. The most difficult task you have in your position now is to reconcile minds and hearts, which have been so deeply alienated from one another. To achieve this you must do two things: one concerns yourself, while the other involves the government of the Society.
>
> In what regards yourself, now you must be more gentle, more humble, more loving, more patient, in the measure that others are less. You will achieve nothing by dominance but a great deal by being affable. That is what I mean by the letters I advised you write. But it is not my intention that you should apologise. It is only that you speak kindly and gently, as if you had nothing against them in your heart. Then, do you not see that if you have to go farther towards them, you have to do it for the sake of Jesus Christ who is always the first to come to us despite our faults?
>
> As for the other matter which concerns the government of the Society, in as much as being gentle and kind towards all, so you must also act firmly and with authority in the fullest sense. To achieve this you must not compromise your freedom or your affection with anyone. You must open your arms to all in the love of Our Lord and nothing else.[86]

This invitation went to the heart of Sophie Barat's life and leadership. She was the founder and the leader of the Society of the Sacred Heart. She led the Society in the initial years and ensured that in 1815 its impulse was articulated in the Constitutions. She presided over the rapid growth of the Society and after 1833 planned consolidation and structural reform. All those years her inner world had been in turmoil, as she struggled to reach inner peace and confidence, and most of all become free of the scourge of scruples. Joseph-Marie Favre accompanied her in this dark night, repeatedly inviting Sophie to trust in the love of the Heart of Christ, to let that love fill her heart. Then she would truly govern the Society of the Sacred Heart according to the spiritual impulse she had initiated and which she was called to embody in her life.

Now in February 1843 Sophie found herself at a crossroads, refusing an invitation to reach out and forgive her four assistants general. At this point she could become lost in bitterness and self-righteousness, or she could take a step across the abyss, go out of herself, out of her pride and hurt and anger, and take the initiative with her colleagues. Césaire Mathieu's words, 'It is only that you speak kindly and gently, as if you had nothing against them in your heart', gave Sophie courage to act in a way which had seemed quite impossible to imagine. She took up her pen and wrote to each of her assistants general, inviting them to join her, if they wished, and work together towards restoring harmony in the Society.

This decision was the act of trust which Sophie Barat had been trying to make for so long. It was the fruit of her years of inner struggle to accept the love of God revealed in the Heart of Christ. In Sophie Barat's case her decision to act was made for the life of the Society. By reaching out 'as if she had nothing in her heart against them', Sophie entered upon another stage of her spiritual journey, one that truly transformed and liberated her inner being. During these critical years some had compared Sophie's life to that of St Francis of Assisi. Although she did not bear the wounds of Christ exteriorly she understood in March 1843 that for the rest of her life she would govern the Society from that place in her heart which had indeed been pierced and wounded. In her gesture of forgiveness she liberated both herself and the Society and by so doing she took her leadership onto a new plane. Having lost her reputation and good name, and accepted her own errors in the creation of the crisis, she found a new space within herself where the old shadows and doubts no longer had a place. She had taken the path of humble love and reached out to all.

She moved forward with a deeper sense of herself and her task, and freer inwardly than she had ever been. Césaire Mathieu continued to support her as she found a balance between asserting her authority and avoiding individuals or groups feeling crushed or defeated.[87] From the spring of 1843 she set about restoring union and peace in the Society by re-establishing, as far she could, the relationships fractured during the crisis. She did this with dignity, without flattery or obsequiousness, gradually assessing where each one stood with her. In the summer of 1846 Sophie moved her residence from Conflans (outside Paris) to the rue de Varenne, which signalled her assertion of her authority as superior general. Reconciliation was most delicate of all with Louise de Limminghe, her old friend from the days of Joseph-Marie Favre. When they eventually resumed correspondence only the language and memory of former times in Chambéry with Joseph-Marie Favre seemed to bridge their differences.

By the time Sophie convened the next General Council in 1851 she had restored regularity of government in the Society and divisions around the past were lessening. Her letter to the Society in December that year showed that she had re-established her leadership.[88] Few in the Society, if any, would have known the extent of the inner journey Sophie had made over the years. But they would have seen the effects of her finally breaking free of old fetters and inner attachments which had bound and constrained her. In the course of the years of crisis she had transformed her image of a Jansenist God and come home at last to a warm, loving presence within her. The years of encouragement from Joseph-Marie Favre had prepared her for the years of isolation and rejection, and all had borne fruit, inwardly and outwardly. Now Sophie could live alone, with herself, with her God, and with the fruits of her life, both sweet and bitter to the taste. She had found a spiritual path that was liberating and joyful, even if it was not always easy to live out with consistency. Of course, she could readily fall back into her old images, especially in times of difficulty and depression. The difference lay in knowing now what to do, how to journey out into the light again. At the age of seventy-two she felt she was in the right place, with the right task, in the Society of the Sacred Heart:

> What a life we have, and while we were young we thought that we would bury ourselves in a Carmelite monastery. The ways of God are unfathomable. I would always regret not going to Carmel if I did not have the assurance that God so designed it. But at least we must unite solitude to the work we do, and counter this whirlwind with a deep cavern where the soul can take refuge as often as possible. For us this cavern in the rock is the Heart of Jesus![89]

Sophie Barat's guidance of the Society, 1843–1865

Sophie Barat's spiritual guidance of the members of the Society became even more demanding as she grew older. The broad lines of her teaching remained the same. She continued to insist on self-knowledge and reflection, on a spirit of self-giving (generosity) which would lead to transformation in Christ and flow out in the gift of self in community and in the fulfilling of tasks. She was convinced that if this process was begun in the period of noviceship and during the years of preparation for final vows, and retained throughout life, then the Society of the Sacred Heart's spiritual task would be assured. But after 1843 Sophie Barat's spiritual teaching had a new accent, or new insistence, on humility, a direct consequence of her own journey.[90] She insisted on humility as the basis of all spiritual growth. With that as foundation for living, love would form each one into the likeness of Christ. Those who lived with her in Paris, especially after 1846, noticed greater ease, more light-heartedness, more spontaneous laughter in Sophie Barat. Much of her intensity and anxiety had gone. Yet even at her worst, Sophie's wry humour did not desert her. During the Roman winter of 1839, when her life was descending into chaos, Sophie wrote to a friend:

> A case is currently being examined [in Rome] that could lead to a process of beatification or even canonisation at the Sacred Congregation. It is the case of a young Carmelite from Florence who was regarded as a holy person when she died at age twenty-three. The devil's advocate, in his attempt to stop the process, quoted one particular remark attributed to her confessor which I found to be intriguing. Her sisters, touched by her virtuous ways – or maybe just surprised – asked her confessor one day: 'Father, what do you think of Sister so and so, is she not a very holy person?' 'Very holy?' he replied, 'She is as mischievous (*impertinente*) as everyone else.' *Impertinente*, at that time, meant lively, joyful. So, saints retain their humanity, but they transform it and use it to act in a virtuous way. I hope this reply will be given to the Devil's Advocate. As a result, it will prove that for this young Saint a lively, sensitive nature was the source of her sanctification.[91]

Sophie noted with some relief that the seventeenth-century Carmelite retained her humanity. Over the years Sophie had faced her own humanity and made peace with herself. After 1850 she travelled less and concentrated her energies on governing the Society from her desk in Paris. Her correspondence greatly increased in volume as Sophie maintained contact with the communities in different parts of the world. Her letters continued to be honest and direct, at times quite severe in tone, always trying to speak the truth. In the course of her canonisation process (1879–1925) several devil's advocates were taken aback at such forthrightness in her correspondence and questioned if Sophie Barat should be canonised at all, something which would not have concerned her in the least. As far as she was concerned, her task was to give spiritual leadership and guidance to those who would carry the Society into the future.

The older she grew, the greater was her sense of urgency. Time was passing and she had so much yet to do. On 18 May 1859 Sophie wrote to Henriette Granon:

> It is getting late for us and the sun of our life is more than just beginning to decline. Let us imitate this healing planet, at the moment when it sinks over the horizon. Just before it disappears, its flames seem to rekindle, casting an even greater burning, bright glow. May it be the same for us.[92]

In a few short years Sophie Barat would cross the threshold of death. In the course of her life, begun in Joigny in 1779 and completed in Paris in 1865, Sophie had gone on a profound inner path which touched every aspect of her biography. Out of the wisdom gleaned on that journey she gradually embodied the spirituality of the Heart of Christ and transmitted it to the members of the community she founded in 1800.

Conclusion

The five essays in this book present some of the collective and individual biographies of members of the Society of the Sacred Heart in nineteenth-century France. Central to their experience was the form of life they created, which responded to their spiritual ideals and was socially possible for them to live. That form of life was established relatively quickly and articulated in the text of the Constitutions in 1815. While this gave them a basis on which to build their lives and pursue their educational projects, it contained from the beginning a core ambivalence common to religious groups in all religious traditions: how to embody a spiritual ideal in a given historical time and place. In the case of the Society of the Sacred Heart, the task was how to reconcile the spiritual equality of all the members in their day-to-day living, in this instance in nineteenth-century France, where class differences were firmly embedded in society. While recognising the spiritual equality of all the members, the Society adopted a two-rank system in the community, that of choir and coadjutrix sisters. A similar social pattern was reflected in the schools of the Society: the boarding schools catered for the upper class and the poor schools served the poor class, usually established in separate buildings on the same properties.

This model was pragmatic and effective and met the expectations and indeed the experience of those who joined the Society. What is remarkable, however, is the rapidity with which the model took root and developed from 1800. Along with many other religious communities of women of the time, the Society of the Sacred Heart took advantage of the new spaces created inadvertently for women by the decision of the Legislative Assembly in August 1792 to suppress religious life in France.

This break with the past, however ruthless, created the possibility of new forms of life, capable in time of meeting the new realities of revolutionary and post-revolutionary France. Another factor helped the Society of the Sacred Heart. The Roman Catholic Church had been weakened by the Revolution and the Civil Constitution of the Clergy divided the church in France. The Revolutionary armies sacked Rome twice and the papacy was humiliated when the pope was forced to witness Napoleon crown himself emperor in Paris. In such a position the church welcomed the initiatives taken by women in the early nineteenth century, in the field of education and health, and used them as vehicles to re-build its power and influence.

Many of the women in the Society of the Sacred Heart, especially in the early years, were gifted and independent, and their background, capacity and spiritual convictions made them strong leaders. Together they created their form of life, their community and their schools, which they ran like villages, self-contained and effective. This was an exciting time for women in the Society, with so many opportunities opening out for them with the scope to act decisively. They learnt how to resist clerical or government interference, and knew what to do if they were opposed. While they never questioned the rightful authority of state or church, they contested any encroachment on the rights of the Society as enshrined in the 1815 Constitutions. The independence of the Society was helped by its central form of government led by a superior general. To safeguard this, and the goods of the Society, Sophie Barat and her companions sought early on, in 1826/7, to have the Society recognised legally in France and in Rome. However, the property and inheritance rights of individual religious remained confused; nuns did not fit the categories of mother, wife, daughter, sister, aunt. The vast number of legal cases, concerning wills and legacies, which Sophie Barat had to deal with bear witness to this anomaly.

Members of the Society were devout Catholics and they were committed to rebuilding the church in France after the Revolution, and many of the clergy recognised their contribution in this regard. In the sphere of the sacraments, the regulations concerning religious life, as well as the running of schools in dioceses, the authority of bishops and priests was usually accepted without question, unless the rights of the Society were infringed. However, tensions with local clergy tended to exist below the surface and could erupt easily into struggles for authority in the community, or around finance and ownership of properties. In such cases, and this usually affected only the leaders of communities who had to deal with these issues, there was a line of conscience to which the Society held.

In the case of conflict with local bishops, it is remarkable how Sophie Barat's authority was supported by the popes. It was in their interest to do so at a time when Gallican and Ultramontane tensions were being played out in the church. But for women coming into the public sphere in a new way in the nineteenth century, it was a difficult balancing act to deal with the clergy and government authorities.

The Society of the Sacred Heart maintained a strong independent stance with regard to the French government throughout the nineteenth century. Such was its conviction around this position that when the state threatened to encroach on the Society's rights in 1904, it preferred to close the schools and be expelled from France rather than submit. Such an independent stance was not possible with the church. The delicate balance of power and influence between the Society and church authorities became harder to hold in the measure that the institutional church regained confidence in the course of the nineteenth century. This became especially marked after Pius IX became pope in 1846. The loss of the Papal States from 1848 led the papacy to reject the modern world, and focus inwards on its spiritual empire. It turned to education in particular as a sphere of influence and where it could gain ascendency. The declaration of papal infallibility only underpinned this stance, as well as the call to codify canon law.

By the end of the century, the church familiar to Sophie Barat and her companions in 1800 had disappeared. They had created their community and established their schools within the ideals of that religious consciousness. Busy and enclosed in their world, they were unaware of the women's movement which was growing rapidly internationally, though rather more slowly in nineteenth-century France. They could not have known that their experiences and struggles mirrored that of their contemporaries. Indeed, the Society's concern to protect its independence and legal rights would have been readily appreciated by Mary Wollstonecraft and her successors in the nineteenth century. But these were two parallel worlds which did not meet then. They would in time and that is another story for another day. This story records the lives of many nineteenth French women in the Society of the Sacred Heart whose most extraordinary achievements remain unseen and whose place in history endures.

Notes and References

INTRODUCTION

1 Jeanne de Charry (1914–2000)

2 Canonical decrees for canonisation were established by Pope Urban VIII in 1642. These were judicial processes which examined a candidate for evidence of holiness and canon lawyers were appointed to argue either for or against each particular case. The lawyers who opposed the candidate were called Promoters of the Faith, commonly known as the devil's advocate. Lawyers who defended the person's sanctity based their case on testimonies of living witnesses, writings of the candidate and posthumous miracles attributed to the candidate.

3 [Adèle Cahier], *Vie de la Vénérable Mère Madeleine-Sophie Barat, Fondatrice et Première Supérieure Générale de la Société du Sacré-Cœur,* 2 vols (Paris, 1884). Louis Baunard, *Histoire de Madame Barat, Fondatrice de la Société du Sacré-Cœur,* 2 vols (Paris, 1876). This work reached its sixth edition by 1892. An illustrated edition was published in 1900 for the centenary of the Society of the Sacred Heart, and reprinted for the canonisation of Madeleine Sophie Barat in 1925.

4 *Official Documents: Canonisation,* 8 vols, 1872–1876; 17 vols, 1882–1897; 19 vols, 1877–1908; 8 vols, 1881–1910 (General Archives, Rome, C-I., A-a).

5 GA, Rome, C-I., E, Box 1, Cahier.

6 GA, Rome, C-I., A, 1-e, Box 1. Also, Phil Kilroy, 'The Use of Continental Sources of Women's Religious Congregations and the Writing of Religious Biography: Madeleine Sophie Barat, 1779–1865', in Maryann Gialanella Valiulis and Mary O'Dowd (eds), *Women and Irish History* (Dublin, 1997), pp. 59–70. Also, Phil Kilroy, 'Les Archives de Congrégations Religieuses Féminines et la Rédaction d'une Biographie: Exemple de Madeleine-Sophie Barat, 1779–1865', *Revue d'Histoire de l'Eglise de France,* tome 85, no. 215 (Juillet–Decembre 1999), pp. 359–71. Many scholarly women have endured the same experience. See Natalie Zemon Davis, 'Women and the World of the *Annales',History Workshop Journal,* no. 33 (1992), pp. 121–37.

7 Adèle Cahier to Matilde Garabis, Paris, 31 December 1871/2 January 1872 (GA, Rome, C-I., E, Box 1, Cahier).

8 However, spiritual conferences attributed to her were based on the notes of those who heard them. Sophie Barat rarely wrote out an entire conference. She tended to speak from brief notes rather than from a text. See [Madeleine-Sophie Barat]

Conférences aux Religieuses, 2 vols, (Roehampton, Londres, 1900). For Jeanne de Charry's comments on these editions, see de Charry, *Histoire des Constitutions de la Société du Sacré-Cœur: La Formation de l'Institut*, vol. I, nos XXVI–XXVII (Rome, 1975).

9 [Madeleine-Sophie Barat], *Lettres Choisies Adressées aux Religieuses*, 5 vols (Roehampton, Londres, 1920); (Rome, 1928–1957); *Lettres Choisies pour les Seules Supérieures*, 5 vols (Rome 1922–1965); *Lettres aux Mères en Charge* (Rome, 1924).

10 [Madeleine-Sophie Barat], *Lettres Circulaires Adressées aux Religieuses*, 2 vols. *Première partie: Lettres Adressées à Toute la Société* (Roehampton, Londres, 1917); *Seconde partie: Lettres pour les Supérieures: Leur Conseil et les Économes* (Roehampton, Londres, 1904).

11 Mary Cecilia Wheeler was general archivist of the Society of the Sacred Heart from 1976 to 1980.

12 Jeanne de Charry, *Histoire des Constitutions de la Société du Sacré-Cœur, Ière partie: La Formation de l'Institut*, 2 vols (Rome, 1975; 2de éd 1981); *2de partie: Les Constitutions Définitives et leur Approbation par le Saint-Siège*, 3 vols (Rome 1979). These have been translated into English. de Charry (ed.), *Correspondance Sainte Madeleine Sophie Barat, Sainte Philipine Duchesne: Texte des Manuscrits Originaux Présenté avec une Introduction, des Notes et un Index Analytique*, 1804–1815 (Rome 1988); 1818–1821 (Rome; 1989); 1821–1826 (Rome 1992); 1826–1852 (Rome 2001). de Charry (ed.) *Lettres à Sainte Madeleine Sophie Barat (1801–1849): Texte Intégral, d'Après les Manuscrits Originaux, Présenté, avec une Introduction, des Notes et un Index Analytique* (Rome 1982).

13 This task took from 1976 to 1985. The transcriptions are in process of being verified and computerised in preparation for being placed online.

14 Batchelor, John, *The Art of Literary Biography* (Oxford, 1995); Bostridge, Mark (ed.), *Lives for Sale: Biographers' Tales* (London, 2004); France, Peter and St Clair, William (eds), *Mapping Lives: The Uses of Biography* (Oxford, 2002); Lee, Hermione, *Body Parts: Essays on Life-Writing* (London, 2005), and *Biography: A Very Short Introduction* (Oxford, 2009); Holroyd, Michael, *Works on paper: The Craft of Biography and Autobiography* (London, 2002).

15 Laurel Thatcher Ulrich, *Well-Behaved Women Seldom Make History* (New York, 2007); Perrot, Michelle, *Mon Histoire des Femmes* (Seuil, 2006); *Les Femmes ou les Silences de l'Histoire* (Flammarion, 1998); Olwen Hufton, *The Prospect Before Her: A History of Women in Western Europe*, vol. I, 1500–1800 (London, 1995); Heilbrun, Carolyn, *Writing a Woman's Life* (London, 1989); *Women's Lives. The View from the Threshold* (Toronto, 1999).

16 French, Spanish, Japanese, Polish and Korean translations followed.

17 Simon Skinner, 'History Versus Hagiography: The Reception of Turner's *Newman*', *Journal of Ecclesiastical History*, vol. 61, no. 4 (2010), pp. 764–81.

18 For a study of contemporary groups of women in France engaged on a similar search, Sarah A. Curtis, *Civilizing Habits: Women Missionaries and the Revival of French Empire* (Oxford, 2010).

19 A collection of Marie d'Olivier's letters and documents was discovered in the Jesuit Archives in Paris in 1996 by Fr Robert Bonfils, SJ. This material is now lodged in the Provincial Archives of the Society in Poitiers, France.

CHAPTER 1

1 Marie Lataste to the Abbé Dupérier, Rennes, 21 November 1846.

2 Pauline Perdrau, *Les Loisirs de l'Abbaye*, 2 vols (Rome, 1934, 1936).

3 Langlois, Claude, *Le catholicisme au féminin: Les congrégations françaises à supérieure générale au XIXe siècle* (Paris, 1984). Also, Olwen H. Hufton, *Women and the Limits of Citizenship in the French Revolution* (Toronto, 1992), pp. 140–54.

4 Perdrau, *Les Loisirs de l'Abbaye*, vol. i, pp. 422–4.

5 Recognition of final solemn vows of religion implied full restoration of religious life. Napoleon accepted women living in religious communities because he needed the social services they offered.

6 Emmanuel Fureix, *La France des Larmes: Deuils Politiques à l'Âge Romantique, 1814–1840* (Champ Vallon, 2009), pp. 43–52, 138–67; Carla Hesse, *The Other Enlightenment: How French Women became Modern* (Princeton, NJ, 2003), pp. 104–6; Suzanne Desan, *The Family on Trial in Revolutionary France* (California, 2006).

7 The rank accorded each member in the Society of the Sacred Heart, as a choir sister or a coadjutrix sister, is placed in the footnotes.

8 Olwen Hufton and Timothy Tallett, 'Communities of Women, the Religious Life, and Public Service in Eighteenth-Century France', in *Connecting Spheres: European Women in a Globalizing World, 1500 to the Present* (Oxford, 2000), pp. 93–103; Gwenaël Murphy, *Les Religieuses dans la Révolution Française* (Bayard, 2005).

9 Phil Kilroy, *Madeleine Sophie Barat: A Life* (Cork, 2000), pp. 7–25.

10 Octavie Bailly (1768–1825) was born at Forge les Eaux, near Rouen. In 1804 she entered the Carmelite community at rue St Jacques (later rue d'Enfer) in Paris where her sister (1765–1850) entered in 1801. Notice sur Béatrix de la Conception (Octavie Bailly); Notice sur Anne de Saint Barthélemy (Archives, Carmel de Clamart, Registres et Circulaires); Notice sur Octavie Bailly, Carmel rue d'Enfer (General Archives, Rome, A-II., 2-c, Biographical information); de Charry, *Histoire des Constitutions de la Société du Sacré-Cœur: La Formation de l'Institut*, vol. 1, pp. 227, 245–6.

11 No family records exist for Marguerite. Later on in Amiens she was called Marguerite Boulanger, referring to her skill as a baker in the community.

12 Loquet published: *Cruzamante, ou la Sainte Amante de la Croix* (Paris, 1786); *Voyage de Sophie et d'Eulalie au Palais du Vraie Bonheur: Ouvrage pour Servir de Guide dans les Voies du Salut, par une Jeune Demoiselle* (Paris, 1789); *Entretiens d'Angélique, pour Exciter les Jeunes Personnes à l'Amour et à la Pratique de la Vertu*, no. 2 ed., (Paris, 1782); *Le Miroir des Âmes*, 6 ed. (Paris, 1822).

13 Joseph-Désiré Varin d'Ainville (1769–1850) went to the seminary of Saint Sulpice in Paris and left it to join the counter-revolutionary army led by the prince de Bourbon-Condé. The campaigns of 1792 and 1793, along with his mother's death by guillotine in Paris in 1794, with 1,300 others, convinced him of the futility of violence and he resumed his studies for the priesthood. AFSJ, Vanves, Fonds Varin; Achille Guidée, *Vie du R.P. Joseph Varin* (Paris, 1854); *Dictionnaire de Spiritualité*, fascicules CII–CIII, no. 16 (1992), pp.288–90; AF Poitiers, A2, Les fondateurs.

14 Kilroy, *Madeleine Sophie Barat*, pp. 26–30.

15 de Charry, *Histoire des Constitutions de la Société du Sacré-Cœur: La Formation de l'Institut*, vol. III, Textes, 96*–103*; Cahier, *Vie de la . . . Mère Madeleine-Sophie Barat*, vol. i, pp. 30–1; Mario Colpo, 'Una Lettera del P. Varin al P. Paccanari del [18 Mars] 1801', *ARSI*, vol. LVII (1988), pp. 315–29.

16 Henriette Grosier (1774–1842), LA 1842, Poitiers, p. 29; Paris, p. 33 (she died in Paris). Choir sister.

17 After a time Hyacinthe Devaux withdrew from the new community.

18 Ménologes (GA, Rome, C-VII, Box 8, Juillet; C-VII, Box 2, Juillet). Geneviève Deshayes, Premiers Jours de la Société du Sacré-Cœur de Jésus. Notes Manuscrites de la Mère Deshayes; Geneviève Deshayes, 'Notes sur notre . . . Fondatrice et les Commencements de la Société', no. 3, f. 10 (GA, Rome, A-II, 1-a, Box 1). LA, 1848–1849, pp. 19–20. Geneviève Deshayes corresponded with the German mystic Catherine Emmerich and with Emmerich's secretary, Clemens Brentano. Clemens Brentano, *Sämtliche Werke und Briefe*, Band 22, 1, Religiöse Werke 1, 1 (Stuttgart, Berlin, Köln, Mainz, 1985), pp. 501–4; *Sämtliche Werke und Briefe*, Band 22, 2. *Religiöse Werke*, 1, 2 (Stuttgart, Berlin, Köln, 1990), pp. 358–62. Also, in French, *Extrait du Journal de Dülmen*, le 14 et 15 Décembre 1823 (GA, Rome, Dossiers Jeanne de Charry, Lettres Geneviève Deshayes et Clemens Brentano; also A-II, 1-a). Jeanne de Charry transcribed and edited this correspondence but did not have time to publish it before her death in 2000.

19 For a time Geneviève Deshayes assisted Madame de Rumigny, a wealthy widow, who ran a boys' school in the Hôtel des Douze Pairs de France. Deshayes, 'Notes sur notre . . . Fondatrice et les Commencements de la Société', ff. 33–4. See, ff. 25–32 for Joseph Varin's long exposé on the Dilette di Gèsu, and on the new members in Paris. [Josephine de Coriolis], 'Histoire de la Société du Sacré-Cœur de Jésus, fondée en 1800 par . . . Madeleine Louise Sophie Barat, f. 26v (G.A. Rome, A-II., 2-b), ff. 35v–36.

20 Catherine Maillard (1784–1854). No family records exist regarding her origins, but since she entered service at such a young age it may be presumed that she was a native of Amiens. LA Charleville, 1852–1855, vol. II, p. 11; de Charry, *Histoire des Constitutions de la Société du Sacré-Cœur: La Formation de l'Institut*, vol. ii, p. 401, n.179. Catherine Maillard and Geneviève Deshayes were professed as choir sisters in 1806. Later Catherine Maillard was designated as a coadjutrix sister.

21 de Coriolis, 'Histoire de la Société du Sacré-Cœur', ff. 39v–40v; Achille Guidée, *Vie du R.P. Varin* (Paris, 1854), pp. 68–76.

22 Kilroy, *Madeleine Sophie Barat*, pp. 35–6. Adèle Jugon later married the Comte de La Rivière. She retained her friendship with the Society of the Sacred Heart, especially during the 1830 July Revolution. Cahier, *Vie de la . . . Mère Madeleine-Sophie Barat*, vol. i, p. 520.

23 Adele Bardot (1761–1828) had some degree of education since she taught writing in the school and looked after the children's health. LA 1818–1834, pp. 324–5. She died in La Ferrandière. Choir sister.

24 Marguerite-Rosalie Debrosse (1786–1854) was born in the region around Verdun and entered at the age of eighteen. She died in Charleville. No family details survive. LA 1854–1855, p.11. Choir sister.

25 Barthélémy Roux (1779–1870). LA 1870–1872, Première partie, pp. 4–6. Coadjutrix sister. Later in Cuignières she taught in the village and cared for the sick including those wounded in the wars of Napoleon. Souvenirs d'une élève de Cuignières (AF, Poitiers, B05/117 Beauvais).

26 Félicité Desmarquest (1780–1869) from Guillaucourt, in the district of Rosières. Her father was a farmer and shopkeeper; she was the eleventh of sixteen children. Notice de la révérende Mère Desmarquest (GA, Rome, B-Des. RSCJ); also, Ménologes (GA, Rome C-VIII, 2). Choir sister.

27 Thérèse Joséphine Pelletier (1785–1853). LA 1852–1853, Quimper, p. 58. Aso, GA, Rome, C-VII, 2, NOP. Her father was a baker and her mother a skilled dressmaker. See p. 51, n. 229. Coadjutrix sister.

28 Josephine Pelletier (1788–1855). She died in Niort on 4 October 1855. GA, Rome, Circulaires de nos RSCJ, 1818–1863, Box 31, pp. 141–3. Coadjutrix sister. Scholastique Pelletier (1789–1831) became a sister of Notre Dame in 1805. She entered the community at Amiens in 1816. LA 1805–1833, pp. 400–7. Choir sister.

29 Augustine Huchon (1790–1830) came from Bretagne. Her family were forced to flee home during the Revolution and for a time were imprisoned in a boat on the Loire. She died in Niort. LA 1805–1833, pp. 325–9. Coadjutrix sister.

30 Marie de la Croix (1792–1879). Little is known of her family background, except that her parents valued education. LA, 1879–1880, pp. 249–57. Marie de la Croix à son père, Amiens, 3 Mai 1812; à sa mère, Amiens, 15 Mai 1812; à Pierre Ronsin, Amiens, 22 Avril 1812; à Pierre Ronsin, Amiens, 25 Juillet 1812 (AFSJ, Dossier Pierre Ronsin, SJ. H Ron 12 a). Kilroy, *Madeleine Sophie Barat*, pp. 88–91, 104–8. Choir sister.

31 Suzanne Labart (1790–1848). She died on 19 December 1848 in Poitiers, LA 1848–1852, p. 33. Coadjutrix sister.

32 This was the first Clarissan monastery founded in France in the lifetime of St Clare. de Charry, *Histoire des Constitutions de la Société du Sacré-Cœur: La Formation de l'Institut*, vol. ii, p. 335, n. 42.

33 de Charry, *Histoire des Constitutions de la Société du Sacré-Cœur. Seconde partie: Les Constitutions Définitives et leur Approbation par le Saint-Siège*, vol. ii, *Documents et Correspondances*, p.12.

34 de Coriolis, 'Histoire de la Société du Sacré-Cœur', ff. 39v–40v; Achille Guidée, *Vie du R.P. Varin* (Paris, 1854), pp. 68–76. Mlle Capy's Christian name is not known.

35 Teresa Copina (nd) de Charry, *Histoire des Constitutions de la Société du Sacré-Cœur: La Formation de l'Institut*, vol. ii, p. 493; de Charry, *Exposé Historique*, pp. 16, 33–6; Joseph Varin to Sophie Barat, Belley, 8 October [1803], p. 66, n. 6. No biographical details exist for Teresa Copina. She left the Society of the Sacred Heart in 1814/15 and went to Rome with Anne Baudemont. J.M. Vidal, *Saint-Denis aux Quatre Fontaines à Rome* (Rome/Paris 1934), pp. 41–6.

36 de Charry, *Histoire des Constitutions de la Société du Sacré-Cœur: La Formation de l'Institut*, vol. ii, p. 494. Also, Madame de Gramont d'Aster to Pierre-Vincent Dombidau de Crouseilles, Amiens, 7 January [1810]. (GA, Rome, de Gramont d'Aster, C-VII, 2).

37 Anne-Marie de Coërville (1754–1820). This was possibly a community founded in Paris in 1636. LA 1809–1834 (7), p. 30. She died in Poitiers on 15 November 1820; de Charry, *Exposé Historique*, pp. 16, 41, n. 144. Choir sister.

38 Madeleine Raison (1761–1837). She died in Paris. No biographical details have survived. Coadjutrix sister.

39 Clarisse Langlet (1792–1834) was a dressmaker (ouvrière en linge). de Charry, *Exposé Historique*, pp. 13, 16, 17, n. 43. LA 1818–1834, Lyon, La Ferrandière. No pagination. Choir sister.

40 Catherine-Emilie de Charbonnel de Jussac (1774–1857) was fearless during the Revolution when her family home was attacked and her mother imprisoned. *Vie de la Mère [Catherine] de Charbonnel, Assistante et Économe Générale de la Société du Sacré-Cœur de Jésus* (Paris, c.1870). Her level of education allowed Catherine de Charbonnel teach and to mentor her own colleagues. Choir sister.

41 Marie d'Olivier (1778–1866). *Mémorial Catholique*, Février 1868, pp. 70–4. Papiers Hypolite Martin, SJ (AF Poitiers, Beauvais, B05/117, Box 2). Marie d'Olivier published *Les Trois Paulines* (Lille, 1834); *L'Imagination ou Charlotte de Drelincourt*

(Lille, 1858); *Dialogues des Vivants au XIXe Siècle* (Paris, 1859); *Lettres aux Jeunes Femmes du Monde Élégant* (Avignon, 1866). Choir sister.

42 The Abbé Lamarche was chaplain to the Carmelite community of Compiègne. When the community was condemned to death he gave absolution to each Carmelite as she went to the guillotine in Paris in 1792. He supported the community in Amiens from the beginning. Abbé Lamarche to Madame Barat, Cuignières, 17 February 1816 (GA, Rome. A-II, b-2, Amiens- Affaires, no. 51).

43 See note 19.

44 Marie-Elizabeth Prevost (1785–1871) was born in St Dominique. She went to school with the Ursulines at Clermont-en-Beauvaisis where her eldest sister was already a member of the community. Choir sister.

45 She entered again in 1828 and made final profession in 1835; some years later, c.1842, she left once more (GA, Rome, Vow and Profession Register, 1820–1845). In 1845 she asked to return and Sophie Barat refused. SB to Eugénie de Gramont , Rome, 27 May 1845. However, when she asked again to re-enter in 1857, at the age of eighty-two, she was accepted. SB to Aimée d'Avenas, Paris, 11 November 1857; Paris, 24 December 1857 (*Passim*). When she left Amiens in 1804 Cécile de Cassini (1777–1867) entered La Trappe in Switzerland for a time, as well as several other communities. She also spent time in Castelnaudary, ancient site of the Cathars, and was in contact with the stigmatist Catherine Emmerich and Clemens Brentano. Cécile de Cassini died in Orleans in 1867.

46 (AN 101 AP, Maison de Gramont, Series D, Carton 3).

47 Both were pupils at the boarding school in Amiens. Madame de Gramont d'Aster to Pierre-Vincent Dombidau de Crouseilles, Amiens, 11 October 1807; Amiens, 7 January [1810] (GA, Rome, de Gramont d'Aster, C-VII, 2). Pierre-Vincent Dombidau de Crouseilles (1751–1823) was bishop of Quimper from 1805 to 1823. Eugénie de Gramont was born with a spinal defect and by the age of eight this handicap had become a chronic condition. For the rest of her life she was obliged to wear a steel corset, to support her back and enable her to breathe.

48 *Notice sur la Vie de Madame la Comtesse de Gramont, Née de Boisgelin* (Paris, 1836); Jean Jaurgain et Raymond Ritter, *La Maison de Gramont, 1040–1967*, 2 vols (Les Amis du Musée Pyrénéen, 1968), pp. 658–65; Olivier Ribeton, *Les Gramonts: Portraits de Famille, XVIe–XVIIIe Siècles* (J et D Éditions, 1992), pp. 41, 128; *Dictionnaire de Biographie Française* (1985), pp. 916–26. [Jeanne de Charry] *Une Tryptique. Les Mères de Gramont d'Aster: La Mère et ses Filles* [GA, Rome, Papiers de Charry]. The three de Gramonts were choir sisters.

49 She was educated by the Canonesses of Remiremont, an order established in the thirteenth century for women from noble families. The Princess de Bourbon-Condé (1757–1824) was Abbess of the noble chapter of Remiremont in 1786. The Society of the Sacred Heart had direct links with the Princess de Bourbon-Condé which began in 1797 and ended only with her death in 1824, in the rue Monsieur, Paris. de Charry, *Histoire des Constitutions de la Société du Sacré-Cœur*, vol. i, pp. 131–40. Also, Dom J. Rabory, *La Princess Louise de Bourbon-Condé: Fondatrice du Monastère du Temple* (Paris, 1888); Marguerite Savigny-Vesco, *La Princess Louise-Adélaïde de Bourbon-Condé: Le Double Reflet de l'Étoile* (Paris, 1932).

50 She was presented at the court at Versailles in 1781 and appointed Dame du Palais to the Queen, Marie-Antoinette, in 1778. Her uncle, Cardinal Jean de Dieu-Raymond de Boisgelin de Cucé (1732–1804), archbishop of Aix, went into exile, as did her aunt, Marie-Catherine de Boufflers (1744–1794). Madame de Gramont

d'Aster fled to London with her husband and children, where she was joined by her sister, Cornélie Zoé Vitaline de Boisgelin-Pléhédel (†1852), Marquise de Chabannes. They ran a small school in Hyde Park to support the family. In 1795 the Comte de Gramont d'Aster died; in 1796 Madame de Gramont d'Aster felt it safe enough to return to Paris with her children.

51 Marie du Terrail (1771–1813) was professed in Amiens in 1804 and was sent to Belley in 1805 and later to Grenoble in 1807, where she took charge of the poor school. She died on 30 November 1813. LA 1805–1830 (2), p. 15. SB to Philippine Duchesne, 10 December 1813. Also, note in Jeanne de Charry (ed.), *Lettres Madeleine-Sophie Barat et Philippine Duchesne, Première Partie: Période de Grenoble (1804–1815)*, p. 200, n. 2. Choir sister.

52 de Charry, *Histoire des Constitutions de la Société du Sacré-Cœur*, vol. ii, no. 62, pp. 343–4. Dominique Picco, *Des Méridionales à la Cour: l'Exemple des Demoiselles de Saint-Cyr (1688–1793). Bulletin du Centre de Recherche du Château de Versailles. Les Méridionales à Versailles. Mis en ligne 6 Juin 2008*, pp. 1–18; de Charry, *Histoire des Constitutions de la Société du Sacré-Cœur*, vol. ii, pp. 493. The educational vision of the Society of the Sacred Heart was influenced by St Cyr and the Maison de L'Enfant Jésus in Paris.

53 Henriette Ducis (1772–1844). LA Circulaires de nos RSCJ, 1818–1863. Biographies des défuntes de la Société. vol. 3, 1839 a 1854, pp. 51–4. Her uncle and guardian was the poet Jean-François Ducis. Choir sister.

54 Jean-Baptiste-Louis Sambucy de Saint-Estève (1771–1847) was born in Millau en Rouergue and went to Paris to train for the priesthood, first at the Collège de Juilly and later in 1787 at St Sulpice.

55 Louis de Sambucy de St Estève to Eugénie de Gramont, Millau, 6 January 1846 (Archives Historiques, Diocèse de Paris, Fonds de Quelen, 1D IV 12); R. Limouzin-Lamothe, *Monseigneur de Quelen, Archevêque de Paris*, 2 tomes (Paris, 1955), vol. i, p. 28; *Histoires des Catéchismes de Saint-Sulpice, 1830*, pp. 150–1, 167, 182.

56 de Charry, *Histoire des Constitutions de la Société du Sacre-Cœur*, vol. ii, p. 494.

57 Philippine Duchesne, 1769–1852. de Charry (ed.), *Correspondance Sainte Madeleine Sophie Barat, Sainte Philippine Duchesne*. Sarah A. Curtis, *Civilizing Habits: Women Missionaries and the Revival of French Empire* (Oxford, 2010); Louise Callan, *Philippine Duchesne: Frontier Missionary of the Sacred Heart, 1769–1852* (Maryland,1957); Catherine Mooney, *Philippine Duchesne: A Woman with the Poor* (New York, 1990). Choir sister.

58 de Coriolis, 'Histoire de la Société du Sacré-Cœur', ff. 52–67; de Charry, *Histoire des Constitutions de la Société du Sacré-Cœur*, vol. ii, pp. 349–51; Curtis, *Civilizing Habits*, pp. 23–36; Callan, *Philippine Duchesne*, pp. 61–76; Mooney, *Philippine Duchesne*, pp. 79–84.

59 Pierre-Aimé-Alexandre Roger (1763–1839). *DS*, Fascicules 89–90, no. 13 (1988), pp. 871–5.

60 Sophie Barat was accompanied by Rosalie Debrosse and Catherine Maillard from Amiens, and by two priests, Pierre Roger and the Abbé Coidy. *Journal de la Maison de Grenoble. Depuis sa fondation, le 13 Décembre 1804 jusqu'au 27 Décembre 1813. Par la Mère Duchesne, 13 Décembre 1804*, f 1 (GA, Rome, A-II., 1-d); de Charry, *Histoire des Constitutions de la Société du Sacré-Cœur*, vol. ii, pp. 400–1.

61 de Coriolis, 'Histoire de la Société du Sacré-Cœur', ff. 52–52v; Curtis, *Civilizing Habits*, pp. 37–40; Callan, *Philippine Duchesne*, pp. 14–38.

62 Marie Rivet (1768–1841). Her brother, Pierre Rivet, was a priest and vicar general

in Grenoble. LA 1833–1847 (20), pp. 257–8. de Charry (ed), *Lettres Madeleine-Sophie Barat et Philippine Duchesne, Première Partie: Période de Grenoble (1804–1815)*, n. 1, pp. 5–6. No further biographical details survive. She died in Chambéry in 1841. Choir sister.

63 Marie Balastron (1784–1862). No family details survive. Her obituary notes that as a child during the Revolution Marie Balastron did not recall ever seeing a church open. As she taught soon after her arrival in Grenoble this may indicate that she had received a basic education at home. She died in Marseilles. Choir sister.

64 Emilie Giraud, 1783–1856. LA Circulaires de nos RSCJ. *Biographies des Défuntes de la Société*, vol. 3, 1839 a 1854, pp. 148–59. de Charry, *Exposé Historique*, p. 13; de Charry, *Histoire des Constitutions de la Société du Sacré-Cœur*, vol. ii, p. 353. Also GA, Rome, C-I, A, 1-C, Box 2. She died in Lille. Choir sister.

65 Adélaïde Second (1782–1847), LA 1833–1847 (20), pp. 518–20. No family details have been recorded. She died in Le Mans in 1847. Choir sister.

66 Henriette Girard (1761–1828). LA 1806–1830 (2) p. 255; GA, Rome, C-VII, 2, G; A-II, 1-a. Also, SB to Philippine Duchesne, Lyon, 19 April 1805; Amiens, 20 January 1806; Poitiers, 1 August 1806. Henriette Girard was a member of the General Council in 1815 and died in Amiens in 1828. Choir sister.

67 Marie-Louise de Vaulserre des Adrets (1759–1812). LA 1805–1830 (2), p. 10. Choir sister.

68 Françoise Leridon (1793–1857). LA Circulaires de nos RSCJ, 1818–1863. *Biographies des Défuntes de la Société*, vol. 3, 1839 à 1854, pp. 255–8. She died in Marseilles. de Charry, *Histoire des Constitutions de la Société du Sacré-Cœur, Seconde Partie*, vol ii, *Documents et Correspondances*, p. 15. Choir sister.

69 Caroline Messoria (1783–1838). She died in Bordeaux. No biographical details survive. Choir sister.

70 Angelique Lavauden (1789–1872) died in Montfleury on 10 January 1872. de Charry, *Exposé Historique*, pp. 288, 394–5, 397, 418, 446; de Charry (ed.), *Correspondance Sainte Madeleine Sophie Barat et Sainte Philippine Duchesne, 1818–1821*, SB to Philippine Duchesne, Paris, 5 November 1818, pp. 178–9, n. 4. Choir sister.

71 Bertille Chauvin (1780–1834), LA Circulaires de nos RSCJ, 1818–1863. She hoped Sophie Barat would found a community in Joigny, but despite pressure from her brother Louis Barat and the local priest, Abbé Fromenteau, Sophie declined. de Charry, *Exposé Historique*, p 17 and n. 49; de Charry, *Histoire des Constitutions de la Société du Sacré-Cœur*, vol. ii, pp. 431–2; M.T. Virnot (ed.), *Sainte Madeleine-Sophie Barat, Journal, Poitiers 1806–1808* (1977), pp. 64, 90. Choir sister.

72 Euphrosine Jouve (1797–1821). On entry she took the name Aloysia and in the course of her short life gained a reputation for sanctity. Chantal Paisant, *Litanie Pour une None Défunte* (Paris, Cerf, 2003).

73 Christine de Crouzas (1771–1828/9). Her family was from Pont de Beauvoisin and was deeply affected by the Revolution. She entered against the wishes of her family in 1806, and had to leave for two years due to ill-health. She entered again in 1809. LA 1805–1830 (2) pp. 245–8. She died in Grenoble. Choir sister.

74 Hélène du Tour (1788–1849). She died in Natchitoches. LA 1848–1849, p. 260. Choir sister.

75 Octavie Berthold (1787–1833). While few family details survive, her life in the Society of the Sacred Heart is well documented. See Jeanne de Charry (ed.), *Correspondance Sainte Madeleine Sophie Barat et Sainte Philippine Duchesne, passim;*

Chantal Paisant, *Les Années Pionnières, 1818–1823. Lettres et Journaux des Premières Missionnaires du Sacré-Cœur aux États-Unis.* Textes rassemblés, établis et présenté par Chantal Paisant (Paris, 2001) *passim.* Callan, *Philippine Duchesne*, pp. 550–1. LA 1834–1852, St Louis. No pagination; her obituary was written by Philippine Duchesne. Choir sister.

76 Hypolite Lavauden (1792–1867). She died in Rome on 2 April 1867. GA, Rome, Ménologes, C-VIII, 2, Box 7. Choir sister.

77 Eugénie Audé (1792–1842). de Charry, *Correspondance Sainte Madeleine Sophie Barat, Sainte Philippine Duchesne, 1818–1821*, pp. 2, 28–9; de Charry, *Exposé Historique*, p. 201, n. 41, p. 220.

78 de Charry, *Histoire des Constitutions de la Société du Sacré-Cœur*, vol. iii, Textes, No. 22, La Mère Barat raconte les débuts de la fondation de Grenoble, p. 130.*

79 The Dilette di Gesù was dissolved in Rome in 1802 due to scandals concerning the life of the founder, Nicolas Paccanari. Kilroy, *Madeleine Sophie Barat*, pp. 37–40.

80 Kilroy, *Madeleine Sophie Barat*, pp. 42–4.

81 Curtis, *Civilizing Habits*, pp. 4–7; Silvia Evangelisti, *Nuns: A History of Convent Life* (Oxford, 2008), pp. 41–65, 201–4; Mary Laven, *Virgins of Venice: Broken Vows and Cloistered Lives in the Renaissance Convent* (Harmondsworth, 2004).

82 On the other hand, Anne Baudemont, formerly a Clarissan nun, had accepted in Amiens that some monastic practices and forms had to be laid aside. de Charry, *Histoire des Constitutions de la Société du Sacré-Cœur*, vol. ii, pp. 362–8.

83 Following the practice of the Dilette, Sophie Barat considered silent prayer more suitable for women who taught all day.

84 de Charry, *Histoire des Constitutions*, vol. ii, pp. 370–82; de Charry, *Histoire des Constitutions*, vol. iii, Textes, no. 22, La Mère Barat Raconte les Débuts de la Fondation de Grenoble, pp. 132–3; Curtis, *Civilizing Habits*, pp. 37–40; Callan, *Philippine Duchesne*, pp. 93–9.

85 Kilroy, *Madeleine Sophie Barat*, pp. 49–61.

86 Marie-Thérèse Virnot (ed.), *Sainte Madeleine-Sophie Barat, Journal de Poitiers 1806–1808. Texte Intégral* (Poitiers, 1977), pp. 25–6, 28, 124 n. 6, 129 n. 34.

87 Lydie Choblet (1765–1832). Choir sister.

88 She founded an Ursuline community in Tours as well as a boarding school for girls. In the 1830s there were unsuccessful attempts to fuse this community with the Society of the Sacred Heart.

89 Joséphine Bigeu (1779–1827). LA 1805–1833 (3), pp. 257–66; GA, Rome, C-VII, 2. Bigue. Choir sister.

90 de Coriolis, 'Histoire de la Société, 1806–1807', Ch. II, ff. 5v–6v; *Journal de Poitiers*, pp. 15–16, 25–8, 124. Lambert was a Father of the Faith and a colleague of Joseph Varin.

91 SB to Philippine Duchesne, Poitiers, 1 August 1806.

92 de Coriolis, 'Histoire de la Société, 1806–1807', Ch. II, f. 8v.

93 de Coriolis, 'Histoire de la Société, 1806–1807', Ch. II, ff. 7–9v; *Journal de Poitiers*, pp. 28–34, 125; 'Manuscrit de la Mère Thérèse Maillucheau. Premier Noviciat de la Société, Formé à Poitiers par ma Mère Générale en Année 1806', ff. 78–85; 3–5 (GA, Rome, A-II, a-1, Box 1); Souvenirs des recréations de notre . . . Mère Générale au Noviciat de la Maison Mère, Juillet 1835 (Society of the Sacred Heart National Archives, USA)

94 *Journal de Poitiers*, pp. 30–3.

95 de Coriolis, 'Histoire de la Société, 1806–1807', Ch. II, ff. 10v–11.

96   Susanne Geoffroy (1761–1845) came from a large family with little fortune. She was brought up by an aunt and uncle. *Vie de Madame Geoffroy* (Oudin, Poitiers, 1854), pp. 7–30; *Journal de Poitiers*, pp. 49, 99–101, 108–11, 126–7; LA 1834–1847, pp. 236–50; de Charry, 'Histoire des Constitutions de la Société du Sacré-Cœur', vol. i, 73ff. Choir sister.

97   Josephine Bonnet (1786–1852). After four months she returned to her former community but soon asked to rejoin Les Feuillants. Sophie Barat was reluctant to receive her back but finally allowed her another attempt. *Journal de Poitiers*, pp. 49, 71, 107; LA Beauvais, 1852–1853, p. 19. Choir sister.

98   Madeleine du Chastaignier (1774–1832). LA Niort, 1818–1834, p. 452ff. She died in Niort. Choir sister. Her father was a lawyer in Poitiers. Her mother died when she was a child and Madeleine was brought up by her relations.

99   Marie-Madeleine de Chasseloup, née Lafitte (1761–1836). *Journal de Poitiers*, p.107; de Charry, *Exposé Historique*, pp. 16 and 206, n. 54. LA 1834–1847 (21), pp. 75–8. She died on 14 May in Annonay. Choir sister.

100 Henriette Bernard (1766–1830). *Journal de Poitiers*, pp. 47, 69–70, 119. LA Bordeaux, 1818–1834, pp. 215–16. She died in Bordeaux. Choir sister.

101 In 1808 Henriette Bernard returned to Niort, accompanied by Susanne Geoffroy to continue the poor school. The community expanded and later a boarding school was established.

102 Gertrude Lamolière (1769–1818) died on 17 May 1818 in Poitiers. LA 1805–1833, pp. 22–3.

103 Marinette Guiégnet (1782–1808) was a native of Bordeaux and was orphaned as a child. She died in Poitiers on 24 December 1808. LA 1805–1833, pp. 1–2; *Journal de Poitiers*, p. 122.

104 Mélanie Demelin (1778–1827) died on 22 June 1827 in Bordeaux. LA 1805–1833, pp. 240–4; de Charry, *Histoire des Constitutions de la Société du Sacré-Cœur. Seconde Partie: Documents et Correspondances*, p. 15. Choir sister.

105 Brigette Berniard (1780–1851). LA Beauvais 1850–1851, p. 21; de Charry, *Histoire des Constitutions de la Société du Sacré-Cœur*, p. 15. Choir sister.

106 Louise Macqué Olivier (1778–1810). She died in Poitiers on 28 February 1810. LA 1805–1833, pp. 4–5. de Charry, *Histoire des Constitutions de la Société du Sacré-Cœur. Seconde Partie: Documents et Correspondances*, p. 15. Choir sister.

107 Félicité Boulard (1785–1866) died in La Ferrandière. LA 1867–1868, vol. iii, pp. 12–13. de Charry, *Histoire des Constitutions de la Société du Sacré-Cœur. Seconde Partie: Documents et Correspondances*, p. 15. Coadjutrix sister.

108 Elizabeth Boué (1777–1861). LA Poitiers, 1859–1862, p. 149. Choir sister.

109 (NN) Froissard, *Journal de Poitiers*, p. 123. Coadjutrix sister.

110 Gabrielle Benoit (1771–1848) died on 2 January 1848. LA Poitiers, 1848–1849, p. 33. Sophie Barat remarked on her remarkable qualities. *Journal de Poitiers*, pp. 113–14, 123. Coadjutrix sister.

111 Marthe Maugenet (1790–1867) died in Poitiers on 27 April 1867. LA 1867–1868, vol. vii, pp. 3–4. Coadjutrix sister.

112 Amélie Colas (1789– 1849) died in Bourges. No biographical details survive. Coadjutrix sister.

113 Célestine Desnos (1793–1837) died in Quimper. LA 1834–1847 (21), pp. 131–4. Choir sister.

114 Julie Barré (1780–1859). LA Poitiers, 1859–1862, p. 149. Choir sister.

115 No biographical details survive for Gabrielle Hinard. *Journal of Poitiers*, pp. 37–8.

116 Listed in de Charry, *Histoire des Constitutions de la Société du Sacré-Cœur. Seconde Partie: Documents et Correspondances*, pp. 15, 20.

117 *Journal de Poitiers*, 1806–1808.

118 Sophie Barat to Madeleine Chastaignier, Grenoble [nd] December 1812.

119 Records are sparse for many of those who entered the communities, especially in Grenoble and Poitiers. Some indication of social background is given by the later designation of choir sister and coadjutrix sister. Records from Amiens are richer due to the fact that early controversies (1802–1815), concerning the purpose and the leadership of the Society, were largely played out there. In addition, some of the women who came from nobles families had family archives which survived the Revolution.

120 Further biographies of women who joined the Society and for the most part died early on can be found in GA, Rome in the collections LA 1805–1830 (2), pp. 1–46; LA 1805–1833 (3), pp. 1–20.

121 In Poitiers Sophie Barat invited each one to share their life story, speaking in turn each evening. Thérèse Maillucheau, premier noviciat de la Société, 1806, ff. 83, 93, 95; Souvenirs des recréations, Juillet 1835. Kilroy, *Madeleine Sophie Barat*, p. 59.

122 de Charry, *Exposé Historique*, pp. 14–15.

123 Madame de Gramont d'Aster to Pierre-Vincent Dombidau de Crouseilles, bishop of Quimper, Amiens 7 January [1810]. (GA, Rome, de Gramont d'Aster, C-VII, 2). In 1802 newspapers commented on the 'learned women' in the school in Amiens; de Coriolis, 'Histoire de la Société', f. 36.

124 Kilroy, *Madeleine Sophie Barat*, Chapters 2–5.

125 de Charry, *Exposé Historique*, p. 14.

126 *Journal de Poitiers*, pp. 38–9.

127 Statuts des Sœurs ou Dames de l'Instruction Chrétienne, Osterode, le 10 Mars 1807. Art. 4 (GA, Rome, A-IV, 1. Box 2), Art. 4; de Charry, *Histoire des Constitutions de la Société du Sacré-Cœur. Seconde Partie: Documents et Correspondances*, pp. 165–9.

128 État du matériel des Associations religieuses de femmes, existantes dans le Département de la Vienne. Association des Dames de l'Instruction Chrétienne de la ville de Poitiers (GA, A-II, 2) e-f-g) [1807].

129 Many of the choir sisters did not know Latin either. In 1820 the General Council specifically asked that choir sister novices be taught Latin so that Office could be said properly. Despite Sophie Barat's wish to replace Office with silent prayer, the recitation of Office became more formalised and solemn in the Society after 1815, especially on feast days and during the celebration of Christmas and Easter, when the Society adopted the full Roman breviary. In 1839 another effort to have Office replaced with silent prayer also failed.

130 Fureix, *La France des Larmes: Deuils Politiques à l'Âge Romantique*; Bettina Frederking, 'Il ne Faut pas être le Roi de Deux Peuples: Strategies of National Reconciliation in Restoration France', *French History*, vol 22, no 4 (December 2008), pp. 446–68.

131 The first General Council was held in Amiens in 1806, when Sophie Barat was elected superior general for life by a majority of one.

132 For a detailed account of this process, de Charry, *Histoire des Constitutions de la Société du Sacré-Cœur. Second Partie: Les Constitutions Définitives et Leur Approbation par le Saint-Siège*, 3 volumes (Rome, 1979).

133 Society of the Sacred Heart, 1815 Constitutions, nos 1, 4–6.

134 de Charry, *Exposé Historique*, p. 10 ff.

135 GA, Rome, A-II, c-d. Box 3.

136 1815 Constitutions, nos 8, 89 and *passim*. The term *sujet* also meant the one who is governed. Sophie Barat used the word in that sense when writing to leaders of communities.

137 1815 Constitutions, nos 4, 60, 167, 180, 246, 300, 309, 329 and *passim*

138 1815 Constitutions, nos 74, 134, 136, 328; de Charry, *Exposé*, pp. 118–21.

139 1815 Constitutions, no. 7.

140 1815 Constitutions, no. 231.

141 1815 Constitutions, nos 169–74; 186, 195, 201–3, 207–8, 217, 223–5, 227, 237, 241 and *passim*.

142 1815 Constitutions, nos 100, 106.

143 On 16 July 1816 Philippine Duchesne noted that each of the nine members of the new community was dressed according her rank in the Society. de Charry, *Exposé Historique*, p. 213.

144 1815 Constitutions, no. 16, 20.

145 1815 Constitutions, no. 51.

146 1815 Constitutions, nos 10, 106.

147 1815 Constitutions, 332, no. 3.

148 1815 Constitutions, 334, no. 5; de Charry, *Exposé Historique*, p.245, n. 190; p. 252, n. 200.

149 Procès Verbaux des Conseils, Amiens 1816–1828, f. 20 (AF Poitiers, BOI Amiens 116).

150 1815 Constitutions, no. 68.

151 1815 Constitutions, nos 98–9.

152 1815 Constitutions, no. 101.

153 1815 Constitutions, nos 147, 151–6, 162. Also, de Charry, *Exposé Historique*, p.150, n. 307.

154 Procès Verbaux des Conseils, Amiens 1816–1828 (AF Poitiers, BOI Amiens 116).

155 This was Thérèse Pelletier. See note 27.

156 Procès Verbaux, f. 4, no. 2.

157 Procès Verbaux, ff. 4–5, no. 3; f. 8, no. 3.

158 Procès Verbaux, Samedi 11 Janvier 1817, f 8. no. 2.

159 Procès Verbaux, Samedi 11 Janvier 1817, f. 7, no. 1–2. By 1831 financial requirements for those entering as choir sisters were established. If the candidate entered in Paris the family was asked to pay 800 francs a year until final vows; if the candidate entered in the provinces ('pour la province'), the family paid 600 francs. On the other hand, if families wished to give a dowry on entry, then they were asked to give in proportion to wealth and the number of children in the family. SB to the Marquis d'Aigremont, Chambéry, 26 April 1831.

160 Procès Verbaux, Mercredi 12 Février 1817, f. 12 ff.

161 Emplois des Sœurs. Procès Verbaux, 19 Février, 1817, ff. 15–17. From c. 1838/9 the Society of the Sacred Heart catalogues of the houses and members of the Society began, as well as a description of each one's task. These were circulated annually to all communities. Records of visitations of communities and schools also began then. For example, Paris, 1825 and 1827 (AF Poitiers, B06/111); Charleville, 1835 and 1842 (AF Poitiers, B22/117); Louisiana, 1842 (Visitation Book, 1840–1859 Society of the Sacred Heart National Archives, USA, Series IV. St Louis Province, City House St Louis-1, Box 1); Lemberg (Poland), 1847 (GA, Rome, C-IV, Lemberg/Lvov 1847). *Passim.*

162 Procès Verbaux, 19 Février, 1817, f. 17, 19.

163 Madame Piorette (dépensière) was charge of house supplies and monitored the use of soap, only allowed for washing clothes by hand.

164 Procès Verbaux, 19 Février, 1817, f. 19, 20.

165 Maison de Beauvais (GA, Rome A-II., 1-a, Box 2, Dossier 3)

166 SB to Philippine Duchesne, Paris, 21 April 1818.

167 Liste générale des charges de la maison, Beauvais (GA, Rome, C-IV, I, Beauvais 1818).

168 Reading religious texts during the midday and evening meal was a monastic practice adopted in the Society of the Sacred Heart.

169 At this period the family names of coadjutrix sisters are not always recorded and can only be verified from the Register of Vows.

170 Amiens Affaires, no. 39, Réponse à Mr Lambert, Paris, 1 Décembre 1815.

171 The Society of the Sacred Heart retained its independence by invoking the requirement of cloister, hereby limiting access to its properties to pupils, parents and the chaplains officially assigned. The observance of cloister for religious women laid down at the Council of Trent was adopted in a mitigated form by the Society of the Sacred Heart. Later in the century the Society used cloister to protect itself from government inspection of schools. Philippine Duchesne to Sophie Barat, St Louis, 7 October 1827; SB to Emilie Giraud, Paris, 20 January 1829; SB to Aimée d'Avenas, Paris, 19 January 1859; Paris, 23 January 1859.

172 For the way of life in stately homes, see Mark Girouard, *La Vie dans les Châteaux Français, du Moyen Age à nos Jours* (Editions Scala, 2001); *Life in the French Country House* (London, 2001); Amanda Vickery, *Behind Closed Doors: At Home in Georgian England* (Yale, 2009).

173 Olwen Hufton, 'Altruism and Reciprocity: The Early Jesuits and their Female Patrons', *Renaissance Studies*, vol. 15, no. 3, September 2001, pp. 328–53.

174 Kilroy, *Madeleine Sophie Barat*, pp. 135–8, 144–6.

175 The Institute of the Society of Jesus [10]–7–[16]–12; also, The Bull of Julius III, Esposcit Debitum, July 21 1550 [2].

176 The Institute of the Society of Jesus, Ch. 6 [112]–1. This fourth grade became an issue for the Jesuits in France in 1816, following their restoration in 1814. P.J. de Clorivière avec T. Brzozowski, Paris, 4 Juin 1816; Paris, 20 Aout 1816; Paris, 17/29 Septembre 1816. Chantal Reynier (ed.), 'La Correspondance de P.J. de Clorivière avec T. Brzozowski, 1814 à 1818' *AHSI*, vol. LXIV, no. 10 (1995), pp. 106, 114–17. John W. Padberg, *Colleges in Controversy: The Jesuit Schools in France from Revival to Suppression, 1815–1880* (Cambridge, MA, 1969) p. 9. By 1824 in Paris there were 104 Jesuit priests, 131 Jesuit scholastics and 81 Jesuit brothers.

177 This is evident in Sophie Barat's letters at this time, as she sought to maintain balance in numbers and ranks between choir and coadjutrix sisters. See: SB to Emilie Giraud, Amiens, 5 October 1814; SB to Thérèse Maillucheau, Amiens, 22 April 1816; Paris, 11 July 1816; Paris, 9 September 1816; Paris, 18 September 1816; Paris, 28 September 1816; Paris, 3 January 1817; Paris, 8 January 1817; Paris, 16 June 1817; Paris, 13 October 1817; Paris, 12 March 1819; Paris, 18 April 1819; Paris, 19 July 1819; Paris, 19 January 1820; SB to Eugénie de Gramont, Grenoble, 11 August 1818; SB to Marie Prevost, Paris, 25 March 1819; Lyon, 2 December 1819. Silvia Evangelisti, 'To Find God in Work? Female Social Stratification in Early Modern Italian Convents', *European History Quarterly*, vol 38, no. 3 (2008), pp. 398–416.

178 de Charry, *Exposé Historique*, pp. 219–22; Callan, *Philippine Duchesne*, pp. 202 ff;

Kilroy, *Madeline Sophie Barat*, pp. 127–30; Curtis, *Civilizing Habits*, pp. 41–50.

179 Philippine Duchesne to Sophie Barat, New Orleans, 17 June 1818.

180 SB to Philippine Duchesne, Paris, 5 November 1818.

181 Philippine Duchesne to Sophie Barat, en route from Bordeaux to New Orleans, Cuba, 16 May 1818. See also New Orleans, 7 June 1818; New Orleans, begun 9 July 1818.

182 Philippine Duchesne to Sophie Barat, New Orleans, 7 June 1818.

183 Philippine Duchesne to Sophie Barat, St. Louis, 22 August 1818.

184 de Charry, *Exposé Historique*, pp. 160–1. The practice of working outside with the people ended in 1827 when the Society accepted a mitigated form of cloister in order to achieve papal recognition.

185 Philippine Duchesne to Sophie Barat, St Charles Missouri, 25 January 1819. In 1822 a third community was being formed in Louisiana and Sophie Barat suggested that Catherine Lamarre become part of it, tacitly acknowledging the tension between the two women. SB to Lucile Mathevon, Paris, 30 July 1822.

186 The Ursuline community in New Orleans.

187 Philippine Duchesne to Sophie Barat, New Orleans, 9 July 1818.

188 Philippine Duchesne to Louis Barat, St Charles Missouri, 15 March 1819.

189 Philippine Duchesne to Sophie Barat, St Charles Missouri, 29 July 1819.

190 1815 Constitutions. Règles de la Sœur Commissionnaire, pp. 476–7, nos I–IX. SB to Thérèse Maillucheau, Paris, 11 July 1816; SB to Henriette Grosier, Chambéry, 20 March 1831; Chambéry, 10 April 183; SB to Marie Toussenel, Paris, 23 October 1855.

191 Philippine Duchesne to Sophie Barat [Florissant, 15 November] 1819. For the form of dress worn by the commissioner sisters and the nature of their commitment in the Society of the Sacred Heart (GA, C-I, C-3, Box 3, 1815, 1820, 1826, 1833); de Charry, *Histoire des Constitutions de la Société du Sacré-Cœur. Second Partie: Les Constitutions Définitives et Leur Approbation par le Saint-Siège, vol iii, Constitutions, Sommaire, Cérémonial*, pp. 158–9.

192 Annabelle M. Melville, *Louis William Dubourg: Bishop of Louisiana and the Floridas, Bishop of Montauban and the Archbishop of Besançon, 1766–1833*, 2 vols (Chicago, 1986).

193 Bishop Dubourg to Sophie Barat, Florissant, Territiore du Missouri, 30 October 1819.

194 Philippine Duchesne to Sophie Barat [Florissant, 1 December 1819]. In 1831, when mulatto women wished to enter the Society, Philippine Duchesne suggested that a separate congregation be set up for them, under the initial guidance of some members of the Society. Philippine Duchesne to Joseph Rosati (bishop of St Louis), St Louis, 11 April 1831.

195 SB to Philippine Duchesne, Paris, 11 April 1820.

196 SB had experience of such issues in Paris. On 27 December 1820 Neline Bruyer de Warvilliers (1791–1841), a Creole, was born in Domingo and went to school in Amiens. She entered the Society and made her first vows in Paris, and was finally professed in Bordeaux on 26 April 1822. Régistres des Vœux, no. 1, 1820–1839, f. 3 (GA, Rome, Notes de la Mère Girard, A–II, 1–a, f. 72). In 1837 there was a Creole woman in the noviceship in Paris. SB to Eulalie de Bouchaud, Rome, 8 March 1837; SB to Aloysia Hardey, Rome, 30 June 1840. Also, SB to Matilde Garabis, Paris, 4 July 1852.

197 SB to Philippine Duchesne, Paris, 16 April 1820.

198 SB to Philippine Duchesne, Paris, 24 May 1820; Philippine Duchesne to Sophie Barat, St Ferdinand, 1 September 1824.

199 The two-rank structure in the Society remained a source of tension in Louisiana, within and without the communities. This was linked with the need for domestic help. Unable to hire white people for domestic work, the Society was confronted with the reality of slavery in southern Louisiana where the internal slave market was active. To maintain the communities and schools the Society hired black men and women slaves to work in the houses and on the farms. Philippine Duchesne to Madame de Rollin [Florissant], 29 August 1820; Philippine Duchesne to Sophie Barat, Florissant, 14 September 1825. Xavier Murphy to Sophie Barat, Grand Coteau, 9 October 1826 (GA, C-III, Provinces. Dossier 6, North America); SB to Lucile Mathevon, Montet, 2 September 1836. Curtis, *Civilizing Habits*, pp. 53–61.

200 Philippine Duchesne to Sophie Barat, St Ferdinand, 18 February 1821. For details of Eulalie Hamilton see de Charry (ed.), *Correspondence Sainte Madeleine-Sophie Barat et Sainte Philippine Duchesne* (1818–1821), p. 348, n. 7.

201 de Charry (ed.), *Correspondence Sainte Madeleine-Sophie Barat et Sainte Philippine Duchesne* (1827–1852), p.144, n. 18.

202 Lucile Mathevon to Sophie Barat, St Charles de Missouri, 11 February 1833 (GA, Rome, C-III, Provinces. Dossier 6, North America). For Lucile Mathevon, see Agnès Brot et Guillemette de la Borie, *Héroines de Dieu: L'épopée des Religieuses Missionnaires du XIXème* (Paris, 2011).

203 Bordeaux, 20 Novembre 1819. Lettres du Père Barat. Communauté de Niort (AF Poitiers, B04/117). Another version of these letters, addressed to the community in Poitiers, is in the Jesuit Archives in Paris (AFSJ, Règles et Avis pour un ordre religieux de femmes. Oeuvre du P. Louis Barat, Ms. no. 6861, Carton Barat).

204 Arrêts, Décrets, 1815, 1820, 1826, 1833, ff. 38–40. (GA, C-I, C-3, Box 3); also, Arrêts, Décrets, 1834, 1851, 1874,1894 , ff. 36–8 (GA, Rome, C-I, c-2, Box 2); For details, de Charry, *Exposé Historique*, pp. 284–5 and p. 284, n. 316; The General Council of 1833 specified that three times a week the coadjutrix sisters were to have fifteen minutes of spiritual reading followed by a half hour of instruction and the recital of the Rosary. Décrets des Congrégations Générales de la Société du Sacré-Cœur. Ire Partie. Pour être Lus Devant Tout le Monde (Paris, 1867), no. 1, p. 9.

205 Another signal of spiritual equality in the Society was given when the 1826 General Council decided on the number of Masses to be offered on the death of the members. It indicated that both coadjutrix sisters and choir sisters were to have the same numbers of Masses said for them. Décrets des Congrégations Générales de la Société du Sacré-Cœur. Ire Partie. Pour être Lus Devant Tout le Monde (Paris, 1867), no. 10, 1826, p. 8.

206 This was recognised in 1864 when the eighth General Council stipulated that in each house of the Society the coadjutrix sister novices were to be given four religious formation sessions a week. Décrets des Congrégations Générales de la Société du Sacré-Cœur. Ire Partie. Pour être Lus Devant Tout le Monde (Paris, 1867), no. 3, p. 9.

207 de Charry, *Exposé Historique*, p. 493 and notes 380–2.

208 de Charry, *Histoire des Constitutions de la Société du Sacré-Cœur. Les Constitutions Définitives et Leur Approbation par le Saint-Siège, vol ii, Documents et Correspondances*, pp. 111–17.

209 The inherent ambivalence in this distinction in vows persisted in the Society until Vatican II. Many choir sisters, who did not teach or have contact with students, found it difficult to integrate the vow into their spiritual life, despite efforts to explain it or justify it. Similarly many coadjutrix sisters had daily contact with students and had real influence in the schools.

210 Thérèse Pelletier, who entered the Amiens community in 1805, recounted later in life how the bonnets made by her mother for her trousseau were used as the model for the coadjutrix sisters' headdress. Notes sur la Sœur Thérèse Pelletier (GA, Rome, C-VII, 2, NOP).

211 Arrêts, Décrets, ff. 3, 5 (GA, C-I, C-3, Box 3, 1815, 1820, 1826, 1833); de Charry, *Exposé Historique*, p. 75 n. 71.

212 Arrêtés des Conseils pour Servir d'Explication ou de Supplément aux Constitutions (GA, Rome, C-I, C-A, 1-b. Box 3). In 1833 it was also decided that in the Italian houses a rosary would be worn around the waist (this was extended to the whole Society in 1839). In addition, new, simpler choir cloaks were prescribed to be worn in winter from 1833; this was extended to all year round in 1839.

213 Sophie Barat to Henriette Grosier, Paris, 17 December 1837.

214 Arrêtés des Conseils, ff. 7–10. Sophie Barat to Henriette de Clausel, Paris, 26 September 1835.

215 Arrêtés des Conseils, f. 9.

216 Arrêtés des Conseils, ff. 1–6.

217 Arrêtés des Conseils, f. 6.

218 Arrêtés des Conseils (1834), f. 18.

219 Arrêtés des Trois Conseils en une Seule Rédaction, vol 1 (1815, 1820, 1826), ff. 51–6 (GA, Rome, C-1, C-3, Box 3).

220 SB to Philippine Duchesne, Paris, 29 November 1827.

221 Kilroy, *Madeleine Sophie Barat*, pp. 225–32. Also, Philippine Duchesne to Joseph Rosati, (Bishop of St Louis), St Louis, 1 May 1828; St Louis, 7 November 1828; St Louis, 4 January 1829. Joseph Rosati to Sophie Barat, New Orleans, 14 April 1829.

222 SB to Philippine Duchesne, Paris, 14 February 1830: Annex: For the houses in America, nos 3 and 21.

223 Philippine Duchesne to Sophie Barat, St Louis, 1 August 1831. However, there also were difficulties in assessing vocations. Cf. Philippine Duchesne to Sophie Barat, St Louis, 2 March 1834.

224 *Mémoires, Souvenirs et Journaux de la Comtesse d'Agoult*, 2 tomes (Le Temps retrouvé, LVIII, Paris, 1990), vol. i, p. 136. Marie Sophie Catherine de Flavigny (1805–1876), later the Comtesse d'Aghoult and writer under the pseudonym Daniel Stern, began her studies in the rue de Varenne on 28 April 1821.

225 Cinquième Congrégation 1833. *Journal des Séances*, 5 Octobre 1833. In French society 'de' before a family name signified nobility. For a description of this issue in 1833, see SB to Adelaide de Rozeville, Rome, 8 January 1833.

226 It took a long time before this decree was put into practice. Décrets des Congrégations Générales de la Société du Sacré-Cœur. Ire partie: Pour être Lus Devant Tout le Monde (Paris, 1867), no. 16, 1833, p. 28.

227 SB to Eugénie de Gramont, Chambéry, 19 May 1831. When the parents objected to their daughter being ranked as a coadjutrix sister Sophie Barat decided to educate her for two years and provide her trousseau, thus enabling her to become a choir sister. SB to Eulalie de Bouchaud, Paris, 12 March 1843.

228 SB to Elisa de Bouchaud, Paris, 18 February 1851.

229 Souvenirs de Sœur Virginie Roux, ff. 75–6 (GA, Rome, C-I, A, 1-e, Box 4); SB to Eugénie de Gramont, Chambéry, 17 March 1831; Chambéry, 27 March 1831. Maria Cutts. LA, 1854–1855, vol. X, pp. 5–7; SB to Maria Cutts, Chambéry, 16 October 1836.

230 Souvenirs de Sœur Virginie Roux, ff. 76–7. Comments on women who changed rank also came from outside the Society. SB to Joséphine Buesen, Paris, 20 January 1838.

231 Abbé Briand, *Vie de Pauline de Saint André de la Laurencie de Villeneuve, de Saint-Jean-d'Angély* (La Rochelle, 1847). For further details, Alfredo Peri-Morosini, *La Sainte Madeleine-Sophie Barat, Fondatrice de la Société du Sacré-Cœur et le Château de Middes en Suisse* (Toulouse, 1925), pp. 82–3. The family were linked with the kings of France, with Henry III, Louis XIII and Louis XIV. One member served Louis XIV as marshal of France. *Vie de Pauline de Saint André*, pp. 13–14; Sophie Barat to Clara Quirin, Rome, 7 March 1840.

232 *Vie de Pauline de Saint André*, pp. 61–2.

233 SB to Josephine Buesen, Paris, 1 July 1834. While waiting to go to Paris for her noviceship, Sophie Barat suggested that Pauline de Saint André could work in the school linen room, as 'because of her class she will not be used to heavy housework'.

234 SB to Josephine Buesen, Paris, 16 July 1834.

235 On Pauline de Saint André's death, her sister, Sophie de Saint André, forwarded the dowry due her sister by succession. In appreciation, Sophie Barat used it to support one of the foundations in Italy. SB to Clara Quirin, Paris, 18 December 1840.

236 Peri-Morosini, *La Sainte Madeleine-Sophie Barat . . . et le Château de Middes en Suisse*, p. 83.

237 SB to Clara Quirin, Rome, 7 March 1840.

238 Sophie Barat was dismayed at such a change and noted that no signs of ill-health appeared during the noviceship, and she could only conclude that the change in climate was the cause. SB to Louise de Limminghe, Turin, 6 September 1840; Turin, 7 September 1840.

239 SB to Louise de Limminghe, Besançon, 24 September 1840; SB to Clara Quirin, Besançon, 25 September 1840. Sophie Barat tracked this request for some years until her wishes were carried out. SB to Clara Quirin, Paris, 5 October 1840; SB to Alix de Kérouartz, Conflans, 20 September 1843; SB to Anna du Rousier, Conflans, 3 October 1843.

240 SB to Clara Quirin, Paris, 18 October 1840.

241 A case in point was that of Delphine Martigny, 1833–1855. LA, 1854–1855. Paris, Maison Mère. Also, Pauline Perdrau, Delphine Martigny, novice coadjutrice, 1852 (GA, Rome, C-I, A, i-e, Box 4).

242 Among them was Adèle Davidoff. SB to Adèle Davidoff, Montet, 25 August 1836. Also re Elisa Croft: see SB to Eugénie de Gramont, Rome, 4 May 1839. And Aymardine de Nicolay. See: SB to Aimée d'Avenas, Paris, 6 October 1859.

243 SB to Anna de Lommessen, Paris, 19 May 1855.

244 SB to Adelaide de Rozeville, Paris, 21 January 1826; Paris, 2 May 1826; Paris, 13 May 1826; Paris, 4 August 1826; Paris, 26 August 1826; Paris, 13 April 1827; Paris, 18 May 1827; Paris, 7 June 1827; Paris, 17 June 1827; Paris, 29 June 1827; Paris, 1 June 1828; Paris, 2 September 1829. SB to Henriette Grosier, Paris, 30 May 1830; SB to Elizabeth de Castel, Paris, 21 September 1845; SB to Louise de Limminghe, Paris, 28 July 1851; SB to Anne Marie Ganon, Paris, 22 April 1855; SB to Lucie Merilhou, Paris, 5 August 1860. *Passim.*

245 SB to Josephine Buesen, Paris, 10 December 1835; Rome, 20 January 1838; SB Léonie de Brives, Paris, 27 May 1856.

246 SB to Anne Marie Ganon, Paris, 11 March 1843; Paris, 1 April 1844; Conflans, 18 May 1844; Rome, 25 April 1845; SB to Adèle Lehon, Paris, 17 September 1858.

247 SB to Henriette Grosier, Chambéry, 20 March 1831; Chambéry, 10 April 1831; SB

to Anna du Rousier, Conflans, 10 June 1843; SB to Elizabeth de Castel, Conflans, 13 April 1845; SB to Gertrude de Brou, Paris, 21 May 1856.

248 SB to Gertrude de Brou, Paris, 13 June 1857. SB ensured that those who left the Society had enough money to live on initially and a means to earn their living. SB to Joséphine Buesen, Paris, 20 February 1838. *Passim.*

249 Some of the poor schools received funds from town authorities for the education of poor children.

250 Sophie Barat consistently stated that the Society could not respond to all requests for foundations. Yet she responded quickly in a crisis and set up emergency plans for schools or communities, either during bouts of cholera (frequent in her lifetime) or in the course of the several revolutions which marked her lifetime. However, in her judgement such responses were exceptional and temporary, and would not alter the symmetry of what she and her companions had created.

251 For a discussion of these issues see Jeanne de Charry, *The Canonical and Legal Evolution of the Society of the Sacred Heart from 1827 to 1853* (Rome, 1991).

252 Kilroy, *Madeleine Sophie Barat*, pp. 242–52.

253 Jean Rozaven à Sophie Barat, Rome, 15 Octobre 1835. Also, Jean Rozaven [à Louise de Limminghe] [Rome], 24 Juin 1835 (GA, Rome, C-I., C-3, Box 7).

254 SB to Thérèse Maillucheau, Paris, 22 May 1821; Paris, 25 May 1821; Paris, 12 June 1821; Paris, 17 August 1821; Paris, 26 October 1821; Paris, 8 February 1822; SB to Eugénie Audé, Paris, 16 July 1824; Paris, 7 June 1827; SB to Susanne Geoffroy, Paris, 16 August 1824; Paris, 7 March 1826; SB to Adelaide de Rozeville, Paris, 21 December 1825; Paris, 14 September 1826; Paris, 11 February 1830 (*passim*); SB to Philippine Duchesne, Paris, 2 September 1826; Paris, 26 June 1829; SB to Alexandrine Riencourt, Paris, 13 April 1827; SB to Henriette Grosier, Paris, 19 March 1830.

255 SB to Thérèse Maillucheau, Lyon, 16 December 1819.

256 SB to Elizabeth Galitzine, Rome, 6 February 1838. For similar comments, see Geneviève Deshayes to Clemens Brentano [Tours], 4 September 1837 (GA, Rome, Dossiers Jeanne de Charry).

257 SB took this practice from the Jesuits, who maintained a balance of two-thirds priests to one-third brothers. Reynier, *La Correspondance de P.J. de Clorivière avec T. Brzozowski*, pp. 114–19. SB to Emilie Giraud, Amiens, 5 October 1814; SB to Thérèse Maillucheau, Amiens, 22 April 1816; Paris, 9 September 1816; Paris, 16 September 1816; Paris, 28 September 1816; Paris, 13 October 1817; Paris, 18 April 1819. SB to Marie Prevost, Lyon, 2 December 1819. SB to Adelaide de Rozeville, Paris, 21 January 1826; Paris, May 1827. *Passim.*

258 A case in point was Chambéry in 1839. The household consisted of twelve choir sisters and eighteen coadjutrix sisters. Of the twelve choir sisters only three were professed and nine were aspirants (first vows); of the coadjutrix sisters, four were professed, three were aspirants, nine were novices and two were postulants (AF Poitiers, B08/111,114, 117). For the numbers of novices in Montet (founded in Switzerland after the July 1830 Revolution in Paris), 1833–1835, see AF Poitiers, B90/111,114,117.

259 For details, de Charry (ed.), *Lettres Sophie Barat et Joseph Varin (1801–1849)*, pp. 331–2, n. 4.

260 SB to Eugénie Audé, Rome, 29 May 1837; SB to Alexandrine de Riencourt, Paris, 31 December 1838. Later Sophie Barat suggested that girls trained for housework in the orphanages of the Society could be employed by the Society, to lessen the

tendency of superiors to accept women, not for their vocation, but for the work they could do. SB to Adèle Lehon, Paris, 18 March 1852; Paris, 28 September 1855; SB to Esther de Ban, Paris, 25 June 1853; La Ferrandière, 11 August 1853.

261 This was especially so in the rue de Varenne in Paris. In 1852 Sophie Barat lamented the poor discernment of coadjutrix sisters vocations exercised in Paris by Eugénie de Gramont, Elisa Croft and Stephanie Cardon. SB to Emma de Bouchaud, Paris, 16 March 1852. Also, SB to Eugénie de Gramont , Rome, 23 July 1839; Conflans, 26 November 1845; SB to Eulalie de Bouchaud, Rome, 23 June 1840; SB to Elisa Croft, Paris 12 January 1847. Sophie Barat also criticised the number of coadjutrix sisters assigned by Eugénie de Gramont to look after Mgr de Quelen, archbishop of Paris, when he resided at the rue de Varenne from 1830 until his death in 1839. SB to Eulalie de Bouchaud, Rome, 23 June 1840.

262 Sophie Barat was concerned for some time about the spiritual formation of the coadjutrix sisters. SB to Alexandrine de Riencourt, Paris, 12 August 1828; Paris, 31 December 1838; SB to Louise de Limminghe, Paris, 1 June 1828; SB to Eugénie de Gramont, Chambéry, 1833; SB to Josephine Buesen, Paris, 20 February 1843. In 1827 Louise de Limminghe asked Joseph-Marie Favre if the coadjutrix sisters were receiving sufficient spiritual formation for their religious life. He thought it was adequate. Indeed, based on his experience of visits to houses of the Society and talking with the coadjutrix sisters, he suggested their prayer life was too demanding. Joseph-Marie Favre to Louise de Limminghe, Chambéry, 1 March 1827. Nevertheless, he recommended the Society to a woman who wished to enter as a coadjutrix sister. Joseph-Marie Favre to Louise de Limminghe, Conflans, 24 December 1837.

263 For a description of the process in action, SB to Adelaide de Rozeville, Rome, 7 June 1842. Also, SB to Louise de Limminghe, Rome, 19 September 1839.

264 Articles fondamentaux des Décrets du Conseil Général, Tenu à Rome en Juin 1839, p. 2 (GA, C-I, C-3. Box 4-1839), f. 2. Also, C-I, C-3, Box 3, 1839 [f. 10], Conseils Particuliers, Juillet 1839–Juin 1840.

265 de Charry, *The Canonical and Legal Evolution of the Society of the Sacred Heart of Jesus from 1827 to 1843*, pp. 4–8. Eugénie de Gramont to Sophie Barat, Paris, 28 August 1839. Elizabeth Galitzine, 'Histoire Secrète de la Société du Sacré Cœur. Depuis 1839 jusqu'à Juillet 1840', ff. 35–6 (GA, Rome. C-1., C-3, Box 2, 1839), ff. 15–16; Kilroy, *Madeleine Sophie Barat*, Chapters 15–16.

266 Aimée d'Avenas à Sophie Barat, Paris [nd c. Août] 1839. Histoire Secrète de la Société, ff. 16–17. Aimée d'Avenas was in charge of school studies in the rue de Varenne.

267 The Institute of the Society of Jesus, Ch. 6 [119]-8; also 209–17. See Esposcit Debitum, July 21 1550/6.

268 Articles Fondamentaux des Décrets du Conseil Général, Tenu à Rome en Juin 1839, p. 2 (GA, C-I, C-3. Box 4-1839), ff. 18–19.

269 Alongside the decree concerning final vows of the members, provincials were to limit the number of coadjutrix sisters in each house and ensure that their number did not exceed actual needs of each house. Règles des Supérieures Provinciales de la Société du Sacré-Cœur. Congrégation Tenue à Rome en 1839. Limiter le Nombre des Sœurs Coadjutrices. Ch. IV, p. 9. (GA. Rome, C-1, C-3, Box 4. 1839).

270 Lettres Circulaires de . . . Madeleine Sophie Barat, Seconde Partie (Roehampton, 1904), Rome, 13 Juillet 1839, p. 83; Ganss, George E. *Saint Ignatius of Loyola: The Constitutions of the Society of Jesus. Translated, with an Introduction and Commentary* (St Louis, 1970) p. 65, n. 6.

271 Joseph Varin to Sophie Barat, Paris, 19 August 1839.
272 Elizabeth Galitzine à Joseph Varin, Rome, 16 Septembre 1839. From July 1839. Also, [Elizabeth Galitzine] Conseils Particuliers, avec les Assistants [Générales], 7 Juillet–8 Juin 1840 (GA, Rome, C-I., C-3, Box 3, 1839).
273 Histoire Secrète de la Société, ff. 35–6.
274 SB to Louise de Limminghe, Rome, 7 September 1839.
275 SB to Eulalie de Bouchaud, Rome, 15 February 1840.
276 SB to Louise de Limminghe, Paris, 12 November 1840. Also, Paris, 18 November 1840; Paris, 23 November 1840.
277 SB to Eulalie de Bouchaud, Rome, 5 September 1839; SB to Thérèse Gilbert, Rome, 8 September 1839.
278 Césaire Mathieu à Sophie Barat, 14 Septembre 1839. 'Histoire Secrète de la Société du Sacré-Cœur Depuis 1839 Jusqu'à Juillet 1840', ff. 38–41 (GA, Rome. C-1., C-3, Box 2, 1839).
279 Mémoire de Césaire Mathieu. Exposé des Décrets de 1839 Comparés avec les Constitutions de Léon XII et les Statuts Approuvés par l'Autorité Civile [Février 1839] (Archives de Diocèse de Besançon, Boite 2476), ff. 11–12. Also ff. 13–14. For a similar comment, Curé de Noyon à Marie d'Olivier, Noyon, 25 Octobre 1839 (AF Poitiers, Affaire d'Olivier, B05/117 Beauvais). Also the letters of Catherine de Charbonnel to Sophie Barat, Autun, October/November 1839 (GA, Rome, C-I, e-I, Box 3).
280 SB to Henriette Grosier, Rome, 31 December 1839.
281 Lettres Circulaires, Seconde Partie, Rome, 19 Novembre 1839, pp. 115–16.
282 Kilroy, *Madeleine Sophie Barat*, pp. 355–75. In fact, the next General Council in the Society was held only in 1851. Sophie Barat could not convene a council in 1845 due to the opposition of the archbishop of Paris, Denys Affre. After his death in 1848 Sophie Barat was still unable to call a council due to the 1848 Revolutions in Europe and unrest in the Papal States.
283 Lettre de Mgr Tharin, et note de Sophie Barat [hiver 1839] (Archives de Diocèse de Besançon, Boite 2477). Until 1851 Sophie Barat continued to hope for this structure of government but Pope Pius IX refused on the grounds that the issue was still too contentious within and without the Society. The Society of the Sacred Heart did not adopt the structure of provinces and provincials until 1967.
284 SB to Elizabeth Galitzine, Rome, 6 February 1838. Also, SB to Eugénie de Gramont, Chambéry, 27 March 1831; SB to Valerie de Bosredont, Paris, 22 April 1846; SB to Alida Dumazeaud, Paris, 13 June 1849; SB to Emma de Bouchaud, Paris, 28 March 1852.
285 Minutes, 8 Juin 1839 (GA, Rome, C-I, C-3, Box 3 1839); Améliorations pour le Conseil Général de 1839. Pensionnat (AF Poitiers, A4). SB to Eugénie Gramont, Rome, 28 May 1839.
286 Décrets des Six Conseils (GA, Rome, C-I, C-3, Box 4, 1839). For a policy statement on the necessity of having French superiors in all houses, as far as possible, see Pour Italie; à Garder au Secretariat. Conseil de 1851 (GA, Rome, C-I, C-3, Box 8. 1851; 1864). In 1851 Aimée d'Avenas insisted on the hegemony of France in the Society. Note Pour le Conseil [1851] 'At this time more than ever, the superior general must not think of having her residence outside of France. The origin, the vitality, the spirit of the Society is French, and our foundations abroad can never be more than branches of the trunk' (GA, Rome, C-I, C-3, Box 8, 1851).
287 This had been the practice in Louisiana. Sophie Barat to Eugénie Audé, Paris, 7 June 1827.

288 SB to Maria Cutts, Paris, 2 May 1844 [Reorganisation of Louisiana, after the sudden death of Elizabeth Galitzine in 1843]. GA, Rome, C-I, A, 1-F, Box XVII bis; also, H-II, 1, Box 1 bis. For the reaction of Maris Cutts to this policy, Maria Cutts to Sophie Barat, St Louis, 18 July 1844 (GA, Rome, C-VII, 2, C, Box 2). Also, SB to Aloysia Hardey, Berrymead (London), 17 June 1844; Lille, 7 July 1844; Paris, 27 September 1844. For Elizabeth Galitzine's views on the issue of young religious in Louisiana, see Mémoire des Visites Provincials. Maison de St Charles, Missouri, 5 Avril 1840. Visite de Elizabeth Galitzine, Assistante Général et Provinciale, ff. 1–12; (Society of the Sacred Heart, National Archives, USA, M. St Charles, Box 2); Ire visite en Octobre 1840 par M. E. Galitzine [St Louis], (National Archives, USA, Series IV, St Louis Province, City House St Louis -1. Box 1, Community Visitation Book, 1840–1859); Notes pour les Supérieures Seules. Visits of Mother Galitzine to the Houses of North America 1840–1843 (GA, Rome, C-III. Provinces. US early history). For Maria Cutts, LA 1855–1858 (27), pp. 713–16.

289 SB to Elizabeth Galitzine , Rome, 19 January 1842.

290 Lettre Circulaires, vol. ii, Paris, 10 February 1844, pp. 169–71. Also, Lettres Circulaires, vol. ii, Conflans, 29 December 1845, pp. 200–2; Paris, 5 April 1848, p. 224.

291 SB to Thérèse Maillucheau, Lille, 5 July 1844. Delenda est Carthago/Carthage must be destroyed (Cato the Elder, 234–149 BC). Also, SB to Louise de Limminghe, La Ferrandière, 18 September 1840; Paris, 12 November 1840; Paris, 8 December 1840; Metz, 12 September, 1845; Conflans, 3 January 1846; SB to Thérèse Maillucheau, Paris, 21 March 1844; SB to Lucie Merilhou, Paris, 6 April 1844; SB to Anne Marie Ganon, Paris, 22 April 1855; SB to Adèle Lehon, Paris, 31 January 1856; Paris, 17 September 1858; SB to Aimée d'Avenas, Paris, 2 September 1858. *Passim.*

292 For those choir sisters who proved to have no vocation but who neither could nor would not leave the Society, Sophie Barat decided that they would not make final profession. SB to Elizabeth de Castel, Conflans, 13 April 1846; Conflans, 29 June 1846; SB to Emma de Bouchaud, Paris, 17 October 1855; Paris, 19 January 1856; Paris, 14 February 1856; SB to Emma de Bouchaud, Paris, 26 July 1860; SB to Aloysia Hardey, Paris, 4 April 1861; Paris, 18 April 1861; Paris, 28 April 1861.

293 There is a prolonged correspondence on this theme: SB to Anne-Marie Granon, Paris, 11 March 1843; Paris, 1 April 1844; SB to Elizabeth de Castel, Rome, 8 May 1845; Paris, 20 October 1845; Paris, 29 October 1845; Conflans, 9 November 1845; Conflans, 30 November 1845; Paris, 21 December 1845; Paris, 10 February 1846; Paris, 4 March 1846; Paris, 18 March 1846; Conflans, 24 April 1846; Conflans, 27 April 1846; Conflans, 30 April 1846; Paris, 6 September 1848; Paris, 13 July 1849. SB to Alida Dumazeaud, Poitiers, 20 January 1849; Tours, 29 January 1849; Paris, 13 June 1849; Paris, 7 March 1855; SB to Onesime de Curzon, Poitiers, 20 June 1849; SB to Elisa de Bouchaud, Paris, 23 April 1855; SB to Louise de Limminghe, Paris, 23 June 1853; SB to Adèle Lehon, Paris 1 November 1859; Paris 31 March 1860; Paris 27 July 1860; Paris, 11 August 1860; Paris, 18 August 1860; Paris, 5 January 1861; Paris, 12 January 1861; Paris, 15 January 1861. SB warned against what she called 'vocations de position', career vocations, or seeking security. SB to Matilde Garabis, Paris, 26 January 1853; SB to Aloysia Hardey Berrymead (London), 17 June 1844. SB to Elisa de Bouchaud, Nancy, 14 July 1855; SB to Gertrude de Brou, Paris, 3 June 1857. *Passim.*

294 SB to Thérèse Maillucheau, Amiens, 22 April 1816; Paris, 9 September 1816; Paris, 6 August 1817; SB to Lucile Mathevon, Paris, 12 December 1820; Paris, 4

September 1821; SB to Louise de Limminghe, Paris, 22 June 1829; SB to Lucie Merilhou, Chambéry, 8 March 1831; SB to Marie Dieudonnée, Paris, 21 July 1834; SB to Adèle Lehon, Conflans, 23 June 1846; SB to Matilde Garabis, Paris, 14 October 1853. After the Revolution some noble families were financially impoverished; others regained some of their wealth. Sophie Barat noted wryly that the richest families were often the least generous when settling dowries on those entering the Society.

295 SB to Adèle Lehon, Autun, 24 September 1841; Paris, 4 June 1852 (2 letters); Paris, 14 October 1852; Nancy, 15 September [1852]; Paris, 24 January 1853; Paris, 14 March 1853; Paris, 28 September 1855; SB to Louise de Limminghe, Paris, 21 January 1853.

296 SB to Alexandrine de Riencourt, Paris, 5 November 1824; SB to Louise de Limminghe, Paris, 18 November 1825; SB to Louise de Limminghe, Paris, 31 August 1827 (re dowries and vow of stability); Paris, 13 September 1850; Paris, 5 August 1858; Paris,7 May 1859; SB to Eulalie de Chezelles, Paris, 4 October 1862.

297 Sophie Barat normally asked those who donated finances to the Society to make a will to that effect, but never insisted on it. A case in point was that of Autun. The superior there, Aglae Fontaine, gave permission for her family inheritance to be used for the upkeep and development of the buildings. When she died, without making a will in favour of the Society, her family took a lawsuit against the Society. The case lasted beyond the lifetime of Sophie Barat and was used by the devil's advocate during the process of canonisation. It was definitively refuted by Sophie Barat's secretary, Adèle Cahier. Process Apost. Ven. M. Barat, Cahier-Fontaine, Sessio 86, 23 Avril 1885, 1591ff, and f 1555ff; Sessio III. 65A, 114A (GA, Rome, C-I, e-I; C-IV, Autun, Box 1); Histoire de la Société jusqu'au 1865 (AF Poitiers, A15). SB to Alexandrine Riencourt, Paris, 20 April 1847; SB to Matilde Garabis, Paris, 4 October 1858.

298 SB to Elisa de Bouchaud, Paris, 19 March 1846; SB to Joséphine de Coriolis, Paris, 10 May 1856; Paris, [nd] June 1856; Paris, 1 December 1856.

299 SB to Thérèse Maillucheau, Paris, 29 December 1818.

300 For example, Marie Adeline Henrion de Magnoncour[t] (1816–1878), was an only child of a wealthy noble family in Franche-Comté. When her father died her mother moved to Paris and sent her daughter to school at the rue de Varenne. Marie Adeline decided to enter the Society in 1835, made first vows in 1837 and final profession in 1847. Madame de Magnoncourt was permitted to live in the grounds of the rue de Varenne, in separate quarters. SB to Adeline Magnoncourt, Rome, 27 February 1845; LA, 1877–1878, pp. 8–9. Virginie Roux, Notes confidentielles, f. 139 (GA, C-I, A, i-e, Box 4); Journal du Noviciat, du 9 Juillet 1835 au Décembre 1835, f. 14 (AF Poitiers, B06, Paris 119, II).

301 SB to Eugénie de Gramont, Grenoble, 14 March 1823; Blaye [nd, end of May] 1825; Bordeaux, 31 May 1825; Bordeaux, 12 June 1825.

302 Jan Roothaan to Louise de Limminghe, Rome, Villa Lante, 1851 (GA, Rome, C-I, C-3, Box 8, 1851).

303 For a discussion of the relationship between the aristocracy and servant class in late nineteenth-century France, Elizabeth C. Macknight, 'A "Theatre of Rule"? Domestic Service in Aristocratic Households under the Third Republic', *French History*, vol. 22, no. 3 (September 2008), pp. 316–36.

304 Notes pour le Conseil et communauté (GA, Rome, C-I, C-3, Box 8 (1851)). This was noted again in 1864.

305 Marie-Louise-Armande de Causans was born in December 1785, at the Château de Suzy near Soissons. Before the Revolution the Marquis and Marchioness de Causans lived at the French court and were close to Madame Elizabeth, sister of Louis XVI. In 1822, at the age of thirty-six, Armande de Causans entered the Society of the Sacred Heart at the rue de Varenne; soon after her profession Sophie Barat appointed Armande de Causans as her private secretary. Cahier, *Vie de la . . . Mère Madeleine-Sophie Barat*, vol. i, pp. 468–9.

306 SB to Henriette Grosier, Paris, 27 May 1819.

307 These decisions were enshrined in state law in 1853. Tribunal civil de la Seine, 2ieme Chambre. Mémoire. Pour la Congrégation du Sacré-Cœur de Jésus. Préfecture de la Seine. Statuts de la Congrégation du Sacré-Cœur de Jésus. Approuvés par Décret du 5 Août 1853, Art. 11, 13, 18, 19, pp. 27–30 (GA, Rome, C-I, A, I-c, Box 2); [Notes] Pour les Supérieures, leurs Conseil et les Économes, 1851 (GA, Rome, C–I, C–3, Box 8 (1851); Henriette Coppens, Paris, 11 Octobre 1852. Pour les Supérieures, leur Conseil et les Économes, 1852, nos 2, 4, 6 (GA, Rome, C-I, C-3, Box 8, 1851).

308 Conseil Générale, Temporel (GA, Rome, C-I, C-3, Box 8 (1864)). This is found extensively in Sophie Barat's correspondence. SB to Elizabeth Galitzine, Paris, [nd] November 1825; Paris, 6 June 1826; Paris, 8 June 1826; Paris, 31 October 1826; SB to Césarie de Bouchaud, Paris, 14/18 October 1850; Paris, 4 June 1852. SB to Louise de Limminghe, Paris, 31 August 1827. These letters describe the legal position of the Society regarding the legacies, dowries and pensions of the members. Also, Paris, 18 November 1825; SB to the Marquis d'Aigremont, Chambéry, 26 April 1831; SB to Amélie de Savonnieres, Paris, 8 June 1861; SB to Monsieur Brice, Paris, 1 September 1861. Sophie Barat usually discussed the issue of dowries with individual members, and sometimes over several decades, according as family and legal matters arose. SB to Alexandrine de Riencourt, Paris, 5 November 1824; Conflans, 29 August 1846; Paris, 13 September 1850; Paris, 5 August 1858; Paris, 7 May 1859; Paris, 9 April 1862; Paris, 13 February 1864. *Passim.*

309 This was listed under the subject of Religious Poverty. See GA, Rome, C-I, C-3, Box 8, 1851; 1864. SB to Alexandrine Riencourt, Paris, 9 April 1862; Paris 13 February 1864.

310 SB to Adèle Lehon, Paris, 30 March 1856. This was a sensitive issue if the person entered as a choir sister with a dowry and then became a coadjutrix sister later. SB to Anna du Rousier, Conflans, 10 June 1843.

311 See Temporal (GA, Rome, C-I, C-3, Box 8, 1864).

312 SB to Emma de Bouchaud, Paris, 27 February 1857; Paris, 12 April 1858; SB to Sophie Toussenel, Paris, 17 January 1853.

313 SB to Stephanie Cardon, Paris, 18 November 1833; Paris, 23 September 1838; Paris, 16 January 1853. For a discussion of some of these issues, Caroline Ford, *Divided Houses: Religion and Gender in Modern France* (Ithaca, NY, 2005).

314 The financial records of the Society are vast. Apart from the 14,000 letters of Sophie Barat which deal with the Society's finance on a daily basis, the treasury records and the house and school journals/registers contain vast information on the finances of the Society of the Sacred Heart. See also Dossiers Jeanne de Charry. Further material is contained in the legal cases concerning dowries which were taken against the Society in the lifetime of Sophie Barat. See, for example, A.N., F19 6322 1858; F19 6254, 1860–1868. Congrégations et communautés religieuse. Jurisprudence des cours et tribunaux. Affaires diverses. No. 1 Succession d'une religieuse, Société du

Sacré-Cœur de Jésus de Paris (Famille de Louise Kœnig, décédée); GA, Rome, C-I, A, I-C, Box 3, and E-I, 2, 3. See SB to Adelaide de Rozeville, Rome, 25 March 1837; Rome, 27 June 1837; Paris, 29 October 1838; SB to Anne Marie Granon, Rome, 21 October 1839; SB to Aimée d'Avenas, Paris, 19 January 1859; SB to Stanislas Dusaussoy, Paris, 29 January 1859; Paris, 13 March 1860. *Passim.* For an example of how the Society dealt with mental breakdown, and consequent issues with families, see Renseignements sur Sœur Elizabeth Chevalier, religieuse professe de la Société du Sacré-Cœur de Perpignan. (GA, Rome, E-I, 1, Box 4); C-VII, 3–9, Box 1.R, 1858. The family of Emilie Giraud, one of the earliest members of the Society, claimed her personal possessions on her death in 1856 with financial compensation, even though the Society had supported the family financially throughout the Emilie Giraud's lifetime (GA, Rome, C-I, A, 1-C, Box 2). See note 297, re the case of Autun.

315 Arrêtés/Décrets, 1834, 1851, 1874, 1894, pp. 57, 61. For the financial issues with the de Gramont family concerning the foundation at Le Mans, see SB to Olympie Rombeau, Paris, 4 December 1849; Rome, 30 January 1851; Paris, 29 October 1852.

316 Odile Arnold, *Le Corps et l'Âme. La Vie des Religieuses au XIX Siècle* (Seuil, 1984), pp. 177–200.

317 Sophie Barat constantly commented on the financial state of the houses and on the management of finances by superiors and bursars. SB to Aloysia Hardey, Paris, 8 March 1844; Conflans, 21 May 1844; Berrymead (London), 5 June 1844 and 17 June 1844; Paris, 3 December 1852; Paris, 31 January 1853; SB to Gertrude de Brou, Rome, 30 May 1851.

318 Avis pour les Supérieures Vicaires. 8ième Congrégation Générale, Juillet 1864, Clôture, Nos 2, 3, 4 (GA, Rome, C-I, C-3, Box 8, 1864).

319 Arrêtés/Décrets, 1834, 1851, 1874, 1894, pp. 48, 50; Conseil Générale, Pensionnat (GA, Rome, C-I, C-3, Box 8, 1864).

320 SB to Elizabeth de Castel, Paris, 5 July 1853; SB to Louise de Limminghe, Paris, 4 January 1856; SB to Sophie Toussenel, Paris, 28 October 1855. Also, SB to Adelaide de Rozeville, Avignon, 12 March 1832; SB to Eugénie de Gramont, Rome, 4 May 1833. Lettres Circulaires, vol. ii, Paris, 11 Novembre 1833, pp. 21–2; Lettres Circulaires, vol. i, Conflans, 29 Décembre 1845, pp. 120–1.

321 Lettres Circulaires, vol. i, Conflans, 29 Décembre 1845, p. 126. See Marie Prevost à Louise de Limminghe, Aix, 24 Décembre 1844 (GA, Rome, C-I, C-3, Box 3, 1839).

322 Travail de la Commission pour les Études, et le Pensionnat. 7ième Congrégation Générale 1851 (GA, Rome, C-I, C-3, Box 8, 1851).

323 GA, Rome, A-IV, 1, Boxes 1 and 2; D-I, 1-f.

324 AN, F/17/12434/D Inspections des écoles, Paris, 26 Janvier 1854; Perdrau, *Les Loisirs de l'Abbaye*, vol. i, pp. 254–63. Lettres circulaires, vol. i, La Ferrandière, 13 Décembre 1851, pp. 155–6; Lettres circulaires, vol. ii, Paris, 1 Août 1856, pp. 292–303; Paris, 21 Septembre 1859, pp. 303–5; Paris, 5 Août 1863, pp. 309–18. SB to Pauline Pellisson de Valencise, Paris, 26 October 1855.

325 Avis pour les Supérieures Vicaires. 8ième Congrégation Générale, Juillet 1864. Pensionnat, Petit Pensionnat, Écoles Externes, Discipline Religieuse, No. 11 (GA, Rome, C-I, C-3, Box 8, 1864); Décisions prises dans la 8ième Congrégation Générale, et modifications apportées à plusieurs de celles des congrégations précédentes. Art. XIX. Orphelines; Art. XX demi-Pensionnat, Externat. Décisions diverses: Pensionnat. Études (GA, Rome, C-I, C-3, Box 8, 1864). In 1862 Sophie

Barat asked Josephine Gœtz, then mistress of novices at Conflans (near Paris), to draw up plans for teacher training for presentation at the 1864 General Council which were implemented after Sophie Barat's death in 1865.

326 SB to Elizabeth de Castel, Paris, 30 December 1842; Conflans, 3 July 1846; Conflans, 8 July 1846; Conflans, 18 July 1846; Paris, 17 August 1846; Conflans, 29 August 1846; SB to Onesime de Curzon, Paris, 19 April 1846; Paris, 6 December 1856; SB to Esther de Ban, Paris, 14 June 1852; SB to Cecile de Chalais, Paris, 22 September 1860; SB to Louise de Limminghe, Paris, 10 April 1859.

327 For the daunting challenges of leadership in Louisiana, see letters of Sophie Barat and Philippine Duchesne (1804–1852) edited and published in four volumes by Jeanne de Charry; similarly, in Lemberg, Gallicia from 1843, see letter of Sophie Barat to Marie de la Croix; and in Chile, see letters of Sophie Barat to Ana du Rousier from 1853. Also, SB to Emma de Bouchaud, Paris, 18 October 1840; Paris, 13 June 1857; SB to Marie Dieudonnée, Paris, 9 June 1855; SB to Marie de Tinseau, Paris, 9 October 1858; SB to Cécile de Chalais, Paris, 22 September [1860]. SB intervened directly if she found local superiors demanded too much work of the choir and coadjutrix sisters, or if they stinted on the quality and quantity of food in the communities and schools. SB to Emma de Bouchaud, Paris, 13 October 1859; SB to Adeline Assailly, Paris, 12 April 1858; SB to Adèle Lehon, Paris, 6 April 1861. *Passim.*

328 SB to Aloysia Hardey, Conflans, 13 November 1845; Paris, 16 September 1849; Paris, 31 January 1856; SB to Louise de Limminghe, Paris, 29 January 1863; Paris, 3 February 1863.

329 SB to Thérèse Maillucheau, Paris, 17 July 1821; SB to Elisa de Bouchaud, Paris, 27 November 1852; SB to Léonie de Brives, Paris, 12 February 1857. *Passim.*

330 SB to Alida Dumazeaud, Paris, 21 July 1835; Paris, 15 March 1836; Besançon, 7 August 1843; Paris, 17 March 1850; Paris, 13 March 1862. SB to Matilde Garabis, Conflans, 4 November 1849; Lyon, 4 January 1852; Paris, 2 August 1855. Concerning sheep: SB to Matilde Garabis, Paris, 10 December 1852; Paris, 13 December 1852; Paris, 20 December 1852; Paris, 8 March 1853. Concerning cows: SB to Eugénie Audé, Rome, 3 October 1837; SB to Matilde Garabis, Paris, 13 October 1857; Paris, 16 October 1857. *Passim.* Also: SB to Adelaide de Rozeville, Paris, 22 August 1828; Paris, 28 August 1828; Paris, 5 September 1828; Paris, 22 September 1828. For the care taken of the rue de Varenne gardens by Eugénie de Gramont, see Dominique Viéville, Guide de l'hôtel Biron, Musée Rodin (Paris, 2010), pp. 23–30, 83–92.

331 See, SB to Emilie Giraud, Amiens, 19 January 1814; SB to Thérèse Maillucheau, Paris, 9 September 1816 and *passim* 1816–22; SB to Henriette Grosier, Paris, 17 May 1818; Paris [nd], October 1827; SB to Susanne Geoffroy, Paris, 10 July 1819; SB to Philippine Duchesne, *passim*; SB to Marie Prevost, Lyon, 19 August 1822; Paris, 28 October 1822; Paris, 21 December 1822; Paris, 3 February 1823; Grenoble, 11 March 1823; SB to Eugénie de Gramont, Bordeaux, 31 May 1825; SB to Eugénie Audé, Paris, 4 August 1825; Paris, 28 February 1826; Paris, 28 March 1826; Paris, 7 September 1826; Paris, 14 September 1828; SB to Adelaide de Rozeville, Paris, 5 March 1826; SB to Elizabeth Galitzine, Lyon, 5 October 1841; Rome, 14 March 1842; Montet, 23 August 1843; SB to Elizabeth de Castel, Paris, 21 April 1843; Paris, 20 November 1846; SB to Eugénie de Gramont, Amiens, 11 October 1843; SB to Valerie de Bosredont, Rome, 24 February 1851; SB to Eliane Cuënot, Paris, 18 August 1851; Paris, 26 December 1862; SB to Onesime de

Curzon, Paris, 15 October 1859; SB to Lucie Merilhou, Paris, 18 October 1859. *Passim*. Sophie Barat would not tolerate delay in paying the wages of workers engaged by the Society. SB to Olympie Rombau [Paris], 1 June 1864; Paris, 13 June 1864; Paris, 16 June 1864. *Passim*.

332 SB to Eugénie de Gramont, Conflans, 3 November 1845; Conflans, 26 November 1845; SB to Emma de Bouchaud, Conflans, 23 February 1846.

333 Réponses aux Observations faites contre les Décrets du Conseil Général tenu à Rome en 1839, et contre la réunion d'une nouvelle congrégation à Lyon no. 10 (GA, Rome , C-I, C-3, Box 4, 1839).

334 Points de la rédaction de 1839 qui présentent quelques difficultés. 1. Decrees Fondamentaux. (GA, Rome, C-1, C-3, Box 5, 1851; 1864), f. 3. Adèle Cahier's comments were made when discussing the issue with Philippe de Villafort, secretary general of the Jesuits.

335 Sophie Barat to Elisa de Bouchaud, Paris, 17 July 1852. Sophie Barat to Alida Dumazeaud, Paris, 13 June 1849; Paris, 17 September 1854.

336 Confesseurs et aumôniers (GA, Rome, C-1, C-3, Box 8, 1851; 1864).

337 These were called 'extraordinary confessors' and they came to hear the confessions of the community at regular intervals during the liturgical year.

338 Marie Lataste to the Abbé Dupérier (Director of the Grand Séminaire at Dax, France), Rennes, 21 November 1846. Marie Lataste was a mystic who asked to enter the Society as a coadjutrix sister. Her sister joined the community of the Filles de la Charité in the rue de Bac, Paris. Abbé Dupérier to Alex Kerouartz, Dax, 19 May 1847 (concerning the educational background of Marie Lataste). Letters of Marie Lataste to her family and to the Abbé Pascal Darbins, the parish curé: *La Vie et les Oeuvres de Marie Lataste, Religieuse du Sacré-Cœur par M. L'Abbé Paschal Darbins*, 3 vols (Paris, 1862); *Vie de Marie Lataste par Marguerite Lataste, Sacré-Cœur, Rennes, 11 November 1866* (GA, Rome, C-VII, 2, Lataste Box 2). Also, P.P. Toulement, Les Écrits de Marie Lataste in *Études religieuses, historiques et littéraires, par les des pères de la compagnie de Jésus. Nouvelle Série. Janvier–Février 1863*. Numéro 7, pp. 66–91). Sophie Barat's secretary, Adèle Cahier, published a biography: *Vie de Marie Lataste, Soeur Coadjutrice de la Society du Sacré-Cœur* (Paris, 1866). SB to Louise de Limminghe, Paris, 13 February 1863; SB to Camille Bruté, Paris, 10 August 1864 (bis).

339 The General Council of 1851–2 assimilated as much as possible of the 1839 proposed Constitutions, as well as drawing up detailed regulations for the roles and offices in the Society. Constitutions et Règles de la Société du Sacré-Cœur (Lyon, 1852).

340 Articles fondamentaux des Décrets du Conseil Général, tenu à Rome en Juin 1839, p. 2 (GA, C-I, C-3. Box 4, 1839). In the course of her two visits to Louisiana in 1840 and 1843, Elizabeth Galitzine rescinded the permission given by Sophie Barat (in 1830) allowing the coadjutrix sisters to learn to write (GA, Rome, C-III. Provinces. US Early History. Visits of Mother Galitzine to the houses of North America, 1840–1843, no. 8). Sophie Barat encouraged Sister Agnes Verney to learn to write. SB to Matilde Garabis, Paris, 22 January 1854; Paris, 28 November 1855. In 1859 Sophie Barat requested a coadjutrix sister for the poor school in Calais, asking specifically that she could teach the art of writing to the children. It is clear also that generations of coadjutrix sisters in the rue de Varenne in Paris worked in the printing house of the Society, under the guidance of Adèle Cahier, the secretary general. Notes de la Soeur Victorine [Godefroy], Paris, Janvier 1869 (GA, Rome,

C-I, A-1-d, Box 2). Victorine Godefroy (1831–1873), LA 1873–1874, pp. 321–2. Soeur [Constance] Beauve (1814–1874), Petite notice sur la vie et les vertus de Notre Très Révérende Mère Générale, 18 June 1865 (GA, Rome, C-I, A-1-d, Box 2).

341 In 1851 the Council commented that women of poor health were accepted too easily into the Society as coadjutrix sisters; or that superiors assigned coadjutrix sisters work that was too heavy. SB to Valerie de Bosredont, Paris, 26 February 1852; Paris 12 March 1852.

342 GA, Rome, C-1, C-2, Box 2. Arrêts/Décrets 1834, 1851, 1874, 1894, p. 67 (1833 version in C-1, C-3, Box 3).

343 Constitutions (GA, Rome, C-I, C-3, Box 8, 1851).

344 Constitutions/Conseil Général de 1839 (Le Mans). Améliorations pour le Conseil Général de 1839. Trop tard (AF Poitiers, A4).

345 As early at 1816 the issue of overwork in the Society was raised by a priest and by a past pupil in Beauvais. AF Poitiers, B05/117, Beauvais; Sophie Barat to Thérèse Maillucheau, Paris, 18 September 1816. Virginie Roux, a coadjutrix sister, commented on overwork generally in the rue de Varenne and of a coadjutrix sister in particular in 1838. Souvenirs de Soeur Virginie Roux, ff. 81, 104–14 (GA, Rome, A-II, i-a, Box 1). For Virginie Roux, 1810–78, LA, 1877–8, pp. 31–4. In 1835 Sophie Barat warned Eugénie de Gramont that everyone, choir and the coadjutrix sisters, were overworked in the orphanage in Conflans. SB to Eugénie de Gramont, Paris, rue Monsieur, 21 November 1835. She repeated this warning in 1839: SB to Eugénie de Gramont, Rome, 23 July 1839.

346 Louis Sellier à Sophie Barat, St Acheul [Amiens], 18 Novembre 1849 (GA, Rome, C-IV, 2, Amiens. Letters, Box 3). A similar situation obtained in Poland around this time in Lemberg. Monita de la Visite faite dans la maison de Lemberg le 20 Août 1847 par la Mère [Anna] du Rousier (GA, C-IV, Lemberg).

347 Notes données par la Soeur Adélaide Edouard, en 1896 (AF Poitiers, La Neuville, B35, 111, 115, 118). The community at Amiens was in urgent need of reform at this time. Kilroy, *Madeleine Sophie Barat*, pp. 409–11.

348 Discipline religieuse (GA, Rome, C-I, C-3, Box 8, 1864).

349 Discipline religieuse (GA, Rome, C-I, C-3, Box 8, 1864).

350 Noviciat (GA, Rome, C-I, C-3, Box 8, 1864). While Sophie Barat planned to have a general noviceship for choir and coadjutrix sisters, this never materialised. SB to Alida Dumazeaud, Tours, 29 January 1849; SB to Emma de Bouchaud, Paris, 5 June 1855.

351 Tableau sommaire de la visite des maisons, d'après la Règle et les Décrets. Discipline religieuse, Observations des Règles, Nos 5, 6, 7 (GA, Rome, C-I, C-3, Box 8, 1864). Sophie Barat to Stephanie Cardon, Quadrille (Bordeaux), 31 October 1848; Paris, 5 June 1852.

352 The issue of overwork and health breakdown in both ranks was addressed again in 1864. Supérieures locales, gouvernement (GA, Rome, C-I, C-3, Box 8, 1864).

353 SB to Elisa de Bouchaud, Paris 11 April 1855. Also, SB to Aimée d'Avenas, Paris, 8 November 1856; Paris, 19 October 1857.

354 SB to Eugénie de Gramont, Conflans, [nd] September 1844.

355 SB to Cécile de Chalais, Paris, 14 January 1858. Sophie Barat bought cows from the Jesuits in Amiens and arranged to have them brought to the rue de Varenne in Paris. SB to Alexandrine de Riencourt, Paris 15 [August] 1828. Also, letters of SB to Adelaide de Rozeville, superior at Amiens at this time.

356 SB to Cécile de Chalais, Paris, 31 December 1857. Also, SB to Charlotte Goold,

Paris, 20 July 1846; SB to Gertrude de Brou, Paris, 23 July 1858.

357 Lettres Circulaires de Marie-Joséphine Goetz, Lettres XVII, Paris, 12 Février 1870.

358 Témoignages des personnes de la Société, ayant servi à Mgr Baunard (GA, Rome, C-1, A, 1-e, Box 1, bis).

359 Témoignages, nos 123, 157.

360 Témoignages, nos 151, 153, 405, 407, 425.

361 Témoignages, no. 15.

362 Témoignages, no. 124.

363 Témoignages, no. 124, Virginie Roux. A past pupil of Amiens, Aimée Herbert, recalled that in 1818 Sophie Barat was recovering from an illness and that Marguerite Boulanger used to look after her. She remembered watching Sophie being pushed around the garden in a type of garden chair, an arduous exercise for both women. Aimée Herbert, Amiens, 18 Novembre 1868 (GA, Rome, C-I, A, i-e, Box 1, bis).

364 Témoignages, nos 25, 282, 306.

365 Témoignages, nos 37, 124, 136, 147, 148, 151. This remark is repeated extensively.

366 Témoignages, nos 124, 147, 153, 154, 432.

367 Témoignages, nos 136, 338. Also nos 25, 139, 151–6, 158, 178, 205, 299, 338.

368 Témoignages, no. 447; Souvenirs de Sœur Virginie Roux, ff. 108–9 (GA, Rome, A-II, 1-a, Box I). This work was edited by Adèle Cahier and Pauline Perdrau; each used material from it for their respective biographies of Sophie Barat. One section of this ms, ff. 133–40, is listed as confidential; and ff. 1–52 are missing. Virginie Roux (1811–1878), LA, 1877–1878, Paris, rue de Varenne, pp. 31–4.

369 Témoignages, nos 136, 144, 145, 147, 153, 205, 301, 432.

370 Témoignages, nos 25, 282, 306.

371 SB to Alida Dumazeaud, Paris, 7 June 1864. Françoise Bruchet (1814–1880) died in La Ferrandière (Lyon) on 1 September 1880. She taught in the poor schools of the Society for most of her life. LA, 1879–1880, pp. 148–50.

372 Témoignages, nos 147, 148, 149, 151, 153–6, 158, 159, 205, 281, 296, 299.

373 Témoignages, nos 205, 282 *passim.*

374 Témoignages, nos, 153, 155.

375 Témoignages, nos 25, 56, 139, 147, 154, 155, 159, 283, 285, 296, 408, 454.

376 Témoignages, nos 145, 147–9.

377 Témoignages, nos, 446, 454.

378 Témoignages, nos 136, 139, 147, 151, 153, 155, 156, 158, 296, 298, 299, 301, 432. Most called it economy (or 'poverty') and did not connect this with Sophie Barat's experience of fire at her birth.

379 Témoignages, nos 147, 149, 153, 205; and nos 136, 144, 145, 432.

380 Témoignages, nos 144, 153, 158, 296, 447, 448, 454.

381 Témoignages, nos 146, 147, 149, 283, 298, 208, 338.

382 Lettres Circulaires de Marie-Joséphine Gœtz, Lettres XVII, Paris 12 Février 1870.

383 Témoignages, nos 85, 92, bis, 96. Also 228.

384 Témoignages, nos 30, 188.

385 Témoignages, nos 17, 61, 96, 301.

386 Témoignages, nos 61, 121, 338. Also 22.

387 Témoignages, no. 231 (Marie Prevost). Also 400 (Olympie Rombau); 173 (Constance Bonaparte); 231 (Rosine Granon); 50 (Marie du Chelas); 54 (Louise Combalot).

388 Témoignages, nos 20, 50, 85, 92, 121, 173, 226, 396.

389 SB to Eugénie Desmarquest, Paris, 2 January 1843. Codes of behaviour in community were called the *Rules of Modesty* in Society of the Sacred Heart. See also SB to Elizabeth de Castel, Paris, 4 September 1848; SB to Louise de Limminghe, Paris, 26 January 1857; Paris, 25 February 1857; Paris, 12 March 1863; Paris, 20 March 1863. SB to Rameau Rambaud, Paris, 26 May 1858. Also, Arnold, *Le Corps et l'Âme. La Vie des Religieuses au XIX Siècle.*

390 SB to Aimée d'Avenas, Paris, 27 May 1852; SB to Joséphine de Coriolis, Paris, 7 June 1855; Paris, 24 October 1855.

391 SB to Elisa de Bouchaud, Paris, 21 March 1861, Document 57, no. 1; SB to Emma de Bouchaud, Paris, 16 October 1852; SB to Elisa de Bouchaud, Paris, 21 March 1861. Document 57, Note 1. SB to Gertrude de Brou, Paris, 23 June 1853; Paris, 29 August 1853. *Vie de Madame Geoffroy*, pp. 82, 85.

392 SB to Emilie Giraud, Paris 5 April 1821; SB to Thérèse Delêtret [Paris, c. September 1843], a coadjutrix sister, 1795–1852 (A.F. Poitiers, Affaire d'Olivier, B05/117, Beauvais). SB to Aimée d'Avenas, Paris, 6 December 1861; Paris, 8 December 1861; Paris, 22 January 1862.

393 Marie Patte (1796–1848). LA, 1848–1852, Paris, pp. 1–2. Kilroy, *Madeleine Sophie Barat*, pp. 203, 216, 275, 280, 367, 391, 395.

394 There are constant references to Marie Patte in Sophie Barat's letters. For example, SB to Louise de Limminghe, Parme, 2 June 1838; SB to Stanislas Dusaussoy, Paris, 24 January 1839; SB to Elizabeth de Castel, Conflans, 28 May 1844; SB to Emilie Giraud, Conflans, 28 February 1846. *Passim.*

395 Canonisation Process. Romana seu Parisiensis. Beatificationis et Canonizationis v.s. Dei Magdalena Sophia Barat. Postulatio virili. Testis juxta 30 interr. proc. pag. 2335 respondit, ff. 801–2. SB to Louise de Limminghe, Parme, 2 June 1838; Turin, 30 June 1838; Paris, 31 August 1838.

396 SB to Stanislas Dusaussoy, Bourges, 28 July 1848. See also SB to Adèle Lehon, Paris, 2 July 1848.

397 SB to Stanislas Dusaussoy, Paris, 12 August 1848. See also SB to Stanislas Dusaussoy, [Paris], 24 January 1839; Conflans, 3 June 1846. For an account of Marie Patte's death, Pauline Perdrau, *Les Loisirs de l'Abbaye*, vol. i, pp. 218–22; LA, 1848–1852, Paris, pp. 1–2. Agnès Verney succeeded Marie Patte. Sophie Barat speaks of Agnès Verney with affection and felt her loss when Agnès died in 1863. Perdrau, *Les Loisirs de l'Abbaye*, vol. i, p. 439; Notes de la Soeur Victorine [Godefroy], Paris, Janvier 1869, ff. 1–3a (GA, Rome, C-I, A-1-d, Box 2); SB to Matilde Garabis, Paris, 29 May 1863. Honorine Monnet cared for Sophie Barat from 1863 until Sophie's death in May 1865. Honorine Monnet died in September 1865. Agnès Verney, (1817–1863), LA Paris, Maison-Mère, XLIII 1863–1866; Honorine Monnet (1810–1865), LA Paris, Maison-Mère, XLIII 1863–1866.

398 SB to Anna du Rousier, Rome, 10 April 1842; SB to Anna du Rousier, Conflans, 10 June 1843.

399 SBto Elisa de Bouchaud, Paris, 5 October 1852; SB to Clémence de la Roulière, Paris, 1 May 1861.

400 In her image of the queen bee who remains in the hive, Perdrau included those choir sisters who held offices of responsibility within the community, such as the mistress of novices, the local superiors, bursars and other offices within the houses. Pauline Perdrau (Souvenirs de la Mère Perdrau. Ma Révérende Mère Henriette Coppens (GA, Rome, C-I, A, 1-e, Box 4).

401 Pauline Perdrau, Souvenirs de la Mère Perdrau. Ma Révérende Mère Desmarquest

(GA, Rome, C-I, A, 1-e, Box 4), ff. 3–4.

402 Marie Lataste to Abbé Dupérier, Rennes, 21 November 1846.

403 For example, the General Council of 1864 noted that some coadjutrix sisters bypassed the choir sisters in charge and went directly to the superior. Avis pour les Supérieures Vicaires. 8ième Congrégation Générale, Juillet 1864, Discipline religieuse, No. 11 (GA, Rome, C-I, C-3, Box 8 (1864).

404 SB to Henriette Grosier, Paris, 24 May 1834; Paris, 16 October 1838.

CHAPTER 2

1 Josephine de Coriolis, 'Histoire de la Société', f. 36.

2 Sophie Barat generally held to this model of education but encouraged flexibility in certain circumstances. In her later years she recognised that social boundaries were fast changing. SB to Philippine Duchesne, Paris, 9 May 1830; Paris 2 July 1830; SB to Emma de Bouchaud, Conflans, 28 October 1845; Conflans, 17 November 1845; SB to Adèle Lehon, Paris, 14 July 1847; Paris, 29 September 1849. SB to Aloysia Hardey, Conflans, 8 November 1845; SB to Eliane Cuënot, Paris, 2 September 1851; SB to Louise de Limminghe, Paris, 17 December 1853; Paris, 22 October (bis) 1855; SB to Stephanie Cardon, Paris, 1 February 1856; SB to Anne Marie Granon, Paris, 29 March 1856; SB to Esther de Ban, Paris, 20 November 1856; SB to Onesime de Curzon, Paris, 11 October 1859; Paris, 4 November 1859. *Passim.*

3 de Coriolis, 'Histoire de la Société', f. 36, 1802. While permitting exceptions in some cases, Sophie Barat held to this model throughout her lifetime. SB to Philippine Duchesne, Paris, 9 May 1830; Paris, 2 July 1830; SB to Emma de Bouchaud, Conflans, 28 October 1845; Conflans, 17 November 1845; Paris, 29 September 1849. SB to Aloysia Hardey, Conflans, 8 November 1845; SB to Anne Marie Granon, Paris 29 March 1856. *Passim.*

4 Maison d'Amiens, rue de l'Oratoire, no. 7, Programme des différents Exercices qui seront soutenus par les Élèves et suivie de la distribution solennelle des Prix, Septembre 19, 20, 21, 23, 1805 (AF Poitiers, Archives de la maîtresse générale des Études françaises, 1820–1940).

5 Plan d'Etudes provisoire à l'usage de la maison d'Amiens (GA, Rome Séries D. External History of the Society. D–1, Activities of the Institute: School Rule and Plan of Studies). Nicholas Loriquet became a Jesuit in 1815. John W. Padberg, *Colleges in Controversy: The Jesuit Schools in France from Revival to Suppression 1815–1880* (Cambridge, MA, 1969), pp. 54–64. During the General Council of the Society in 1820 Sophie asked Nicholas Loriquet to further advise the Society on a revision of the Plan of Studies. The Plan of Studies was updated also in 1833 and 1851

6 GA, Rome, A-III, 1, Box 3, ff. 223–37. Also, SB to Emma de Bouchaud, Paris, 18 September 1849. SB to Eulalie de Bouchaud, Rome, 3 August 1839, and Rome, [nd] August 1839. SB to Aglaé Bazin, Paris, 25 August 1855 (re an orphan from Joigny); SB to Adrienne Michel, Paris, 6 February 1852; SB to Matilde Garabis, Paris, 7 April 1858; SB to Olympie Rombau, Paris, 14 July 1860.

7 Rebecca Rogers, *From the Salon to the Schoolroom: Educating Bourgeois Girls in Nineteenth-Century France* (Pennsylvania Press, 2005) p. 58. French edition: *Les Bourgeoises au Pensionnat: L'éducation féminine au xix Siècle* (Presses Universitaires de Rennes, 2007).

8 SB to Clémence de la Roulière, Paris, 5 January 1858; Paris, 16 October 1859; SB to Stephanie Cardon, Paris, 1 February 1856. Sophie Barat acknowledged that the demanding task of teaching could put off women entering the Society. SB to

Emma de Bouchaud, Paris, 28 June 1859; SB to Louise de Limminghe, Paris, 31 May 1847.

9   SB to Aimée d'Avenas, Paris, 16 April 1833; Rome, 21 September 1837; Rome, 22 June 1839; Paris, 25 August 1847; SB to Louise de Limminghe, Paris, 4 January 1856. Despite proposals in 1851 and 1864 teacher training colleges were not seriously addressed until after Sophie Barat's death. SB to Elizabeth de Castel, Paris, 5 July 1853; SB to Aimée d'Avenas, Paris, 7 July 1864; Paris, 30 August 1864.

10 For details, see letters of Sophie Barat to the superiors of communities, to headmistresses, and teachers: SB to Adrienne Michel, Grenoble, 11 August 1810; Amiens, 4 June 1811; Amiens, 11 July 1811; Amiens, 4 October 1814; Paris, 24 November 1818; Paris, 24 January 1819; Chambery, 14 November 1819; Paris, 26 May 1820; SB to Thérèse Maillucheau, Paris, 11 July 1816; Amiens, 19 August 1816; Paris, 17 February 1818; SB to Emilie Giraud, Paris 27 January 1817; Paris, 26 March 1818; Sophie Barat to Philippine Duchesne, Paris, 21 April 1818; Philippine Duchesne to Sophie Barat, New Orleans, 7 June 1818; St Louis, 31 August 1818; St Charles, [nd] November 1818; Florissant, 30 October 1820; Florissant, 14 September 1825; St Louis, 23 August 1829; SB to Marie Prevost, Lyon, 2 December 1819; SB to Eugénie de Gramont, La Ferrandière (Lyon) 12 December 1819; Grenoble, 14 March 1823; Bordeaux, 12 June 1825; SB to Adelaide de Rozeville, Paris, 5 March 1826, and *passim* 1826–1830; SB to Eulalie de Bouchaud (in charge of novices), Turin, 9 December 1836; Rome, 8 July 1837; SB to Aimée d'Avenas, Paris, 25 August 1847; Rome, 8 February 1851; SB to Onesime de Curzon, Paris, 9 April 1859; SB to Césarie de Bouchaud, Paris, 24 April 1861; SB to Elisa de Bouchaud, Paris, 13 November 1862. *Passim*. Also, *Lettres Circulaires de Madeleine Sophie Barat*, vol. ii, Paris, 11 Novembre 1833.

11 For the services needed to support the schools. SB to Léonie de Brives, Paris, 9 October 1853; SB to Mary Josephine Thompson, Paris, 14 February 1856; Paris, 26 February 1856; SB to Sidonie de Barroux, Paris, 24 February 1862.

12 Prior to the French Revolution religious communities of women were bound by strict rules of cloister laid down by the Council of Trent in the sixteenth century. The suppression of religious life during the Revolution enabled religious women in France to make a certain break with such strictures. Silvia Evangelisti, *Nuns: A History of Convent Life* (Oxford, 2008), pp. 41–65, 201–4.

13 AF Poitiers, Affaire d'Olivier, B05/117. This is a major collection of letters and documents concerning Marie d'Olivier (1782–1868) which were discovered in the Jesuit Archives in Paris in 1996 by Fr Robert Bonfils, SJ and forwarded to the Provincial Archives of the Society in France in Poitiers.

14 SB to Thérèse Maillucheau, Paris, 8 February 1822. Despite searches in the diocesan archives in Avignon, no family details of Marie d'Olivier have been found to date.

15 SB to Thérèse Maillucheau, Paris, 17 February 1818; Adèle Cahier, *Vie de la . . . Mère Madeleine-Sophie Barat*, vol. i, p. 334.

16 SB to Emilie Giraud, Grenoble, 9 July 1812; Grenoble, 6 August 1812. Also, Paris, 22 April 1812.

17 SB to Henriette Grosier, Paris, 27 May 1819.

18 Journal de la maison de La Ferrandière, 14 Février 1822. SB to Thérèse Maillucheau, Paris, 8 February 1822. Also, SB to Joséphine Lédo Thénevin, Paris, 10 February 1822.

19 Journal de la maison de La Ferrandière, 22 Aout 1822; SB to Eugénie de Gramont, La Ferrandière [Lyon], 22 August 1822.

20 Journal de la maison de La Ferrandière, 1 Janvier 1824.

21 The de Gramont d'Aster family traced its origins to the early Middle Ages and were court nobles (de cour). The d'Olivier family came from landed nobility (noblesse terrienne de province).

22 Marie d'Olivier expressed her educational vision not only in the Mémoires addressed to Sophie Barat but also in the Prospectus drawn up for the schools. For example: Pensionnats des Religieuses du Sacré-Cœur de Marie, établis à Saignes, Cantal. (AF Poitiers, Beauvais B05/117–2, Affaire d'Olivier).

23 Sophie Barat encouraged other members of the Society to write and publish text books for the Society. In 1861 she welcomed a document on education, which contained similar views to Marie d'Olivier. SB to Thérèse Gilbert, Paris, 12 October 1861.

24 16ème séance, Mardi 10 Octobre [1826] (GA, Rome, C-I., C-3, Box 1. 1815; 1820; 1826; 1833). Sophie Barat remarked in 1819: Our pupils [in Paris] especially cause us much concern. They are full of themselves and like only what pleases them. I put them to shame one day when I informed them that we were really punished by having only the nobility and that henceforth I would prefer [to have] the middle classes . . . One in particular objected strongly to this threat (SB to Thérèse Maillucheau, Paris, 13 January 1819).

25 In 1808 the Society made a foundation in Cuignières which was transferred to Beauvais in 1816.

26 Bibliothèque de la Compagnie de Saint-Sulpice, Paris. Fonds Frayssinous, Communautés Religieuses, Sacré-Cœur, Cuignières/Beauvais 1815–1828; A.N. F 19, 6340 Cuignières/Beauvais. Sophie Barat asked Eugénie de Gramont to assist Marie d'Olivier in the negotiations with the local authorities. SB to Eugénie de Gramont, Aix, 12 May 1831; Avignon, 20 February 1832; Turin, 28 May 1832; Turin, 9 July 1832; Turin, 18 August 1832. SB to Eulalie de Bouchaud, Rome, 7 April 1840. Journal de la Maison de Beauvais, 1828–1831; Journal de la Communauté de Beauvais, 1837–1856 (AF Poitiers, B05/115).

27 For a similar comment see: Esther de Liniers to Marie d'Olivier, Beauvais, 14 August 1833 (AF Poitiers, , Affaire d'Olivier, B05/117). Esther de Liniers (1808–1839) was a member of the Society.

28 Sophie Barat to Nicolas Loriquet, Paris, 5 June 1828 (GA, Rome C-I, 1-F, Lettres. Holographs. Carton XVII, Lettres à divers ecclésiastiques (1814–1864), à des religieux et religieuses; Also, C-I, G. Box 28. B Lettres aux ecclésiastiques); SB to Adélaïde de Rozeville, Paris, 9 October 1828.

29 SB to Adrienne Michelle, Paris, 9 November 1827. Also, SB to Eugénie de Gramont, Rome, 19 May 1840.

30 Marie d'Olivier to Nicholas Loriquet, Beauvais 28 May 1828 and Beauvais 24 June 1828; Nicholas Loriquet to Marie d'Olivier, Paris 28 June 1828 (GA, Rome, B-IV, 3, Box 9).

31 *Les Trois Paulines* (Lille, 1834). Others followed later: *L'Imagination ou Charlotte de Drelincourt* (Lille, 1858); *Dialogues des Vivants au XIXe Siècle* (Paris, 1859); *Lettres aux Jeunes Femmes du Monde Élégant* (Avignon, 1866).

32 From 1832 Sophie Barat became concerned about the number of works being carried out in Beauvais and she doubted that Marie d'Olivier had the capacity to oversee and sustain them all. SB to Eugénie de Gramont, Turin, 9 July 1832.

33 Sophie Barat anticipated that such diverse projects, not only in Beauvais but also in other foundations, would create serious administrative problems. SB to Eugénie de Gramont, Avignon, 29 March 1832.

34 SB to Eugénie de Gramont, Rome, 23 July 1839; Rome, 2 May 1840; Rome, 14 May 1840; Rome, 19 May 1840. Eugénie de Gramont to Sophie Barat, [Paris, 18 Avril 1840]; Eugénie de Gramont to Sophie Barat, [Paris], 4 May [1840]. GA, Rome, C-IV, Box 3, Paris (Closed Houses).
35 Kilroy, *Madeleine Sophie Barat*, pp. 326–8.
36 SB to Elizabeth de Castel, Paris, 21 April 1843; Conflans, 29 June 1846. Also, SB to Elisa de Fonsabelle, Paris, 22 January 1858.
37 Sophie Barat to Cardinal Patrizzi, secretary of the Sacred Congregation of Bishops and Religious. Paris, 2 April 1841 and Paris, 5 June 1841 (GA, Rome, Dossier Jeanne de Charry); Sophie Barat to Pierre Cotteret, bishop of Beauvais, Paris, 30 May 1841; Eugénie Audé to Cardinal Patrizzi, Rome, Trinité des Monts, 15 June 1841. Dossiers Jeanne de Charry (GA, Rome, Dossiers Jeanne de Charry).
38 Marie d'Olivier to Sophie Barat, Letter no. 7, c. autumn 1841. She considered her vocation as pioneering as that of Philippine Duchesne who set out for Louisiana in 1818. Marie d'Olivier to Sophie Barat, Beauvais, 7 April 1841.
39 SB to Henriette Grosier, Paris, 5 June 1841. SB to Eugénie Audé, Paris, 5 June 1841; SB to Adélaïde de Rozeville, Paris, 6 June 1841.
40 Jean-Francois-Marie Cart, bishop of Nîmes to Marie d'Olivier, 8 March 1839.
41 SB to Adelaide de Rozeville, Rome, 28 August 1841; Paris, 6 June 1841; Paris, 20 August 1841; SB to Eugénie Audé, Paris, 5 April 1841; Paris, 5 June 1841.
42 Eulalie de Bouchaud to the Comtesse de Bassignac, Paris, 26 August 1841. SB to Eulalie de Bouchaud, Jette 19 July 1841; Amiens, 1 August 1841.
43 Oeuvre de Lavorr (AF Poitiers, Beauvais, Affaire d'Olivier, B05/117–2).
44 The new prospectus indicated that three schools (for the rich, the middle class and the poor) would be run by the new congregation called the 'Religieuses du Sacré-Cœur de Marie Pensionnats des Religieuses du Sacré-Cœur de Marie établie à Saignes' (Cantal) (AF Poitiers, Beauvais, Affaire d'Olivier B05/117–2). No mention was made of a nursery, day school, orphanage and the other works originally advocated by Marie d'Olivier.
45 Sophie Barat thought then that Marie d'Olivier should not leave the Society, that it would not help her personally. SB to Eulalie de Bouchaud, Rome, 17 January 1842. Also, Abbé Thiebla to Marie d'Olivier, Noyon, 21 December 1842.
46 For the extensive correspondence on Marie d'Olivier's departure and financial settlement with the Society of the Sacred Heart, see AF Poitiers, Beauvais, Affaire d'Olivier B05/117–2. Also, SB to Eliane Cuënot, St Joseph (Marseilles), 10 November 1850.
47 Bruno Béthouart, *Religion et Culture en Europe Occidentale de 1800–1914* (Éditions du Temps, 2001).
48 Later Marie d'Olivier expressed her distress that during the final days in Beauvais, when she had to pack and leave quickly, her personal papers and writings had been lost, or taken to Paris and destroyed by Eugénie de Gramont.
49 *Mémorial Catholique*, 1868, Une vénérable religieuse [Marie d'Olivier], pp. 71–4. The obituary was written by Louis-Francois Guérin (1814–1872), editor of *Mémorial Catholique* from 1849 to 1870. Papiers Hypolite Martin, SJ (AF Poitiers, Beauvais, B05/117, Box 2). *Mémorial Catholique* was owned by Louis-Francois Guérin, and published monthly from 1841 to 1870.
50 AF Poitiers, Affaire d'Olivier, B05/117.
51 The author gratefully acknowledges the translation of these documents into English by Mary Maher.

52 Pluche, Noël-Antoine, abbé (1686–1761). *Spectacle de la Nature*, 9 vols (1732–50).

53 Photius was patriarch of Constantinople in the ninth century.

54 Rebecca Rogers is Professor in the History of Education at Université Paris Descartes. Specialist in the history of girls' education in France, she has published widely in both English and French on the subject. Her most recent publications include *From the Salon to the Schoolroom: Educating Bourgeois Girls in Nineteenth-Century France* (Penn State University Press, 2005) and *Girls' Secondary Education in the Western World: From the 18th to the 20th Century*, with James Albisetti and Joyce Goodman (Palgrave, 2010).

55 For the emergence and growth of these congregations, see Claude Langlois, *Le Catholicisme au Féminin: Les Congrégations Françaises à Supérieure Générale au XIXe Siècle* (Paris: Cerf, 1984).

56 For a general overview of the educational context in these years, Rebecca Rogers, *From the Salon to the Schoolroom: Educating Bourgeois Girls in Nineteenth-Century France* (University Park: Pennsylvania State University Press, 2005), Chapters 1 and 2.

57 The subtitle of this journal was *Lectures Religieuses, Morales et Littéraires pour les Jeunes Personnes et les Jeunes Gens*. For information on Lévi-Alvarès, see Françoise Mayeur, *L'Éducation des Filles en France au XIXe Siècle* (Paris, Hachette, 1979; 2nd ed. Perrin, 2008), pp. 69–72.

58 One of the few studies that analyses the functioning of teaching congregations is that of Sarah Curtis, *Educating the Faithful: Religion, Schooling, and Society in Nineteenth-Century France* (Dekalb: Northern Illinois Press, 2000). See, as well, Alice-Marie Puga, *Histoire de la Congrégation du Saint-Nom de Jésus de Toulouse: de 1800 à 1953* (Toulouse: Privat, 2006).

59 See Rebecca Rogers, 'La place de la Religion dans la Formation des Enseignantes Religieuses et Laïques avant les Années 1880', in Jean-François Condette (dir.), *Religion, Fait Religieux et Laïcité dans la Formation des Enseignants XVIe –XXe Siècles* (Lille, 2010).

CHAPTER 3

1 A shorter version of this paper was given in October 2006 in the Gregorian University, Rome.

2 Martial Marcet, *Jésuites Modernes pour Faire Suite au Mémoire de M. le Comte de Montlosier* (Paris, 1826). Similarly, in April 1823 the Comte Lanjuinais, speaking in the Chambre des Pairs, wildly exaggerated the links of the Society of the Sacred Heart with the Jesuits. Archives Parlementaires, 2 Avril 1823. t.39.

3 Lettres de Sophie Barat et les Dames du Sacré-Cœur (AFSJ, H Ra 102/6); Sophie Barat to Marie Prevost, Paris, 10 July 1819; Lyon, 2 December 1819; Paris, 21 December 1822; Paris, 17 February 1824; SB to Susanne Geoffroy, Paris, 16 August 1824; SB to Thérèse Maillucheau, Paris, 17 August 1821; Paris, 5 December 1821; SB to Eulalie de Bouchaud, Rome, 18 February 1842. Also, Rome, 23 November 1841; SB to Léonie de Brives, Paris, 7 November 1855. Sophie was careful in her choice of the Jesuits who ministered to the communities. SB to Eugénie de Gramont, Bordeaux, 5 March 1834; SB to Eulalie de Bouchaud, Rome, 8 July 1837. The title 'extraordinary confessor' was given to those priests who heard the confessions of the community in Advent and Lent. This was to ensure the community had access to different confessors from time to time.

4 Letters of Vicars, 1844–1852; 1885–1889 (GA, Rome, C-III. Italy); also, Philippe de Villafort à Adèle Cahier, Rome, 4 Février 1853; Rome, 8 Février 1853; Rome, 24

Juillet 1854 (GA, Rome, B-IV, 3, Box 9, Roothaan). SB to Emma de Bouchaud, Paris, 14 May 1859; Paris, 20 July 1859; Paris, 30 July 1859; Paris, 11 September 1859; Paris, 19 November 1859. SB to Matilde Garabis, Paris, 8 November 1853; Paris, 8 November, 9 November, 3 December, 5 December 1853; Paris, 5 and 7 October 1853. Sophie Barat on occasion asked a Jesuit to withdraw from their ministry in the communities and schools. For example, SB to Alida Dumazeaud, Paris, 10 May 1863; Paris, 18 May 1863; Paris, 20 May 1863. In this instance Sophie Barat asked that a Jesuit not give the school retreat in Marmoutier, citing inappropriate behaviour.

5 Lettres aux religieux et religieuses: au Père Général, Compagnie de Jésus à Rome. Lettre 1, Sophie Barat au Père Fortis, Paris, 15 Juin 1828; Lettre 2, Sophie Barat et les assistantes générales au Père Fortis, Paris, 20 Octobre 1828 (GA, Rome, C-I, 1-F, Letters. Holographs. Carton XVII, Lettres à divers ecclésiastiques, 1814–1864, à des religieux et religieuses; C-I, G. Box 28.B); Roothaan/Beckx; Letters of Vicars, 1844–1852; 1885–1889 (GA, Rome, C-III, Italy); Re foundation in Westphalia [1851] (GA, Rome, B-IV, 3, Box 9). Lettres de Sophie Barat et les Dames du Sacré-Cœur (AFSJ, H Ra 102/6); Correspondence Sophie Barat and Jean Roothaan (ARSI, Monial I, Fasc. I, VI, 6, Dossier Barat).

6 Alison Weber, *Teresa of Avila and the Rhetoric of Femininity* (Princton, 1990).

7 GA, Rome, Canonisation Process. Romana seu Parisien. Beatificationis et canonizationis servae Dei Magdalenae Sophiae Barat. Animadversiones. See also C-I, A, i-a, Box 5. SB to Louise de Limminghe, Paris, 24 October 1828; Paris, 27 October 1838; Paris, 21 November 1838; Paris, 9 December 1853; SB to Emma de Bouchaud, Conflans, 20 May 1843. Témoignages des personnes de la Société, ayant servi à Mgr Baunard, no. 298. Eléonore Buire, Original version, f. 2 (GA, Rome, C-1, A, 1-e, Box 1, bis).

8 With regard to the Jesuits, see the correspondence between Sophie Barat and Philippine Duchesne, especially in the 1823–30 period. Also, SB to Aloysia Hardey, Rome, 30 December 1837 and Rome, 9 January 1838, suggesting that Aloysia Hardey offer money to Jesuits and the bishop of St Louis in return for their support of the Society in Louisiana; SB to Adèle Lehon, Paris, 11 February 1846, re money lent to a Jesuit in Rome; SB to Aimée d'Avenas, Rome, 21 January 1842; SB to Lucie Merilhou, Paris, 22 February 1843; SB to Louise de Limminghe, Paris, 21 May 1853; SB to Olympe Rombau, Paris, 29 May 1859; Paris, 29 June 1859. See also SB to Elizabeth Galitzine, Rome, 5 May 1838; Jan Roothaan à Sophie Barat, Rome, 26 Juin 1849 (GA, Rome B-IV, 3, Box 9, Roothaan); Olwen Hufton, 'Altruism and Reciprocity: The Early Jesuits and their Female Patrons', *Renaissance Studies*, vol. 15, no. 3 (September 2001), pp. 328–53.

9 SB to Thérèse Maillucheau, Amiens, 2 February 1816; Paris, 12 March 1817; Paris, 16 June 1817; Paris, 2 July 1817; Paris, 4 August 1817; Paris, 12 February 1820; Paris, 18 May 1820; SB to Emilie Giraud, Paris, 26 March 1818; SB to Eugénie Audé, Paris, 16 July 1824; SB to Louise de Limminghe, passim, September 1828–October 1829; SB to Henriette Grosier, Paris, 21 September 1835; Montet, 23 August 1836; Turin, 4 November 1836; Rome, 12 March 1837; Rome, 10 April 1837; SB to Stanislas Verhulst, Paris 9 March 1847; SB to Thérèse du Lac, Paris, 31 March 1855; SB to Marie Dieudonnée, Paris, 3 April 1856; SB to Joséphine Goetz, Paris, 8 May 1856; Paris, 26 May 1856; SB to Esther d'Oussières, Paris, 8 December 1857; SB to Sophie Toussenel, Paris 9 August 1859. SB also had to deal with bishops or clerics who took offence if they were not asked to preside over school prizegvings or over religious events in the community. SB to to Olympie

Rombau, Paris, 14 July 1859. Passim. At one point, in exasperation, Sophie Barat drew up a rule for chaplains, in the hope that this could keep their interference in the communities and schools within the bounds she considered appropriate. Règlement l'aumônier de la maison du Sacré-Cœur, Chambéry, 19 Juin 1838 (Society of the Sacred Heart, General Archives, Rome, C-IV, 4, Chambéry, Box 3).

10 André Rayez et Louis Fèvre, *Foi Chrétienne et Vie Consacrée: Clorivière Aujourd'hui* (Paris, 1971), pp. 118–22; André Rayez, 'Clorivière et les Pères de la Foi', *AHSJ*, vol. xxi (1952), pp. 300–28.

11 P. Fidèle de Grivel, Breve Ragguaglio de Principje Progressi della Società del Sacro Cuore di Gesù, 18 à 20. Récit de la première inspiration du P. de Tournély concernant l'Institut féminin voué au Sacré-Cœur. Original text and translation in de Charry, *Histoire des Constitutions de la Société du Sacré-Cœur*, vol. ii, Textes, no. 1, pp. 1*–7*. Also, *Notice sur ... Léonor François de Tournély et sur son oeuvre La Congrégation des Pères du Sacré-Cœur* (Vienne, 1886), pp. 104–12.

12 de Charry, *Histoire des Constitutions de la Société du Sacré-Cœur: La Formation de l'Institut*, vol. i, pp. 115–31. Kilroy, *Madeleine Sophie Barat*, p.27.

13 *Vie de Madame Geoffroy* (Poitiers, 1854). She entered the Society of the Sacred Heart in Poitiers in 1807.

14 Prophétie du R.P. Nectou[x] (GA, Rome, A-I, 1, a-b); *Vie de Madame Geoffroy*, p. 17. In this text Drouard is spelt Draut.

15 Beatificationis et canonizationis servae Dei, Leopoldinae Naudet fundatricis sororum a Sacra Familia Veronae (1773–1834). Relatio et Vota, 5 Novembre 1996 (Rome, 1996), pp. 12–18.

16 By this time de Tournély had died and was succeeded as leader by Joseph Varin.

17 Achille Guidée, *Vie du P. Joseph Varin ... Suivie de Notices sur Quelques-uns de ses Confrères* (Paris, 1854), pp. 48–60, 94–99. Notice XV, Le P. Nicolas Paccanari, pp. 323–35; de Charry, *Histoire des Constitutions de la Société du Sacré-Cœur: La Formation de l'Institut*, vol. i, pp. 149–51.

18 Beatificationis et canonizationis servae Dei, Leopoldinae Naudet, pp. 18–23.

19 SB to Emma de Bouchaud, Paris, 18 June 1853.

20 Kilroy, *Madeleine Sophie Barat*, pp. 37–40.

21 Jean Baptiste Louis de Sambucy Saint-Estève was born in Millau en Rouergue in 1771 and went to Paris to train for the priesthood. He studied at first in the Collège de Juilly and later in 1787 at St Sulpice. Kilroy, *Madeleine Sophie Barat*, pp. 44–8.

22 Amiens Affaires, Lettre no. 2, Lettre de la Mère Barat à l'abbé de Saint-Estève, Paris, 11 Septembre [1814]; Kilroy, *Madeleine Sophie Barat*, pp. 62–9, 74–80.

23 At this time the Association was sometimes called the Ladies of the Faith.

24 Amiens Affaires, no. 4, Lettre de l'abbé de Saint-Estève à la Mère Barat, Rome, 23 Octobre [1814].

25 Chantal Reynier, 'Le Père de Clorivière et le Rétablissement des Jésuites en France (1814–1818)', *Revue Mabillon*, n.s., t.6 (=t.67), 1995, pp. 267–93.

26 Barat à Panazzoni, 27 Novembre 1814; de Charry, *Histoire des Constitutions de la Société du Sacré-Cœur*, vol. ii, Textes, 48*, p. 242.

27 Amiens Affaires, no. 11, Copie de la réponse à trois lettres de M. de Sambucy.

28 Julien Druilhet (1768–1845) was a priest of the diocese of Orléans. He became a Jesuit in Paris in 1814.

29 Affaires Amiens, no. 19, Lettre de la Mère Barat au P. de Clorivière [Été 1815].

30 Affaires Amiens, no. 20, À Madame Barat, Maison de l'Instruction Chrétienne à Cuignières. Paris, 18 Août 1815.

31 For an extensive treatment of the influences of other religious and educational traditions on the content of the 1815 Constitutions, see de Charry, *Exposé Historique*, pp. 80–115.

32 Kilroy, *Madeleine Sophie Barat*, pp. 95–9.

33 Sophie Barat signalled this change from 1833. SB to Eugénie de Gramont , Rome, 9 February 1833; Rome, 5 March 1833; Rome, 13 April 1833; Turin, 1 July 1833; Chambéry, 23 July 1833; SB to Henriette Grosier, Rome, 18 April 1833.

34 Affaires Amiens, no. 52, Joseph Varin à Madame Barat, Paris 19 Février 1816.

35 Jean Louis de Lessègues de Rozaven (1772–1851). Achille Guidée, *Vie du . . . P. Joseph Varin, Suivie de Notices sur Quelques-uns de ses Confrères* (Paris, 1854), pp. 225–35.

36 Catherine the Great refused to acknowledge the decision of the pope in 1773 to suppress the Jesuits and permitted them to minister in Russia.

37 The boys' school in Amiens, Saint-Acheul, was run by the Fathers of the Faith; it became a Jesuit school in 1814. One of the teachers there, Nicholas Loriquet, drew up a Plan of Studies in 1803 for the girls' school run by the Dilette di Gèsu. Twice a week he helped those learning to teach, giving them teaching methods and practical class preparation. Achille Guidée, *Les Pères de la Foi* (Paris, 1854), pp. 33–105; de Charry, *Pédagogie-Spiritualité dans l'Activité Éducative Originelle*, p. 15, note 47. Geneviève Deshayes, 'Notes sur notre . . . Fondatrice et les Commencements de la Société. Premiers Jours de la Société du Sacré-Cœur de Jésus', p. 24 (GA, Rome, A-II, 1-a, Box 1). *Vie du Père Loriquet* (Paris, 1845), p. 75; John W. Padberg, *Colleges in Controversy: The Jesuit Schools in France from Revival to Suppression, 1815–1880* (Cambridge, MA, 1969), pp. 52–54, 74. Nicholas Loriquet continued to advise the Society of the Sacred Heart on educational matters over many years.

38 Jean Louis Rozaven to Sophie Barat, Rome, 19 August 1824 (GA, Rome, C-I., A, I-F, Box R). The contacts continued down the years, and not just at the level of education. Sophie Barat regularly bought hens and cows from the Jesuit farm in Amiens. SB to Marie Prevost, Paris, Holy Thursday 15 April 1824; Paris, 17 February 1824; SB to Alexandrine Riencourt, Paris, 15 August 1828; SB to Adelaide de Rozeville, Paris, 22 August 1828; Paris, 28 August 1828; Paris, 5 September 1828; Paris, 22 September 1828.

39 Elizabeth Galitzine's mother also converted to Roman Catholicism. Kilroy, *Madeleine Sophie Barat*, pp. 178–9. Achille Guidée, *Notices Historiques sur Quelques Membres de la Société du Pères du Sacré-Cœur et de la Compagnie de Jésus*, Tome 1 (Paris, 1860). Lettres du Père Jean Rozaven à Madame de Elizabeth Galitzin, pp. 170–267.

40 Notes sur la vie de Mme Elizabeth Galitzine (GA, Rome, C-VII, 2, Galitzine, Box 3); *Notice sur Madame Elizabeth Galitzin, Religieuse du Sacré-Cœur, 1795–1843* (Tours, 1858); Prince Augustin Galitzin, *Mélanges: Une Religieuse Russe*, Le Correspondent, Août 1862 (GA, Rome, C-VII, 2, Galitzine, Box 3).

41 Jean-Louis Rozaven to Sophie Barat, Rome, 19 August 1824; also Rome, 7 October 1824.

42 Jean-Louis Rozaven to Sophie Barat, Rome, 23 January 1825; 27 November 1825; 13 April 1826; 21 June 1826; 23 January 1827. SB to Elizabeth Galitzine, Paris, November 1825; Paris, 4 January 1826; Paris, 6 July 1826; 21 July 1826. For Elizabeth Galitzine's letters to Sophie Barat, 1825–6, GA, Rome, C-I., A, I-F, Box R.

43 SB to Elizabeth Galitzine, Paris, 6 May 1825; Paris, 26 August 1825; Paris, 2 October 1825.

44 After the demise of the Dilette di Gesù, Léopoldine Naudet (1773–1834) founded the congregation of the Holy Family of Verona, Italy.

45 Correspondance Jean-Louis Rozaven et Léopoldine Naudet, Rome, 9 Mai 1821 (GA, Rome, H-I, 3, de Charry).

46 Jean-Louis Rozaven to Sophie Barat, Rome, 20 February 1827; Jean-Louis Rozaven to Joséphine Bigeu, Rome, 13 March 1827; 24 March 1827; 7 May 1827.

47 SB to Philippine Duchesne, Paris, 28 October 1824; SB to Marie de la Croix, Paris, 6 December 1826. Kilroy, *Madeline Sophie Barat*, pp. 182–7.

48 Archives de la Trinité des Monts, Rome, Histoire de la Fondation de Rome en 1828, ff. 1–2; Archives de l'Ambassade de France près le Saint-Siège. Dossier: Religieuses du Sacré-Cœur (1838–1904); Mgr Fourier Bonnard, *Histoire du Couvent Royale de la Trinité du Mont Pincio à Rome* (Rome/Paris, 1933), pp. 279–307.

49 Archives de la Trinité des Monts, ff. 2–9. Cahier, *Vie de la . . . Mère Madeleine-Sophie Barat*, vol. i , pp. 468–74; Luigi M. Manzini, *Il Cardinale Luigi Lambruschini* (Vatican, 1960), pp. 126–31; 438–42.

50 Archives de la Trinité des Monts, f. 46.

51 SB to Philippine Duchesne [Paris], 9 May 1828.

52 GA, Rome, Lettres aux religieux et religieuses: au Père Général, Compagnie de Jésus à Rome. Lettre 1, Sophie Barat au Père Fortis, Paris, 15 Juin 1828; Lettre 2, Sophie Barat et les assistantes générales au Père Fortis, Paris, 20 Octobre 1828 (GA, Rome, C-I, 1-F, Letters. Holographs. Carton XVII, Lettres à divers ecclésiastiques (1814–1864), à des religieux et religieuses; Also, C-I, G, Box 28.B).

53 SB to Armande de Causans [Rome], 13 September 1828 (GA, Rome, C-IV, 4, Rome, Box 1).

54 SB to Louise de Limminghe, Rome, 12 March 1833.

55 Louis Sellier (1772–1854) was originally a Father of the Faith in Amiens and became a Jesuit in 1814. Guidée, *Les Pères de la Foi*, pp. 33–105.

56 Armande de Causans to Sophie Barat, Trinité des Monts, 11 June 1828 (GA, Rome, C-IV, 4, Rome, Box 1).

57 Jean-Louis Rozaven to Joseph Varin, Rome, 5 March 1823 (GA, Rome, C-I, A, I-F, Box R).

58 Armande de Causans to Sophie Barat, Trinité des Monts, 11 June 1828 (GA, Rome, C-IV, 4, Rome, Box 1).

59 Armande de Causans to Sophie Barat, Rome, 20 September 1828 (GA, Rome, C-IV, 4, Rome, Box 1). Also, SB to the Countess de la Grandville, Paris, 9 January 1829.

60 Armande de Causans to Sophie Barat, Trinité des Monts, 11 June 1828 (GA, Rome, C-IV, 4, Rome, Box 1).

61 Archives de la Trinité des Monts, f. 61. See also ff. 45, 46, 52, 58–60; Jean Rozaven to Sophie Barat, Rome, 8 January 1833; Rome, 3 February 1833 (GA, Rome, B-IV, 3, Box 9).

62 Sophie Barat to Eugénie de Gramont, Turin, 14 July 1832. Also, Turin [nd] July 1832; Turin, 9 July 1832; Casino, près de Turin, 11 July 1832; SB to Hypolite Lavauden, Paris, 21 November 1838. Natalie Rostopchine (1787–1875) entered the Society in 1821. SB to Emilie Giraud, Paris, 26 April 1821; SB to Thérèse Maillucheau, Paris, 13 May 1821; SB to Catherine de Charbonnel, Paris, 11 May 1821; SB to Philippine Duchesne, Paris, 14 June 1821. After a time Natalie Rostopchine left the Society and re-entered in 1858 at the age of seventy-one. She made her final profession in 1861 and died in the Trinité des Monts, Rome, in 1875.

63 Kilroy, *Madeleine Sophie Barat*, pp. 221–2, 242–3.
64 Jean Rozaven to Sophie Barat, Rome, 15 October 1835; Jean Rozaven [to Louise de Limminghe, Rome], 24 June 1835.
65 Jan Roothaan (1785–1853) was born in Amsterdam and became a Jesuit in Russia. He was expelled from Russia in 1820 and went first to Switzerland and then to Turin where he taught at the Collège des Nobles. He was elected superior general in 1828.
66 Lettre du P. Roothaan à Mère de Limminghe, supérieure à Turin. Rome, 15 Janvier 1833 (AFSJ, Dossier Barat). SB to Louise de Limminghe, Rome, 14 February 1833; Rome, 23 February 1833; Rome, 6 March 1833; Rome, 12 March 1833; Rome, 13 April 1833. For the differing views between Jan Roothaan and Rozaven, see SB to Louise de Limminghe, Rome, 17 January 1833 and Rome, 22 January 1833. Tensions between the Jesuits and the Society of the Sacred Heart continued in Turin, Rome and Paris. Sophie Barat to Louise de Limminghe, Turin, 21 June 1838; Jette [Brussels], 8 July 1841; SB to Elizabeth Galitzine, Rome, 6 February 1838. Louise de Limminghe continued to request Jesuits for retreats and spiritual direction. Pierre Beckx à Louise de Limminghe, Rome, 18 Juillet 1854; Rome, 19 Octobre 1861 (GA, Rome B-IV, 3, Box 9. Roothaan/Beckx).
67 Evangelisti, *Nuns: A History of Convent Life*, pp. 41–65; Laven, *Virgins of Venice: Broken Vows and Cloistered Lives in the Renaissance Convent* (Harmondsworth, 2002).
68 de Charry, *Exposé Historique*, pp. 152–62, 274–84, 339–49. Passim.
69 Armande de Causans to Sophie Barat, Rome, 10 Décembre 1829 (GA, Rome, C-IV, 4, Rome, Box 1). Also, Armande de Causans to Sophie Barat, Turin, 7 May 1827 (GA, Rome, C-IV, 1. Torino, 1822–1848, Box 2).
70 *Vie de . . . Catherine de Charbonnel* (Paris, c. 1870), p. 191.
71 SB to Eugénie de Gramont, Rome, 13 May 1842. Also, SB to Aimée d'Avenas, Rome, 7 April 1840; SB to Adèle Lehon, Paris, 22 September 1863.
72 In that context, Sophie Barat considered removing Armande de Causans in 1834 from her position as superior of the Trinité, but Rozaven thought a sudden change could give the Society an image of instability in Rome. SB to Eugénie de Gramont, Bordeaux, 20 March 1834.
73 St Ruffine was founded in 1833 and the Villa Lante in 1837, both in the Trastevere.
74 SB to Louise de Limminghe, Parme, 2 June, 1838; Turin, 27 June 1838; La Ferrandière, (Lyon), 17 July 1838; La Ferrandière, 21 July 1838.
75 SB to Louise de Limminghe, La Ferrandière, 26 July 1838.
76 SB to Louise de Limminghe, La Ferrandière, 27 July 1838. Also, SB to Louise de Limminghe, La Ferrandière, 30 July 1838; SB to Hypolite Lavauden, Paris, 31 October 1838.
77 SB to Louise de Limminghe, Lyon, 21 July 1838; SB to Louise de Limminghe, La Ferrandière, 1 August 1838.
78 SB to Louise de Limminghe, La Ferrandière, 4 August 1838. Also, La Ferrandière, 1 August 1838. Sophie chided Hypolite Lavauden for abandoning the Trinité community at this time. SB to Hypolite Lavauden, Autun, 20 August 1838.
79 SB to Louise de Limminghe, Autun, 19 August 1838. Also, La Ferrandière, 9 August 1838; Autun, 14 August 1838; Paris, 12 November 1838.
80 SB to Louise de Limminghe, Autun, 27 August1838. Also, Paris, 12 November 1838.
81 SB to Louise de Limminghe, Paris, 8 September 1838.
82 SB to Louise de Limminghe, Paris, 10 September 1838.
83 SB to Louise de Limminghe, Paris, 19 October 1838.

84 SB to Louise de Limminghe, Paris, 19 November 1838.
85 SB to Louise de Limminghe, Paris, 26 November 1838. See also Paris, 3 December 1838 (bis).
86 SB to Louise de Limminghe, Paris, 28 November 1838.
87 SB to Louise de Limminghe, Paris, 21 January 1839. Also, Paris, 18 January 1839 (bis).
88 Kilroy, *Madeleine Sophie Barat*, pp. 278–82. Passim.
89 Sophie Barat à Cardinal Pedicini, Paris, 7 Octobre 1838 (GA, Rome, Lettres aux Ecclésiastiques, C-1, G, Box 28B).
90 Kilroy, *Madeleine Sophie Barat*, pp. 287–96.
91 Elizabeth Galitzine, Histoire Secrète de la Société, ff. 35–6.
92 For the part Joseph Varin played during these years, see Kilroy, *Madeleine Sophie Barat*, pp. 290–3, 302–3, 332, 342. Also, the letters of Catherine de Charbonnel to Sophie Barat, October/November 1839 (GA, Rome, C-I, e-I, Box 3).
93 Clément Boulanger à Jean Roothaan, 27 Octobre 1839. Clément Boulanger became Jesuit provincial in Paris in 1842.
94 Jean Rozaven à Achille Guidée, Rome, 9 Novembre 1839. Also, E. Solente à Jean Roothaan, 12 Janvier 1840.
95 Achille Guidée à Jean Roothaan, 30 Octobre 1839.
96 Jean Roothaan à Achille Guidée, Rome, 5 Novembre 1839.
97 Thomas Morrissey, *As One Sent. Peter Kenny SJ, 1779–1841: His mission in Ireland and North America* (Dublin, 1996), pp. 283–8; Elizabeth Galitzine contacted Louis Barat in Paris hoping he could influence his sister to side with the Ultramontane group in the Society. Kilroy, *Madeleine Sophie Barat*, pp. 365–6.
98 Journal de la retraite commencée au Grand Coteau le 13 Décembre 1841, achevée le 22 Décembre, f. 28 (GA, Rome C-VII., 2, Galitzine, Box 3).
99 Journal de la retraite, f. 28. At the end of this retreat Elizabeth Galitzine took two vows. One was to work for the Society of the Sacred Heart without concern for her own reputation, the other to offer her life in return for the 1839 decrees being implemented in the Society. Grand Coteau, 29 Décembre 1841; 12 Janvier 1842 (GA, Rome C-VII, 2, Box 3). For a discussion on victim spirituality in the nineteenth century, *DS*, fasc. CII–CIII, no. 16 (1992), pp. 537–45.
100 SB to Eulalie de Bouchaud, Rome, 2 December 1841; Rome, 22 January 1842.
101 In 1827 no mention was made of expansion of the Society beyond the frontiers of France. Papal approbation of the Society and the nomination of a Roman Cardinal Protector of the Society were not alluded to either. These issues were considered too sensitive, given the Gallican stance of the French government.
102 Antonio Garibaldi à Césaire Mathieu, Lettre 102, Paris, 30 Décembre 1842. Paul Poupard, *Correspondance Inédite entre Mgr Antonio Antonio Garibaldi, Internonce à Paris et Mgr Césaire Mathieu Archevêque de Besançon. Contribution à l'Histoire de l'Administration Ecclésiastique sous la Monarchie de Juillet* (Rome, 1961), pp. 382–5.
103 Clément Boulanger à Jean Roothaan, [Paris], 1 Janvier 1843; 19 Janvier 1843; 25 Juin 1843, Graves difficultates, Franc. 5-II, 16, 18, 27. Jesuits in Paris appealed to Pope Gregory XVI over their difficulties with Archbishop Affre. P.F. Grandidier, *Vie du . . . Père Guidée de la Compagnie de Jésus* (Amiens/Paris, 1867), pp. 192–204, 404–10.
104 Paul Tharin à Jean Roothaan, Paris, 10 Janvier 1843. Graves difficultates, Monial 5-I, 19.
105 B.U. du Trousset d'Héricourt (1797–1851), bishop of Autun to Césaire Mathieu, Rome, 14 Février 1843 (Diocèse de Besançon. Archives Historiques, Boite 2476).
106 Jean Roothaan à Paul Tharin, Rome, 6 Février 1843 (ARSI, Responsa ad externos,

1840–3, vol. v, pp. 292–4). See also GA, Rome, C-I, C-3, Box 3.

107 Ambassadeur de France à Rome à Mons. Le Ministre, Rome, 8 Novembre 1842 (Archives des Affaires Etrangères, Paris. Correspondance Politique, Rome, vol. 984, Rome, 1842–43, f. 156); A.A.F. Dossier: Religieuses du Sacré-Cœur (1838–1904), Dépêches du Département 1842–43, no. 133, Paris, 14 Décembre 1842. Also, Jean Roothaan à Césaire Mathieu, Rome, 28 Mars 1843 (ARSI, Responsa ad externos, 1840–43, vol. v, p. 312).

108 Garibaldi à Lambruschini, Paris, 20 Décembre 1842 (ASV, Fonds Segretario di Stato Esteri, Busta 616, Rubrica 283, Fascicolo 1, no. 1768).

109 Sophie Barat to Henriette Grosier, Rome, 31 December 1839.

110 Jean Rozaven à Ferdinand Donnet, Rome, 13 Octobre 1842 (GA, Rome, H-I, 6. Box 1, de Charry). Kilroy, *Madeleine Sophie Barat*, pp. 344–5, 353. In France the Jesuit provincial, François Renault, also made known his criticism of the Society and in particular of Sophie Barat. SB to Eulalie de Bouchaud, Rome, 1 March 1842.

111 SB to Césaire Mathieu, 5, Lyon, 25 September 1842. Until this point Sophie Barat did not acknowledge the extent of Rozaven's criticisms of her, nor of the influence of the Jesuits on the 1839 General Council; SB to Adelaide de Rozeville, Rome, 10 November 1839; SB to Eugénie Audé, Paris, 27 October 1840; Paris, 5 December 1840; Paris, 29 May 1841; SB to Henriette Grosier, Rome, 26 December 1841. Kilroy, *Madeleine Sophie Barat*, pp. 317–18, 326–8.

112 Cited by Elizabeth Galitzine in a letter to Louise de Limminghe. Elizabeth Galitzine to Louise de Limminghe, Lyon, 16 September 1842. See also Kilroy, *Madeleine Sophie Barat*, pp. 329, 352.

113 Paul Poupard, *Correspondance Inédite*, Paris, 26 Septembre 1842, p. 377.

114 SB to Césaire Mathieu, [Paris, 17 November 1842]. Also Paris, 15 November 1842; Césaire Mathieu to Sophie Barat, Besançon, 16 November 1842. Sophie Barat's assistants general were Louise de Limminghe, Catherine de Charbonnel, Félicité Demarquest and Elizabeth Galitzine.

115 Adèle Lehon à Elizabeth Galitzine, St Rufine, 14 Mars 1843 (Affaires concernant la Société, no. 2, 1839 à 43, ff. 67–8 (GA, Rome, C-I, C-3, Box 2, 1839). Adèle Lehon remarked that, although Elizabeth Galitzine was a gifted woman, 'her aristocratic background led her to believe that people could be led like machines'.

116 Louis Barat à Elizabeth Galitzine, [Paris, Juin 1843], Affaires concernant la Société, ff. 85–6. Elizabeth Galitzine quoted from Louis Barat's letter when she wrote to Laure d'Avernioz in June 1843: Elizabeth Galitzine à Laure d'Avernioz, Conflans, 13 Juin 1843 (GA, Rome, C-I, C-3, 1839, Box 6).

117 Adèle Lehon, Récit historique des événements de 1839–1843 (General Archives, Rome, C-I, c, Box 2, 1839, f. 8).

118 SB to Adèle Lehon, Rome, 24 September 1839; Paris [nd] October 1840; Paris, 31 October 1840; Paris, 23 August 1841.

119 SB to Stanislas Dusaussoy, Paris, 26 October 1840.

120 Joséphine de Coriolis to Sophie Barat, Rome, [February] 1844; Rome, 4 March 1844 (GA, Rome, C-IV, 4, Rome, Box 1). For Sophie Barat's comments some years later on the role of Rozaven, SB to Adèle Lehon, Paris, 20 April 1855.

121 Note demandée Monseigneur l'Archevêque sur les communautés Religieuses et sur les prêtres attachés aux dites communautés, 1843 (Archives de l'Archevêché de Paris, Fonds Affre, 1840–1848, 1 D V 2).

122 SB to Caesar Mathieu, Conflans, 23 February 1846. Also, Paris, 20 September 1845. Denys Affre à Sophie Barat, Paris, 20 Octobre 1846 (AF Poitiers, Paris, B06,

151, II, Evêché); Notes en forme de journal, ff. 19–22; Souvenirs de Soeur Virginie Roux, Notes Confidentielles, ff. 139–40. Also, SB to Eugénie de Gramont, Rome, 27 May 1845.

123 SB to Caesar Mathieu, Paris, 15 March 1846; Paris, 24 December 1847.

124 A further source of tension between the Society and Archbishop Affre was his decision in March 1846 to hold a canonical visitation of the houses of the Society in Paris. Sophie resisted this action and asked that it not be carried out. Archbishop Affre was predictably furious and insisted it take place. SB to Caesar Mathieu, Conflans, 6 May 1846. Also, SB to Luigi Lambruschini (cardinal protector of the Society of the Sacred Heart) [Conflans], [nd] May 1846 (GA, Rome, B-II, Box 1, Dossier 3). Notes en forme de journal, ff. 24–5; Lettres de Alexis Gaume (AF Poitiers, Paris, B06, 151, I, Evêché); Limousin-Lamothe, Leflon, Mgr Denys-Auguste Affre, pp. 257–8.

125 Luigi Lambruschini à Sophie Barat, Rome, 20 Mai 1846 (GA, Rome, B-II., Box 1, Dossier 3); Notes en forme de journal, f. 21.

126 Sophie Barat à Jean Roothaan, Trinité des Monts, 11 Février 1851 (ARSI, Monial I, I-VI, 2); Notes ou mémoire pour son Éminence le cardinal protecteur [Luigi Lambruschini] (GA, Rome, Lettres aux Cardinal Protecteur, Document 21, Lettres aux ecclésiastiques).

127 SB to cardinal Lambruschini, Trinité des Monts, 8 March 1851.

128 Léon de Chazournes, *Vie de . . . Père Joseph Barrelle*, 2 tomes (Paris, 1870), vol. ii, pp. 120–1; also, 119, 122–42. Also, GA, Rome, B-IV, 3, Box 4. SB to Matilde Garabis, Paris, 19 May 1853; Paris, 3 December 1853. SB to Adèle Lehon, Paris, 2 June 1853.

129 SB to Louise de Limminghe, Paris, 2 April 1855. Referring to letters from Jesuits in Latin America, asking for foundations in Argentina and Guatemala.

130 Sophie Barat complained that some Jesuits opposed the Society's foundations in different countries. For example, in Ireland and England from 1842. SB to Aimée d'Avenas, Rome, 11 February 1842; Rome, 3 March 1842; SB to Charlotte Goold, Rome, 17 March 1842; SB to Lucie Merilhou, Conflans, 15 May 1843; Paris, 15 August 1857; Paris, 18 October 1857; SB to Gertrude de Brou, Paris, 7 March 1853. Similarly in France. SB to Gertrude de Brou, Paris, 1 October 1852; Paris, 7 October 1852; SB to Esther d'Oussières, Paris, 31 May 1857; Paris, 25 December 1857; Paris, 29 December 1857; Paris, 8 June 1858. Sometimes public perception of links between the Society of the Sacred Heart and the Jesuits worked against the Society, as when Sophie Barat was making foundations in Prussia and Tuscany. SB to Anne Marie Ganon, Paris, 21 March 1846.

131 Sophie Barat à Jean Roothaan, Paris, 10 Avril 1852 (ARSI, Monial I, Fasc. I, VI, 6); SB to Elizabeth Galitzine, Rome, 6 February 1838.

132 Jean Roothaan à Sophie Barat, Paris, 3 Mai, 1852 (ARSI, Monial I, Fasc. I, VI, 6).

133 Philippe de Villafort (1799–1866) entered the Jesuits in 1821. From 1834 he was in Rome, as sub-assistant general for France and secretary to Jean Roothaan.

134 Philippe de Villafort à Adèle Cahier, Rome, 30 Avril 1852 (GA, Rome, B-IV, 3, Box 9).

135 Sophie Barat à Jean Roothaan, Paris, 10 Avril 1852 (ARSI, Monial I, Fasc. I, VI, 8).

136 Philippe de Villafort à Adèle Cahier, Rome, 30 Avril 1852. Also, Rome, 4 Octobre 1852. For this and extensive correspondence with Philippe de Villafort see GA, Rome B-IV, 3, Box 9, Roothaan/Beckx. Sophie Barat herself recognised that not every superior or community welcomed Jesuits as retreat givers or confessors. SB to

Alida Dumazeaud, Paris, 11 November 1856.

137 Sophie Barat was not alone in experiencing clerical dominance. Many in the Society endured it, especially at times of foundation. See Philippine Duchesne's struggles with the Jesuit Charles van Quickerborne in Louisiana. Sarah A. Curtis, Civilizing Habits: Women Missionaries and the Revival of French Empire (Oxford, 2010), pp. 78–82; Louise Callan, Philippine Duchesne: Frontier Missionary of the Sacred Heart, 1769–1852 (Maryland, 1957), pp. 384–90; Catherine Mooney, Philippine Duchesne: A Woman with the Poor (New York, 1990), pp. 154–66; Jeanne de Charry, Correspondance Sainte Madeleine Sophie Barat, Sainte Philippine Duchesne. Texte des manuscrits originaux présenté avec une introduction, des notes et un index analytique, 1821–1826, 1826–1852 (Rome, 1988–2001). For the Jesuits in Louisiana, see Morrissey, As One Sent, pp. 271–313.

CHAPTER 4

1 Members of the Society kept the letters Sophie Barat wrote to them personally and 14,000 were collected after her death. However, Sophie Barat usually disposed of personal letters sent to her once she had replied. She only retained letters concerning the governance of the Society, or written during a time of crisis, and sent these to the Archives.

2 Iain Bamforth (ed.), *The Body in the Library: A Literary Anthology of Modern Medicine* (London, 2003).

3 Notice sur l'enfance et la jeunesse du R.P. Barat avec lettre d'envoi autographe de Ste Sophie Barat, 1846 (AFSJ, Vanves, Carton Louis Barat). Also, Pauline Perdrau, *Les Loisirs de l'Abbaye*, vol. i, p. 390.

4 Edme-Joachim de la Mothe, 'Éloge du Climat de Joigny (1783)', *L'Écho de Joigny*, no. 7 (1971–2), pp. 13–18. *Almanach Historique de la Ville, Bailliage et Diocèse de Sens 1782* (Sens, 1782), p. 49.

5 A.D. Yonne, 2 E 206/21.

6 Sophie Barat to Eugénie de Gramont, Grenoble, 23 August 1818.

7 Adrienne Michel, 'Journal du Second Voyage de . . . Mère Barat à Gand 1811'.

8 de Coriolis, 'Histoire de la Société', f. 30.

9 A.D. Yonne, L 610, Collège de Joigny, Auxerre, 20 Août 1791; 16 Janvier 1792. The 1791/2 report on the Collège St Jacques commented on Louis Barat's learning, and on his austerity.

10 Deshayes, 'Notes sur notre . . . Fondatrice et les Commencements de la Société' (GA, Rome, A-II, 1-a, Box 1); de Coriolis, 'Histoire de la Société', ff. 26–26v; Perdrau, *Les Loisirs de l'Abbaye*, vol. i, pp. 93, 165–7, 239, 375.

11 Un cas de possession diabolique à Joigny, en 1791 [1790]. Récit de l'abbé Fromentot in *L'Écho de Joigny*, no. 15 (1974), pp. 13–18; Deshayes Premiers jours de la Société [f. 5]; Michel, 'Journal du Second Voyage de . . . Mère Barat à Gand 1811'.

12 Michel, 'Journal du Second Voyage de . . . Mère Barat à Gand 1811'.

13 A.D. Yonne Registre de St Thibault de Joigny, Série 2 E, 11 J 206/16, 1792–1800; Archives Municipales de Joigny, Bibliothèque de Joigny, Paroisse de St Thibault, Registres des Naissances, no. 63, 2 Mars 1792; no. 151, 4 Septembre 1795; A.D. Yonne, Série 2 E, 11 J 206/31, Registre des concessions des places et bancs d'Église. Paroisse St Thibault, 1761–1824, no. 38, f. 38.

14 Michel, 'Journal du Second Voyage de . . . Mère Barat à Gand 1811'. Also, Cahier, *Vie de la . . . Mère Madeleine-Sophie Barat*, vol. i, p. 7; Samuel Richardson, *Clarissa, or the History of a Young Lady* (London, 1747–8). French edition, 1751.

15 de Coriolis, 'Histoire de la Société', ff. 31–31v.
16 Récits de . . . Thérèse Maillucheau (c. 1846), ff. 9, 11(GA, Rome, A-II, a-1, Box 1); de Coriolis, 'Histoire de la Société', ff. 32–32v; Perdrau, *Les Loisirs de l'Abbaye*, vol. i, pp. 170–1.
17 de Coriolis, 'Histoire de la Société', f. 33; Récits de . . . Thérèse Maillucheau (c. 1846), ff. 15, 19. Deshayes, 'Notes sur notre . . . Fondatrice et les Commencements de la Société', ff. 6–7; Michel, 'Journal du Second Voyage de . . . Mère Barat à Gand 1811'; Perdrau, *Les Loisirs de l'Abbaye*, vol. i, p. 121.
18 Déposition Adèle Lehon, Paris, 23 Février 1882, ff. 541–2 (GA, Rome, Copia Publica, Transumpti processus apostolica auctoritate constructi in curia ecclesiastica Parisiensi . . . Magdalena Sophia Barat, vol. ii, 1897).
19 Kilroy, *Madeleine Sophie Barat*, pp. 26–30.
20 de Coriolis, 'Histoire de la Société', ff. 45v (i)–45v (ii); Joseph Varin to Sophie Barat, Besançon, 27 June [1803]; Lyon, 24 July [1803]; Tours, 6 March [1804]; Tours, 10 March [1804].
21 Louis Barat to Marie-Louise Dusaussoy, St Galmier [Loire], 9 September 1803 (AFCJ, Fonds Barat).
22 de Coriolis, 'Histoire de la Société', f. 45; Joseph Varin to Sophie Barat, Tours, 22 March [1804].
23 de Coriolis, 'Histoire de la Société', f. 45v (i).
24 Charles Bruson (1764–1838) joined the Fathers of the Faith in 1800 and was rector of the college at Amiens at this time.
25 Joseph Varin to Sophie Barat, Tours, 6 March 1804.
26 de Coriolis, 'Histoire de la Société', f. 45v (ii).
27 SB to Philippine Duchesne, Poitiers, 1 August 1806; also, Bordeaux, 30 August 1806. Cahier, *Vie de . . . Mère Madeleine-Sophie Barat*, vol. i, pp. 119–20.
28 Thérèse Maillucheau. Premier noviciat de la Société, 1806, ff. 102–3, 128.
29 Thérèse Maillucheau. Premier noviciat de la Société, 1806, f. 154 and ff. 93, 97, 107, 109–13, 130, 140, 142. For further examples of Sophie's conduct at this time, see de Coriolis, 'Histoire de la Société', Ch. II, ff. 12v–13, 21v.
30 Michel, 'Journal du Second Voyage de . . . Mère Barat à Gand 1811'.
31 SB to Philippine Duchesne, Poitiers, 15 July 1807.
32 SB to Emilie Giraud, Paris, 29 November 1809.
33 SB to Eugénie de Gramont, Paris, 21 September 1817.
34 SB to Thérèse Maillucheau, Paris, 29 December 1818.
35 Kilroy, *Madeleine Sophie Barat*, Chapters 3–5.
36 SB to Philippine Duchesne, Poitiers, 7 September 1807; Gand, 17 February 1811; Gand, 23 April [1811].
37 Joseph Varin to Sophie Barat, Lyon, 14 June 1810.
38 SB to Emilie Giraud, Paris, 19 July 1811.
39 SB to Philippine Duchesne, Poitiers, 19 August 1811; Poitiers, 9 September 1811; Poitiers, 7 October 1811; Niort, 14 February 1812.
40 SB to Emilie Giraud, Grenoble, 14 March 1814.
41 SB to Thérèse Maillucheau, Paris, 7 July 1816.
42 SB to Thérèse Maillucheau, St Genis, 6 September [1818].
43 SB to Stanislas Dusaussoy, Paris, 24 November 1818; Joséphine de Coriolis to Eugénie de Gramont, Grenoble, 11 August 1818 (GA, Rome, C-I, A, 1-F, Box I, no. 46).
44 SB to Eugénie de Gramont, Amiens, 7 September 1817; Paris, 24 September 1817.

45 SB to Eugénie de Gramont, Beauvais, 16 September 1817; SB to Thérèse Maillucheau, Beauvais, 16 September 1817; SB to Eugénie de Gramont, Paris, 24 September 1817.

46 SB to Stanislas Dusaussoy, Paris, 13 February 1817; Lettre d'une professe de la maison de Paris to F. Desmarquest, Paris, 16 February 1818, in Sophie Barat to Philippine Duchesne, 1818–1821, p. 31; SB to Thérèse Maillucheau, Paris, 26 February 1819.

47 SB to Marie-Louise Dusaussoy [Barat], Paris, 12 July 1819; also, SB to Thérèse Maillucheau, Paris, 19 July 1819.

48 SB to Thérèse Maillucheau, Lyon, 8 December 1819.

49 SB to Marie Balastron, Paris, 28 April 1819; SB to Marie Prevost, Paris, 28 April 1819; SB to Thérèse Maillucheau, Paris, 6 May 1819.

50 Sophie Barat had to find the money to close the bid on the property. She raised money by petitioning Louis XVIII who donated 50,000 francs in 1820, with a promise of another 50,000 the following year. The king's gift was conditional upon his right to nominate five free places in the school annually. The rest of the money was borrowed. The Marquis de Montmorency and two businessmen in Amiens, Laurent and Morand, between them lent the Society 265,000 francs at a reduced interest. She agreed to pay all her debts by 1824. In September 1820 the Society bought the house and gardens of the Hôtel Biron for 365,000 francs.

51 SB to Marie Balastron, Paris, 17 April 1821; SB to Marie Balastron, Paris, 28 June 1822.

52 SB to Thérèse Maillucheau, 20 April (Good Friday), 1821; Paris, 7 November 1821; Paris, 10 November 1821; Paris, 16 November 1821. Passim.

53 SB to Thérèse Maillucheau, Paris, 15 April 1822. Also, Paris, 20 April 1822. SB to Suzanne Geoffroy, Paris, 8 July 1822.

54 SB to Philippine Duchesne, Paris, 30 July 1822; Philippine Duchesne to Sophie Barat, [Florissant], 16 January 1823; SB to Thérèse Maillucheau, Paris, 18 May 1822, and Paris, 27 June 1822.

55 SB to Philippine Duchesne, Paris, 18 June 1823; Paris, 7 August 1823; Paris, 5 December 1823.

56 Mr Bilou, Grenoble, à Mr Ferral, Amiens. Grenoble, 4 Mai 1823; Marie de la Croix (1867). Note sur le séjour et la maladie de la Mère Barat à Grenoble [1823] (GA, Rome, C-I, A, 1-d, Box 1); Cahier, *Vie de la . . . Mère Madeleine-Sophie Barat*, vol. i, pp. 393–4.

57 Joseph-Marie Favre (1791–1838). Abbé Pont, *Vie de l'Abbé Favre, Fondateur des Missions de Savoie* (Montiers, 1865); François Bouchage, *Le Serviteur de Dieu, Joseph-Marie Favre, Maître et Modèle des Ouvriers Apostoliques, 1791–1838* (Paris, 1901); *DS, Fascicules CII–CIII*, pp. 120–1.

58 SB to Adelaide de Rozeville, Paris, 21 May 1826.

59 SB to Philippine Duchesne, Paris, 6 August 1826.

60 SB to Eugénie Audé, Paris, 15 April 1828.

61 SB to Adelaide de Rozeville, Paris, 12 July 1828.

62 SB to Eugénie de Gramont, La Ferrandière (Lyon), 2 February 1832.

63 SB to Eugénie Audé, Paris, 6 April 1829; SB to Adelaide de Rozeville, Paris, 22 April 1829.

64 SB to Louise de Limminghe, Paris, 22 June 1829. Also, Chevalier Rossi, Turin, 15 August 1832. Témoignage autographe du chevalier Rossi sur la guérison de la Mère Barat à Turin en 1832 (GA, Rome, C-I, A, 1-d, Box 1).

65 SB to Henriette Grosier, Paris, [c. 12–16] May 1829; SB to Madeleine du Chastaignier, Paris, 16 May 1829; SB to Adelaide de Rozeville, Paris, 18 May 1829. SB hurt her foot badly in 1806 while in Poitiers. Journal de Poitiers, p. 34.

66 SB to Henriette Grosier, Paris, 30 May 1829.

67 SB to Eugénie de Gramont, Chambéry 13 February 1831.

68 SB to Eugénie Audé, Paris, 12 June 1829; SB to Adelaide de Rozeville, Paris, 13 June 1829; Paris, 13 June 1829; SB to Louise de Limminghe, Paris, 22 June 1829.

69 SB to Madeleine Duchastaignier, Paris, 16 August 1829.

70 SB to Emilie Giraud, Paris, 8 December 1829. Also, SB to Adelaide de Rozeville, Paris, 22 April 1829; Paris, 18 May 1829; Paris, 17 June 1829; Paris, 19 March 1830; Paris, 26 May 1830; Paris, 7 June 1830; Paris, 8 June 1830. SB to Henriette Grosier , Paris, [nd] December 1829; Paris, 28 December 1829; Paris, 11 February 1830; [Paris], 18 April 1830; Paris, 26 July 1830. SB to Eugénie Audé, Paris, 12 June 1829. SB to Louise de Limminghe, Paris, 31 August 1829; Paris 18 September 1829; Paris, 12 October 1829; Paris, 7 July 1830.

71 SB to Henriette Grosier, Paris, [November] 1829; Paris, [December] 1829; Paris, 11 February 1830; Paris, 18 April 1830; Paris, 26 July 1830. SB to Adelaide de Rozeville, Paris, 19 March 1830; Paris, 23 March 1830; Paris, 26 May 1830; Paris, 7 June 1830; SB to Louise de Limminghe, Paris, 31 May 1830; Paris, 7 July 1830.

72 Cahier, *Vie de la . . . Mère Madeleine-Sophie Barat*, vol. i, pp. 518–22. From 1830 Marie Patte was Sophie's constant travelling companion (GA, Rome, C-VII, 2-P).

73 The thermal baths at Aix-les-Bains were known from Roman times for their healing properties. On 8 September Sophie went on pilgrimage with Eugénie de Gramont and Hypolite Lavauden to the shrine St Pierre d'Albigny to pray for a cure for her foot. Chambéry, Journal de la Maison, 1818 jusqu'à 1836 (copie), ff. 112–15 (AF Poitiers, Chambéry, B08, 114/115).

74 Cahier, *Vie de la . . . Mère Madeleine-Sophie Barat*, vol. i, pp. 527–31. 'Sainte Sophie Barat et le diocèse de Lausanne, Genève et Fribourg', *La Semaine Catholique de la Suisse Romande*, nos 20, 21, 22 (1952), pp. 306, 308–23, 338–9. *Dictionnaire Historique et Statistique des Paroisses Catholiques du Canton de Fribourg*, vol. 7 (Fribourg, 1891), pp. 498–500. Chambéry, 'Journal de la Maison', f. 111.

75 SB to Henriette Grosier, Middes, 11 November 1830; Middes, 20 November 1830; Middes, 21 November 1830.

76 Récamier worked as a doctor during the Revolution and Empire. By 1805 he had become chief doctor in the Hôtel Dieu Paris. He was professor in the Collège de France from 1821 to 1830, chair of the Collège de France from 1826 until his resignation in 1830, and a member of the Academy of Medicine from its foundation in 1820. He maintained independence from the monarchy and refused to become physician to either Louis XVIII or Charles X. He was, however, a loyal Bourbon and refused to recognise the July Monarchy of Louis Philippe in 1830 and chose exile for a time in Fribroug. Henri Gouraud, *Éloge de M. Récamier* (Paris, 1853); Paul Triaire, *Récamier et ses Contemporains 1774–1852: Étude d'Histoire de la Médecine aux XVIIIe et XIXe Siècles* (1899); J. Eyraud, *Conférence sur le Professeur Joseph-Claude-Anthelme Récamier* (Belley, 1913); Louis Sauve, *Le Dr Récamier (1774–1852)* (Paris, 1838). Récamier was a pioneer in the study of cancer. His colleague, Henri Gouraud, became Sophie Barat's doctor when Récamier died in 1852.

77 SB to Eugénie de Gramont, Bordeaux, 18 June 1825. *Mémoires, Souvenirs et Journaux de la Comtesse d'Aghoult*, 2 vols (Le Temps Retrouvé, LVIII, Paris, 1990),

vol. i, p. 139. The Comtesse d'Aghoult commented on the poor quality of food in the rue de Varenne, vol. i, pp. 139–41, 151–2, as did Sophie Barat. SB to Eugénie de Gramont, Rome, 24 November 1832. See also Arnold, *Le Corps et l'Âme: La Vie des Religieuses au XIXe Siècle*, pp. 171–200.

78 SB to Adelaide de Rozeville, Paris, 13 May 1830; SB to Eugénie de Gramont, Rome, 20 December 1832; Rome, 19 January 1833; Turin, 1 July 1833; [Bordeaux], 30 March 1834; Rome, 9 May 1837; Paris, 9 October 1840; Conflans, 29 April 1844; [Conflans], 29 September 1845; Conflans, 30 October 1845; Conflans, 1 November 1845; Conflans, 28 November 1845; Conflans, 24 January 1846; Conflans, 21 May 1846.

79 SB to Stanislas Dusaussoy, Rome, 21 June 1839; 15 July 1849. SB to Eulalie de Bouchaud, Lille, 27 June 1841; Jette, 9 July 1841. SB to Adelaide de Rozeville, Paris, 21 November 1846. SB to Louise de Limminghe, Paris, 25 February 1847. SB to Henriette de Clausel, Poitiers, 19 January 1849. SB to Elianne de Cuënot, Paris, 1 May 1852.

80 SB to Stanislas Dusaussoy, Paris, 3 July 1852. Also, SB to Louise de Limminghe, Paris, 2 July 1852. SB to Ana du Rousier, Paris, 3 July 1852. SB to Joséphine Gœtz, Paris, 9 January [1856]. Indeed Récamier even lent Sophie Barat money in a moment of difficulty. SB to Elianne de Cuënot, Rome, 25 May 1851; SB to Madame Récamier, Paris, 30 June 1852.

81 SB to Eugénie de Gramont, [Chambéry], 1 January 1831.

82 SB to Eugénie de Gramont, [Chambéry], 16 January 1831.

83 SB to Eugénie de Gramont, [Chambéry], 30 January 1831.

84 SB to Eugénie de Gramont, [Chambéry], 8 January 1831.

85 SB to Eugénie de Gramont, Chamb[éry], 22 March 183; Chamb[éry], 3 April 1831; Aix, 8 April (1831).

86 SB to Eugénie de Gramont, Aix, 6 April 1831; Chambéry, 14 April 1831, 19 April 1831. Notes des passages de notre . . . Mère Générale au Sacré-Cœur de Chambéry, 1818–1842 (AF Poitiers, B08, 114/115).

87 SB to Eugénie de Gramont, Chambéry, 23 April 1831; Chambéry, 3 May 1831; Aix, 4 May 1831; Aix, 14 May 1831; Aix, 19 May 1831; Aix, 29 May 1831.

88 SB to Eugénie de Gramont, Aix, 27 July 1831; Aix, 2 August 1831, 3 August 1831.

89 SB to Eugénie de Gramont, Paris, 21 September 1817; Lyon, 13 June 1818; Grenoble, 22 June 1818; Grenoble, 18 July 1818; Grenoble, 11 August 1818; Grenoble, 24 August 1818.

90 SB to Eugénie de Gramont, Bordeaux, 12 June 1825; Niort, 4 July 1825.

91 SB to Eugénie de Gramont, [Chambéry], 1 January 1831; Aix, 29/30 May 1831; Chambéry, 3 September 1831, 7 September 1831, 8 September 1831; Lyon, 13 January 1832. Passim.

92 SB to Eugénie de Gramont, Chambéry, 3 September 1831. Also, SB to Henriette Grosier, Chambéry, 11 September 1831.

93 SB to Eugénie de Gramont, Chambéry, 11 September 1831.

94 SB to Eugénie de Gramont, Payerne, 15 September 1831.

95 SB to Eugénie de Gramont, Middes, 17 September 1831, 19 September 1831.

96 SB to Stanislas Dusaussoy, Besançon, 11 October 1831.

97 SB to Eugénie de Gramont, Tarrare, 22 November 1831. Passim, winter–spring 1831–2.

98 SB to Adelaide de Rozeville, Aix, 8 May 1832. Cahier, *Vie de la . . . Mère Madeleine-Sophie Barat*, vol. i, pp. 564–5.

99   Notes dictées par . . . [Louise] de Limminghe, sur les voyages de notre . . . mère
     fondatrice, f. 7 (GA, Rome, C-I, A, 1-c, Box 1). Louise de Limminghe states that
     Sophie Barat's right foot was treated. Rossi indicates he treated the left foot.
     Chevalier Rossi, Turin, 15 August 1832. Témoignage autographe du chevalier Rossi
     sur la guérison de la Mère Barat à Turin en 1832 (GA, Rome, C-I, A, 1-d, Box 1).
100 SB to Eugénie de Gramont, Turin, 16 June 1832.
101 SB to Eugénie de Gramont, Turin, 1 June 1832; SB to Emilie Giraud, Turin, 17
     June 1832; SB to Henriette Grosier, Turin, 2 July 1832; also, Turin, 15 August
     1832; SB to Stanislas Dusaussoy, Turin, 30 June 1832. Cahier, *Vie de la . . . Mère
     Madeleine-Sophie Barat*, vol. i, pp. 566–9. SB to Eugénie de Gramont, Turin, 18
     June 1832; Turin, 6 August 1832.
102 Kilroy, *Madeleine Sophie Barat*, pp. 210–19.
103 Joseph-Marie Favre to Sophie Barat, Chambéry, 27 August 1832.
104 Louise de Limminghe was a member of the Society and a trusted friend of both.
105 SB to Eugénie de Gramont, Turin, 6 August 1832.
106 SB to Louise de Limminghe, Rome, 26 February 1833; Rome, 2 March 1833;
     Rome, 21 March 1833; Rome, 26 March 1833. SB to Adelaide de Rozeville, Rome,
     14 March 1833. Also, Joseph-Marie Favre to Sophie Barat, Tamié par Conflans, 12
     January 1834.
107 SB to Henriette Grosier, Lyon, 25 January 1835; Jette, 27 June 1835.
108 SB to Eugénie de Gramont, Rome, 2 May 1837; also, SB to Henriette Grosier,
     Rome, 16 May 1837; SB to Eugénie de Gramont, Rome, 12 August 1837.
109 SB to Henriette Grosier, Turin, 4 November 1836; Rome, 23 February 1838; Rome,
     20 March 1838; Paris, 16 October 1838; Rome, 14 October 1839; Paris, 27 March
     1841.
110 Joseph-Marie Favre to Sophie Barat, Albertville, 14 February 1837.
111 SB to Eugénie Audé, Rome, 23 December 1837.
112 SB to Louise de Limminghe, [Rome], 24 January 1838.
113 SB to Eugénie de Gramont, Rome, 15 February 1838; SB to Henriette Grosier,
     Rome, 26 February 1838, and Rome, 20 March 1838; SB to Eugénie de Gramont,
     Rome, 25 April 1838. For comments on the diet, SB to Louise de Limminghe,
     Turin, 9 June 1838.
114 SB to Louise de Limminghe, Parma 25 May 1838.
115 SB to Louise de Limminghe, Parma, 2 June 1838.
116 SB to Louise de Limminghe, Turin, 8 June 1838.
117 SB to Louise de Limminghe, Turin, 9 June 1838; Turin, 11 June 1838; Turin, 13
     June 1838; Turin, 16 June 1838; Turin, 21 June 1838; Turin, 27 June 1838; Turin,
     28 June 1838.
118 SB to Louise de Limminghe, Turin, 27 June 1838.
119 SB to Louise de Limminghe, Turin, 2 July 1838.
120 SB to Louise de Limminghe, Lyon, 12 July 1838; Lyon, 13 July 1838; Lyon, 14 July
     1838.
121 SB to Henriette Grosier, La Ferrandière (Lyon), 16 July 1938.
122 SB to Louise de Limminghe, La Ferrandière (Lyon), 27 July 1838.
123 SB to Louise de Limminghe, La Ferrandière (Lyon), 30 July 1838; La Ferrandière
     (Lyon), 1 August 1838.
124 SB to Louise de Limminghe, Autun, 19 August 1838; Autun, 27 August 1838.
125 SB to Louise de Limminghe, Paris, 31 August 1838. Also, SB to Hypolite Lavauden,
     Autun, 20 August 1838.

126 Kilroy, *Madeleine Sophie Barat*, pp. 262–78.

127 SB to Louise de Limminghe, Paris, 5 September 1838; Paris, 7 September 1838; Paris, 11 September 1838.

128 SB to Louise de Limminghe, Paris, 18 (bis) September 1838; Paris, 24 September 1838.

129 SB to Louise de Limminghe, Paris, 17 and 18 September 1838.

130 SB to Louise de Limminghe, Paris, 26 November 1838.

131 SB to Henriette Grosier, Paris, 16 October 1838. Also, SB to Louise de Limminghe, Paris, 12 October 1838; Paris, 14 October 1838.

132 Kilroy, *Madeline Sophie Barat*, Chapters 15–20.

133 SB to Louise de Limminghe, Paris, 13 February 1839; Paris 15 February 1839; Montet, 10 March 1839. SB to Elizabeth Galitzine, Montet, 12 March 1839; Montet, 24 March 1839.

134 SB to Louise de Limminghe, Montet, 23 March 1839; Rome, 4 May 1839.

135 SB to Henriette Grosier, Rome, 14 November 1839.

136 SB to Henriette Grosier, Rome, 8 May 1840; SB to Adèle Lehon, Rome, 29 April 1840.

137 SB to Louise de Limminghe, Parma, 30 August, 1840; La Ferrandière, 18 September 1840; Paris, 7 October 1840.

138 SB to Eugénie Audé, Paris, 6 November 1840.

139 SB to Eugénie de Gramont, Paris (rue Monsieur), 13 October 1840.

140 SB to Eugénie Audé, Paris, 13 March 1841. Also, SB to Henriette Grosier, Paris, 27 March 1841.

141 SB to Eugénie Audé, Paris, 6 April 1841. SB to Louise de Limminghe, Paris, 22 May 1841.

142 SB to Eugénie Audé, Paris, 23 May 1841; Paris, 26 May 1841; Paris, 15 June 1841. SB to Henriette Grosier, Paris, 5 June 1841. Eulalie de Bouchaud to the Comtesse de Roissy, Paris, 5 June 1841. (AF Poitiers, A33, II. La Fondatrice et ses écrits. Lettres reçues par Armandine de Castillion de St Victor, Vicomtesse de Roissy et la Marquise de Calvière, Paris, Lettre no. xxiv.)

143 SB to Eulalie de Bouchaud, Amiens, 20 June 1841; Amiens, 21 June 1841; Amiens, 24 June 1841; Lille, 27 June 1841; Lille, 30 June 1841; Lille, 2 July 1841; SB to Anna du Rousier, Lille, 2 July 1841.

144 SB to Elizabeth Galitzine, Lille, 1 July 1841. Also, SB to Louise de Limminghe, 28 June 1841.

145 SB to Eulalie de Bouchaud, Jette, 9 July 1841; Jette, 19 July 1841; Jette, 22 July 1841. SB to Eugénie de Gramont, Jette, 9 July 1841; Jette, 21 July 1841. SB to Adèle Lehon, Jette, 17 July 1841.

146 SB to Eulalie de Bouchaud, Jette, 16 July 1841; Jette, 17 July 1841; Jette, 24 July 1841.

147 SB to Elizabeth Galitzine, Jette, 16 July 1841.

148 SB to Eulalie de Bouchaud, Beauvais, 7 August 1841; SB to Eugénie de Gramont, Beauvais, 9 August 1841.

149 SB to Stanislas Dusaussoy, Autun, 20 September 1841. Also, SB to Eulalie de Bouchaud, Autun, 19 September 1841.

150 Beer was suggested as a help for digestion and Sophie wondered what Dr Récamier would advise. SB to Eulalie de Bouchaud, La Ferrandière, 2 October 1841.

151 SB to Louise de Limminghe, Rome, 15 April 1842; Rome, 16 April 1842; Rome, 17 April 1842; SB to Eulalie de Bouchaud, Rome, 1 March 1842; Rome, 9 March 1842.

152 SB to Eulalie de Bouchaud, Rome, 3 December 1841; Rome, 16 December 1841.

153 SB to Eulalie de Bouchaud, Rome, 1 March 1842.

154 SB to Eugénie de Gramont, Rome, 7 February 1842.

155 SB to Louise de Limminghe, Rome, 12 February 1842.

156 SB to Louise de Limminghe, Rome, 15 April 1842; 16 April 1842; 17 April 1842.

157 SB to Elizabeth Galitzine, Rome, 9 December 1839; SB to Eulalie de Bouchaud, Rome, 13 January 1842; SB to Adèle Lehon, [no date] April 1842; SB to Louise de Limminghe, Rome, 12 January 1842.

158 SB to Eugénie Audé, Jette, 15 July 1841.

159 SB to Stanislas Dusaussoy, Jette, 15 July 1841. Also, SB to Elizabeth Galitzine, Paris, 7 September 1841.

160 Elizabeth Galitzine to Louise de Limminghe, Lyon, 4 September 1842.

161 Kilroy, *Madeleine Sophie Barat*, Chapter 18.

162 In the course this process, Césaire Mathieu acted as negotiator and friend. The extensive correspondence between Sophie Barat and Césaire Mathieu over the months of September 1842 to June 1843 is in the General Archives in Rome.

163 SB to Eugénie de Gramont, Besançon, 30 July 1843.

164 SB to Charlotte Gould, Conflans, 19 May 1844; Adèle Cahier, *Vie de la . . . Mère Madeleine-Sophie Barat*, vol. ii, pp. 125–30.

165 SB to Adèle Lehon, Lille, 8 July 1844.

166 *Lettres Circulaires*, vol. ii, Marseille, 16 Janvier 1845, p. 198; SB to Matilde Kersabie, La Ferrandière, 23 November 1844.

167 SB to Eugénie de Gramont, Aix, 7 January 1845. Also SB to Charlotte Goold, 5 January 1845.

168 SB to Césaire Mathieu, Aix, 8 January 1845. Also, 'Notes en Forme de Journal', ff. 14–15. Cahier, *Vie de la . . . Mère Madeleine-Sophie Barat*, vol. ii, pp. 131–3; SB to Eugénie de Gramont, La Ferrandière, 21 November 1844; Aix, 3 January 1845; St Joseph [Marseille], 15 January 1845; SB to Eugénie de Gramont, Rome, 28 March 1845.

169 SB to Eugénie de Gramont, Rome, 5 February 1845.

170 SB to Eugénie de Gramont, Rome, 28 March 1845.

171 SB to Eugénie de Gramont, Conflans, 14 January 1846.

172 SB to Eugénie de Gramont, Paris, 24 January 1846; SB to Anne Marie Granon, Paris, 9 February 1846.

173 Sophie Barat to Eugénie de Gramont, Grenoble, 23 August 1818.

174 Sauve, *Le Dr Récamier*, pp. 175–6.

175 SB to Stanislas Dusaussoy, Paris, 19 February 1848; Paris, 27 February 1848; Paris, 5 March 1850; SB to Amélie Jouve, Paris, 17 June 1850; Paris, 12 April 1858; Paris, 30 January 1863; Paris, 2 October 1863; SB to Eliane Cuënot, Paris, [no date; end of] August, 1854; Paris, 3 January 1855; SB to Euphémie Josset, Paris, 21 January 1855; Paris, 6 April 1858; Paris, 5 January 1861; Paris, 10 December 1861; SB to Josephine de Coriolis, Paris, 22 March 1856; Paris, 10 May 1856; Paris, 2 November 1856; Paris, [no date] January 1857; SB to Euphémie Josset, 6 April 1858; SB to Julia Prost, Paris, 15 June 1858. SB to Eliane Cuënot, Paris, 27 June 1858; SB to Stanislas Dusaussoy, Paris, 13 March 1860; Paris, 10 April 1860; SB to Adèle Lehon, Paris, 24 March 1860; Paris, 31 March 1860 (right foot very painful); SB to Esther d'Oussières, Paris, 16 November 1860; SB to Euphémie Josset, Paris, 5 January 1861. Notes de la Soeur Victorine [Godefroy], Paris, Janvier 1869, ff. 7–8 (GA, Rome, C-I, A-1-d, Box 2).

176 SB to Stanislas Dusaussoy, Paris, 7 January 1858. In June 1858 Sophie Barat noted that she had an accident which required minor surgery. SB to Eliane Cuënot, Paris, 27 June 1858; SB to Euphémie Josset, Paris, 21 June 1858. Passim.

177 SB to Julia Prost, Paris, 14 April 1859.

178 SB to Camille Sappey, Paris, 16 October 1862.

179 SB to Sophie Dusaussoy, Paris, 16 February 1857. Also, SB to Louise de Limminghe, Paris, 7 July 1830. 'Procès de Madame Barat, 1–28 Mai 1872', f. 471 (Archives de l'Archidiocèse de Paris); SB to Adèle Lehon, Paris, 6 February 1857; Paris, 12 March 1859.

180 SB to Sophie Dusaussoy, Paris, 20 February 1863.

181 When Agnes Verney died in June 1863 Sophie said that no one in Paris could make the gougère properly. She wrote to her niece, Zoe Cousin, in Joigny and asked her to send the recipe to Paris. SB to Zoe Cousin, Paris, 29 June 1863; Paris, 10 June 1863; Paris, 23 June 1863.

182 SB to Amélie Jouve, Paris, 30 January 1863; SB to Stanislas Dusaussoy, Paris, 14 February 1863.

183 SB to Esther d'Oussières, Paris, 9 January 1864; Paris, 13 January 1864; SB to Eulalie de Chezelles, 26 February 1865; SB to Camille Sappey, Paris, 6 March 1865.

184 SB to Stanislas Dusaussoy, Paris, 22 March 1862. Passim.

185 Lettres Circulaires de . . . Marie-Joséphine Goetz, Paris, 2 Juin 1865, pp. 1–8. Sophie asked not to be buried until three days after her death, and this request was honoured. Her funeral took place on Monday 29 May 1865 in the rue de Varenne and she was laid to rest in Conflans.

186 Frederick Holmes, MA, MD, FACP, Hashinger Distinguished Professor of Medicine Emeritus, University of Kansas Medical Center, has spent most of his career as a consultant physician in academic medical centres, while managing a large research programme in cancer epidemiology. Late in his career he sought a vocation for his retirement and studied British history with Professor John P. Kenyon. His thesis on the medical problems of the English Stuart monarchs was published as *The Sickly Stuarts: The Medical Downfall of a Dynasty* (Sutton, 2005). Presently he is Professor of the History and Philosophy of Medicine at the University of Kansas in the US. He finds particular pleasure in refining the medical diagnoses of historical figures.

187 Mary d'Apice is a doctor, psychotherapist and spiritual director and she combines these three disciplines in her professional work. She has been involved in education at secondary and tertiary levels, and as principal of the Catholic Women's Colleges of Sydney and Queensland Universities has been actively engaged with young adults. Her practice in psychotherapy has been largely with those in their middle and later years, concentrating especially on the impact of early-life experiences on psychological and personality development. She has been extensively involved in the therapy of victims of both physical and sexual abuse. Widely known for her workshops on Midlife and Ageing, she has lectured on these topics and directed retreats internationally. Her book, *Noon to Nightfall: A Journey through Midlife and Ageing* (Harper Collins, 2nd edition 1995) reflects her interest in this area. Mary d'Apice is a member of the Society of the Sacred Heart.

188 Kilroy, *Madeleine Sophie Barat*, p. 70.

189 Kilroy, *Madeleine Sophie Barat*, p. 214.

CHAPTER 5

1 A shorter version of this paper was given in November 2010, to mark the return of

Sophie Barat's remains from Brussels to the church of St Francois Xavier in Paris, opposite the Hôtel Biron, now the Rodin Museum.

2 Sophie Barat to Esther d'Oussières, Paris, 26 December 1853. Also, SB to Louise de Limminghe, Paris, 9 March 1859.

3 Jeanne de Charry noted that the letters of Sophie Barat, edited and published at the end of the nineteenth century, often had passages omitted, especially issues regarding Sophie Barat's family, her feelings or finance.

4 Sophie Barat's letters between 1804 and 1820, especially to Philippine Duchesne, Thérèse Maillucheau, Emilie Giraud and Adrienne Michel, track the early development of Sophie Barat as a spiritual leader.

5 SB to Louise de Limminghe, Paris, 2 October 1824.

6 Sophie Barat to Marie de la Croix, Paris, 22 August 1828. Also, SB to Marie Balastron, Amiens, 11 March 1809; SB to Hypolite Lavauden, Paris, 17 October 1838; SB to Marie de Tinseau, Conflans, 11 December 1845; SB to Emma de Bouchaud, Conflans, 17 Juillet 1849; SB to Onésime de Curzon, Paris, 19 August 1846 and 6 December 1856; SB to Eléanore Clifford, Paris, 24 June 1847; SB to Jeanne Cabagni, Paris, 19 November 1852; Paris, 21 March 1853; SB to Marie Dieudonnée, Paris, 30 September 1855; SB to Stéphanie Cardon Paris, 8 November 1856; SB to Adèle Lehon, Paris, 8 January 1859; SB to Adèle Lehon, Paris, 25 August 1860; SB to Sidonie de la Roulière, Paris, 23 March 1862; Paris, 24 September 1862; Paris, 1 May 1863; Paris, 24 August 1863; SB to Clémence de la Roulière, Paris, 27 March 1862; Paris, 26 August 1863; Paris, 16 September 1863; Paris, 21 September 1863.

7 SB to Marie de la Croix (at Lemberg), Conflans, 30 September 1845. Also, SB to Susanne Geoffroy, Paris, 27 July 1821; SB to Aimée d'Avenas, Poitiers, 2 January 1849; Poitiers, 22 January 1849; Paris, 8 April 1859; SB to Sophie Dudrunska, Paris, 25 July 1860; Paris, 11 October 1862.

8 SB to Alexandrine de Riencourt, Paris, 23 October 1828. Also, SB to Marie d'Olivier, Paris, 24 December 1828; SB to Adeline Assailly, Paris, 12 April 1858; SB to Sophie Dudrunska, Paris, 11 October 1862; Paris, 18 October 1862; Paris, 25 October 1862.

9 SB to Josephine Buesan, Conflans, 13 December 1845. Also, SB to Louise Combalot, Paris, 13 October 1838; SB to Eugénie de Bouchaud, Paris, 27 August 1852.

10 SB to Alida Dumazeaud, La Ferrandière, 12 January 1852. Also, SB to Alida Dumazeaud, Quadrille (Bordeaux), 23 November 1848; Paris, 13 June 1849; SB to Adèle Davidoff, Montet, 25 August 1836; SB to Eulalie de Bouchaud, Rome, 21 February 1837; SB to Valerie de Bosredont, Rome, 26 May 1845; SB to Stanislas Verhulst (Manhattanville), Paris, 23 April 1856; SB to Constance Thomassin, Paris, 21 May 1858.

11 SB to Irène de Ferry, Paris, 15 September 1862. Also, SB to Elisa de Bouchaud, Paris, 13 November 1862; [Paris], 29 October [1864].

12 SB to Irène de Ferry, Paris, 29 October 1856. Also, SB to Irène de Ferry, Paris, 26 November 1856; SB to Rosalie Debrosse, Paris, 25 May 1852.

13 SB to Eliane Cuënot, La Ferrandière, 29 December [1851]. Also, SB to Eliane Cuënot, La Ferrandière, 30 December 1851; SB to Gertrude de Brou, [Paris], 15 August [1854].

14 SB to Eliane Cuënot, Paris, 27 November 1862.

15 SB to Marie de Tinseau, Paris, 18 September 1858. Also, SB to Emma de Bouchaud, Paris, 1 June 1849; SB to Amélie de Savonnières, Paris, 20 August 1849; SB to Elisa

de Bouchaud, Paris, 18 February 1851. Correspondence of SB with Aloysia Hardey and with Ana du Rousier, particularly after 1842.

16 SB to Elizabeth Galitzine, Rome, 6 February 1838. SB to Louise de Limminghe, Avignon, 19 March 1832.

17 SB to Eliane Cuënot, Paris, 18 September 1856.

18 SB to Noémi de Gères, Paris, 29 July 1849.

19 SB to Louise de Limminghe, Paris, 25 February 1852. See also SB to Louise de Limminghe, Rome, 19 February 1833; La Ferrandière, 13 January 1852; Paris, 25 September 1853. SB to Victoire de Joigny de Pamèle, Conflans, 20 November 1845. Passim.

20 SB to Alida Dumazeaud, Paris, 22 March 1853. Also, SB to Emma de Bouchaud, Paris, 1 June 1849; SB to Cécile de Chalais, Rome, 3 April 1845. Passim.

21 SB to Adèle Lehon, Paris, 12 May 1860.

22 SB to Adèle Lehon, Paris, 4 August 1860. Also, SB to Aloysia Jouve, Paris, 12 November 1857. SB to Alida Dumazeaud, Paris, 21 July 1835; Besançon, 7 August 1843; Paris, 16 April 1844. To a superior battling with depression, SB to Emma de Bouchaud, Aix, 5 January 1845; Rome, 22 April 1845; Paris, 12 March 1852; Paris, 4 November 1854.

23 SB to Adrienne Michel, Paris, 31 March 1816. Sophie Barat cites the letters of St Paul to the Romans (6. 3–4), and to the Colossians (3.3). She underlines the quotations in her letter. Also, SB to Madeleine de Chastaignier, Grenoble, 15 May 1813.

24 SB to Louise de Limminghe, Chambéry, Easter, 2 April 1831. Also, SB to Louise Combalot, Rome, 3 April 1842; SB to Alexandrine de Riencourt, [Avignon], 2 April 1832; Rome, 4 April 1845; SB to Eulalie de Bouchaud, Rome, 28 March 1840; SB to Eugénie de Gramont, Rome, 22 April 1842; SB to Emma de Bouchaud, Paris, 15 April 1843; Paris, 25 April 1843; SB to Elisa de Bouchaud, Paris, 22 April 1846 and Paris, 24 June 1855; SB to Clémence de la Roulière, Paris, Good Friday, 6 April 1849; SB to Jeanne Cabagni, Paris, 31 May 1858; Paris, [nd] April 1859; Paris, 24 October 1859; SB to Adèle Gérard, Paris, 14 April 1861.

25 SB to Louise de Limminghe, Paris, 4 April 1853. Also, SB to Césarie de Bouchaud, Paris, 14/18 October 1850; Paris, 19 January 1863. For the reference to Teresa of Avila, see *The Interior Castle*, vol. V, Chapter 2; also Chapter 3.

26 SB to Marie de Tinseau, Paris, 3 November 1853. Also, SB to Louise de Limminghe, Paris, 17 March 1853; SB to Emma de Bouchaud, Paris, 20 July 1859.

27 SB to Marie de Tinseau, Paris, 22 March 1853. Also, SB to Eulalie de Bouchaud, Rome, 28 March 1840; SB to Marie de Tinseau, Paris, 21 March 1855; Paris, 6 April 1862; SB to Emma de Bouchaud, Paris, 14 May 1859; SB to Sophie Dudrunska, Paris, 8 October 1862.

28 SB to Valérie de Bosredont, Paris, 27 July 1853. The feast of Mary Magdalene is on 22 July.

29 SB to Blanche Ghirelli, Paris, Good Friday 1865. Blanche Ghirelli (1836–1908) was born in Rome and entered the Society in 1855. She was an artist. In 1865 she was a young professed (aspirant) at the rue de Varenne; she was finally professed in 1867. SB to Alix de St Victor, Paris, 6 June 1864. In 1904 Blanche Ghirelli remarked: 'Only now . . . I am beginning to understand more clearly what she was calling me to.' She attempted a portrait of Sophie Barat, probably after Sophie's death. This appears to be unknown.

30 Kilroy, *Madeleine Sophie Barat*, pp. 192–6. SB to Elisa de Bouchaud, Paris, 27

November 1852; Paris, 24 May 1855; SB to Esther d'Oussières, Paris, 8 June 1858; Paris, 31 July 1863. SB to Adèle Davidoff, Montet, 26 September 1836; Turin, 31 October 1836; Paris, 7 May 1837; Rome, 17 September 1839; Rome, 9 February 1845; Amiens, 12 August 1850; Paris, 4 September 1864. SB to Alix de St Victor, Paris, 15 January 1863; Paris, 17 March 1863; Paris, 9 June 1864.

31 SB to Madame Tallandier de Chaudeney, Paris, 11 June 1852. On the other hand, Anne Marie Ganon became terminally ill soon after she entered the Society. She worried about her mother in the event of her death, and Sophie Barat assured her that the Society would care for her, if necessary until death. SB to Anne Marie Ganon, Amiens, 1 August 1841.

32 SB to Marie Tallandier, Paris, 15 June 1852. Sophie Barat counselled Marie Tallandier that the offer of marriage she had received was very positive and should be considered seriously. SB to Marie Tallandier, Paris, 21 June 1852; Paris, 5 July 1852; Paris, 25 October 1852; Paris, 20 January 1853. Marie Tallandier decided to enter the Society.

33 SB to Emma de Bouchaud, Paris, 23 May 1849; Paris, 25 May 1849; Paris, 29 May 1849; Paris, 11 July 1849; Conflans, 17 July 1849.

34 SB to Eulalie de Bouchaud, Montet, 12 March 1839; SB to Louise de Limminghe, Paris, 16 April 1855; SB to Aimée d'Avenas, Paris, 25 November 1859; SB to Elisa de Bouchaud, Paris, 20 December 1862.

35 SB to Matilde Kersabie, Paris, 24 September 1845. Also, SB to Olympie Romabu, Paris, 6 October 1855.

36 SB to Matilde Kersabie, Bordeaux, 26 October 1848; also, SB to Matilde Kersabie, Paris, 19 August 1851. Their correspondence continued until October 1864. Sophie Barat's letters to those who left the Society are held in the General Archives in Rome.

37 SB to Eugénie de Gramont, Rome, 15 February 1838. Also, SB to Eliza Croft, Paris, 31 December 1845. For the vocation of Antonine de Maudajor, SB to the Marquise de Calvière, Paris, 22 May 1844. Eugénie de Gramont to the Marquise de Calvière, Paris, 22 August 1844 (AF Poitiers, A33, II. La Fondatrice et ses écrits. Lettres reçues par Armandine de Castillion de St Victor, Vicomtesse de Roissy and the Marquise de Calvière, Paris, Lettre nos xxvii, xxviii).

38 SB to Eulalie de Bouchaud, Rome, 15 February 1840. Also, SB to Gertrude de Brou, Paris, 22 June 1855.

39 SB to Elizabeth Galitzine, Rome, 19 January 1842. See also SB to Adèle Lehon, Paris, 4 August 1860 and Paris, 11 August 1860. SB to Alida Dumazeaud, Paris, 22 March 1853.

40 *Lettres Circulaires*, vol. ii, Paris, 10 February 1844, pp. 169–71. See also *Lettres Circulaires*, vol. ii, Conflans, 29 December 1845, pp. 200–2; Paris, 5 April 1848, p. 224.

41 SB to Thérèse Maillucheau, Lille, 5 July 1844.

42 SB to Matilde Garabis (Kientzheim), Paris, 15 March 1849; SB to Alida Dumazeaud, Berrymead (England), 23 June 1844; SB to Sophie Dudrunska, Paris, 4 August 1859; Paris, 24 August 1859; Paris, 25 July 1860; Paris, 8 August 1860.

43 SB to Joséphine de Coriolis, Paris, 1 December 1856; Paris, 19 December 1856; Paris, 25 January 1857; SB to Gertrude de Brou, Paris, 3 June [1857]; Paris, 4 July 1857. SB to Onésime de Curzon, Poitiers, 20 January 1849; SB to Onésime de Curzon, Paris, 6 December 1856. SB to Alida Dumazeaud, Paris, 13 December 1851; Paris, 14 March 1864; SB to Valerie de Bosredont, Paris, 31 January 1852; Paris, 16 May 1859; Paris, 5 July 1860; SB to Adèle Lehon, Paris, 4 August 1860;

Paris, 11 August 1860. SB to Esther d'Oussières, Paris, 8 December 1857; Paris, 26 January 1863; Paris, 13 January 1864; SB to Maria Cutts, Paris, 2 May 1844; SB to Philippine Duchesne, Paris, 16 September 1849; Paris, 16 February 1852. Passim.

44 SB to Aimée d'Avenas, Paris, 14 December 1858. Also, SB to Aimée d'Avenas, Paris, 13 December 1852 and Paris, 13 December 1853. Also SB to Louise de Limminghe, La Ferrandière, 13 December 1851; Paris, 19 December 1857. Also, SB to Louise de Limminghe, La Ferrandière, 13 December 1851.

45 Kilroy, *Madeleine Sophie Barat*, pp. 7–10.

46 SB to Stanislas Dusaussoy, Turin, 9 July 1832.

47 *Manuel du Chrétien, Contenant les Psaumes, le Nouveau Testament et l'Imitation de Jésus Christ: De la Tradition de M le Maître de Saci* (Paris, 1751). Sophie wrote her name inside the front cover in large, childish handwriting; Cahier, *Vie de la . . . Mère Madeleine-Sophie Barat*, vol. i, pp. 8–9. Deshayes, 'Notes sur notre . . . Fondatrice et les Commencements de la Société', f. 4; de Coriolis, 'Histoire de la Société', f. 31.

48 Dale K. Van Kley, *The Religious Origins of the French Revolution: From Calvin to the Civil Constitution, 1560–1791* (Yale, 1996); *Le Jansénisme dans l'Yonne: Les Cahiers des Archives no. 4* (Auxerre, 1986); Edmond Franjou, *La Querelle Janséniste à Joigny et dans le Jovinien au XVIIIe Siècle*, première partie (Auxerre, 1970).

49 Franjou, *La Querelle Janséniste à Joigny et dans le Jovinien au XVIIIe Siècle*, pp. 3–11, 30–45, 51–81. Also, Kilroy, *Madeleine Sophie Barat*, pp. 11–13.

50 Perdrau, *Les Loisirs de l'Abbaye*, vol. i, p. 165.

51 Récit de la Mère Barat . . . 30 Mai 1856 (GA, Journal de la Probation 1855–1856, 36); de Charry, Histoire des Constitutions de la Société du Sacré-Cœur, vol. iii, Textes, no. 10, 89*, 89–90)

52 Van Kley, *The Religious Origins of the French Revolution*, pp. 114–18. It was widely believed that while awaiting execution in 1793 Louis XVI promised to dedicate France to the Sacred Heart. Certainly after the Revolution, devotion to the Sacred Heart was linked with those who worked for a restoration of the Bourbons.

53 Deshayes, 'Notes sur notre . . . Fondatrice et les Commencements de la Société'.

54 Michel, 'Journal du Second Voyage de . . . Mère Barat à Gand 1811'; Perdrau, *Les Loisirs de l'Abbaye*, vol. i, pp. 93, 165–7, 239, 375.

55 Un cas de possession diabolique à Joigny, en 1791 [1790]. Récit de l'abbé Fromentot in *L'Écho de Joigny*, no. 15 (1974), pp. 13–18. Deshayes, 'Premiers Jours de la Société', f. 5; Michel, 'Journal du Second Voyage de . . . Mère Barat à Gand 1811'. Later in life Sophie Barat spoke of these matters to her nephew, Stanislas Dusaussoy. SB to Stanislas Dusaussoy, Paris, 19 May 1853; Paris, 29 May 1853.

56 de Coriolis, 'Histoire de la Société', ff. 31–31v; Michel, 'Journal du Second Voyage de . . . Mère Barat à Gand 1811'; Cahier, *Vie de la . . . Mère Madeleine-Sophie Barat*, vol. i, p. 7.

57 Kilroy, *Madeleine Sophie Barat*, pp. 21–4; Perdrau, *Les Loisirs de l'Abbaye*, vol. i, pp. 170–1.

58 Deshayes, 'Notes sur notre . . . Fondatrice et les Commencements de la Société', f. 10.

59 Michel, 'Journal du Second Voyage de . . . Mère Barat à Gand 1811', f. 15; de Coriolis, 'Histoire de la Société', ff. 33–33v; 'Récits de . . . Thérèse Maillucheau (c. 1846)', f. 27.

60 Journal de Mantes, 1846,1848 et 1849, no. 11, Diverses anecdotes très intéressantes (AFSJ, Vanves, Fonds Varin); de Coriolis, 'Histoire de la Société', f. 25.

61 Kilroy, *Madeleine Sophie Barat*, Chapters 2–5.

62 [Abbé Lamarche à] Madame Barat, Cuignières, 17 Février 1816. The Abbé Lamarche was chaplain to the Carmelites of Compiègne. The community was guillotined during the Terror.

63 La Mère Barat présente à ses soeurs les nouvelles Constitutions, Paris, 17 Décembre 1815.

64 Joseph–Marie Favre, 1791–1838. Abbé Pont, *Vie de l'Abbé Favre, Fondateur des Missions de Savoie* (Montiers, 1865); François Bouchage, *Le Serviteur de Dieu, Joseph-Marie Favre, Maître et Modèle des Ouvriers Apostoliques, 1791–1838* (Paris, 1901); *Dictionnaire de Spiritualité, Fascicules CII–CIII* (Paris, 1992), pp. 120–1.

65 Bouchage, *Le Serviteur de Dieu*, p. 234. Louise de Limminghe was a member of the Society of the Sacred Heart.

66 Joseph-Marie Favre to Louise de Limminghe, Tamié par Conflans, 27 June 1834; Chambéry, 14 September 1833; Chambéry, 30 September [1833]; Chambéry, 24 November 1834; [np], October 1835; Albertville, 22 January 1836; Conflans, 24 December 1837.

67 Joseph-Marie Favre to Sophie Barat, Arith, 15 December 1824; also, Chambéry, 25 January 1832.

68 Joseph-Marie Favre to Louise de Limminghe, Chambéry, 5 May [1830/31/32]; Chambéry, 1 March 1827.

69 Joseph-Marie Favre to Sophie Barat, Chambéry, 27 August 1832.

70 Joseph-Marie Favre to Louise de Limminghe, Chambéry, 27 August 1832.

71 Joseph-Marie Favre to Sophie Barat, Tamié, par Conflans, 27 June 1834. Also, Tamié, par Conflans, 12 January 1834.

72 Joseph-Marie Favre to Sophie Barat, [nd], Tamié, par Conflans, July–September 1834.

73 Joseph-Marie Favre to Louise de Limminghe, Chambéry, 24 November 1834.

74 Joseph-Marie Favre to Sophie Barat, Albertville, 14 February 1837. He died in 1838.

75 Joseph-Marie Favre to Louise de Limminghe, Conflans, 24 December 1837.

76 For details of this crisis in the Society of the Sacred Heart, see Kilroy, *Madeleine Sophie Barat*, Chapters 15–20.

77 Archbishop Affre claimed he was the superior of the Society of the Sacred Heart and by right should have the official role of the cardinal protector, then held by Cardinal Pedicini in Rome. Manuscript evidence shows that Césaire Mathieu, Antonio Garibaldi, Gregory XVI, Luigi Lambruschini and some of the French episcopacy rejected Affre's claims and were shocked at his rudeness to Sophie Barat. They admired her firm refusal to cede to his demands. Before Affre died in 1848 he sent a message of apology to Sophie Barat, asking for forgiveness.

78 'From the retreat of 1839. Renewed in retreat of 1852 and 1855' (GA, Rome, C-I, A, 1-f, Box XVII, bis). The prayer is based on a text of the seventeenth-century Jesuit, Jacques Nouet (1605–1680), with Sophie's own additions. Cahier, *Vie de la . . . Mère Madeleine-Sophie Barat*, vol. ii, pp. 394–5. Before the 1839 Council Sophie Barat had premonitions of death. SB to Emilie Giraud, Rome, 16 May 1839. Also, SB to Henriette Ducis, Paris 18 March 1844.

79 Lettres Madeleine Sophie Barat et Césaire Mathieu (GA, Rome); Dossiers Dames du Sacré-Cœur, Boites 2476, 2477 (Archives de l'Archevêché de Besançon); Paul Poupard, *Correspondance Inédite entre Mgr Antonio Garibaldi, Internonce à Paris et Mgr Césaire Mathieu Archevêque de Besançon. Contribution à l'Histoire de l'Administration Ecclésiastique sous la Monarchie de Juillet* (Rome, 1961).

80 Césaire Mathieu to SB, Paris, 8 October 1842.

81 SB to Césaire Mathieu, Paris, 2 December 1842. See SB to Joséphine Bigeu, Paris, 9 May 1826; SB to Louise de Limminghe, Besançon, 16 September 1842; Lyon, 3 October 1842; Paris, 13 January 1843; Paris, 15 February 1843; SB to Emma de Bouchaud, Paris, 18 June 1853.

82 Césaire Mathieu to SB, Besançon, 6 December 1842. For a later comment, SB to Mary Josephine Thompson, Paris, 15 February 1852.

83 Césaire Mathieu to SB, Besançon, 21 December 1842.

84 Césaire Mathieu knew how difficult this task would be for Sophie Barat. Césaire Mathieu to B.U. du Trousset d'Héricourt (Bishop of Autun), Rome, 2 March 1843; Florence, 12 March 1843; Besançon, 10 April 1843 (Archives de l'Archevêché de Besançon, Boite 2476).

85 SB to Césaire Mathieu, [Paris, 15 February 1843].

86 Césaire Mathieu to SB, Rome, 17 February 1843. Also, Rome, 2 February 1843; Rome, 8 February 1843; Toulon, 26 March 1843.

87 Césaire Mathieu to SB, Florence, 10 March 1843.

88 *Lettres Circulaires*, vol. i, La Ferrandière, 13 Décembre 1851.

89 SB to Emma de Bouchaud, Paris, 18 June 1853.

90 SB to Elizabeth Giraud, Paris, 30 January 1857; SB to Adèle Gérard, Paris, 14 January 1861; SB to Clémence de la Roulière, Paris, 20 October 1862.

91 SB to Adelaide de Rozeville, Rome, 23 November 1839.

92 SB to Henriette Granon, Paris, 18 May 1859. Also, SB to Rosalie Debrosse, Paris, 10 July 1847; Paris, 25 May 1852; SB to Juliette Desoudin, Paris, 25 September 1863.

Bibliography

Select Manuscript Sources

Archives of the Society of the Sacred Heart, Rome[1]
Original letters of Madeleine Sophie Barat, October 1800–May 1865 (14,000+)
Transcriptions of the original letters (68 volumes)
Lettres Annuelles de la Société du Sacré-Cœur
Ménologes des religieuses du Sacré-Cœur
Minutes and Decrees of the General Councils of the Society of the Sacred Heart
Collected manuscripts and papers of Jeanne de Charry

Select Printed Primary Sources

Bouchage, François, *Le Serviteur de Dieu, Joseph-Marie Favre, Maître et Modèle des Ouvriers Apostoliques, 1791–1838* (Paris, 1901)

Baunard, Louis, *Histoire de Madame Barat, Fondatrice de la Société du Sacré-Cœur*, 2 vols (Paris, 1876)

Briand, Abbé, *Vie de Pauline de Saint André de la Laurencie de Villeneuve, de Saint-Jean-d'Angély* (La Rochelle, 1847)

[Cahier, Adèle], *Vie de la Vénérable Mère Madeleine-Sophie Barat, Fondatrice et Première Supérieure Générale de la Société du Sacré-Cœur*, 2 vols (Paris, 1884)

[Cahier, Adèle], *Vie de Marie Lataste, Sœur Coadjutrice de la Society du Sacré-Cœur* (Paris, 1866)

Charbonnel, Vie de la Mère [Catherine de] assistante et économe générale de la Société du Sacré-Cœur de Jésus (Paris, c.1870)

Calvimont, Comte Louis de, *Quelques Traits de la Vie et de la Mort de Madame Eugénie de Gramont: Extrait de la Quotidienne du 25 Janvier 1847*

Eyraud, J. *Conférence sur le Professeur Joseph-Claude-Anthelme Récamier* (Belley, 1913)

Geoffroy, *Vie de Madame* (Poitiers, 1854)

Gondran, Chanoine, *Éloge Historique de M. l'Abbé Favre en Joseph-Marie Favre: Théorie et Pratique de la Communion Fréquente et Quotidienne à l'Usage des Prêtres qui Exercent le Saint Ministère*, 2 tomes (Lyon, 1840)

Gœtz, Joséphine, *Première Lettres et Bulletins Relatifs à la Maladie et la Mort de Notre Vénérée Mère Fondatrice* [Mai 1865]

Gouraud, Henri, *Éloge de M. Récamier* (Paris, 1853)

Grandidier, P.F. *Vie du . . . Père Guidée de la Compagnie de Jésus* (Amiens/Paris, 1867)

Guidée, Achille, *Vie du R.P. Joseph Varin* (Paris, 1854)

[Lataste, Marie] *La Vie et les Oeuvres de Marie Lataste, Religieuse du Sacré-Cœur par M. L'Abbé Paschal Darbins*, 3 vols (Paris, 1862)

L.F. Guérin, *Mémorial Catholique, Février 1868: Une Vénérable Religieuse*

— *Vie de Marie Lataste par Marguerite Lataste, Sacré-Cœur, Rennes, 11 Novembre 1866* (GA, Rome, C-VII, 2, Lataste Box 2)

Vie du . . . Père Loriquet (Paris, 1845)

Manuel du Chrétien, Contenant les Psaumes, le Nouveau Testament et l'Imitation de Jésus Christ: De la Tradition de M le Maître de Saci (Paris, 1751)

Marcet, Martial, *Jésuites Modernes pour Faire Suite au Mémoire de M. le Comte de Montlosier* (Paris, 1826)

Mémoires, Souvenirs et Journaux de la Comtesse d'Agoult, 2 tomes (Le temps retrouvé, LVIII, Paris, 1990)

[NN] *Notice sur la Vie de Madame la Comtesse de, Née de Boisgelin* (Paris, 1836)

[Olivier, Marie d'], *Les Trois Paulines* (Lille, 1834); *L'Imagination ou Charlotte de Drelincourt* (Lille, 1858); *Dialogues des Vivants au XIXe Siècle* (Paris, 1859); *Lettres aux Jeunes Femmes du Monde Élégant* (Avignon, 1866)

Perdrau, Pauline, *Les Loisirs de l'Abbaye, Souvenirs inédits de . . . Pauline Perdrau sur la Vie de notre Sainte Mère*, 2 vols (Rome, 1934, 1936)

Pont, Abbé, *Vie de l'Abbé Favre, Fondateur des Missions de Savoie* (Montiers, 1865)

Reynaud, François-Dominique de, Comte de Montlosier, *Les Jésuites, les Congrégations et le Parti Prêtre, en 1827: Mémoire à M. le Comte de Villèle* (Paris, 1827)

Sauve, Louis, *Le Dr Récamier (1774–1852)* (Paris, 1838)

— *Notice sur le Révérend Père Léonor François de Tournél, et son oeuvre La Congrégation des Pères du Sacré-Cœur* (Vienne, 1886)

Triaire, Paul, *Récamier et ses Contemporains, 1774–1852: Étude d'Histoire de la Médecine aux XVIIIe et XIXe Siècles* (1899)

'Un Cas de Possession Diabolique à Joigny, en 1791 [1790]: Récit de l'Abbé Fromentot', *L'Écho de Joigny*, no. 15 (1974)

Virnot, Marie-Thérèse, (ed.), *Sainte Madeleine-Sophie Barat, Journal de Poitiers 1806–1808. Texte Intégral* (Poitiers, 1977)

SELECT CONTEMPORARY BIBLIOGRAPHY

Arnold, Odile, *Le Corps et l'Âme: La Vie Religieuse au XIXe Siècle* (Paris, 1984)

Bamforth, Ain (ed.), *The Body in the Library: A Literary Anthology of Modern Medicine* (London, 2003)

Bates, David W. *Enlightenment Aberrations: Error and Revolution in France* (Ithaca, NY, 2002)

Béthouart, Bruno, *Religion et Culture en Europe Occidentale de 1800–1914* (Nantes, 2001)

Boudon, Jacques-Olivier, *L'Épiscopat Français à l'Époque Concordaire, 1802–1905* (Cerf, 1996)

Brot Agnès et Borie, Guillemette de la, *Héroines de Dieu: L'Épopée des Religieuses Missionnaires du XIXème* (Paris, 2011)

Burton, Richard D.E. *Blood in the City: Violence and Revelation in Paris, 1789–1914* (Ithaca, NY, 2001)

Callan, Louise, *Philippine Duchesne: Frontier Missionary of the Sacred Heart, 1769–1852* (Maryland, 1957)

Callan, Louise, *The Society of the Sacred Heart in North America* (New York, 1937)

Charry, Jeanne de, *Histoire des Constitutions de la Société du Sacré-Cœur: La Formation de l'Institut*, 3 vols (Rome, 1975)

Charry, Jeanne de, *Histoire des Constitutions de la Société du Sacré-Cœur, Second Partie: Les Constitutions Définitives et leur Approbation par le Saint-Siège*, 3 vols (Rome, 1979)

Charry, Jeanne de (ed.), *Joseph Varin SJ, Lettres à Sainte Sophie Barat (1801–1849): Texte Intégral, d'après les manuscrits originaux, présenté avec une introduction, des notes et un index analytique* (Rome, 1982)

Charry, Jeanne de, *Évolution Canonique et Légale de la Société du Sacré-Cœur de Jésus de 1827 à 1853* (Rome, 1991)

Choudhury, Mita, *Convents and Nuns in Eighteenth-Century French Politics and Culture* (Ithaca, NY, 2004)

Conrad, Glenn R. (ed.), *Cross, Crozier and Crucible: A Volume Celebrating the Bicentennial of a Catholic Diocese in Louisiana* (New Orleans, 1993)

Curtis, Sarah A. *Civilizing Habits: Women Missionaries and the Revival of French Empire* (Oxford, 2010)

Davies, Natalie Zemon, *Women on the Margins, New Worlds: Marie de l'Incarnation* (Cambridge, MA, 1995)

Desan, Suzanne, The *Family on Trial in Revolutionary France* (California, 2006)

Doyle, William, *Aristocracy and its Enemies in the Age of Revolution* (Oxford, 2009)

Driskel, Michael Paul, *Representing Belief: Religion, Art and Society in Nineteenth-Century France* (Pennsylvania, 1992)

Dufourcq, Elizabeth, *Les Aventurières de Dieu: Trois Siècles d'Histoire Missionnaire Française*, 4 vols (Paris, ed. 2009)

Evangelisti, Silvia, *Nuns: A History of Convent Life* (Oxford, 2008)

Ford, Caroline, *Divided Houses* (Ithaca, NY, 2005)

Foster, Margaret, *Lady's Maid* (Harmondsworth, 1991)

Franche, Brigitte, *Marquoirs et Trousseaux en Bourgogne ou de l'Éducation des Filles* (Armançon, 2002)

Franjou, Edmond, *La Querelle Janséniste à Joigny et dans le Jovinien au XVIIIe Siècle* (Auxerre, 1970)

Fureix, Emmanuel, *La France des Larmes: Deuils Politiques à l'Âge Romantique, 1814–1840* (Champ Vallon, 2009)

Gibson, Ralph, *A Social History of French Catholicism* (London, 1989)

Girouard, Mark, *La Vie dans les Châteaux Français, du Moyen Age à nos Jours* (Paris, 2001); *Life in the French Country House* (London, 2001)

Goldberg, Rita, *Sex and Enlightenment: Women in Richardson and Diderot* (Cambridge, 1984)

Gough, Austin, *Paris and Rome: The Gallican Church and the Ultramontane Campaign 1848–1853* (Oxford, 1986)

Gueber, Jean, *Le Ralliement du Clergé Français à la Morale Liguorienne. L'Abbé Gousset et ses Précurseurs* (Rome, 1973)

Hamon, Léo (ed.), *Du Jansénisme à la Laïcité: Le Jansénisme et les Origines de la Déchristianisation* (Paris, 1987)

Heilbrun, Carolyn, *Writing a Woman's Life* (London, 1989)

Heilbrun, Carolyn, *Women's Lives: The View from the Threshold* (Toronto, 1999)

Hesse, Carla, *The Other Enlightenment: How French Women became Modern* (Princeton, NJ, 2003)

Heyden-Rynsch, Verena von der, *Salons Européens: Les Beaux Moments d'une Culture Féminine Disparue* (Luçon, 1993)

Hildesheimer, Françoise, *Le Jansénisme* (Paris, 1992)

Hufton, Olwen, *The Prospect Before Her: A History of Women in Western Europe*, vol. I, 1500–1800 (London, 1995)

Hufton, Olwen, *Women and the Limits of Citizenship* (Toronto, 1992)

Le Jansénisme dans l'Yonne. Les Cahiers des Archives No. 4 (Auxerre, 1986)

Jaurgain, Jean et Ritter, Raymond, *La Maison de Gramont, 1040–1967*, 2 vols (Les Amis du Musée Pyrénéen, 1968)

Jonas, Raymond, France *and the Cult of the Sacred Heart: An Epic Tale for Modern Times* (California, 2000)

Langlois, Claude, *Le Catholicisme au Féminin: Les Congrégations Françaises à Supérieure Générale au XIXe Siècle* (Paris, 1984)

Laven, Mary, *Virgins of Venice: Broken Vows and Cloistered Lives in the Renaissance Convent* (New York, 2004)

Lerner, Gerda, *The Creation of Feminist Consciousness: From the Middle Ages to Eighteen-Seventy* (Oxford, 1993)

Limouzin-Lamothe, R. *Monsignor de Quelen, Archevêque de Paris*, 2 tomes (Paris, 1955, 1957)

Limouzin-Lamothe, R. et Leflon, J. *Mgr Denys Affre, Archevêque de Paris, 1793–1848* (Paris, 1971)

Martin-Fugier, Anne, *La Vie Élégante ou la Formation du Tout-Paris, 1815–1848* (Paris, 1990)

Martin-Fugier, Anne, *La Place des Bonnes: La Domesticité Féminine à Paris en 1900* (Paris, 2004)

Martin, J.P. *La Nonciature de Paris et les Affaires Ecclésiastiques de France sous le Règne de Louis-Philippe, 1830–1848* (Paris, 1949)

Mayeur, Françoise, *L'Éducation des Filles en France au XIXe Siècle: Complément Bibliographique par Rebecca Rogers* (Paris, ed. 2008)

Maza, Sarah, *The Myth of the French Bourgeoisie: An Essay on the Social Imaginary* (Cambridge, MA, 2003)

Melville, Annabelle M. *Louis William Dubourg, Bishop of Louisiana and the*

Floridas, Bishop of Montauban and the Archbishop of Besançon, 1766–1833, 2 vols (Chicago, 1986)

Michel, Marie-José, *Jansénisme et Paris* (Paris, 2000)

Mooney, Catherine M. *Philippine Duchesne: A Woman with the Poor* (New Jersey, 1990)

Morrissey, Thomas, *As One Sent: Peter Kenny, SJ, 1779–1841* (Dublin, 1996)

Murphy, Gwenaël, *Les Religieuses dans la Révolution Française* (Bayard, 2005)

Naudet, Léopoldine, *Beatificationis et Canonizationis Servae Dei. Leopoldinae Naudet Fundatricis Sororum a Sacra Familia Veronae (1773–1834). Relatio et Vota. 5 Novembre 1996* (Rome, 1996)

Padberg, John W. *Colleges in Controversy: The Jesuit Schools in France from Revival to Suppression, 1815–1880* (Cambridge, MA, 1969)

Paisant, Chantal, *Litanie pour une None Défunte* (Cerf, 2003)

Paisant, Chantal, *Les Années Pionnières, 1818–1823: Lettres et Journaux des Premières Missionnaires du Sacré-Cœur aux États-Unis*. Textes rassemblés, établis et présenté par Chantal Paisant (Paris, 2001)

Peri-Morosini, Mons, *La Sainte Mère Madeleine Sophie Barat, Fondatrice de la Société du Sacré-Cœur et le Château de Middes en Suisse* (Toulouse, 1925)

Perrot, Michelle, *Mon Histoire des Femmes* (Seuil, 2006)

Perrot, Michelle, *Histoire des Chambres* (Seuil, 2009)

Porter, Roy, *The Greatest Benefit to Mankind: A Medical History of Humanity from Antiquity to the Present* (London, 1997)

Poupard, Paul, *Correspondance Inédite entre Mgr Antonio Antonio Garibaldi, Internonce à Paris, et Mgr Césaire Mathieu, Archevêque de Besançon: Contribution à l'Histoire de l'Administration Ecclésiastique sous la Monarchie de Juillet* (Rome, 1961)

Price, Munro, *The Perilous Crown: France between Revolutions, 1814–1848* (London, 2007)

Rémond, René, *L'Anticléricalisme en France: De 1815 à nos Jours* (Bruxelles, 1992)

Ribeton, Olivier, *Les Gramonts: Portraits de Famille, XVIe–XVIIIe Siècles* (Tours, 1992

Rogers, Rebecca, *From the Salon to the Schoolroom: Educating Bourgeois Girls in Nineteenth-Century France* (Pennsylvania, 2005)

Rogers, Rebecca, *Les Bourgeoises au Pensionnat: L'Éducation Féminine au XIXe Siècle* (Rennes, 2007)

Rogers, Rebecca, *Girls' Secondary Education in the Western World: From the 18th to the 20th Century*, with James Albisetti and Joyce Goodman, (London, 2010)

Sevrin, Ernest, *Les Missions Religieuses en France sous la Restauration, 1815–1879* (Paris, 1959)

Smith, Bonnie G. *Ladies of the Leisure Class: The Bourgeoisies of Northern France in the Nineteenth Century* (Princeton, NJ, 1981)

Sonnet, Martine, *L'Éducation des Filles au Temps des Lumières* (Paris, 1987)

Ulrich, Laurel Thatcher, *Well-Behaved Women Seldom Make History* (New York, 2007)

Vickery, Amanda, *Behind Closed Doors: At Home in Georgian England* (Yale, 2009)

Viéville, Dominique, *Guide de l'Hôtel Biron, Musée Rodin* (Paris, 2010)
Weber, Alison, *Teresa of Avila and the Rhetoric of Femininity* (Princeton, NJ, 1990)
Webster, Kathryn (ed.), The *Correspondence between Bishop Joseph Rosati and Blessed Philippine Duchesne* (St Louis, 1950)
Woolf, Virginia, *A Room of One's Own* (London, 1929)
Woolf, Virginia, *Three Guineas* (London, 1938)
Woodrow, Alain, *The Jesuits: A Study of Power* (London, 1995)

SELECT PERIODICALS/ARTICLES

Andress, David, 'The Shifting Landscape of Revolutionary Interpretations: A Death of the Past and a Rebirth of History?' *French Historical Studies*, vol. 32, no. 4 (Fall, 2009), pp. 647–53
Bourdin, Philippe, and Boutry, Philippe, 'L'Église Catholique en Révolution: L'Historiographique Récente', *Annales Historiques de la Révolution Française*, no. 1 (2009), pp. 3–23
Ford, Caroline, 'Private Lives and Public Order in Restoration France: The Seduction of Emily Loveday', *The American Historical Review*, vol. 99, no. 1 (February 1994), pp. 21–43
Frederking, Bettina, 'Il ne Faut Pas Être le Roi de Deux Peuples': Strategies of National Reconciliation in Restoration France', *French History*, vol. 22, no. 4 (December 2008), pp. 446–68
Gibson, Ralph, 'Le Catholicisme et les Femmes en France au XIXe Siècle', *RHEF*, tome LXXIX, no. 202 (Janvier–Juin, 1993)
Hufton, Olwen, 'Altruism and Reciprocity: The Early Jesuits and their Female Patrons', *Renaissance Studies*, vol. 15, no. 3 (September 2001), pp. 328–53
Hufton, Olwen and Tallett, Timothy, 'Communities of Women: The Religious Life, and Public Service in Eighteenth-Century France', *Connecting Spheres: European Women in a Globalizing World, 1500 to the Present* (Oxford, 2000)
Kilroy, Phil, 'The Use of Continental Sources of Women's Religious Congregations and the Writing of Religious Biography: Madeleine Sophie Barat, 1779–1865', in Maryann Gialanella Valiulis and Mary O'Dowd (ed.), *Women and Irish History* (Dublin, 1997), pp. 59–70
Kilroy, Phil, 'Les Archives de Congrégations Religieuses Féminines et la Rédaction d'Une Biographie: Exemple de Madeleine-Sophie Barat, 1779–1865', *Revue d'Histoire de l'Église de France*, tome 85, no. 215 (Juillet–Décembre 1999), pp. 359–71
Kley, Dale Van, 'The Rejuvenation and Rejection of Jansenism in History and Historiography: Recent Literature on Eighteenth–Century Jansenism in France', *French Historical Studies*, vol. 29, no. 4 (Fall, 2006), pp. 649–84
MacKnight, Elizabeth C. 'A "Theatre of Rule"? Domestic Service in Aristocratic Households under the Third Republic', *French History*, vol. 22, no. 3 (September 2008), pp. 316–36
Peri-Morosini, Alfredo, 'Sainte Sophie Barat et le Diocèse de Lausanne, Genève et Fribourg', *La Semaine Catholique de la Suisse Romande*, nos 20, 21, 22 (1952)
Reynier, Chantal, 'La Correspondance de P.J. de Clorivière avec T. Brzozowski,

1814 à 1818: Le Rétablissement de la Compagnie en France', *AHSI*, vol. LXIV (1995), pp. 83–167

Rogers, Rebecca, 'La Place de la Religion dans la Formation des Enseignantes Religieuses et Laïques avant les Années 1880', in Jean-François Condette (dir.), *Religion, Fait Religieux et Laïcité dans la Formation des Enseignants XVIe–XXe Siècles* (Lille, 2010)

Rogers, Rebecca, 'Retrograde or Modern? Unveiling the Nun in Nineteenth-Century France' *Social History*, vol. 23, no. 2 (May, 1998)

Rogers, Rebecca, 'Boarding Schools, Women Teachers and Domesticity: Reforming Girls' Secondary Education in the First Half of the Nineteenth Century', *French Historical Studies*, no. 19 (1995), pp. 153–81

Rogers, Rebecca, 'Competing Visions of Female Education in Post-Revolutionary France', *History of Education Quarterly* (Summer 1994)

Skinner, Simon, 'History Versus Hagiography: The Reception of Turner's *Newman*', *Journal of Ecclesiastical History*, vol. 61, no. 4 (2010), pp. 764–81

Stone, Judith F. 'Anticlericals and Bonnes Sœurs: The Rhetoric of the 1901 Law of Associations', *French Historical Studies*, vol. 23, no. 1 (Winter, 2000), pp. 109–11

Toulement, P.P. 'Les Écrits de Marie Lataste', *Études Religieuses, Historiques et Littéraires, par les Pères de la Compagnie de Jésus*, Nouvelle Série, no. 7 (Janvier–Février 1863), pp. 66–91

1 Since the General Archives of the Society of the Sacred Heart in Rome are extensive only essential references are included here. Details of the collection can be found in *Madeleine Sophie Barat. A Life*. The archives in Rome are classified in English. The archives of the Society in France, held in Poitiers, are classified in French.

Index

Affre, Denys-Auguste 155, 156, 158, 161, 191, 226
Aix-en-Provence 192
Aix-les-Bains 180, 181–3
Amiens 11, 12–15, 24–5, 27, 31–2, 36–7, 75, 86, 87–8, 137–8, 141–2, 146, 171–5, 189, 220–21
ancien régime 11, 14, 25, 67, 85, 131
Annals 89, 113–14, 120–22, 124–8, 130, 131
Annonay 191
Apice, Mary d' 197–200
Association of the Ladies of Christian Education 17, 19, 23, 137–9, 140; *see also* Society of the Sacred Heart
Audé, Eugénie 17, 39, 49, 188
Avenas, Aimée d' 67, 70
Avignon 191–2

Bailly, Octavie 11, 12
baking 32, 33
Balastron, Marie 16, 177
Barat, Jacques 11, 168, 169, 197, 216, 217
Barat, Louis 11–12, 42, 45–6, 141, 160, 169–72, 174, 195, 197–9, 216–19, 226
Barat, Madeleine Sophie
  in Aix-les-Bains 180, 181–3
  in Amiens 12, 15, 32–4, 171–5, 189, 220–21

appointed leader of Dilette di Gèsu 136, 172, 220
assigns duties 31–4
assigns ranks 51–4
in Beauvais 35
biographies of 2, 3–4, 5, 6
birth 169, 198, 216
in Bordeaux 19
canonisation 2–3, 201
childhood 168–70, 216–18
and the choir sisters 51–4, 70–71
and the clergy 134, 161
and the coadjutrix sisters 31–4, 51–4, 55–63, 72–7
correspondence: with Adelaide de Rozeville 178, 233; with Adèle Lehon 209–10; with Adrienne Michel 210; with Alexandrine de Riencourt 205; with Alida Dumazeaud 78, 205, 209; with Armande de Causans 144–5, 147–8; with Cécile de Chalais 76; with Césaire Mathieu 158, 159, 192, 228–30; with Eliane Cuënot 206–7, 208; with Elisa de Bouchaud 76; with Elizabeth Galitzine 64, 189, 207–8, 212, 215; with Emilie Giraud 174; with Emma de Bouchaud 232; with Esther d'Oussières 201; with Eugénie Audé 188; with Eugénie de Gramont 148, 178, 181, 182, 192–3, 212, 214;

with Eugénie Desmarquest 81; with Eulalie de Bouchaud 60–61, 215; with Henriette Granon 233; with Henriette Grosier 179, 187, 188; with Irène de Ferry 205–6; with Jan Roothaan 163–4; with Jean Rozaven 141–3; with Joseph Varin 5, 139, 152, 172; with Josephine Buesan 205; with Josephine de Coriolis 161, 215; with Joseph-Marie Favre 184, 185, 222, 223–5; with Louis de Sambucy de St Estève 138–9; with Louis Panazzoni 139; with Louise de Limminghe 60, 144, 148–51, 186, 208–9, 210–11, 212; with Maria Cutts 64; with Marie Balastron 177; with Marie de la Croix 204–5; with Marie de Tinseau 207, 211; with Marie-Louise Barat 176; with Marie Tallandier 213; with Matilde de Kersabie 214; with Matilde Garabis 215; with Noémi de Gères 208; overview 201–3; with Philippine Duchesne 5, 39–44, 50, 143, 173, 212, 220; with Pierre de Clorivière 140; publication of 4–5; with the Society 62, 64, 215, 221; with Sophie Dusaussoy 193; with Stanislas Dusaussoy 82, 183, 189, 191, 193; with Thérèse Maillucheau 64, 88, 175, 176, 177; use of citations 203
creation of the Society 1, 7, 10, 15–21, 137–40
death 194–5, 197
death of mother 177
diet 167–8, 186, 187, 190, 193–4, 218–19; *see also* fasting
discernment of vocations 52–4, 56–7, 64–5, 67, 77, 212–16
and education 70–71, 88, 90, 91–2
education of 22, 169–71, 218–19
elected as superior general 25–6, 137, 173, 175, 220
in England 191
and the finances of the Society 68–9, 71, 177
and friendship 81–2, 141, 200, 220

and the General Council of 1839: 55–6, 58–65, 152–9, 187, 188, 190–91, 225–8
in Grenoble 15–16, 17–18, 175
health: burn to foot 185; colds 182–3, 185–6, 188–9, 190, 191–2, 196; coughing 182–3, 186, 190, 192, 196; depression 186, 199; digestive problems 171, 173, 175, 176, 177, 184, 185–6, 187, 188–9, 192, 197, 199; during childhood 168–70; during years 1795–1801: 170–71; during years 1800–1806: 171–5; during years 1823–1824: 177–8; during years 1830–1839: 81, 180–83, 186–8; during years 1839–1845: 188–92; during years 1846–1865: 192–4; after election as superior general 140, 176–7; exhaustion 175, 177, 184, 190, 221; eye problems 175, 176, 177, 178, 195, 196; falls 178–9, 180–81, 191, 192; fevers 175, 176, 177–8, 182–3, 184, 185, 187, 190, 192, 195, 196; gout 178, 195; gynaecological problems 172–3, 178, 195, 199; headaches 177, 178, 184, 187, 199; impact of administration demands upon 184–6; injury to foot 179, 180, 181–3, 196–7; insomnia 178, 184, 186, 188–9, 192, 199; observations on medical history 195–200; psychological effects 176, 199; rashes 186, 189, 196; rheumatism 176, 178, 182, 195; stress 175, 178, 184, 199; throat problems 186–7, 190, 192, 193, 194, 196; weight problems 182
and healthcare in the Society 167–8
and the Jesuits 133–4, 137–44, 145–6, 148–51, 152–9, 162–4
in Jette 189
in Le Ferrandière 88
leadership 6, 8, 12, 24–6, 158–9, 165–6, 172, 220, 228; *see also* spiritual leadership
in Lille 189
and Louisiana communities 39–45, 49–50, 64

in Montet 180, 183
and papal approval for Constitutions 141–3, 147
in Paris 11–12, 46–7, 140, 170–71, 183, 187, 191, 193, 218–21, 232–4
in Poitiers 18–21, 175
proposed change of residence 57, 62–3, 146, 152–3, 154–5, 187–8, 226
reform of the Society 55–6, 58–65
in Rome 147–8, 162, 183, 185–6, 188, 190, 192
spiritual leadership: and the contemplative life 207–10; and discernment of vocations discernment of vocations 52–4, 56–7, 64–5, 67, 77, 212–16; guidance of Society members 203–4, 232–4; origins of 216–21; and self-knowledge 204–7; and transformation in Christ 210–12, 232
spirituality 216–34
testimonies of Society members 77–80
travels 81–2, 173, 176, 180–83, 185–7, 188, 189–90, 191–2, 193
in Turin 183, 186
views on religious life 17–18, 37–8
see also Society of the Sacred Heart
Barat, Marie-Louise 169, 172, 176, 183, 184, 189, 216
Barbot, Prudence 32
Bardot, Adele 12
Barré, Julie 21
Barrelle, Joseph 162
Baudemont, Anne 13, 15, 25
Baunard, Louis 2, 3
Beauvais 35–7, 40, 90–91
Benoit, Gabrielle 20–21
Bernard, Henriette 20
Berniard, Brigette 20
Berthold, Octavie 16, 39
Bigeu, Josephine 18, 19, 22
Bilon, Dr 177–8
biographies 2, 3–4, 5, 6
boarding schools *see* schools
Boisgelin, Gabrielle-Charlotte-Eugenie de *see* Gramont d'Aster, Madame de
Bonald, Cardinal de 158

Bonnet, Josephine 20
Bordeaux 18, 19
Borgèse, princess 160–61
Bouchaud, Elisa de 76
Bouchaud, Emma de 232
Bouchaud, Eulalie de 60–61, 215
Boulanger, Clement 152–3, 156
Boulard, Félicité 20
Bourbon-Condé, Louise-Adélaïde de 135
Bourbons, the 7, 129, 131, 180
Brouillard, Philippe de 220
Bruchet, Françoise 78
Buesan, Josephine 205

Cahier, Adèle 2, 3–4, 72–3, 163, 164, 191, 201, 206, 211
Capy, Mlle 13, 172
Cardon, Rosalie 33
Cart, Jean-Francois-Marie 91
Cassini, Cécile de 13–14
Cassini, Jean-Dominique 13–14
Catholicism 113, 142, 146, 155, 236
Causans, Armande de 67, 143–5, 147–9, 150–51, 158
Cayolle, Dr 187
Chalais, Cécile de 76
Chambéry 180–83, 190, 222
Charbonnel de Jussac, Catherine-Emilie de 13, 22, 148
Charles X, King of France 180, 226
Charry, Jeanne de 2, 3, 4
Chasseloup, Marie-Madeleine de 20
Chauvin, Bertille 16
Chiavarotti, Mgr 147
Choblet, Lydie 18, 19
Choblet, Pulcherie 18
choir sisters
    assignment of rank 24–5, 40, 44–5, 49–50, 51–2, 54
    and the Constitutions 29
    dress 28, 41, 47, 48
    financial contribution 31–2, 65–6, 68–9
    form of address 28, 36–7
    in Louisiana 41–4, 49–50
    numbers of 26–7, 56–7
    roles and duties 25, 34, 35–6, 48–9, 69–71

and social class 66–8
testimonies 79–80
training 28–9, 46–7, 70–71
trousseaus 47–8, 65
vows 47, 58, 63
clergy 73, 82, 133–4, 161
cloister 17–18, 147–51
Clorivière, Pierre de 138, 139, 140, 220
clothing *see* dress; laundry
coadjutrix sisters
admissions 56, 72
assignment of rank 24–5, 40, 44–5, 49–50, 51–2, 54
and the Constitutions 29, 45–6
decree upon 58–63
dismissal of 58, 72
dress 28, 41, 47, 48
envy of vocation 29–30, 52–4
financial contribution 31–2
form of address 28, 36–7
in Louisiana 40–45, 49–50
numbers of 26–7, 56–7
roles and duties 25, 32–4, 36, 45–6, 48–9, 72–7
testimonies 77–9
training 28–9, 46–7, 72
trousseaus 47–8
vows 47, 58–63
Coërville, Anne-Marie de 13
Colas, Amélie 21
Collin, Victorine 130
commissioner sisters 42, 43–4, 54
Constantin, Anna de 180
Constitutions
admission and dismissal policies 28, 57
description of members 27–30, 42, 43, 45–6
establishment of 26, 138, 139–40, 235
and health of members 167
modifications to 57–8, 74, 146, 152
papal approval for 89, 141–3, 147, 157
reinstatement of 63, 191
training of members on 75
convent education 87, 98–9
conversion 113, 142, 146, 155
Copina, Teresa 13, 25

Coppens, Henriette 206
Coriolis, Josephine de 149, 161, 215
Council of Trent 10, 135, 147, 150
Crouzas, Christine de 16
Cuënot, Eliane 206–7, 208
Cuignières 27, 40, 41, 137
Cutts, Maria 51–2, 64

dancing 86
Davaux, Hyacinthe 12
Debrosse, Marguerite-Rosalie 12
Demelin, Mélanie 20
deportment 35, 70
Desbordes-Valmore, Marceline 130
Deshayes, Geneviève-Françoise-Nicole 12, 24, 37, 59–60, 152
Desmarquest, Eugénie 81
Desmarquest, Félicité 12–13, 22
Desnos, Célestine 21
Despines, Dr 182
Diessbach, Nicholas 136, 141
Dilette di Gesù 11–12, 13, 15, 17, 23, 136–7, 140, 146, 171–2, 219; *see also* Society of the Sacred Heart
domestic economy 86
Donnet, Ferdinand 158
dowries 32, 38, 51, 53, 54, 65, 68–9, 142
drawing 70, 86
dress 28, 41, 43, 47–8, 50, 74
Drouard, Fr 135, 140–41
Druilhet, Julien 140
du Rousier, Ana du 212
du Chastaignier, Madeleine 20, 21
du Terrail, Marie 14, 25
Duchesne, Philippine
correspondence with Sophie Barat 5, 39–44, 50, 143, 173, 212, 220
education 16, 22
friendship with Sophie Barat 173, 176, 200
joins the Society 15–18
in Louisiana 39–45, 50, 176, 221
and Sophie Barat's health 173, 175, 176
Dumazeaud, Alida 78, 205, 209
Dutour, Hélène 16, 49–50
Dubourg, William 42–3, 44

Duchesne, Pierre François 16
Ducis, Henriette 14, 25
Duneufgerman, Louise 24, 34
Dusaussoy, Sophie 193
Dusaussoy, Stanislas 82, 176, 180, 183, 189,
    191, 193
Dykmans, Claire 5

education
    convent education 87, 98–9
    curriculum 35–6, 70, 86
    Marie d'Olivier's role in *see* Olivier,
        Marie d'
    Plan of Studies 63, 70, 86
    planned reforms 63
    Sophie Barat's 22, 169–71, 218–19
    standards of 70–71, 90
    teacher training 70–71, 86–7, 111–12,
        128, 130
    vow of commitment to 47
    for women 6, 7, 97–105, 111–12, 128–
        32
    see also schools
embroidery 36, 70, 174
Empire 10, 11, 24, 25
England 191
Enlightenment 7, 16, 25, 84, 165
exorcisms 169, 199, 218

farming 71, 74, 76, 78, 167–8
fasting 173–4, 184
Fathers of the Faith 86, 136, 137, 141, 146
Faux, Euphrosine 149, 151
Favre, Joseph-Marie 178, 184, 185, 186,
    200, 221–5, 230, 231, 232
Feldtrappe, Françoise 32–3
Ferry, Irène de 205–6
Flavigny, Marie de 50–51, 180
Florence 144
flower-making 70
food *see* baking; diet; fasting; kitchens
Fortis, Aloysius 144
Fouffé, Madeleine 11, 169, 170, 177, 197–
    8, 216, 217–18
Francis II, Emperor of Austria 136
French government 63, 89, 145, 154–6,

157, 187, 191, 226
French Revolution 1, 7, 9, 11, 14, 22, 23,
    24, 25, 84, 165
Fribourg 183
friendships 80–82, 141, 200, 220
Frossard, Sister 20

Galitzine, Elizabeth
    correspondence with Sophie Barat 64,
        189, 207–8, 212, 215
    and the General Council of 1839: 152,
        153–4, 155, 157, 158–60
    and health of Sophie Barat 191
    and Jean Rozaven 59, 142–3, 145–6,
        153, 158–60
    joins the Society 142–3
    in Louisiana 160, 161, 190
    as secretary general 59, 146, 190
Gand 27, 137, 138
Garabis, Matilde 215
gardens 33, 34, 71, 74, 78, 167–8
Garibaldi, Antonio 63, 155–6, 157, 159,
    191, 227
General Councils
    1815: 26, 37, 47, 138, 140, 175
    1820: 30, 46
    1826: 30, 46, 47, 89
    1833: 30, 47, 50–51, 54, 146
    1839: 57–63, 72, 92, 151–60, 187, 188,
        190, 225–8
    1842: 72, 158, 190–91
    1851: 67–8, 71, 72–5, 162
    1864: 68, 71, 75
Genoa 192
Geoffroy, Susanne 20, 22, 135
geography 86, 142
Gères, Noémi de 208
Ghirelli, Blanche 211–12
Girard, Henriette 16, 19
Giraud, Emilie 16, 88, 174
Givisiers 180
Goetz, Josephine 77, 79, 194
grammar 86, 142
Gramont, Antionette de 14, 22, 25
Gramont, Eugénie-Cornélie de
    and archbishop de Quelen 214, 225

challenge's Sophie Barat's leadership 25–6, 60
correspondence with Sophie Barat 148, 178, 181, 182, 192–3, 212, 214
education 14, 22
friendship with Sophie Barat 25–6, 200, 228
joins the Society 14
pressure for removal of 158, 161
at rue de Varenne 51, 78, 146, 154, 161, 225
travels with Sophie Barat 180
Gramont d'Aster, Madame de 14, 22, 25, 67–8, 88
Grand Coteau 49–50, 154
Granon, Henriette 233
Gregory XVI, Pope 63, 145, 147, 149, 150, 185, 191, 226, 227
Grenoble 11, 15–18, 24, 27, 137, 173, 175, 177, 220
Grosier Henriette 12, 179, 187, 188
Guidée, Achille 153
Guiégnet, Marinette 20

Hamilton, Eulalie 44
Hardey, Aloysia 212
health 8, 53, 69, 76, 167–8, 190; *see also* Barat, Madeleine Sophie: health
Hidden Objectives (d'Olivier) 110–24
Hinard, Gabrielle 21
history
   as school subject 86, 100–105, 129, 142
   of women 5–6
Holmes, Frederick 195–7
Huchon, Augustine 13
humility 115, 118
Ignatius of Loyola, Saint 37, 115, 139, 140, 147, 165
infirmaries 31, 33, 35, 168

Jansenism 165, 198, 200, 216–18, 219, 221
Jesuits
   influence on the Society: overview 7–8, 133–4, 164–6; origins: 135–7; from 1800 to 1815: 137–41; after 1815: 37–9, 141–3; 1839 General Council 55–6,
57–8, 59–60, 134, 151–9, 226; after 1843: 159–62; from 1850 to 1865: 67, 162–4
   Marie d'Olivier's views 90, 107, 114, 122, 131
   and retreats 73, 133, 161, 162
   in Rome 143–5, 147–51
   Sophie Barat's dealings with 133–4, 137–44, 145–6, 148–51, 152–9, 162–4
   suppression of 90, 135
   tensions with the Society 146–59
Jette 189
Joigny 11, 38, 168–71, 177, 183, 189, 197, 216–18
Jouve, Euphrosine 16
Jugon, Adèle 12
July Revolution 51, 82, 225

Kersabie, Matilde de 214
Kilroy, Phil 6
kitchens 32, 33, 78

La Croix, Marie de 13, 37, 204–5
La Ferrandière 88–9, 91, 129, 180
La Fourche 49–50
Labart, Suzanne 13
Lacordaire, Henri 160
Lamarche, Abbé 14, 220–21
Lamarre, Catherine 34, 39, 40–41
Lambert, Louis 18
Lambruschini, Luigi 63, 143, 149, 150, 151, 155, 157, 161, 162, 191, 227
Lamolière, Jeanne Gertrude 20
Langlet, Clarisse 13
languages 86
Languet de Gergy, Jean-Joseph 217
Lataste, Marie 73, 83
Latin 25, 29, 75, 86, 169, 170, 171, 219
Latour-Maurbourg, Marquis de 157
laundry 31, 32, 33, 34
Lavauden, Angelique 16
Lavauden, Hypolite 16
Lavorr 91–2
Le Franc, Thérèse 13, 34
Le Maître de Saci, Louis-Isaac 216
Le Mans 75

leadership 51–2, 69–71, 204–7; *see also*
    Barat, Madeleine Sophie: leadership
Leclère, Josephine 33
legacies 51, 55, 65, 68–9
Lehon, Adèle 159–60, 209–10
Leo XII, Pope 143
Leridon, Françoise 16
letter-writing 35, 168, 175, 184; *see also*
    Barat, Madeleine Sophie: correspon-
    dence
Lévi-Alvarès, David 130
libraries 35
Liguori, Alphonsus de 221
Lille 189
Limminghe, Louise de
    correspondence with Sophie Barat 60, 144,
        148–51, 186, 208–9, 210–11, 212
    and the General Council of 1839: 148–
        51, 152, 153, 155, 157, 158, 161
    and health of Sophie Barat 184–5, 186
    and the Jesuits 144, 147, 148–51, 152,
        153, 155, 157, 158
    and Joseph-Marie Favre 221, 223, 224
    reconciliation with Sophie Barat 231
    and social class 50–51, 67
    spiritual guidance from Sophie Barat
        208–9
literature 35–6, 86, 100–105, 111–12, 129,
    142, 170–71
Loquet, Marie-Françoise 11, 12
Loretto 190
Loriquet, Jean Nicolas 86, 90, 156
Louis XVIII, King of France 140
Louisiana 39–45, 49–50, 52, 64, 154, 160,
    184, 221
Lyon 75–6, 114, 129, 133, 158, 173, 175,
    180, 186–7, 190, 191; *see also* La
    Ferrandière

Magdaleine de Pazzi, Saint 121
Maillard, Catherine 12, 24
Maillucheau, Thérèse 19, 22, 38, 64, 88,
    174, 175, 176, 177, 220
Manteau, Marguerite 39
Manual of the Christian, The (Le Maître de
    Saci) 216–17

Marguerie, Frédéric de 91
Marguerite (maid to Madame Duval) 11,
    12, 24, 37
Marie (maid to Lydie Choblet) 21
Marie-Anne of Austria 136
Marseilles 192
Martinique 40
Massa, Georgio 143
mathematics 86, 169, 170, 219
Mathieu, Césaire 61–2, 63, 155, 157, 158,
    159, 191, 192, 227–31
Maugenet, Marthe 21
Mémoire on Education (d'Olivier) 92–110
Mémorial Catholique 92
Mère Institutrice, La (Lévi-Alvarès) 130
Messoria, Caroline 16
Michel, Adrienne 210
modesty 81, 98, 101, 118
monastic grills *see* cloister
Montaigne, Jean 138, 220
Montet 52, 82, 180, 183
Moura, Henriette 24
music 35, 70, 86, 101
mythology 86

Napoleon 10, 24, 67, 87, 137, 140, 236
natural history 103–4, 129
Naudet, Léopoldine 136
Naudet, Louise 12, 136
Nectoux, Charles 135
Neuville 75
New Orleans 39–42
Nicolay, Marquis de 180
Niort 27, 41, 45, 88, 137
novices 13, 21, 26–7, 29, 46, 56, 70, 75
nurseries 91

Observations and Responses 72
offices, recitation of 17–18, 25, 29, 42
Olivier, Louise Macqué 20
Olivier, Marie d' 7, 13, 68, 87–92
    Annals 89, 113–14, 120–22, 124–8, 130,
        131
    commentary on texts 128–32
    Hidden Objectives 110–24
    Mémoire on Education 92–110

Prospectus 124–8
Les Trois Paulines 90
Orleans 78
orphanages 49, 91
Otsini, Cardinal 143
Oussières, Esther d' 201

Paccanari, Nicholas 136, 137, 141
Panazzoni, Louis 139
Paris 9–12, 31, 46–7, 50–51, 76, 78, 89,
    136–7, 138, 140, 146, 152, 154–5,
    157, 160–61, 170–71, 177, 183, 187–
    8, 191, 193, 218–21, 225, 226, 228,
    232–4
Parma 190
Patte, Marie 82, 180, 185, 190, 191
Pedicini, Cardinal 156, 158–9
Pelletier, Josephine 13
Pelletier, Thérèse 13, 31
pensions 32, 38, 55, 65–6, 68–9
Perdrau, Pauline 83
Périer, Rose-Euphrosine 16
Photius 104
Pignerol 52–3
Piorette, Lucie 32
Pius VI, Pope 136
Pius VII, Pope 138–9
Pius IX, Pope 162, 237
Place, Antoinette 31, 32
Place, Marianne 31, 33, 37
Plan of Studies 63, 70, 86
Pluche, Noël-Antoine 104
Poitiers 11, 18–21, 24–5, 27, 45, 87–8,
    135, 137, 173, 175, 220
Polie, Marie 33
poor schools *see* schools
Port Royal 216–17
postulants 26, 34
prayer 17–18, 29, 34, 75, 93–5, 209, 218,
    227, 229
Prevost, Marie-Elizabeth 14, 15, 80
private sphere 3, 5, 77, 142
Prospectus (d'Olivier) 124–8
Protestantism 113
public speaking 35, 142–3
public sphere 3, 5, 77, 79

Quelen, Hyacinthe de 14, 63, 161, 225,
    226, 227
Quimper 68, 88

race 39, 40–41, 42–4
Raison, Madeleine 13
Récamier, Joseph Claude Anthelme 180,
    183, 189, 193, 196
recreation 34, 36, 46, 75, 109, 112
religion (as school subject) 86
retreats 35, 45, 73, 133, 154, 161, 162, 173,
    222, 226–7
Rey, Dr 181, 182
Richomme, Fanny 130
Riencourt, Alexandrine de 205
Rivet, Marie 16, 18
Rogers, Rebecca 86, 128–32
Roger, Pierre 15
Rome 57, 62–3, 82, 121, 136, 138–9, 143–5,
    146, 147–51, 152–3, 154–5, 160, 162,
    183, 184, 185–6, 187–8, 190, 192, 226
Roothaan, Jan 67, 146–7, 152–3, 156–7,
    160, 162–4
Rossi, Chevalier 183, 186, 196
Rostopchine, Natalie 145–6
Roux, Barthélémy 12, 37
Roux, Virginie 78
Rozaven, Jean 55–6, 59, 141–6, 148, 150–
    53, 155–61, 162, 165, 226
Rozeville, Adelaide de 178, 233
rue de Varenne *see* Paris
Rumigny, Madame de 14
Russia 141, 142

Saignes 92
Saint André de la Laurencie de Villeneuve,
    Pauline de 52–3
St Charles 44
St Louis 41
St Michael's 49–50
Sambucy de St Estève, Félicité de 13, 14, 15,
    25
Sambucy de St Estève, Louis de 14, 17, 25,
    37, 137–9
schools
    at Amiens 10, 12, 32–3, 88

at Beauvais 35–6, 90–91
boarding schools 12, 18, 21, 28, 33, 35–6, 39, 49, 55, 70–71, 85–6, 88, 91, 235
establishment of 85–6
financing of 55, 66, 85, 91
at Grenoble 10
at La Ferrandière 88–9, 91
in Louisiana 49–50
at Niort 88
at Paris 50–51, 161, 177
places offered to families of members 66
at Poitiers 10, 18, 21, 88
poor schools 10, 12, 21, 28, 33, 35–6, 41, 49, 55, 70, 85–6, 88, 145, 235
at Rome 145, 149
state inspections of 70–71
at Tours 18
at Turin 185
see also education
Second, Adélaïde 16
self-knowledge 204–7, 228
Sellier, Louis 75
Sibour, Dominique-Auguste 162
Sisters of Charity 172–3
Sisters of the Cross 49
slavery 39
social class 1, 10–15, 18, 21, 24–6, 50–52, 66–7, 85, 91, 228, 235
Society of St Francis 107
Society of St Ignatius *see* Jesuits
Society of the Sacred Heart
admissions 56–7, 63, 67, 72, 212–16
bicentenary 6
cataloguing of archives 4–5, 201
and the clergy 73, 82, 133–4
commissions biography of Barat 2
communities *see* Aix-en-Provence;Amiens; Annonay; Avignon; Beauvais; Chambéry; Cuignières; Gand; Grenoble; Jette; La Ferrandière; Le Mans; Lille; Louisiana; Montet; Neuville; Niort; Orleans; Paris; Pignerol; Poitiers; Quimper; Trinité des Monts; Turin; Warendorf
conflict with archbishops 63, 134, 155, 187, 191, 226

conflict with French government 63, 154–6, 187, 191, 226
Constitutions *see* Constitutions
creation of 1, 7, 10, 136–40
dismissals 58, 63–5, 72, 212–16
domestic arrangements 31–3
dress 28, 41, 43, 47–8, 50, 74
and education *see* education; schools
educational background of members 22–3
finances 31–2, 34, 38, 51, 55, 65–6, 68–9, 71, 142, 177; *see also* dowries; legacies; pensions
General Councils *see* General Councils
golden jubilee 162
governmental structure 55–6, 57–8, 63, 71, 146, 152, 162, 187, 225
health 8, 53, 69, 76, 167–8, 190
and the Jesuits *see* Jesuits
leaving after final profession 57, 59, 65
motivations for joining 23
ranks within *see* choir sisters; coadjutrix sisters; commissioner sisters; novices; postulants; vicars
reform of 55–6, 58–65
religious life 17–18, 37–9
roles and duties of members 31–7, 45–6
and social class 10–15, 18, 21, 24–6, 50–52, 66–7, 235
training of members 28–30, 46, 70–71, 74–5
trousseaus 31, 47–8, 65
visitors 17, 70
vows 47, 58–62, 63, 72

Tallandier, Marie 213
Terror 9, 11
Teste, Jean-Baptiste 156, 226
Tharin, Paul 156
Theux, John de 154
Thubières de Caylus, Charles de 217
Tinseau, Marie de 207, 211
Tournély, Léonor de 11–12, 135, 136, 137, 139, 140, 152
Tours 18
Trent 136

Trinité des Monts 143–5, 147–51, 158, 183, 185, 187, 190
Trois Paulines, Les (d'Olivier) 90
trousseaus 31, 47–8, 65
Turin 52–3, 136, 143, 144, 147, 183, 186, 189

Urban VIII, Pope 138

Vaillant, Martha 32
Varin, Joseph
  biography of 201
  correspondence with Sophie Barat 5, 139, 152, 172
  difficulties with Sophie Barat as leader 17, 25
  and the General Council of 1839: 59, 60, 152, 226
  and health of Sophie Barat 172, 174, 199
  and the origins of the Society 11–13, 15, 135, 136–40, 141, 171–2, 220

Vaulserre des Adrets, Marie-Louise de 16
Verney, Agnes 194
vicars 71, 162
Vichy 175
Vidal, Dr 181, 182
Villafort, Philippe de 163, 164
vocations, discernment of 52–4, 56–7, 64–5, 67, 77, 212–16
vows 47, 58–62, 63, 72

Warendorf 53–4
Wartel, Catherine 32, 34
Wheeler, Mary Cecilia 5
Wollstonecraft, Mary 237
women
  education for 6, 7, 97–105, 111–12, 128–32
  history of 5–6
  and writing 118–19, 130
writing 70, 86, 118–19, 130